IMMIGRATION AND THE BORDER

LATINO PERSPECTIVES

Gilberto Cárdenas, series editor

The Institute for Latino Studies, in keeping with the distinctive mission, values, and traditions of the University of Notre Dame, promotes understanding and appreciation of the social, cultural, and religious life of U.S. Latinos through advancing research, expanding knowledge, and strengthening community.

IMMIGRATION AND THE BORDER

Politics and Policy in the New Latino Century

Edited by

DAVID L. LEAL AND JOSÉ E. LIMÓN

University of Notre Dame Press

Notre Dame, Indiana

Library of Congress Cataloging-in-Publication Data

Immigration and the border : politics and policy in the new Latino century /
edited by David L. Leal and José E. Limón.
    pages   cm. — (Latino perspectives)
Includes bibliographical references and index.
ISBN 978-0-268-01335-6 (pbk. : alk. paper) —
ISBN 0-268-01335-7 (pbk. : alk. paper)
1. Hispanic Americans—Politics and government. 2. Hispanic Americans—
Social conditions. 3. Immigrants—Political activity—United States.
4. Immigrants—United States—Social conditions. 5. Latin America—
Emigration and immigration. 6. United States—Emigration and
immigration.   I. Leal, David L.
E184.S75I38   2012
305.868'073—dc23
2012044384

CONTENTS

Part II. Immigrants and Civic Life

Part III. Immigration and Public Policy

ACKNOWLEDGMENTS

This volume began as a selection of papers presented at the first Inter-University Program for Latino Research (IUPLR) conference, "Siglo XXI: Latino Research into the Twenty-First Century," held at the University of Texas at Austin in 2005. We subsequently solicited additional papers specifically for the volume.

The editors would like to acknowledge the support of the Irma Rangel Public Policy Institute, the Center for Mexican American Studies, and the College of Liberal Arts at the University of Texas at Austin. We also wish to thank the staff and graduate research assistants of the Irma Rangel Institute who helped to produce the manuscript, particularly Jill Strube, Kyle Enders, Joanne Ibarra, Jennifer Lamm, Rachel Navarre, and Jerod Patterson.

Chapter 14 was originally published in *Latino Studies* 4 (2006): 419–47 and is used here, with minor changes, with permission.

Introduction

GILBERTO CÁRDENAS,
DAVID L. LEAL, AND JILL STRUBE

Borders matter in our world more—and less—than ever before. With international migration at unprecedented levels, immigrants (with or without legal status) are increasingly visible and consequential in both host and sending nations. They are putting down roots, finding jobs, starting families, creating local and transnational networks, remitting money, and engaging in civic life. In doing so, they are deepening globalization, a process as old as human history (Steger 2003) but one that may be the defining characteristic of the twenty-first century. Technology enables individuals to travel vast distances while maintaining close and continuing contact with family, friends, and even political institutions in sending nations (Brettell and Hollifield 2008). In many host countries, immigrants receive social welfare benefits and even political rights. Such changes intertwine the cultures, economies, and politics of nations across the world. Little wonder scholars are asking if such dynamics weaken the traditional role of the nation state and require new ways of understanding the concept of citizenship (Soysal 1994; Sassen 1998), although others note that state power remains robust (Freeman 1988; Hansen 2008; Hagan, Leal, and Rodriguez 2012).

While the increasingly global economy is impatient with barriers to the movement of goods and commodities, the free movement of people has proven more problematic. Immigrants bring fiscal costs as well as economic benefits, and rapid population changes in the United States and Europe engender debates about national identity. In the United States, the nature of immigration has changed quantitatively and qualitatively over the last five decades, adding to a demographic revolution. The Immigration and Nationality Act of 1965 not only eliminated national-origin quotas and restrictions but also created new provisions for family reunification. This led to greater numbers of immigrants as well as more diverse flows. Over one million people currently naturalize each year, and many millions of others receive temporary visas. In addition, large numbers of other migrants have crossed the border clandestinely, overstayed their visas, or otherwise added to an unauthorized population of about ten million people. Despite occasional nativist outbreaks and growing concern about irregular migration, the U.S. immigration system is unchanged in its fundamentals since 1965 (Leal 2010).

Nevertheless, the Westphalian nation-state system is unlikely to disappear, and recent policy developments point out the importance of nations and citizenship. While borders increasingly fail to contain the people, commercial interests, or ideas of any country (Herzog 1990; Zúñiga 1998; Fox 1999; DeLaet 2000), they are an undeniable feature of political life. Contemporary immigration enforcement is characterized by both border control and interior enforcement (Kanstroom 2007). For instance, recent federal budgets have seen a considerable expansion of resources and personnel dedicated to the U.S. Border Patrol. However, in a departure from recent past practices, the United States now deports about four hundred thousand individuals annually, almost ten times more than the yearly average before the Illegal Immigration Reform and Immigrant Responsibility Act (IIRIRA) of 1996 (U.S. Department of Homeland Security 2010). Immigrants are eligible for a declining number of social services, and even legal residents are subject to deportation if they commit—or are discovered to have committed—any of a growing list of crimes. Some states and localities—a small but well-publicized minority—have enacted laws aimed at discouraging or deporting unauthorized immigrants (such as

Arizona's SB 1070) or cooperate in the federal-local 287(g) and Secure Communities programs.

While the Immigration Reform and Control Act of 1986, as well as European amnesties, suggest the possibility of eventual regularization, the prospects for a new amnesty program are unclear. Recent efforts to develop compromise immigration legislation have failed (Leal 2009a), including the Dream Act.[1] For unauthorized immigrants, life in the United States has become more difficult over time, which reflects the theory of "self deportation." Endorsed by Republican presidential candidate Mitt Romney (Preston 2012), the goal is to shrink the number of such immigrants but without more draconian interior enforcement measures.

Analysts often refer to a "thickening" of the U.S. border, which has implications not only for immigrants but also for the economy and relations with Mexico and Canada. The stricter identification requirements for crossing the border affect both citizens and non-citizens. Today, because of the 2006 Secure Fence Act, a new border wall is expanding across parts of the U.S.-Mexico frontier. In a post–September 11 world, with renewed concerns about security and terrorism, the integration of North America heralded by NAFTA in 1993 has encountered serious roadblocks, and the implications for the U.S. future are not well understood.

In addition, the last fifty years have seen dramatic demographic changes in the United States, particularly the growing size and diversity of the Latino population. The resulting political, economic, and cultural changes are not welcome developments for many. Mounting restrictionist sentiment in Congress, state legislatures, and local governments reflects at best a concern about border security and the "rule of law"—and at worst a nativist reaction that indicts all Latinos.

It is not surprising that few contemporary domestic policy issues capture the popular imagination like immigration. It involves issues central to America's character and self-conception, touching on history, religion, culture, and economics. Many Americans find themselves caught between conflicting principles, facts, and frames. Opinion polls are often contradictory and depend on variations in question wording; while some indicate skepticism about migration and migrants, others suggest openness to more generous reform options (Schildkraut 2012). Americans may also be less sympathetic to immigrants as a category than they are to individual immigrants. One question on the 2006 national exit poll gave voters a choice between legalization and deportation of unauthorized immigrants; 56 percent chose the former and 38 percent the latter.

This unique environment calls out for reasoned—perhaps even scholarly—debate, but this is unfortunately rare. The immigration debate often appears to exist in a parallel universe where policymakers ignore research, pundits present opinions as facts, politicians endorse obvious falsehoods, and the media boil complexities down to sound bites. How can the reality of immigration, immigrants, and border politics be discussed in a PowerPoint world?

While no book can comprehensively cover such a broad and multidisciplinary subject (although, see Brettell and Hollifield 2008), this volume offers a timely analysis of key issues important to current national debates. These chapters include discussions of civic engagement, state and local reactions to immigration, transnationalism, immigrant access to social services, and political lives on the border. As a whole, it points out how borders continue to matter as well as how individuals nevertheless live with, and around, them.

A BRIEF HISTORICAL OVERVIEW

Public debates about migration and border issues too often lack an historical understanding of immigration patterns, laws, rules, and key events. We therefore provide a brief—and inevitably non-comprehensive—overview of immigration history in hopes of better contextualizing the discussion of Latinos and immigration.

To understand the political, social, and economic development of the United States requires an understanding of immigration and immigrants. Given its centrality, contentious debates about immigration are unsurprisingly found throughout American history. Contradictory ideas about who should become an American are seen at the very beginning of the Republic. For instance, President George Washington declared an open-door immigration policy for both the "Respectable Stranger" and the "oppressed and persecuted of all Nations And Religions" in a 1793 speech to the Irish Volunteers, but he also signed the 1794 Naturalization Act that restricted citizenship to "free white persons."[2]

As immigration populations diversified throughout the nineteenth century, new racial and ethnic concerns would come to play a role in immigration policymaking. Not only were migrants arriving from non-traditional sending locales in southern and eastern Europe, but the U.S. border itself expanded in southern and westward directions. Territory was added via the Louisiana Purchase from France (1803); the acquisition of Florida from Spain through the Treaty of Adams-Onís (1819); the admission of Texas as the 28th state (1845); the addition of much of the present American southwest after the Mexican-American War and the Treaty of Guadalupe Hidalgo (1848); the addition of land to Arizona and New Mexico through the Gadsden Purchase from Mexico (1853); the purchase of Alaska from Russia (1867); and territory acquired through the Spanish-American War (1898) including Puerto Rico, Guam, and the Philippines.

After a century of Manifest Destiny, the nation grew to the shape we now recognize today—stretching from the Atlantic through the Caribbean to the Gulf of Mexico and then from the Pacific Ocean to the Bering Sea. With each addition, new, diverse populations were absorbed into America, although some new residents enjoyed full citizenship rights while others did not (and still do not, although for complex reasons); see the Supreme Court's *Insular Cases* and the debate over whether "the Constitution follows the flag." (Sparrow 2006). This expansion of people and land was not without controversy. For instance, the question of how much territory to annex after the Mexican-American War was interwoven with discussions—often negative—about the wisdom of incorporating Mexican citizens into the United States. The border reflected in the Treaty of Guadalupe Hidalgo reflected a compromise between maximizing land but minimizing people (Gutiérrez 1995).

The federal government became more involved in immigration policy with the 1875 Immigration Act, which excluded felons and prostitutes and prohibited the transportation of non-consenting Asian labor

(DeLaet 2000; Tichenor 2002). Subsequent immigration laws contained racial dimensions: the Chinese Exclusion Acts (1882) largely closed migration from China, and the so-called Gentlemen's Agreements (1907) ended most immigration from Japan. Later laws were aimed at reducing the growing number of migrants from southern and eastern Europe. The 1917 Immigration Act not only banned migration from Asia but also required literacy (in any language). Most importantly, the National Quota Law of 1921 and the Johnson-Reed Immigration Act of 1924 fixed migrant levels to a small percentage of foreign-born persons of each nationality residing in the United States in 1910 and 1890, respectively. Because the nation was primarily composed of northern European migrants in these earlier time periods, the effect of the law was to restrict eastern and southern European migration without directly saying so.

During this time period, some immigrants were expelled from the United States, and others returned to Europe or moved to Canada due to public hostility and the violence of nativist and vigilante groups (DeLaet 2000). Some state and local lawmakers, frustrated by federal immigration efforts, enacted their own policies (see Zolberg 2006 for a discussion of the "Passenger Acts"). These are broadly reminiscent of contemporary tactics, but sub-federal actions in this policy arena have faced considerable skepticism from the Supreme Court. Furthermore, Congress created the Border Patrol in 1924, and 1929 is commonly seen as the inauguration of the contemporary "illegal alien" (see below).

However, the immigration laws of the early twentieth century largely excluded restrictions on Mexican and Latin American migration, both through legal exemption or administration rule making. For instance, the National Quota Law of 1921 exempted "aliens who had resided continuously for at least one year immediately preceding their application in one of the independent countries of the Western Hemisphere" (this exemption was subsequently changed to five years in 1922). A Western Hemisphere exemption was also part of the 1924 law. The Immigration and Nationality Act of 1952 accorded non-quota status to natives of Western Hemisphere countries, including their families. It also included the "Texas Proviso," which specifically exempted the employment of unauthorized migration from "harboring" provisions (Calavita 1992). In addition, the Border Patrol was not primarily tasked to prevent Mexican or Latin American migration but rather those who were trying to circumvent the aforementioned national-racial restrictions.

These policy decisions largely reflected agricultural and business interests in the southwest. The arguments used at the time would be familiar today—jobs that needed workers, and the importance of economic growth. Other arguments were based on stereotypes and racist beliefs (for example, it was said that Mexicans were particularly suited for hard labor in hot climates). The Dillingham Commission (formally the United States Immigration Commission) essentially concluded in its 1911 report that Mexicans were desirable as laborers but not as settlers (Gutiérrez 1995). Vélez-Ibáñez (1996, 7) saw this use of labor as imposing a "commodity identity" on Mexicans; although these communities resisted this identity, it had considerable repercussions for Mexican and Mexican-American cultures.

Until 1917 the U.S.-Mexico border was virtually unregulated. This reflects the fact that the 1848 border divided an area with long-established travel patterns and community life. After 1917, Mexican migrants needed birth certificates, marriage certificates, certificates of good conduct and good health, proof they would not become a public burden, ten dollars for a visa, and eight dollars for an entry tax (Portes and Bach 1985). The first recruited immigrants from Mexico were contract laborers who entered the country temporarily for purposes of work during World War I but were required to return to Mexico once their contracts were over in 1921. This policy was a compromise representing an effort on the part of the U.S. Congress to mediate between anti-immigrant, anti-Mexican sentiment and the need for cheap labor (Calavita 1992; Lorey 1999).

In addition to some permanent settlement, a large number of Mexicans commuted across the border to work in the United States, and others entered temporarily to work seasonally in labor-intensive industries—agriculture, railroads, mining, stockyards, and related employment sectors. Labor circulation never ceased to be the dominant mode of entry, even when the number of legal immigrants from Mexico was the highest; it steadily rose since the early 1900s and greatly accelerated after the first temporary admission program ended in 1921 (Calavita 1992; Gutiérrez 1995; Lorey 1999).

By 1926, the number of legal immigrants from Mexico had steadily increased due to the heavy recruitment of Mexican workers, the construction of railroad lines connecting the interior of Mexico with the United States, and refugee movements caused by the Mexican Revolution (Portes and Bach 1985; Calavita 1992; Gutiérrez 1995; Lorrey 1999). With this combination of factors, immigration from Mexico outpaced that from all other countries. The U.S. Consular Service was generous in issuing visas until the late 1920s, when public sentiment became concerned that the migrant population was growing too rapidly. The State Department exercised its discretionary authority to bar Mexicans from entering the United States at the onset of the Great Depression.

The 1929 Acts of March 2nd and March 4th for the first time criminalized border crossing without documentation, amending existing immigration law to allow for deportation, fines, and imprisonment for individuals with no record of legal admission to the United States (Portes and Bach 1985; Lorey 1999; Massey, Durand and Malone 2002; USCIS nda). Because the policing and enforcement actions required to uphold this policy were contrary to southwestern agricultural and railroad needs for Mexican labor, such enforcement was usually a low priority. In fact, both Mexico and the United States tolerated, and in some cases actively recruited, unauthorized Mexican workers for decades (Portes and Bach 1985; Andreas 2000).

The tension between politics and economics is visible in the mix of immigration laws of the twentieth century. Some programs increased immigration. The need for labor during World War II led to the 1943 Emergency Farm Labor Program—more commonly known as the Bracero program—which provided temporary agricultural workers from Mexico with workplace and wage guarantees. The 1943 Naturalization Act formally repealed the Chinese Exclusion Acts, although quotas from Asia remained low. The 1946 War Brides Act facilitated the entry of veterans' foreign-born spouses and children (USCIS ndb). Cold War politics extended a safe haven for refugees from certain Communist nations through the 1953 Refugee Relief Act, which allowed refugees to enter at numbers higher than their quota allowed (Salehyan and Rosenblum 2004). The Cuban Adjustment Act (1966) provided substantial financial and legal benefits for those fleeing Castro's Communist government.

On the other hand, the Cold War and McCarthyism gave rise to the 1950 Internal Security Act, allowing for the deportation and exclusion of alien "political subversives." The Immigration and Nationality (McCarran-Walter) Act of 1952 legislated the exclusion and deportation of aliens from thirty-three categories. However, while it largely preserved the national-origin quota system, it also ended the "Asiatic Barred Zone," created a relatively small number of visas for nonwhite immigrants, and abolished racial requirements for citizenship (USCIS ndb; DeLaet 2000; Tichenor 2002).

The key event in contemporary migration history is the 1965 Hart-Celler Act, which abolished the existing quota system (Tichenor 2002; USCIS ndb). The reality of an immigration policy based on race and national-origin was out of touch with American values, and this was also a public relations problem during the Cold War (DeLaet 2000). The new legislation set in place the migration framework still largely in place today, with admissions primarily for family reunification and those with particular skills and professions. It also set a yearly limit of 120,000 individuals from the Western Hemisphere. Public statements at the time suggested that few believed—or wanted to state publicly—that this law constituted a major change to immigration policy or demography. At the signing ceremony, President Lyndon Johnson said "This bill that we will sign today is not a revolutionary bill. It does not affect the lives of millions. It will not reshape the structure of our daily lives" (Tichenor 2002, 218). However, the law would transform America.

As legal immigration became larger and more diverse, a parallel dynamic was the growing number of unauthorized immigrants. By the 1980s, the subject was on the political agenda. The 1986 Immigration Reform and Control Act (IRCA) was designed as a grand compromise between those who favored legalization and enforcement (Massey et al. 2002). On the one hand, IRCA created a process for the regularization of unauthorized immigrants who had continually lived in the United States since January 1, 1982. On the other hand, it enhanced enforcement at the U.S. border and instituted "employer sanctions" for those who knowingly hired the unauthorized.

Ultimately, IRCA led to the legalization of about 2.7 million unauthorized immigrants (U.S. Immigration and Naturalization Service 1992; Baker 2010)—many more than the anticipated one million. However, very little workplace enforcement transpired, and as employers were not held responsible for ascertaining the validity of identification documents, unauthorized immigrants continued to find a warm embrace in many economic sectors.

U.S. policy toward irregular migration would primarily involve augmenting border security and reducing immigrant eligibility for government services. Apart from an occasional (and well publicized) workplace raid, there was little interior enforcement for several decades. However, the 1996 Illegal Immigration Reform and Immigrant Responsibility Act (IIRIRA), as explained below, would dramatically change this status quo.

GLOBALIZATION AND MIGRATION CONTROL

Scholars have long studied the push and pull of economic forces that bring labor and goods across borders, as well as the networks that sustain this constant movement (Portes and Bach 1985; Andreas 2000; Brettell 2008; Ramos 2002). The spectrum of the basic typologies of migrants—seasonal, temporary, recurrent, continuous, permanent, and conflict-related—illustrates the complexity of the relationship between the sending and receiving nations, as well as the social and cultural institutions that facilitate and reflect population movement (Brettell 2008). While the political relationship between Mexico and the United States is historically contentious, this belies their degree of social and economic integration. Controversies involving immigration, narcotics, and crime could pose challenges to this relationship (Brakman and Erie 2001).[3]

Recent years have seen a number of steps that diminish the barrier posed by the U.S.-Mexico border to the regional economy. While IRCA and subsequent legislation were primarily designed to regulate immigration, economic forces—among them, the 1994 North American Free Trade Agreement (NAFTA)[4]—worked to facilitate and encourage cross-border trade. This attempt to deregulate trade without deregulating labor has not stemmed immigration flows, despite some political promises to the contrary. In fact, greater regional integration may have increased migration.

As globalization increasingly calls into question traditional borders, and as migration transforms societies and cultures, some interpret U.S. immigration policies as seeking to reaffirm national authority (Albert and Brock 1998; Saint-Germain 1998) or reassuring the public (Albert and Brock 1998; Andreas 2000; Hollifield 2008; Bailey 2001). These official efforts to control what some call a "global migration crisis" (Weiner 1995) have both real and symbolic elements. Whether any specific policy proposal is genuine or disingenuous is impossible to ascertain, although advocates likely have varying and even mixed motivations.

Until recent years, most enforcement activity involved "disincentive strategies" (Cárdenas 2006) designed to encourage immigrants to remain in or return to their nation of origin. The logic behind this strategy was that the longer immigrants stayed in the United States, the higher the costs to society through increased use of government services. These kinds of societal costs would be minimized in inverse relation to the length of time that migrant workers remained in the United States. Government strategies therefore sought to bar, limit, or discourage unauthorized—and some legal—immigrants from utilizing public services. For instance, the 1996 Personal Responsibility and Work Opportunity Reconciliation Act (PRWORA) enacted restrictions or prohibitions on access to federal public benefits by unauthorized immigrants and even some legal permanent residents (DeLaet 2000; Cohen 2007). These disincentive strategies have since extended beyond the federal level. A relatively small number of locales have enacted ordinances aimed at unauthorized immigrants, such as preventing landlords from renting to unauthorized immigrants. Some states have passed ballot initiatives directed at immigrants or public policies tied to Latinos more broadly, such as bilingual education. More recently, a growing number of states and cities have considered proactive efforts to enforce immigration laws and discourage unauthorized immigrants. For example, the 287(g) and Secure Communities programs are cooperative ventures between federal immigration officials and local law enforcement agencies.

In addition, some states have considered laws designed to deny social services or citizenship to children born in the United States to unauthorized immigrant parents (as either a direct challenge to, or a circumvention of, the Fourteenth Amendment). However, the number of such laws is relatively small, and a study by the Woodrow Wilson Center found that recent state and local immigrant-related laws are just as likely to expand immigrant rights as to restrict them.[5] Whether this recent spate of immigration lawmaking across the federal system represents the start of an important new development—or a short-lived trend that fails to pass constitutional muster—is unclear.

Such efforts often reflect views that are quick to blame unauthorized migration on the individual migrant instead of considering the role of larger economic contexts. For example, certain labor markets in the United States have typically included a sector of temporary, unauthorized workers as a permanent component; the mutual dependency between these businesses and Mexican labor has evolved over time and will be slow to change (Vélez-Ibáñez 1996; Andreas 2000). Lacking avenues for legal entry into the United States that were available for European workers to meet the needs of a previous turn-of-the-century economy, the majority of immigrant workers from Mexico have had few options other than to enter temporarily and usually illegally (Portes and Rumbaut 2006). While some immigration-skeptics argue that prospective immigrants should "get in line," there are essentially no lines available to the vast majority of unskilled and semi-skilled workers needed by sectors of the economy that depend on low-wage labor. Holding immigrants responsible for responding to conditions they did not create may not be the best way to understand or address migration dynamics that are increasingly global in dimension. Many have noted the difficulty of stopping immigrants "when the invisible hand of Adam Smith is waving them across the border" (Leal 2010).

Lastly, the public (not to mention politicians) is often unaware that immigration reform can involve unintended consequences. For instance, the increased border enforcement of the last few decades may have in fact encouraged unauthorized migrants to settle permanently (Massey et al. 2002). As crossing the U.S.-Mexico border became increasingly difficult and dangerous, many responded by bringing their families north and remaining in the United States throughout the year. Seasonal workers thus become de facto permanent residents, and families that might have remained in Mexico are now living in the United States.

STRENGTH IN NUMBERS? THE GROWING LATINO COMMUNITY

Over the last few decades, growing numbers have brought renewed attention to a group once considered the "forgotten people" (Sanchez 1940). Discussions of Latino influence in politics, the economy, and popular culture are difficult to miss. Such demographic changes also force national governments to re-examine old relationships among themselves and with emigrant communities (Bonilla et al. 1998; Ramos 2002; Wood 2004).

However, we should remember that numbers alone do not guarantee influence (de la Garza 1996); the political future of Latinos may be more complicated than a simple story of growing numbers and increasing power. Clearly, cultural changes are obvious in many communities, ranging from signage to conversations to fashions to architecture. Their political implications, however, are not as readily observed. The questionable metaphor of the "sleeping giant" (see Montoya 2000) captures popular perceptions of numbers that do not equal influence, but in a way that seems to blame Latinos themselves.

Between 1990 and 2000, the overall U.S. population grew by 13 percent but the Latino population grew by 58 percent. This represents an increase of almost thirteen million individuals (from 22.4 million to 35.3 million). Latinos therefore grew from 9 percent of the total population to 12.5 percent (Institute for Latino Studies n.d.). Table I.1 shows that Latinos represented about half of the total U.S. population change between 2000 and 2009, due to both natural increase and net international migration. In fact, international migration represented about 37 percent of the total increase of Latinos. The Anglo (non-Hispanic white) population constituted the majority of births but also had the lowest birth-to-death ratio, so it grew only half as much as all other non-Hispanic races, and by only about one-third that of Latinos.

Table I.1. Population Change: Natural Increase and Net International Migration, 2000–2006

	Total Population Change	Natural Increase			Net International Migration
		Total	*Births*	*Deaths*	
Total Population	17,973,882	10,324,372	25,486,569	15,162,197	7,649,510
Hispanic or Latino Origin	9,014,660	5,017,017	5,704,130	687,113	3,997,551
White Alone, not Hispanic	3,167,498	1,804,399	14,083,012	12,278,613	1,362,881
All Other Races, not Hispanic	5,791,724	3,502,956	5,699,427	2,196,471	2,289,078

Source: Population Division, U.S. Census Bureau. Table 5: Cumulative Estimates of the Components of Population Change by Race and Hispanic or Latino Origin for the United States: April 1, 2000 to July 1, 2006 (NC EST2006-05). Release Date: May 17, 2007.
Note: Net International Migration includes persons present in the United States without authorization.

Census data show that the number of Latinos increased by about 43 percent between 2000 and 2010, from 35.3 million individuals to 50.5 million. While this percentage change is lower than the 1990–2000 change (58 percent), the number of people it includes is almost two and a half million larger (from 12.9 million to 15.2 million).

While population projects are complicated and subject to unpredictable future events, most analysts believe that Latino populations will continue to grow throughout the twenty-first century. The recent recession and increase in deportations has led to a decline in unauthorized migration across the U.S.-Mexico border, with recent estimates suggesting almost zero net movement. However, Latino population growth increasingly reflects what demographers call "natural increase" (births minus deaths) as well as immigration.

As Tables I.2 and I.3 illustrate, the Latino population is projected to grow far more rapidly than the non-Latino population. Table I.2 shows the relatively even pace with which the latter are projected to

Table I.2. Current Population and Projections by Race/Ethnicity (in millions)

	2000 (Apr)*	2005 (July)*	2000 to 2005 (Percent change)	2010 (Apr*)	2005 to 2010 (Percent change)	2015 (Est**)	2010 to 2015 (Percent change)
Total	281.4	295.5	5.0	308.7	4.5	325.5	5.4
Not Hispanic/Lat.	246.1	252.5	2.6	258.3	2.3	267.8	3.7
White (one race) – Not Hispanic/Lat.	195.6	196.6	0.5	197.3	0.4	203.2	3.0
Hispanic or Latino	35.3	43.0	21.8	50.5	17.4	57.7	14.3

Sources: *Table 2: Intercensal Estimates of the Resident Population by Sex, Race, and Hispanic Origin for the United States: April 1, 2000 to July 1, 2010 (US-EST00INT-02). U.S. Census Bureau, Population Division. Release Date: September 2011.
**Table 4: Projections of the Population by Sex, Race, and Hispanic Origin for the United States: 2010 to 2050. http://www.census.gov/population/www/projections/index.

increase (about 3.0 percent for Anglos and 3.7 percent for all non-Latinos from 2010–2015). By contrast, the Latino population is projected to increase by 14.3 percent during this time. Table I.3 shows that by 2050, the Latino population is expected to grow by more than 97 million from its 2000 level (nearly 276 percent growth), compared to just 7.7 million for the Anglo population (about 4 percent growth). In addition, while the Latino (white alone) population comprised about 12.5 percent of the nation in 2000, it is expected to increase to nearly one-third of the total population by 2050. In comparison, during the same time period, the black and Asian populations are expected to grow by about 21 million and 24 million, thereby constituting 13.0 and 7.8 percent of the population by 2050, respectively.

While much media coverage and political debate focuses on unauthorized immigration, a large and growing number of individuals gain legal status every year. Table I.4 illustrates the proportion of legal permanent residents (LPR) from various sending locations around the world since 1960. In the aggregate, the number per year has increased from about 320,000 to over a million. Other figures of note include the

Table I.3. Population and Percent by Race and Hispanic Origin (in millions)

	*2000**	*2010**	*2020*	*2030*	*2040*	*2050*
POPULATION						
TOTAL	281.4	308.7	341.4	373.5	405.7	439.0
White alone	228.1	241.9	266.3	286.1	305.2	324.8
Black alone	35.7	40.3	44.4	48.7	52.9	56.9
Asian Alone	10.6	15.2	18.8	23.6	28.8	34.4
All other races	7.0	11.3	11.9	15.1	18.8	22.9
Hispanic (of any race)	35.3	50.5	66.4	85.9	108.2	132.8
White alone, not Hisp.	195.6	197.3	205.3	207.2	206.0	203.3
PERCENT OF TOTAL POPULATION						
TOTAL	100.0	100.0	100.0	100.0	100.0	100.0
White alone	81.1	78.4	78.0	76.6	75.3	74.0
Black alone	12.7	13.1	13.0	13.1	13.0	13.0
Asian Alone	3.8	4.9	5.5	6.3	7.1	7.8
All other races	2.5	3.7	3.5	4.0	4.6	5.2
Hispanic (of any race)	12.5	16.4	19.4	23.0	26.7	30.3
White alone, not Hisp.	69.5	63.9	60.1	55.5	51.0	46.3

Sources: Table 4. Projections of the Population by Sex, Race, and Hispanic Origin for the United States: 2010 to 2050. http://www.census.gov/population/www/projections/index.html.
Table 2: Intercensal Estimates of the Resident Population by Sex, Race, and Hispanic Origin for the United States: April 1, 2000 to July 1, 2010 (US-EST00INT-02). U.S. Census Bureau, Population Division. Release Date: September 2011.
* 2000 and 2010 data are April figures.

sharp decrease in the proportion of European and Canadian LPRs, the almost equally large increase in the proportion from Asia, the growing Mexican share, and the large percentage increase from Africa.

This process is leading to an increasingly multiethnic and multiracial United States. Anglos may well become a plurality within the next half-century if this "Latinization" trend continues (Ramos 2002). In addition, many regions of the United States with historically few Latinos are seeing significant levels of Latino population growth. In 2000, *le I.4.* Legal Permanent Residents by Country of Last Residence: 1961 to 2010 (fiscal years ing in year shown)

on and *try* *irth*	*1960 to 1969,* *10-yr total*	*1970 to 1979,* *10-yr total*	*1980 to 1989,* *10-yr total*	*1990 to 1999,* *10-yr total*	*2000 to 2009,* *10-yr total*	*2010* *1 yr total*
countries	3,213,749	4,248,203	6,244,379	9,775,398	10,299,430	1,042,625
cico	13.75%	14.62%	16.17%	28.21%	16.55%	13.30%
ada	13.48%	4.22%	2.50%	1.99%	2.30%	1.87%
Europe	35.27%	19.43%	10.71%	13.80%	13.10%	9.15%
Asia	11.16%	33.11%	38.30%	29.26%	33.70%	39.34%
Africa	0.74%	1.68%	2.27%	3.54%	7.38%	9.42%
South America	7.80%	6.44%	6.40%	5.84%	8.32%	8.23%
Central America	3.07%	2.83%	5.43%	6.24%	5.74%	4.18%
Caribbean	13.29%	16.69%	12.65%	10.28%	10.23%	13.37%

ce: U.S. Department of Homeland Security, Office of Immigration Statistics, 2010 Yearbook of Immigration Statistics.
lso http://uscis.gov/graphics/shared/statistics/yearbook/index.htm.
: Not all countries or regions are represented in this table, therefore percentages do not add to 100.

the majority of Latinos lived in the western and southern United States (43 and 33 percent, respectively), but many also lived in the Northeast and Midwest (15 and 9 percent respectively). Between 1990 and 2000, the Latino population in all regions grew considerably—81.0 percent in the Midwest, 70.3 percent in the South, 52.4 percent in the West, and 39.9 percent in the Northeast (Institute for Latino Studies n.d.). Some have suggested that the dominant culture of North America will become increasingly "Hispanicized" (see Wood 2004) as Latino settlement moves throughout the nation in concert with neoliberal economic integration between Mexico and the United States.

However, the larger implications of such changes may be less dramatic than contemporary political rhetoric sometimes suggests. Some claim that Latinos are not sufficiently assimilating, others worry that Latino immigration poses a challenge to fundamental American values, and a few even worry about the emergence of a separatist Latino "Quebec" in the southwestern United States (Huntington 2004). However, scholars have found that Latinos—including Spanish-dominant immigrants—express high levels of patriotism and support fundamental American economic and political values (de la Garza et al. 1996). Others have responded more specifically to Huntington, finding little evidence to support such concerns (Fraga and Segura 2006; Citrin et al. 2007; see also Leal 2009b).

What are the implications of Latino population increases for future Latino political influence? As noted above, numbers do not simply translate into power. One restraining factor is that many Latino immigrants have not naturalized. As Table I.5 indicates, foreign-born Latinos have a lower naturalization percentage than do non-Hispanic immigrant populations. This is not necessarily a matter of choice, as legal status matters—as can historical migration patterns and receptions. In addition, socioeconomic status (SES) factors also structure political participation (Wolfinger and Rosenstone 1980; Rosenstone and Hansen 1993). For instance, better educated and older individuals are much more likely to vote than are younger and less-educated citizens. Statistical models reveal generally that few racial-ethnic participation differences remain when such standard SES variables are included (Verba, Schlozman, and Brady 1995). This means that Latino participation is at a rate commensurate with their demographic profile and is not fundamentally different from that of other groups. In addition, while some look to culture—often a stereotyped version—to explain relatively low Latino political engagement, as the term "sleeping giant" implies, this is not necessary.

Regardless of explanation, however, the Latino electorate is a smaller percentage of its population than is the case for Anglos, which is relevant to the translation of numbers into influence. The Pew Research Center (Lopez and Taylor 2009) examined the 2008 electorate, finding turnout differences by race and ethnicity. The group with the lowest turnout percentage of eligible voters is Asian Americans (47 percent), not Latinos (49.9 percent). However, both rates are considerably lower than those of Anglos (66.1 percent) and African Americans (65.2 percent). Over time, the trend is toward an increasingly diverse electorate, yet one with Anglos as the clear majority. In 1988, the electorate was 82.1 percent Anglo, 11.1 percent African American, and 4.7 percent Latino. Twenty years later, the figures were 73.4 percent, 11.8 percent,

Table I.5. Foreign-Born and Percent of Naturalized Citizens within Foreign-Born, 2010

	Total	Hispanic	White alone, Not Hispanic	All Other Races, Not Hispanic	Mexican	Puerto Rican	Cuban	Central American	South American
Total Population (In Thousands)	304,280	48,901	197,436	57,942	32,071	4,406	1,826	3,960	2,737
Native	87.6%	63.0%	96.1%	79.4%	64.7%	99.7%	37.4%	35.8%	34.6%
Foreign-Born	12.4%	37.0%	3.9%	20.6%	35.3%	0.3%	62.6%	64.2%	65.4%
Naturalized Citizen	5.3%	11.0%	2.2%	10.9%	8.4%	0.2%	37.4%	16.7%	28.2%
Not a Citizen	7.1%	25.9%	1.7%	9.7%	26.9%	0.2%	25.2%	47.5%	37.2%

Source: U.S. Census Bureau, Current Population Survey, Annual Social and Economic Supplement, 2010. Derived from Table 7: Nativity and Citizenship Status by Sex, Hispanic Origin, and Race: 2010; and Table 8: Nativity and Citizenship Status by Sex and Hispanic Origin Type: 2010.

and 9.5 percent, respectively (and 3.4 percent Asian American). While the Latino percentage has nearly doubled, almost three-quarters of all voters were Anglo. The Pew report also noted the distinction between voting age and voting eligibility. In 2008, almost 31 million Latinos were of voting age, but just over 19.5 million were voting eligible—or 63 percent. For Anglos, the data were 151 million eligible voters out of 154 total voting age individuals (or 98 percent); for African Americans, the corresponding figure was 95 percent.

As noted above, individuals with higher levels of educational attainment are more likely to participate in politics, one of the strongest relationships found in the political science literature. As Table I.6 illustrates, the Latino (and specifically Mexican) population has lower educational achievement than do Anglos and all other races. About 43 percent of Mexican Americans do not have a high school diploma, a rate more than five times higher than that of Anglos and nearly three times as high as all other non-Whites, non-Hispanics. The percentages for bachelor's degree attainment are approximately the same.

However, we might ask to what degree these data reflect the experiences of native-born Latinos vs. immigrants. This has important implications for debates over Latino integration, immigrant acculturation, and the effectiveness of the public school system. In fact, educational data are more encouraging when seen across the generations. In addition, because many Mexican immigrants have never attended school in the United States, it is problematic to count them as high school "drop outs" when they never "dropped in" (for an extended discussion of Latinos and education, see Leal and Meier 2011).

Furthermore, an emerging literature examines the political implications of health and health care (see Rodriguez 2010). As shown in Table I.7, Latinos were about twice as likely as Anglos and all other races (non-Hispanic) to be uninsured in 2000. Not only does this indicate potentially devastating consequences for the health and well-being of a large segment of this population, but it could also serve to reduce political influence in a way scholars are only beginning to examine.

In the idealized American Dream, life circumstances improve for each generation. One of the key issues in contemporary immigration debates is the degree of intergenerational progress among Latinos. This

Table I.6. Education: Persons 25 and Older by Ethnicity and Race (2010)

	Total population	*Hispanic or Latino (any race)*	*Mex-Am.*	*Not Hispanic or Latino*	*White, not Hispanic or Latino*	*Not White, not Hispanic or Latino*
Total (In Thousands):	199,928	26,375	16,421	173,553	138,482	35,070
Nursery to 12th grade, no diploma	12.9%	37.1%	42.6%	9.2%	7.9%	14.0%
High school graduate (includes equivalency)	31.2%	29.6%	29.6%	31.5%	31.6%	30.9%
Some college, or Associate's degree	26.0%	19.3%	17.1%	27.0%	27.2%	26.2%
Bachelor's degree	19.4%	10.1%	7.9%	20.8%	21.4%	18.6%
Advanced degree	10.5%	3.8%	2.7%	11.5%	11.9%	10.3%

Source: U.S. Census Bureau, Current Population Survey, Annual Social and Economic Supplement, 2010. Internet release date: June 2011. Derived from Table 5: Educational Attainment of the Population 25 Years and Over by Sex, Hispanic Origin, and Race: 2010 and Table 6: Educational Attainment of the Population 25 Years and Over by Sex and Hispanic Origin Type: 2010.

Note: Data based on a sample. For information on confidentiality protection, sampling error, nonsampling error, definitions, and count corrections, see http://factfinder.census.gov/home/en/datanotes/expsf4.htm.

Table I.7. Insurance Coverage by Ethnicity and Race (2010)

Race	Total (In Thousands)	Insured	Not Insured
White, Non-Hispanic	197,436	88.0%	12.0%
All other races, Non-Hispanic	57,942	80.7%	19.3%
Hispanic origin	48,901	67.6%	32.4%
Mexican-American	32,071	65.6%	34.4%

Source: U.S. Census Bureau, Current Population Survey, Annual Social and Economic Supplement, 2010. Internet release date: June 2011. Derived from Table 41: Health Insurance Status by Sex, Age, Hispanic Origin, and Race: 2010. And Table 42: Health Insurance Status by Sex, Age, and Hispanic Origin Type: 2010.

is often seen as a proxy for successful integration (or lack thereof), but this can be problematic. For instance, it is difficult to sort out generational effects; comparisons against other immigrant groups may not be meaningful; there is an implicit reference to an idealized past; and it can be problematic to hold groups responsible for outcomes that may reflect larger structural dynamics. In addition, Duncan and Trejo (2011) found an ethnic attrition dynamic whereby some of the most socioeconomically successful individuals with Mexican heritage cease to identify themselves as Latino. It may be that many Latinos are integrating so well that they self-identify out of the ethnic category.

As Table I.8 illustrates, homeownership rates are higher, and the poverty rate is lower, for the third generation. On the other hand, improvements do not transpire across the generations for every category. While more third-generation members graduate from high school, bachelor's and advanced degrees are more likely to be held by the second generation and members of the first generation who arrived under the age of thirteen. In addition, members of the third generation over sixteen are the least likely to be in the labor force.

Characteristic	New First Generation (post-1960, foreign-born)		New Second Generation (post 1960, US born)			Third Generation and higher (self and parents are US born)
	Arrived 13 or older	Arrived under 13	Two foreign-born parents	One foreign-born parent	Total[1]	
Number[2]						
(in millions)	26.2	9.1	13.5	7.6	30.3	221.6
Age (mean years)	42.9	23.4	14.3	17.6	17.9	36.5
Metropolitan						
residence, %	95.4	93.7	95.7	90.9	93.9	79.2
Both parents						
present, %[3]	NA	78.0	76.8	69.9	75.2	66.2
Own home, %	52.1	54.4	59.8	68.2	60.3	75.7
Poverty Rate, %[4]	17.1	18.0	21.1	13.3	18.2	11.8
Education, %:[5]						
Less than HS	34.6	17.3	9.6	5.8	12.1	11.3
HS graduate						
or more	65.4	82.7	90.4	94.2	87.9	88.7
Bachelor's degree						
or more	27.1	30.6	39.3	37.8	35	27.6
In labor force, %[6]	68.6	71.4	66.4	73.5	70.2	66.0

Source: March 2005 Current Population Survey.

[1] Total of foreign-born persons who arrived after 1960 as children under 13, plus children born in the United States after 1960 of at least one foreign-born parent.

[2] First- and second-generation totals exclude persons born in Puerto Rico or other U.S. territories.

[3] For children under 18 years old.

[4] Below 100 percent of the federal poverty line.

[5] For persons 25 years or older.

[6] For persons 16 years or older.

Incorporation may also involve a transnational dimension. Some theorists see the immigrant incorporation system as dysfunctional for the children of immigrants. Their research suggests that connections to the home country and to immigrant enclaves in the host country, particularly in urban areas, limit access to mobility ladders for the children of nonwhite immigrants, who must then capitalize on their homeland ties as a strategy for economic survival (see Heisler 2000 for discussion). On the other hand, some research finds that the second generation is less likely to engage in transnational behavior (Jones-Correa 2007), which is primarily of interest to the migrating generation.

Lastly, we might ask about the political representation of Latinos in public office, which can provide both substantive and symbolic benefits (see Casellas and Leal 2010; Casellas 2011). As Table I.9 illustrates, Latino elected officials increased their numbers in all categories of state and local offices between 1984 and 2010. What accounts for this change? First, the growing Latino population leads to a larger number of Latino registered voters in both absolute and relative terms. For example, between 1994 and 2002, while the number of non-Hispanic voters in Texas increased by only 2 percent, the number of Latino voters increased by 33 percent (NALEO 2006). Second, the growth of "majority-minority" political districts can lead directly to more minority elected officials (Casellas 2011) but may also have an indirect effect by boosting Latino turnout in these districts (Barreto et al. 2004). Third, as Latino populations disperse across the nation, individuals are finding their way into elected office as members of both parties—and sometimes without actively advertising their Latino roots (Casellas 2011). In addition, coalitions with other racial and ethnic groups hold out the possibility of increasing the representation of minorities (Kaufmann 2004; Sonenshein and Pinkus 2005).

THIS VOLUME

The goal of this book is to contribute to our understanding of immigration and border politics and policies. The chapters cover a wide range

Table I.9. Hispanic Public Elected Officials by Office and State, 1984 to 2010

Year	Total	Total Percent Change	State executives and legislators	County and municipal officials	Judicial and law enforcement	Education and school boards
1984	3,063	-	119	1,276	495	1,173
1988	3,360	9.7%	135	1,425	574	1,226
1992	4,994	48.6%	150	1,908	628	2,308
1994	5,459	9.3%	199	2,197	651	2,412
1996*	3,743	-	162	1,653	546	1,240
2000	5,019	34.1%	217	1,852	447	2,503
2004	4,651	-7.3%	253	2,059	638	1,723
2006	4,932	6.0%	244	2,151	693	1,835
2010	5,739	16.4%	252	2,270	874	2,071
change 1984–2010		87.4%	111.8%	77.9%	76.6%	76.6%

Source: National Association of Latino Elected and Appointed Officials (NALEO) Educational Fund, Washington, DC, National Directory of Latino Elected Officials, formerly published as the National Roster of Hispanic Elected Officials, Annual.
*Prior to 1996, NALEO included elected officials that held a position at any point during the given year. Reports released in 1996 and the following years include elected official that held a position in January of the given year.

of topics that are central to contemporary scholarship and political debates. We hope this research appeals not only to academics but also to wider policy and public audiences and thereby helps to inform contentious debates about migration and migrants.

We arranged these chapters into five sections. The first sets the stage, discussing the binational lives of Mexican migrants. The subsequent four sections are arranged to highlight more specific political and policy themes: civic engagement; public policies; political reactions against immigrants; and immigrant leadership. We therefore show immigrants as both actors and objects in the political system. While they are buffeted by political forces and lines in the sand, they are also actively engaged in determining their individual and collective circumstances. The border structures how Latinos live, work, and organize, but Latino lives span borders as never before.

Part I. Setting the Stage: Binational Lives

For many Mexican families, migration to the United States is a tradition established over multiple generations. This is not a single-direction movement, however. Circular migration, permanent return, and remittances complicate the story and lead to transitional lives for many. These experiences produce "narratives" that serve to establish "coherent identities" for many immigrants (Vila 2000, 15). The two chapters in this section therefore set the stage for the subsequent policy and political chapters in this volume and discuss how transnational experiences and cultural identities affect the lives of Mexican immigrants and Mexican Americans.

The city of San Antonio, Texas, has a large and long-standing Mexican-origin population and has played a central role in U.S.-Mexico history. In chapter 1, Harriett Romo explores the transnational experience through the eyes of over two hundred Mexican-born individuals residing in this city. Her interviews explore how people live their lives in a transnational community, how transnational experiences are different across generations and socioeconomic classes, and how Mexican immigrants and Mexican Americans construct their cultural identities in this urban context. As she notes, the physical, cognitive, and imagined connections they establish to their native, Mexican communities are important in understanding how these individuals live and construct their individual and group identities. Providing a brief overview of the history of these communities and their evolving relationship, Romo then focuses on how institutions like work and family shape the transnational experience and how formal institutions affect national borders. Transnational experience also affects subsequent generations residing in the area as well as important political and economic institutions on both sides of the border.

In chapter 2, Ricardo Ainslie and Daphny Dominguez Ainslie discuss the psychology of the migration experience, the reasons for migrating, and the conflicts that arise in Mexican communities due to migration. These authors explore (1) how Mexican immigrants live the immigrant experience through awareness at both conscious and unconscious levels—what the authors call the "Social Imaginary," and (2) the impact of mass migration on Mexico itself. They argue that culture is integral to immigrant identities, as well as to their perceptions of what it means to be in the United States. The effect of the journey also colors migrants' perceptions of the world they left behind.

Interviews conducted in Mexico City reveal two different reactions: migrants are seen as either heroes or villains. Many Mexicans see migrants as overcoming obstacles and making sacrifices for the sake of their families. Other Mexicans are concerned about the repercussions of long absences on families and see negative changes in the migrants due to their experiences in the United States; these individuals believe their migrant friends have pursued an unhealthy illusion. Opinions about the migration experience by those Mexicans who stay home are ultimately complex, generally reflecting the inner conflicts of the migrants themselves. As a large portion of the Mexican population makes that journey, this study of the psychology of both the migrants and those who remain behind contributes to our understanding of the issue.

Part II. Immigrants and Civic Life

Studies examining globalization and transnationalism find immigrants who participate in nation-building exercises in both countries by preserving ties to their country of origin and building new connections in their adopted country (Brettell 2008; Heisler 2000; Brettell and Hollifield 2008). These individuals have the potential to influence the political and civic life of both nations, and are therefore of significant interest to scholars. To what degree transnational activities are common, and whether this impedes or promotes political engagement in the United States, are important questions (for instance, see McCann, Cornelius, and Leal 2009).

Specifically seeking to "identify, measure and relate" transnationalism as Latino immigrants experience it, John Garcia examines transnationalism and its consequences for the civic life of Mexican immigrants in U.S. communities. Contemporary transnationalism is promoted by technological advances that enable migrants to maintain contacts and interactions in both countries. Immigrants in the United States can affect politics in their home countries, and political parties in sending nations have reached out to immigrants for support. A growing number of home countries also encourage dual citizenship in order to increase opportunities for civic participation on the part of their non-resident citizens.

Using the data collected from the Chicago Area Study conducted by the Institute for Latino Studies at the University of Notre Dame, Garcia analyzes a sample of 765 foreign-born Latinos. Responses indicate that living in the United States creates opportunities to connect immigrants with social-political institutions. As taxpayers, renters, workers, parents, and participants in other community activities, transnationals are engaged in the life of both nations. Garcia finds that those closest to the immigration experience are more involved in transnational activities, and that such participation is associated with higher levels of engagement in community life. Transnational involvement therefore positively affects civic and political engagement in the United States.

In chapter 4, Adrian Pantoja, Rafael Jimeno, and Javier Rodriguez test three hypotheses about the political consequences of Latino immigrant transnational ties for naturalization and voter participation: Do such ties impede, spur, or have no effect on political incorporation in the United States? Using survey data from the 2002 Pew Hispanic Research Center, the chapter finds evidence supporting the third perspective. Most transnational activities have no impact on Latin American immigrant naturalization or voter participation. The strongest correlates are the traditionally important variables in political engagement models—education and age. While certain transnational ties may impede political incorporation (particularly the negative association of dual citizenship and voting abroad with voting in the United States), the evidence in the chapter suggests a complex view of transnationalism's political effects.

In chapter 5, Louis DeSipio examines the relationship between Latino naturalization and political engagement in the United States. Specifically, because immigrants may need time to learn politically relevant skills and knowledge, he hypothesizes that those who have been naturalized for longer periods of time will be more likely to participate in politics. He also hypothesizes that those who are naturalized for political reasons are more likely to become politically engaged, while those who attain citizenship in order to secure access to government services are less likely to do so. The chapter compares the political behavior of naturalized and native-born Mexican Americans and Cuban Americans in 2000 using a Latino dataset that measures involvement in community organizations, parental involvement in schools, voter registration, and voting.

The results indicate that naturalized citizens participate at lower rates than do U.S.-born citizens, and that year of naturalization is a significant predictor of voting patterns. As expected, immigrants with more years since naturalization were more likely to vote than immigrants who naturalized more recently, as were those with political reasons for naturalizing. DeSipio concludes that advocates should focus their efforts on helping immigrants understand their connections to U.S. politics, the benefits and protections of citizenship, and the skills they need to enact those rights.

The chapter by Adrian Pantoja focuses on the transnational political activities of a growing Latino national-origin group—Dominicans. While the majority of Latinos are still members of one of the three traditionally largest groups—Mexicans, Puerto Ricans, and Cubans— recent decades have seen considerable increases in migrants from the Caribbean, Central America, and South America. Using a unique survey of Dominicans in New York City, Pantoja finds that a quarter of the respondents were engaged in at least one form of transnational activity. The regression models show a number of consistent determinants; those who are older and have participated in U.S. politics were more likely to engage transnationally, while U.S. citizenship and the presence of family in the United States were associated with less activity.

Part III. Immigration and Public Policy

Policymaking and implementation can be a complex and difficult process; this is no less true for immigration issues. The chapters in this section discuss three important issues: border security, health care, and education.

In chapter 7, Raymond Padilla examines the educational attainment of both Mexican immigrant and Mexican American students. He finds that "the two independent national educational systems in Mexico and the United States together shape educational achievement for Chicano students." On the Mexican side, the school system under-educates the population and the economy provides few opportunities, which encourages migration. In the United States, school inequality for Mexican Americans is the result of long-standing racialized attitudes and economic interests. The result is diminished achievement for both sets of students. The author recommends the replacement of assimilationist strategies in favor of a new "multicultural diversity with transcultural unity" model; that activists might spend less time on systemic reform efforts and more time advocating for and mentoring individual students; and that Mexico consider educational reforms, such as English instruction, that will help its many young people who will spend some time in the United States.

In chapters 8 and 9, Adela de la Torre, Nuñez de Ybarra, Marisol Cortez, and Emily Prieto address the critical issues of Latino health care utilization as well as culturally innovative interventions. The first chapter outlines four distinct realms of action that are required for migrants to benefit from public health insurance programs: (1) barriers to eligibility; (2) barriers to enrollment; (3) factors associated with under-enrollment; and (4) barriers to effective utilization of care. They also discuss the implications of recent health care reform for Latinos, both citizens and immigrants. Their second chapter examines culturally innovative and competent interventions that help to reduce the gap between Latino health care eligibility and actual enrollment and utilization. The authors search the existing literature to pinpoint specific problems and identify best practices to improve Latino knowledge of and access to public health insurance programs.

These two chapters address a topic with considerable implications for the quality of life for Latino communities (and, as noted above, perhaps for political power). Ultimately, they conclude that health care agencies must develop strategies to successfully reach out to Latino communities, taking into account linguistic and cultural characteristics as well as the mixed legal status of Latino communities.

In chapter 10, Lisa Magaña examines the Immigration and Naturalization Service (INS, subsequently reorganized) and the U.S. Border Patrol from an organizational and administrative perspective. Her chapter uses the issue of immigration, both legal and unauthorized, to illustrate that public agencies do not operate in a vacuum but are accountable to uphold many complex, contradictory, and sometimes illogical policy mandates. She finds that these entities are required to implement immigration policies in a context of frequent new policies and directives, often based on political and economic factors. These directives give little consideration to how they will affect the agency or the target group—in this case, migrants crossing the Mexican border. Magaña utilizes research from macro evaluations and extensive interviews and surveys in order to show that immigration agencies do not implement policy in isolation. They are responsible for multifaceted, often conflicting, tasks under great challenges—such as poor funding, constantly increasing demands, and limited resources—that reduce their ability to function effectively and efficiently to achieve policy objectives.

Part IV. Political Reactions to Immigration

In the early months of the George W. Bush administration, the immigration reform issue was back on the policy agenda. Many expected that the Bush administration would negotiate a new reform plan in coordination with newly elected Mexican President Vicente Fox. However, despite the personal commitment of both presidents, the terror attacks of September 11, 2001, not only displaced the issue from the agenda but also changed future debates by introducing a new security dimension. When President Bush brought renewed attention to immigration reform in mid-decade, many politicians and grass roots activists would favor "law and order" approaches that required a "securing" of the border before considering a legalization (often denounced as "amnesty").

An important part of the policymaking process is therefore the rhetoric used in political discourse; how issues, people, and concerns are framed and discussed can have important consequences. The contributors to this section discuss the often-divergent language, goals, and consequences of the rhetoric found in contemporary immigration debates.

In chapter 11, Rodolfo Espino and Rafael Jimeno consider how the changing political and economic environment affected immigration policy in the post–9/11 years. Specifically, they discuss the rhetoric surrounding immigration policymaking, which can provide insight into how the objective observation of facts and the subjective framing of those facts are used to construct political agendas. They consider two factors: the justification for immigration enforcement along the U.S.-Mexico border and the degree to which security threats are perceived along our northern vs. southern borders. First, they find that over time, the rhetorical justification for the apprehension of unauthorized immigrants has changed from employment to crime to security. Policies continue, but justifications change. Second, they studied congressional debates about immigration from 1988–2004, particularly the association of Mexico and Canada with trade, drugs, and security. They found a sharp spike in the rhetorical connections between security and Mexico after September 11, 2001. In 2004, the association of security with Mexico was nearly six times larger than the association with Canada. This suggests that while debates about immigration policy may have shifted in response to the terrorist attacks, the underlying source of many politicians' angst may continue to be Mexican immigrants.

Examining rhetoric at the policy level, Sylvia Manzano discusses the success of Arizona's Proposition 200 in chapter 12. A citizen's initiative, Proposition 200 (the "Arizona Taxpayer Citizen Protection Act") received strong support from voters in November 2004. The proposition called for government employees to verify citizenship status for those seeking to register to vote, vote, and apply for and use public benefits. They would also be required to report any violations to the federal government. Failure to do so would be a state crime as well as constitute grounds for citizen lawsuits. The success of this proposition was the result of political and social forces at both the state and national levels. Immigration and border policies in the previous decade pushed immigrants specifically toward the Arizona border, creating a spike in unauthorized immigration to the state. High-profile rhetoric painted immigrants as a menace to local and national security, and the success of similar previous initiatives helped pave the way. All of these factors combined to create an ideal political environment for this sweeping policy.

Manuel Avalos and Lisa Magaña also examine Arizona's Proposition 200 in chapter 13. Using precinct data, the authors attempt to explain the influence of the Latino vote, the determinants of the vote, and why a bipartisan coalition was unable to defeat the proposition. They found strong support for the proposition from Anglos, men, Republicans, conservatives, and those who identified terrorism and moral values as the most important issues in the election. Support was especially strong in precincts with a large concentration of Anglo voters. On the other hand, some variables did not behave as expected; registered Democrats, as well as registered Republicans, mostly voted in favor of the bill. Even more unexpected was the fairly strong support in the Latino electorate—although 55 percent were opposed, 44 percent voted yes. The authors postulate that, due to this division in the community, a greater mobilization of Latinos would not likely have changed the outcome of the vote.

René Galindo and Jami Vigil explore media accounts of anti-immigrant statements in terms of their racist and nativist implications in chapter 14 (reprinted from *Latino Studies Journal*). They contend that media accounts of such statements sometimes question whether the statements were racist but less often whether they were nativist. The absence of the term "nativism" in the media is striking given the long history of immigration-skeptic politics in the United States. The absence of nativism also obscures the historical patterns of anti-immigrant sentiment from previous eras. These authors analyze two cases as reported in newspaper articles and as interpreted in editorials. The case studies explore the implications of distinguishing nativism from racism for policy outcomes, for revealing bias against Latinos, and for understanding the place of Latinos within the nation.

Part V. Immigrants and Leadership

Networks of organizations and individuals can improve the social, economic, and political conditions for immigrant communities. Effective leadership is an important component of group effectiveness, and these leaders cannot be taken for granted. The following chapters examine the emergence of Latino leaders in both new and established communities. In chapter 15, Maria de los Angeles Torres interviewed Latino youth about their involvement with and attitudes about political issues, including education, immigration, the war in Iraq, and marginalization. She additionally interviewed directors and organizers of community groups that work with youth in the Chicago area. All the interviewed youth were involved in some political activity, and the author found that parents, family, schools, and reading materials all helped motivate them—with family support and the home environment the best predictors. The author notes that most organizations seeking to empower Latino communities focus on voter registration or naturalization. She suggests, however, that activists cultivate youth involvement through their parents in order to spur the political engagement of Latino communities.

The 1990s to the present have seen a significant surge in the Mexican-origin population of New England. In the final chapter, Martha Montero-Sieburth explores immigrant empowerment through the emergent leadership of Mexican immigrants in community-based organizations (CBOs) in the New England area. Taking a combined qualitative and quantitative approach, Montero-Sieburth gathered data on Mexican leaders in New England communities, including factors such as (1) education and work experience; (2) organizational behavior; (3) leadership experience; and (4) relationship with the Mexican Consulate. Additionally, surveys were given to Mexicans who attended a seminar sponsored by the Gaston Institute of the University of

Massachusetts–Boston and the General Consulate of Mexico in Boston. The chapter discusses their perspectives on leadership development, leadership styles, the relationship of CBOs with local Mexican consulates, the expectations of immigrant leaders about the Mexican and U.S. governments, and implications for the future of local and transnational Mexican immigrant leadership.

NOTES

1. Although there are different proposals, the Development, Relief, and Education for Alien Minors (DREAM) Act would allow individuals who graduated from U.S. high schools but were brought without authorization to the United States as children to gain legal status by graduating from college or serving in the armed forces.

2. See the PBS special website about George Washington at http://www .pbs.org/georgewashington/collection/other_1788dec2.html (last accessed April 18, 2008) for his speech to Irish immigrants. In particular, scholars point to this quote as the "open door" policy Washington sets: "The bosom of America is open to receive not only the Opulent and respectable Stranger, but the oppressed and persecuted of all Nations And Religions; whom we shall wellcome [sic] to a participation of all our rights and privileges, if by decency and propriety of conduct they appear to merit the enjoyment." See also the webpage for the "Official Site of the U.S. Constitution" http://www.us constitution.com/naturalizationactof1795.htm (last accessed April 18, 2008) for the full Naturalization Act of 1795.

3. We might also note the possibility that security concerns will create economic inefficiencies in the U.S.-Canada relationship.

4. See also its predecessor, the 1988 Canadian American Free Trade Agreement (CAFTA).

5. Tara Bahrampour, "More laws have been enacted to help immigrants than restrict them." *Washington Post,* May 11, 2010.

REFERENCES

Albert, Mathias, and Lothar Brock. 1998. "New Relationships between Territory and State: The U.S.-Mexico Border in Perspective." In *The U.S.-Mexico Border: Transcending Divisions, Contesting Identities,* edited by David Spener and Kathleen Staudt, 215–32. Boulder: Lynne Rienner Publishers.

Andreas, Peter. 2000. *Border Games: Policing the U.S.-Mexico Divide.* Ithaca: Cornell University Press.

Bailey, John. 2001. "Nafta's Impacts on Mexico and the United States: Subregional Effects of Trade and Economic Integration." In *U.S.-Mexican Economic Integration: Nafta at the Grassroots,* edited by John Bailey, 1–45. Austin: University of Texas Press.

Baker, Bryan C. 2010. "Naturalization Rates Among IRCA Immigrants: A 2009 Update." Washington, DC: Department of Homeland Security Office of Immigration Statistics. www.dhs.gov/xlibrary/assets/statistics/publications/irca-natz-fs-2009.pdf. Last accessed February 1, 2011.

Barreto, Matt A., Gary M. Segura, and Nathan D. Woods. 2004. "The Mobilizing Effect of Majority-Minority Districts on Latino Turnout." *American Political Science Review* 98 (1): 65–75.

Bonilla, Frank, Edwin Meléndez, Rebecca Morales, and Maria de los Angeles Torres, eds. 1998. *Borderless Borders: U.S. Latinos, Latin Americans, and the Paradox of Interdependence.* Philadelphia: Temple University Press.

Brakman, Harold, and Steven P. Erie. 2001. "Paradoxes of Mexican Integration in Southern California." In *U.S.-Mexican Economic Integration: Nafta at the Grassroots,* edited by John Bailey, 99–135. Austin: University of Texas Press.

Brettell, Caroline B. 2008. "Theorizing Migration in Anthropology: The Social Construction of Networks, Identities, Communities, and Globalscapes." In *Migration Theory: Talking across Disciplines,* edited by Caroline B. Brettell and James F. Hollifield, 113–59. New York: Routledge.

Brettell, Caroline B., and James F. Hollifield, eds. 2008. *Migration Theory: Talking across Disciplines.* 2nd ed. New York: Routledge.

Calavita, Kitty. 1992. *Inside the State: The Bracero Program, Immigration, and the I.N.S.* New York: Routledge.

Cárdenas, Gilberto. June, 2006. "Visualizing Mexican Migration to the United States." Princeton: Working Paper 06–04e, Center for Migration and Development, Princeton University.

Casellas, Jason P. 2011. *Latino Representation in State Houses and Congress.* New York: Cambridge University Press.

Casellas, Jason P., and David L. Leal. 2010. "Minority Representation in the United States Congress." In *The Political Representation of Immigrants and Minorities: Voters, Parties, and Parliaments in Liberal Democracies,* edited by Karen Bird, Thomas Saalfeld, and Andreas M. Wüst, 183–206. London: Routledge.

Citrin, Jack, Amy Lerman, Michael Murakami, and Kathryn Pearson. 2007. "Testing Huntington: Is Hispanic Immigration a Threat to American Identity?" *Perspectives on Politics* 5: 31–48.

Cohen, Robin K. 2007. "PRWORA's Immigrant Provisions." OLR Research Report: 2007-R-0705. December 13. http://www.cga.ct.gov/2007/rpt/2007-R-0705.htm. Last accessed July 16, 2010.

DeLaet, Debra L. 2000. *U.S. Immigration Policy in an Age of Rights*. Westport: Praeger.

de la Garza, Rodolfo. 1996. "El Cuento de los Números and Other Latino Political Myths." In *Su Voto Es Su Voz: Latino Politics in California,* edited by Aníbal Yañez-Chávez, 11–32. San Diego: Center for U.S.-Mexican Studies, University of California San Diego.

de la Garza, Rodolfo, Angelo Falcon, and F. Chris Garcia. 1996. "Will the Real Americans Please Stand Up: Anglo and Mexican-American Support of Core American Political Values." *American Journal of Political Science* 40: 335–51.

Duncan, Brian, and Stephen J. Trejo. 2011. "Tracking Intergenerational Progress for Immigrant Groups: The Problem of Ethnic Attrition." *American Economic Review: Papers and Proceedings* 101, (3): 603–8.

Fox, Claire F. 1999. *The Fence and the River: Culture and Politics at the U.S.-Mexico Border*. Cultural Studies of the Americas. Minneapolis: University of Minnesota Press.

Fraga, Luis R., and Gary M. Segura. 2006. "Culture Clash? Contesting Notions of American Identity and the Effects of Latin American Immigration." *Perspectives on Politics* 4: 279–87.

Freeman, Gary P. 1988. "The Decline of Sovereignty? Politics and Immigration Restriction in Liberal States." In *Challenge to the Nation-State: Immigration in Western Europe and the United States,* edited by Christian Joppke. New York: Oxford University Press.

Gutiérrez, David G. 1995. *Walls and Mirrors: Mexican Americans, Mexican Immigrants, and the Politics of Ethnicity.* Berkeley: University of California Press.

Hagan, Jacqueline M., David L. Leal, and Nestor P. Rodriguez. 2012. "Social Consequences of Mass Deportation by the U.S. Government, 2000–2010." Paper presented at the conference "Citizenship in Question." Sponsored by the Boston College Center for Human Rights and International Justice. Boston, April 19–21, 2012.

Hansen, Randall. 2008. "A New Citizenship Bargain for the Age of Mobility? Citizenship Requirements in Europe and North America." In *Delivering Citizenship,* edited by Bertelsmann Stiftung, European Policy Centre, Migration Policy Institute. Gutersloh: Bertelsmann Stiftung.

Heisler, Barbara Schmitter. 2008. "The Sociology of Immigration: From Assimilation to Segmented Integration, from the American Experience to the Global Arena." In *Migration Theory: Talking across Disciplines,* edited by Caroline B. Brettell and James F. Hollifield, 83–111. New York: Routledge.

Herzog, Lawrence A. 1990. *Where North Meets South: Cities, Space, and Politics on the U.S.-Mexico Border*. Austin: University of Texas Press.

Higham, John. 2006. "Patterns in the Making." In *The Migration Reader: Exploring Politics and Policies,* edited by Anthony M. Messina and Gallya Lahav, 375–83. Boulder: Lynne Rienner Publishers.

Hollifield, James F. 2008. "The Politics of International Migration: How Can We 'Bring the State Back In'?" In *Migration Theory: Talking across Disciplines,* edited by Caroline B. Brettell and James F. Hollifield, 183–237. New York: Routledge.

Huntington, Samuel P. 2004. *Who Are We? The Challenges to America's National Identity.* New York: Simon and Schuster.

Institute for Latino Studies (ILS). n.d. The Latino Population: 1990–2000 (PowerPoint presentation). University of Notre Dame. http://www.nd.edu/~iuplr/downloads.htm. Last accessed November 19, 2007.

Jones-Correa, Michael A. 2007. "Fuzzy Distinctions and Blurred Boundaries: Transnational, Ethnic, and Immigrant Politics." In *Latino Politics: Identity, Mobilization, and Representation,* edited by Rodolfo Espino, David L. Leal, and Kenneth J. Meier, 44–60. Charlottesville: University of Virginia Press.

Kanstroom, Daniel. 2007. *Deportation Nation: Outsiders in American History.* Cambridge, MA: Harvard University Press.

Kaufmann, Karen. 2004. *The Urban Voter: Group Conflict and Mayoral Voting Behavior in American Cities.* Ann Arbor: University of Michigan Press.

Leal, David L. 2009a. "Stalemate: U.S. Immigration Reform Efforts, 2005 to 2007." *People and Place* 17: 1–17.

———. 2009b. "Latinos, Immigration, and Social Cohesion in the United States." In *Nations of Immigrants: Australia and the USA,* edited by John Higley and John Nieuwenhuysen, 132–46. Cheltenham: Edward Elgar.

———. 2010. "Prospects for Change." Room for Debate: Why Congress Falters on Immigration. *New York Times,* December 9.

Leal, David L., and Kenneth J. Meier, eds. 2011. *The Politics of Latino Education.* New York: Teachers College Press.

Lopez, Mark Hugo, and Paul Taylor. 2009. "Dissecting the 2008 Electorate: Most Diverse in U.S. History." Washington, DC: Pew Hispanic Center. http://www.pewhispanic.org/2009/04/30/dissecting-the-2008-electorate-most-diverse-in-us-history/.

Lorey, David E. 1999. *The U.S.-Mexican Border in the Twentieth Century: A History of Economic and Social Transformation.* Wilmington: Scholarly Resources.

Massey, Douglas S., Jorge Durand, and Nolan J. Malone. 2002. *Beyond Smoke and Mirrors: Mexican Immigration in an Era of Economic Integration.* New York: Russell Sage Foundation.

McCann, James A., Wayne Cornelius, and David L. Leal. 2009. "Transnational Political Engagement and the Civic Incorporation of Mexican Immigrants in the United States." Paper presented at Mexico Week, London School of Economics, March 3.

Montoya, Lisa J. 2000. "The Sleeping Giant in Latino Electoral Politics." In *Reflexiones 1999: New Directions in Mexican American Studies,* edited by Richard R. Flores, 29–50. Austin: Center for Mexican American Studies Press.

National Association of Latino Elected and Appointed Officials (NALEO). *2006 Primary Election Profiles: Texas.* http://www.naleo.org/downloads/ TX_Primary_Profile_2_22_06_FIN.pdf. Last accessed January 9, 2008.

Portes, Alejandro, and Robert L. Bach. 1985. *Latin Journey: Cuban and Mexican Immigrants in the United States.* Berkeley: University of California Press.

Portes, Alejandro, and Rubén G. Rumbaut. 2006. *Immigrant America: A Portrait.* Berkeley: University of California Press.

Preston, Julia. 2012. "Romney's Plan for 'Self-Deportation' Has Conservative Support." *New York Times* (The Caucus: The Politics and Government Blog of the Times), January 24. http://thecaucus.blogs.nytimes.com/.

Ramos, Jorge. 2002. *The Other Face of America: Chronicles of the Immigrants Shaping Our Future.* Translated by Patricia J. Duncan. New York: Harper Collins.

Rodriguez, Javier M. 2010. "The Contribution of Mortality Gaps Between African Americans and Whites to Their Disparities in Voter Turnout." Paper presented at the annual meeting of the American Political Science Association. Washington, DC.

Rosenstone, Steven J., and John Mark Hansen. 1993. *Mobilization, Participation, and Democracy in America.* New York: Macmillan.

Saint-Germain, Michelle A. 1998. "Re-Presenting the Public Interest on the U.S.-Mexico Border." In *The U.S.-Mexico Border: Transcending Divisions, Contesting Identities,* edited by David Spener and Kathleen Staudt, 59–81. Boulder: Lynne Rienner Publishers.

Salehyan, Idean, and Marc R. Rosenblum. 2004. "Norms and Interests in U.S. Asylum Enforcement." *Journal of Peace Research* 41 (6): 677–97.

Sanchez, George I. 1940. *Forgotten People: A Study of New Mexicans.* Albuquerque: University of New Mexico Press.

Sassen, Saskia. 1998. "The *de facto* Transnationalizing of Immigration Policy." In *Challenge to the Nation-State: Immigration in Western Europe and the United States,* edited by Christian Joppke, 49–85. New York: Oxford University Press.

Schildkraut, Deborah J. 2012. "Amnesty, Guest Workers, Fences! Oh My! Public Opinion about 'Comprehensive Immigration Reform.'" In *Immigration and Public Opinion in Liberal Democracies,* edited by Gary P. Freeman, Randall Hansen, and David L. Leal. New York: Routledge.

Sonenshein, Raphael J., and Susan H. Pinkus. 2005. "Latino Incorporation Reaches the Urban Summit: How Antonio Villaraigosa Won the 2005 Los Angeles Mayor's Race." *PS: Political Science and Politics* 38 (4): 713–21.

Soysal, Yasemin. 1994. *Limits of Citizenship: Migrants and Postnational Membership in Europe.* Chicago: University of Chicago Press.

Sparrow, Bartholomew H. 2006. *The Insular Cases and the Emergence of American Empire.* Lawrence: University Press of Kansas.

Spener, David, and Kathleen Staudt. 1998. "The View from the Frontier: Theoretical Perspectives Undisciplined." In *The U.S.-Mexico Border: Transcending Divisions, Contesting Identities,* edited by David Spener and Kathleen Staudt, 3–33. Boulder: Lynne Rienner Publishers.

Steger, Manfred B. 2003. *Globalization: A Very Short Introduction.* Oxford: Oxford University Press.

Tichenor, Daniel J. 2002. *Dividing Lines: The Politics of Immigration Control in America.* Princeton: Princeton University Press.

U.S. Citizenship and Immigration Services (USCIS). n.d.a. "Historical Immigration and Naturalization Legislation: Legislation from 1901–1940." http://www.uscis.gov/files/nativedocuments/Legislation%20from%20 1901-1940.pdf. Last accessed January 14, 2008.

———. n.d.b. "Historical Immigration and Naturalization Legislation: Legislation from 1901–1940." http://www.uscis.gov/files/nativedocuments/ Legislation%20from%201941-1960.pdf. Last accessed January 14, 2008.

———. n.d.c. "Historical Immigration and Naturalization Legislation: Legislation from 1981–1996." http://www.uscis.gov/files/nativedocuments/ Legislation%20from%201981-1996.pdf. Last accessed January 14, 2008.

U.S. Department of Homeland Security, 2010. *Yearbook of Immigration Statistics: 2009.* Washington, DC: Office of Immigration Statistics. Online report: http://www.dhs.gov/xlibrary/assets/statistics/yearbook/2009/ois_yb _2009.pdf.

U.S. Immigration and Naturalization Service. 1992. Immigration Reform and Control Act: Report on the Legalized Alien Population. Washington, DC: U.S. Department of Justice.

Vélez-Ibáñez, Carlos G. 1996. *Border Visions: Mexican Cultures of the Southwest United States.* Tucson: University of Arizona Press.

Verba, Sidney, Kay Lehman Schlozman, and Henry E. Brady. 1995. *Voice and Equality: Civic Voluntarism in American Politics.* Cambridge, MA: Harvard University Press.

Vila, Pablo. 2000. *Crossing Borders, Reinforcing Borders: Social Categories, Metaphors, and Narrative Identities on the U.S.-Mexico Frontier.* Austin: University of Texas Press.

Weiner, Myron. 1995. *The Global Migration Crisis.* New York: Harper Collins.

Wolfinger, Raymond E., and Steven J. Rosenstone. 1980. *Who Votes?* New Haven: Yale University Press.

Wood, Andrew Grant, ed. 2004. *On the Border: Society and Culture between the United States and Mexico*. Lanham: Scholarly Resources.

Zolberg, Aristide R. 2006. *A Nation by Design: Immigration Policy in the Fashioning of America*. New York: Russell Sage.

Zúñiga, Victor. 1998. "Nations and Borders: Romantic Nationalism and the Project of Modernity." In *The U.S.-Mexico Border: Transcending Divisions, Contesting Identities,* edited by David Spener and Kathleen Staudt, 35–55. Boulder: Lynne Rienner Publishers.

PART I

Setting the Stage—Binational Lives

ONE

Formal and Informal Institutions in the Construction of Transnational Lives

A Study of Mexican and Mexican American Experiences in San Antonio, Texas—A Mexican-Majority U.S. City

HARRIETT D. ROMO

INTRODUCTION

This study is an exploration of the transnational experiences of Mexican origin residents in San Antonio, Texas. The context of the city of San Antonio, with a history of U.S.-Mexico relations and a majority Mexican origin population, creates an environment of organizations, institutions, work, and family relationships that promote transnational ties. Formal institutions such as religion, schools, and laws shape transnational lives, but work, family, and culture also transcend borders. Variations of Mexican culture permeate all aspects of life in San Antonio. The experiences of Mexican immigrants and Mexican American residents in a majority Mexican U.S. city can advance our basic understanding of the incorporation processes of diverse groups into U.S. society and the complexity of transnational experiences.

The main research questions addressed in this project are the following: How do people live their lives in a transnational community? How do transnational experiences differ across generations and socioeconomic class? How do Mexican immigrants and Mexican Americans construct their cultural identities in a transnational community?

The physical connections that residents in San Antonio sustain to their Mexican communities are critical, but the cognitive and imagined elements of transnational lives are also important (Levitt and Waters 2002). Thus I am interested in how individuals of various generations and socioeconomic backgrounds conduct their daily lives and how these persons construct their identities and social groups within transnational social fields.[1]

In studying the experiences of the Mexican origin population in San Antonio, I recognize that transnational identities are shaped across generations, but, like Eckstein (2002), I propose that generational influences are based on a shared historically contextualized experience. In San Antonio, this involves the heightened emphasis on the Spanish language during the twenty-first century as well as the dynamic borderlands culture promoted in San Antonio due to the city's history as well as increased transnational trade, cultural ties, and immigration. Technology and communication links between sending and receiving communities in Mexico and San Antonio make maintaining connections much easier today than in earlier generations, even if individuals do not physically cross the borders between the two countries. The proximity of Mexico to Texas, the interpenetration of the economies and societies of the two areas, and the emergence of a U.S.-born Mexican-origin population as the majority population in San Antonio have transformed the process of migration and incorporation itself. Residents in San Antonio are constructing new, complex transnational identities that are both Mexican and American.

This chapter explores how transnational families in San Antonio live their lives and how they blend the experiences of Mexico and San Antonio. I focus on how institutions such as work and family shape transnational experiences and how formal institutions expand and restrict national borders.

METHODOLOGY

I directed a research team composed of sociology graduate students and two faculty colleagues[2] who completed 244 in-depth, wide-ranging, life-history interviews, all transcribed, of persons in San Antonio, Texas representing various generations and socioeconomic categories. The sample included individuals representing four main subgroups: (1) elites (high income, college educated, community leaders), (2) working-class people in the 20–50 age group, (3) individuals in their 60s, 70s, and 80s who had transnational business or family lives, and (4) high school students. These subjects provide a good representation of the experiences of transnational families in San Antonio. The subjects were contacted using a snowball technique for the adults. Two high schools from the Westside community, a working-class inner city school that was formerly a vocational high school and a middle-class high school that was initially majority non-Hispanic white students and is now majority Hispanic, agreed to participate in the study. Teachers identified student respondents from English as a Second Language (ESL) classes to reach immigrant students and from regular English classes to reach second-generation students. A selected group of teachers were interviewed to complete the context of the transnational lives of students.

The interviews with adults lasted approximately two hours and those with students approximately an hour. The case studies in this chapter were developed from interviews selected to represent different types of transnational experiences and persons of different social class status.

Target Areas and Groups

Geographic areas in San Antonio with the largest concentrations of Mexican origin families received special consideration in identifying interview subjects. The Westside of San Antonio, one of the oldest Mexican neighborhoods in the city, continues to be the home of many third- and fourth-generation Mexican Americans. Often these families have lived their lives on both sides of the border visiting family, conducting business, or living temporarily in Mexico or San Antonio. The families have extensive contact with Mexican culture and have been influential in shaping the culture of the Westside Mexican American community and San Antonio.

Many of the working-class interviewees, small business owners, and the oldest generation interviewed lived in this Westside Mexican American community. Upper income respondents and many of the professionals interviewed had moved to suburban areas of the city.

Analysis of the Interviews

Questions in the interview guide focused on transnational experiences and the ways families incorporated aspects of American and Mexican culture into their lives on both sides of the border. Other topics covered language, identity, social networks, political participation, and institutional processes that shape transnational experiences. Interviews were coded using Atlas Ti computer software for qualitative research. The research team met frequently to discuss emerging themes and assure consistency of coding.

The case studies of participants used in this chapter illustrate the types of transnational experiences families have in San Antonio and Mexico. I explore themes that arise from the interviews and statements drawn from interviews to identify interpretive frameworks. Mexican-origin middle-class and professional families have quite different transnational experiences compared to low-income Mexican migrants. Interviews with high school-aged students illustrate how transnational fields influence the younger generation's experiences.

THEORETICAL CONSIDERATIONS

Classical ways of viewing ethnicity and assimilation in cities reflect a general belief in incompatibilities between traditional ways of doing things and a more urban, universalistic way of relating to other groups and of conducting one's life. Generation and ethnic origin have been key factors in assessing the assimilation of different ethnic groups in the United States (Alba 1999; Alba and Nee 1997; Gordon 1964; Hirschman 1983; Lieberson 1980; Lieberson and Waters 1988; Perlmann 1988; Portes 1996; Waters 1990, 1999a, 1999b).

Research in the area of racial and ethnic relations has proven that individual ethnic groups vary considerably with respect to the impact of structural assimilation on ethnic group identity, participation in ethnic community activities, and loyalty to members of their ethnic group (McLemore and Romo 2005). Moreover, certain kinds of structural assimilation may in fact strengthen an individual's identification with and participation in the ethnic community (Waters 1999a, 1999b; Gibson 1989). Roger Waldinger (2001) noted also that the functions immigrants fill in an economic system define them. For instance, the children of immigrants and U.S.-born minorities assert different prospects for their future and experience varying levels of acceptance and discrimination (Alba and Nee 1997; Perlmann and Waldinger 1997; Portes and Zhou 1993; Rumbaut and Portes 2001). This chapter proposes that first-, second-, third-, and fourth-generation Mexican-origin persons in San Antonio construct racial, ethnic, class, national, and gender identities in different ways because of distinct transnational interchanges and relationships between Mexico and San Antonio.

Waldinger (2001, 308) points out that the decisions of earlier immigrant settlements exercise a profound effect on the options available to those who come later, especially if they have established ethnic enclaves or have experienced and fought discrimination. Elites who fled Mexico and their descendants, second- and third-generation Mexican Americans, and the contemporary generations in San Antonio often live their lives on both sides of the border (Márquez and Romo 2008). There is also no longer an Anglo "mainstream" in San Antonio (Diehl and Jarboe 1985). Although there are neighborhoods that are predominantly Anglo residents and Anglos remain among the city's elite, Mexican Americans hold prominent elected offices, make influential decisions, and live in all neighborhoods in the city (Montejano 2010; Wolff 1997). As a result, economic mobility and social standing do not depend on full acculturation or pleasing such a "mainstream" class order (Telles and Ortiz 2008).

The case studies presented here show that the Spanish language, Mexican customs, and Mexican institutions are diffused within the San Antonio population. The resulting transnational fields of experiences and social relationships represent an alternative to full assimilation into American culture and strongly suggest that international migration and assimilation can no longer be seen as a one-way process (Kasinitz et al. 2002). In the interviews conducted for this study, Mexican-origin residents in San Antonio talk about how they participate in the social life of Mexico through telephone contacts with family members, radio and TV, personal videos, and members of the community who cross the border frequently. Mexican American residents also participate in the social life of Mexico through work relationships and various social and religious institutions. A study of San Antonio can be presented as a model for understanding the impact of local contexts and institutions on the development of transnational fields and on the processes of incorporation into the economic and social fabric of a city.

Levitt (2001), in a study of Dominican migrants, discussed different types of transnational communities. In some cases, numerous individuals are embedded within transnational social fields and engage in many transnational practices but do not form a viable sense of community. In other sites, transnational migrants become organized and institutionalized sufficiently to think of themselves as a group. Resources, money, or ideas from both sides of the border are used to achieve transnational goals. Younger generations and older generations may experience periodic, selective transnational activities at various stages of their lives (Levitt 2002; Fouron and Glick-Schiller 2002; Glick Schiller, Basch, and Szanton Blanc 1995; Smith 2002), and members of a U.S. community may share identities, occupations, values, or an attachment to their home country—although they may vary greatly in the actual number of migrations back and forth. For example, many individuals from Mexico are living in San Antonio because they have been expelled from their homelands or displaced by security concerns, economic, political, or social forces; many are undocumented. They may live outside the physical boundaries of Mexico but within the defined space of the "borderlands" cemented by institutions, literature, political ideas, religious convictions, music, and lifestyles of Mexico as well as by permanent migrations (Cohen 1997; Levitt 2001,15; Romo, H. 2008).

The perspective that guides this study moves away from the traditional three generation process of assimilation and focuses on evolving adaptive responses to ethnic identifications and institutions that help shape those identifications. Specific cultural content changes as the ethnic group—and different generations and socioeconomic classes within the ethnic group—face different structural exigencies (Lopez and Stanton-Salazar 2001; Smith 2006). Reasons individuals have for maintaining ethnic identification and ethnic community involvement may change with each succeeding generation (Gutiérrez 1995). Ethnicity may also become important as a basis for pursuing interests within a democratic political system and within a transnational or global economic system (Diehl and Jarboe 1985). Historic events are also important in shaping the direction and meaning of a given ethnic community (Lopez and Stanton-Salazar 2001; Montejano 2010; Romo, R. 1993; Telles and Ortiz 2008).

In San Antonio, the long and often conflictual relationship between Anglos and Mexicans has had an impact on the persistence of Mexican identity and the sense of community that many Mexican Americans and Mexican immigrants feel (De Leon 1982; Menchaca 2001; Montejano 1987, 2010). However, relationships within the local context may influence relationships between Mexico and the United States as has been demonstrated in anti-immigrant legislation passed in Arizona, Nebraska, and other states. Public figures in other states and communities as well as researchers have emphasized the strong contributions of Mexican immigrants and Mexican Americans to the economies and social fabric of both countries (Durand, Massey, and Parrado 1999; Stephen 2007; Smith and Bakker 2008). Thus, there need not be a zero-sum relationship among structural and cultural assimilation, the retention of ethnicity, and relations with an ethnic community. Rather, ethnic groups, in varying degrees, transform the nature of their ethnicity and their communities to meet new exigencies that continually arise.

Increasingly, these new exigencies are transnational in nature and perhaps demand that individuals carry on their everyday lives as well as their cultural and community lives in more than one nation-state (Hernandez-Leon 2008). This is especially true in San Antonio where the capacity for Mexican-origin individuals and U.S.-born individuals to maintain interactions among members of Mexican and U.S. communities is high. I explore differences in the experiences of individuals who travel regularly to Mexico to conduct routine economic and political affairs; those whose lives are primarily rooted in San Antonio; and those who do not move but who live their lives in a community that has become transnationalized (see Levitt 2002, 9). All engage in numerous activities and social relationships that span borders.

HISTORICAL AND DEMOGRAPHIC CONTEXT OF SAN ANTONIO

San Antonio's geographical location in the U.S. Southwest allows the city to be considered a borderland despite the fact that it is not located at the U.S.-Mexico border (Romo, H. 2008). Easy accessibility to San Antonio from the Mexican border along the Rio Grande and South Texas corridor is similar to other gateway cities like Los Angeles but distinct from east coast cities such as New York (Smith 2006; Cordero-Guzman, Smith, and Grosfoguel 2001). The demographics of San Antonio, a majority Latino population, make the city similar to Miami and a growing number of other cities with majority-minority populations (Stepick and Stepick 2009).

Many of the Mexican Americans of San Antonio can trace their ancestry back to the time when Texas was a part of Mexico (Arreola 2004; Montejano 1987; Telles and Ortiz 2008). Immigration from Mexico has also continued, largely uninterrupted but with ebbs and flows in response to the economic conditions on both sides of the border (Massey, Durand, and Malone 2003). Today, San Antonio-born Mexican Americans are the majority ethnic population in the city. Skilled workers and Mexican immigrants work in the service and tourism industries, reside in the Westside community where housing costs are low, and return to Mexico for long intervals each year or every few years. In addition, a large group of entrepreneurs, small business owners, professionals, and corporate representatives live both in Mexico and in San Antonio. Intergroup relations are affected by the global economy and the emergence of San Antonio as a transnational trading center with the implementation of the 1994 North American Free Trade

Agreement (NAFTA). As in many other metropolitan regions, demographic shifts in San Antonio are reshaping relationships among Anglos, Hispanics, and African Americans (O'Brien 2008). Between 1980 and 1990, Texas experienced an increase of over 1.3 million Latinos representing a 45 percent increase over the ten-year period. From 1990 to 2000, the Hispanic population of Texas increased by over two million individuals, and the Hispanic share of the state population moved from 25.5 percent to 32 percent (U.S. Census 2000). According to the 2010 census, Hispanics comprised 58.7 percent of the population of Bexar County, Texas—where San Antonio is located—and 84 percent of those Hispanics were of Mexican origin (U.S. Census 2010).

San Antonio has always been an Hispanic city throughout its many national identities (De La Teja 1996; Montejano 1987). The Spanish explorers set up forts and missions in San Antonio to protect Spanish territory in the New World, and the military garrison established along with the missions was composed of northern Mexicans who settled and defended the frontier (Poyo and Hinojosa 1991). After Mexican independence from Spain, while Texas was still a part of Mexico, Santa Anna proposed shutting off the flow of immigrants from the U.S. territories and refused to grant Texas statehood in its own right, which angered Texans and triggered a war for Texan independence. When Texas asserted its independence from Mexico, Tejanos, or native Mexican Texans, were an important part of that struggle and later played an important role in the development of Texas when the area became a U.S. state in 1845 (Poyo and Hinojosa 1991; Weber 1982).

In the early 1900s, Mexican immigration was strongly oriented toward Texas, which had strong financial and material interests in Porfirian Mexico. During the classic era of Mexican migration prior to 1920, immigration policies were not restrictive and no firm border existed between Texas and Mexico (Mora-Torres 2001). People moved back and forth from one nation state to the other as they went about the business of making a living, raising a family, and seeking better opportunities. Family members lived on both sides of the border, and small businessmen and wealthy entrepreneurs established livelihoods in both countries and owned homes in San Antonio and in Mexico, particularly Monterrey and Nuevo Laredo (Mora-Torres 2001).

The unraveling of the Porfirian regime after 1910, massive labor displacements with the implementation of capital-intensive agriculture, ten years of civil war, and the strong demand for Mexican workers in major cities continued Mexican migrations to Texas and the West Coast. In the 1910–1920s, Los Angeles and San Antonio became the refuge of Mexican intellectuals and elites who fled the Revolution (Romo, R. 1993; Wolff 1997). In the twenty year period beginning about 1910 roughly 10 percent of Mexico's population migrated to the United States (Telles and Ortiz 2008). Many of these Mexicans resided in San Antonio, took leadership roles, and shaped the intellectual and social life of the San Antonio community (Garcia 1991). As late as 1920, 50 to 55 percent of all Mexican immigrants living in the United States were in Texas (Durand, Massey, and Charvet 2000, 13). California and Arizona followed Texas in numbers of Mexican immigrants. These three states absorbed approximately 85 percent of all Mexico-U.S. migrants, with just 11 percent going to non-gateway states (Durand, Massey, and Charvet 2000, 3).

The Great Depression triggered a wave of mass deportations and the population of foreign-born Mexicans actually fell during the 1930s (Hoffman 1974; Telles and Ortiz 2008). By 1942, however, the tight wartime labor market caused employers to turn again to Mexico for workers. The United States and Mexican governments negotiated the Bracero Accords to arrange the annual importation of Mexican farm workers under supervision of the U.S. government (Galarza 1978). Although this program was meant as a temporary wartime measure, the arrangement was renewed over some twenty-two years before finally being terminated in 1964 (Clavita 1992). This experience laid the foundation for many patterns of future migrations; workers who had been to the United States as Bracero workers continued to return to U.S. farms and agricultural fields as undocumented workers after the program terminated (Massey, Durand, and Malone 2002). Workers who had lived and worked in the United States were familiar with the labor market, establishing contacts with labor contractors and relationships with employers that facilitated their sons' and later neighbors' and families' migrations to the United States.

In the 1950s, Texas reasserted its dominance as an immigrant destination, increasing its share of Mexican immigrants in the United

States from 40 percent to 45 percent. Late in that decade, the demand for Bracero labor increased, thereby encouraging some 400,000 Mexican workers to enter the United States under this program. A disproportionate share of these migrants were sent to California agricultural growers and by 1960 California had surpassed Texas as home to the largest concentration of Mexican immigrants (Durand, Massey, and Charvet 2000, 7). During the 1970s, however, the demand for unskilled labor in the United States continued unabated and Mexicans expanded their presence in other economic niches in San Antonio and elsewhere in Texas (De Leon 1993; Gutiérrez 1995).

The Immigration Reform and Control Act (IRCA), which the U.S. Congress passed in 1986 and was gradually implemented in the period 1987 through 1989, again changed patterns of immigration (Hagan and Rodriguez 2009). The percentage of foreign-born Mexicans in California peaked at 58 percent in 1990 while the share in Texas decreased to 22 percent. The full effects of the changed immigration law were not felt until after 1990 when the legalization program was completed and employer sanctions were fully implemented. As a result of IRCA's general amnesty and a special legalization program enacted for farm workers, some 2.3 million Mexicans acquired legal documents between 1987 and 1990 (Durand, Massey, and Charvet 2000, 9; U.S. Immigration and Naturalization Service 1991). Newly acquired legal status allowed Mexican immigrants more mobility and greater labor and legal rights. However, IRCA also increased the budget of the U.S. Border Patrol, which launched a series of repressive crackdowns in California and Texas and resulted in heightened tensions in immigrant communities and the institutions they frequented.

Mexico experienced a serious economic crisis in 1994; the peso devaluation led to a recession that created a need for greater income among poor families and fostered new needs for credit and security among middle-class Mexican households. More Mexican families crossed to the United States. As a result of increased immigration, repressive measures sprang up in Texas and California (Valle and Torre 2000). During this period the share of Mexicans located in non-gateway states more than doubled, reaching the highest percentage in the history of Mexico-U.S. migration. New concentrations of Mexican immigrants emerged in Florida, Idaho, Nevada, New York, Utah, Ohio, and the southern states. Houston became a major receiving area of new immigrants and other cities in Texas with booming construction industries and tourist economies, such as San Antonio and Austin, continued to draw new immigrants.

San Antonio, in the meantime, grew a large second-, third-, and fourth-generation Mexican American population (Vigil 1998). Many of these families lived on the south and Westside of San Antonio in majority Mexican American neighborhoods where Spanish was spoken daily and social and work interactions were largely among other Mexican Americans and Mexican immigrants (Pycior 1997). As this population became the majority population of the city, Mexican culture (and Mexican-origin residents) spread to almost all San Antonio neighborhoods, schools, and places of work (Garcia 1991). New immigrants from Mexico, both working class and middle and upper class, strengthened the use of the Spanish language and continued to enrich San Antonio's Mexican cultural milieu.

San Antonio today has reestablished its Hispanic heritage—particularly its Mexican heritage. The total population for the geographic area of the San Antonio city is 1,327,407, and the majority (63.2 percent) is Hispanic (U.S. Census 2010). Of that Hispanic or Latino group, 41.4 percent reported Mexican origin in the 2000 census while 16.5 percent reported they were Other Hispanic or Latino, 0.7 percent reported they were Puerto Rican, and 0.1 percent reported they were Cuban. Approximately 7 percent of the city's population was African American, 1.3 percent American Indian, and 2.1 percent Asian (U.S. Census 2000). By 2010, the Hispanic population of San Antonio represented 63.2 percent of the city's population (U.S. Census 2010).

Obvious racial differences between the majority of Mexican immigrants and most Anglo Americans also contributed to the perseverance of Mexican culture. Darker skinned Mexican immigrants and Mexican Americans were noticeably different in appearance from the white population, and many people of Mexican heritage experienced discrimination similar to that experienced by Asians, American Indians, and African Americans in Texas and in the South.

The history of Mexicans in San Antonio and the new demographics illustrate the complex, multifaceted dimensions of Mexican American and Mexican-immigrant relations and present many possibilities for the social construction of transnational identities.

FORMALIZATION OF TRANSNATIONAL LIVES AND CITIZENSHIP STATUS

Few studies of transnationalism that focus on the links between sending and receiving communities have given much attention to the formalization of citizenship or immigration status. We know that large numbers of Mexicans residing in the United States do not have formal immigration documents. This does not necessarily prevent them from going back and forth between their Mexican communities and U.S. communities, although it complicates border crossings. The events of September 11 have caused increased enforcement of immigration restrictions and surveillance at borders. Student visas and work permits are more difficult to acquire. Recent acknowledgment by the Mexican government of dual nationality has allowed Mexican citizens to acquire U.S. citizenship and maintain their Mexican nationality, facilitating U.S. legal status for many Mexicans eligible for such status who were otherwise reluctant to pursue it if they had to give up Mexican citizenship. Currently, the Mexican government allows anyone with a parent or grandparent who is a Mexican citizen to apply for Mexican nationality. The increased Mexican voters in both Mexican and U.S. presidential elections demonstrated the benefit of this policy to the Mexican-origin population.

The complexity of immigration laws and policy changes contributed to mixed immigration status among family members for an increasing number of families. The families interviewed for this study include members with different citizenship or official immigration status, illustrating the various ways families experience transnationalism. The following case studies illustrate this phenomenon.

Case #1: Working-Class Second-Generation Family

Miriam and Pedro Salinas have recently moved into a new subdivision about 20 miles from downtown San Antonio. Advertisements for the subdivision promoted homes from $70,000. A Mexican flag hangs in the window because they were married on September 16, Mexican Independence Day.

Miriam has dual nationality. She was born in the United States but her parents returned to Mexico when she was seven months old. She stayed there until returning to the United States with her husband at age twenty-six. At that time, she was about five months pregnant with their first child. They moved in with Miriam's brother, also born in the United States, and Pedro got a job as a dishwasher in a restaurant. They lived frugally and as he moved up to the position of cook, they rented their own apartment. They continued to live frugally and saved enough to buy a new car with cash as well as make a cash down payment on the new home.

Miriam stays at home and cares for the house and her son. She fixes tortillas every day for the family. She volunteers at her son's school tutoring children, helping teachers, copying papers, and translating notes and flyers into Spanish. Their seven-year-old son, Oscar, has hung a chart of the multiplication tables on his bedroom wall. Pedro says Oscar has learned English well. Miriam also speaks some English, but Pedro says his English is very poor and it is difficult for him to learn the language because everyone at work speaks Spanish. Both Miriam and Pedro attend free English classes at their child's school. Spanish continues to be the dominant language used in the home because Pedro has difficulty with English.

Most of the people in their neighborhood were first-time homeowners. Before their child was born, Miriam and Pedro saved money for vacations, but now they seldom take a trip except to visit relatives still living in Mexico. Miriam had explored the process of getting Mexican citizenship for her son since his father is a Mexican citizen. The boy has U.S. citizenship because he was born in the United States.

Miriam's kitchen pantry is filled with Mexican label foods—crackers, *leche,* cookies, salsa, and other Mexican products. They go shopping in Monterrey, Mexico, Pedro's home community, which is about a five-hour drive from San Antonio; they also built a home in Monterrey, Mexico. If they cannot go to Monterrey, they go to Laredo, a border city, which is only two hours away. When Mexico recently experienced a bad flood, Pedro helped to gather clothing for people who had to flee their homes.

Oscar greeted the adults in the room with a polite handshake. He brought out a boy doll that spoke a prayer in Spanish. His mother joked that the doll was his little brother. The house was sparsely furnished. A large chair and sofa, upholstered in blue and rose flower prints and purchased in Nuevo Laredo, Mexico, dominated the living room. In a corner of the kitchen on the counter a red candle burned in front of a large picture of Jesus. In front of this altar was a small TV.

Miriam is technically a second-generation U.S.-born Mexican, but she grew up in Mexico. Her U.S. citizenship status allowed her to return as an adult with her husband, a Mexican citizen, to give birth to her son in the United States. The U.S. citizenship status of Miriam and her son helped the family get residency status for Pedro and allows the family members to go back and forth to Monterrey. Pedro's Mexican citizenship facilitated their purchase of property in Monterrey.

Case #2: Working-Class Second-Generation Family

Marcela grew up in a small town near San Luis Potosi. She was the third oldest in a family of twelve children. Her father worked in San Antonio and other U.S. locations as part of the Bracero program for seventeen years. She came to San Antonio at age twenty on a tourist visa. She got a job as a housekeeper and nannie and overstayed her visa. Her immigration status made her fearful during the period that she was "illegal" and she did not see her mother for almost seven years. Her first child was born in San Antonio, but the father of the child did not want to marry Marcela and was not interested in the child. She married her current husband several years later in San Antonio and had another child with him. Both of her children are U.S. citizens because of their birthplace and their fathers' citizenship. Her husband was born in the United States and raised in Mexico, but returned to the United States to work as a teenager. Marcela now has a permanent resident visa and a work permit. She is considering applying for dual citizenship for her children but is reluctant to work with an attorney to do so because of the cost and possible complications due to her past immigration history.

Two of her youngest brothers are working in the United States without documents. She helps them when she can. She regularly sends money by money-gram to her mother and her ailing father, and now that she has immigration papers she returns at least once a year to see her family in Mexico. She explained that her Mexican relatives are "very poor people, so they can't travel, they can't come to visit me." She talks with her mother by telephone on a regular basis and sends letters when the phone bills get too high.

In her neighborhood and at work, she regularly interacts with people in San Antonio who are from Mexico. She worked in the home of an Anglo couple for almost ten years and presently works for a Mexican-American family. A woman about ten years her senior from her hometown community worked alongside Marcela at her previous job. As a child, Marcela worked in her restaurant, and when her parents could not afford to send her to school, this woman paid for Marcela's schoolbooks. Marcela said she likes to help people from Mexico find jobs or provide them with food or clothes because so many people, like her friend, have helped her.

When asked if she felt more or less Mexican now, Marcela described her status in the following way:

I feel on the border. Yes, I'm very Mexican, but my heart is in the United States. I love the United States. United States give [sic] me my job, my food, my opportunities. So United States, I think, is really the first for me. I would like to be a citizen, maybe 'cause I don't have money, too much money for paying my application. But now in Mexico, I can be a Mexican and American citizen. Both. And it's good for me. Very good. I love United States, but I'm still Mexican. . . . I'm authentic Mexican. I tell my children, "You were born in United States by accident." But they are Mexican, too. They were born in United States. But, I tell my children, "M'ijos. You are Mexican. Yes." . . . My son, he say [sic], "I'm American, Mom. I'm American." And it's ok for me because I know he's American. But I told him, "M'ijo, you need to speak Spanish." Because he doesn't speak Spanish. So I told him, "You are American, but you are still Mexican."

Marcela's family's transnational links are complex. While her immigration status was undocumented, she was restricted from physically returning to visit her family but she remained in contact with them. Her children are growing up in the United States and have spent very little time with relatives in Mexico; however, they interact frequently with recent immigrant relatives and Mexican friends living in San Antonio. Marcela communicates with her employers in English and Spanish, but sometimes has difficulties with English outside of the work context. Her children speak predominantly English, but speak Spanish in the home. Marcela lamented that she could not help her son when he had difficulty in his schoolwork, because he did not understand her Spanish and she did not know the math vocabulary in English. Her work experiences have been with Anglo and Mexican American families whom she has occasionally invited to her home, but her primary social networks are with Mexicans of similar socioeconomic backgrounds. She socializes mostly with her husband's extended family who live nearby. The links she maintains with her own family in Mexico through remittances and yearly visits helped form the social structures for migration of her younger brothers. She and her husband helped her brothers find work when they arrived in the United States. Just before the interview she had returned to Mexico to help her mother arrange for an operation for her father who had been ill. While her social and emotional connections to Mexico remain strong, the social relations her children experience in the U.S. schools and with peers reinforce their American identities.

Case #3: Professional Mexican American Family

Lionel Garcia, born in Texas, is fair-skinned and has red hair and hazel eyes. His mother was born in Mexico and came to the United States as a young girl. She married a Mexican American. Dr. Garcia grew up in the United States but visited his mother's family regularly in a rural community north of Monterrey, Mexico. Although this family has not experienced direct discrimination because of their fair complexions and higher educational status, he identified with the Chicano movement in the 1960s and was active in Chicano politics. He completed a Ph.D. in the 1960s through an affirmative action program for Mexican Americans. He has had a successful career as a professor and academic administrator. When his mother's father died, his mother inherited a small family rancho—a working ranch with horses and cattle—in Mexico. Professor Garcia has applied for Mexican citizenship to facilitate his eventual ownership of the family ranch. He goes monthly to the ranch and spends extended time there on his summer vacations and winter and spring breaks.

Professor Garcia and his wife, who is Mexican American, have three sons. The sons do not speak Spanish well and do not identify themselves as Mexican American as strongly as he and his wife do. The children grew up in San Antonio and still participate in Mexican cultural family traditions, such as having tamales for Christmas and showing respect for elderly relatives. Professor Garcia's elderly mother now lives with his family, and the youngest son, who is in high school, interacts regularly with her, which strengthen his ties to his Mexican identity. Professor Garcia's sons are also eligible for dual citizenship through their grandmother's Mexican citizenship and their father's dual citizenship. Professor Garcia is not sure whether they will be interested in acquiring dual status, and he does not know how interested the boys will be in continued participation in the rancho. When Professor Garcia drives his truck down to the ranch, he often takes appliances and other goods requested by relatives in Mexico. He explained that his status has been enhanced among his Mexican relatives since he became a Mexican citizen. Before, his cousins often called him a *pocho* and made fun of his Spanish and Americanized ways. Now, as a Mexican citizen and landowner, his uncles and aunts and cousins treat him more as an equal. He claims that his status is higher in the Mexican community as a landowner than it is in San Antonio as a Mexican American professor. He explained:

It was not until the provision of dual citizenship came into place and I took advantage of that that I was able to get some credentials to be treated as a real Mexican on my own, as opposed to being treated like a gringo. . . . Even though I was through my mother very much tied to Mexico and everybody knew this, they treated me more as an outsider, as a tourist, than as a real Mexican. It has taken me the better part of ten years to get that kind of credibility in Mexico. You can say I went into the other direction. . . . I had to brush up on my Spanish. And now it is clear to them when I speak that I am a Mexican. At first I was a tourist, an outsider. Now I feel good about it. I do feel that I finally achieved a level of literacy within that culture to be taken seriously, or to be taken as one of them.

Professor Garcia is very much assimilated in the United States in a number of ways—he speaks English well, he has achieved upward mobility and success in education and in his profession. Yet he has strongly identified with the Chicano Movement and Mexican American political and social issues. His friendships in San Antonio are largely among Mexican Americans. He works at a university that serves a large number of Mexican American and Mexican students and many of his classes enroll a majority of Mexican-origin students. He belongs to a Mexican American faculty association. Although he lives in a neighborhood that has both Mexican American and Anglo-American residents and his sons attend schools that are ethnically mixed, most of his social interactions are among family and Mexican American friends and colleagues. Professor Garcia emphasized that with increased connections to family in Mexico, particularly as a property owner and citizen of Mexico and with his mother living in his home, the Mexicanness of his experiences is more dominant than before. He explained: "I feel extremely comfortable there [in Mexico]. In Mexico because of the fact that I am a descendent of a landlord that brought my mother's family to Mexico, I have the credentials, and at this point, I am very much considered a player in that arena. Not as a handout, but as a full partner. . . . Even though I spent my entire life living in the United States, aside from my close circle of friends, I don't feel that in this community I would ever be part of the elite or the group of stakeholders. In Mexico, on the other hand, because of my legacy and tie to the landowners in my mother's family, I have achieved that kind of stakeholder status."

This case demonstrates the potential transformation that transnational experiences can have for Mexican Americans in San Antonio.

Some persons of Mexican heritage, like Professor Garcia, feel they still have not been incorporated into the politics and social life of the city as a full "stakeholder." The stakeholders referred to are a group of Anglo businessmen who strongly influenced local elections and civic social life in the past. This respondent, possibly because of the legacy of discrimination in San Antonio and the segregation in the city in the 1950s and 1960s, felt he was able to achieve a higher status as a property owner in a Mexican community of his ancestors where he has never resided, than in San Antonio.

TRANSNATIONAL LIVES ACROSS GENERATIONS

Older generations of Mexican Americans experienced discrimination in schools and social relations during the years of Jim Crow laws and civil rights legislation that younger generations have not experienced. Nonetheless, both generations attended schools with primarily Mexican American student bodies and both generations often lived in neighborhoods that had a majority of Mexican residents. Some communities, like the Westside of San Antonio, remain almost 100 percent Mexican-origin residents. Thus, even when Mexicans have made San Antonio their permanent residence or when they are third- or fourth-generation Mexican American and no longer have family links in Mexico, they may continue to interact primarily with Mexican-heritage people. In addition to school and neighborhood concentrations of Mexicans and Mexican Americans, many work sites require intensive interactions with Mexican nationals or recent Mexican immigrants.

Case # 1: Older-Generation Mexican American

Henry, an eighty-six-year-old, second-generation Mexican American whose parents came to San Antonio from Mexico as teenagers in 1913, described his Westside neighborhood: "I'd say it's 99.5 percent Hispanic families. Maybe about 60 or 70 percent are Mexicans and the rest are from South America. Very few Anglos. We got rid of them [he laughed]. Pushed them out. Where I live now is like at least 75 percent better than it was even sixty years ago. Our streets are well fixed, sewer, water. We have every convenience now that we didn't have before."

Henry noted the improvements in his ethnic community in terms of city facilities, such as paved streets and utilities, that were brought about by Mexican American political activism in the 1960s. Henry's life experiences occur almost exclusively in this predominantly Mexican-origin Westside neighborhood. While his main contacts with Mexico were yearly month-long vacations there, he interacted predominantly with institutions, both formal and informal, in his Westside Mexican American community. His brothers and nephews live about three blocks from his home. His mother, a midwife, lived around the block. She never learned English because all of her clients were Spanish speaking. His father sold fruits and vegetables from a cart and worked for a while as a clerk in the small neighborhood grocery stores run by Chinese businessmen. His father returned to Mexico regularly because he supported a sister there for some twenty-five or thirty years, but the family never owned property in Mexico.

Henry and his wife built a small neighborhood grocery business that was bankrupted when big chain supermarkets moved into the Mexican American neighborhood. He and his wife were able to begin a Mexican restaurant on property they had bought with profits from the store. Over the next twenty-five years they built a profitable Mexican restaurant business. When asked what had changed about Mexican culture over his lifetime, Henry replied, "Actually I haven't seen too many changes. It still feels the same to me. When we were young we were poor and now that we're old, we've got more resources. We have a better life. We have money in the bank. Good children. And we've been happy."

When asked about ethnicity, Henry reflected on changes in terminology over time. He first replied that his ethnicity was "Spanish American." When asked what he calls himself, he replied, "I used to refer to myself at first as Latin American, then Mexican American, now Hispanic American. . . . I changed because the customs changed." He laughed that it was important that he had Mexican American friends because "I didn't have no choice." Henry remembered several significant discriminatory incidents. As a student in junior high, teachers enforced "the English law" punishing students who spoke Spanish. He remembered that, as a young worker, a restaurant manager did not allow him to eat in the restaurant, and police officers once turned his family away from a public park. As a soldier in World War II, he saw discrimination and recalled that Mexicans were seen as "the undergrade people." These incidents caused him to participate in a Mexican American political organization, the American G.I. Forum, and to work to elect Mexican American politicians.

Henry graduated from high school and all five of his children completed high school. His two older sons have graduate degrees and successful professional careers. His youngest son dropped out of college but returned part-time and, taking a few courses a year, earned a BA degree. Henry added, "Now we are seeing the Hispanic group growing more and more and they are seen more favorably than in the past. As time goes forward they are going to prosper more. . . . I think being American has a lot of advantages. We have a lot of privileges that other people don't have. Also, we have a lot of opportunities that other people don't have, so it's great to be an American."

Henry lived all his life in one of the oldest Mexican barrios in San Antonio and had experienced the changes and improvements in city services and civil rights over the years. He was proud to be an American and proud of his service in the U.S. armed forces. He and his wife had only Mexican immigrant or Mexican American friends and socialized mostly with extended family members who lived nearby or with their children and grandchildren. His two older sons married Anglo wives and moved out of the neighborhood, but his younger children still lived in the Westside. His statement that in his early years he had no choice but to have friends of Mexican descent confirms the segregation that most of the older generation of Mexican heritage residents of San Antonio experienced. He directly experienced discrimination against the Spanish language in the schools and remained unsure of his English. He experienced firsthand the banning of Mexicans from public restaurants and parks in the Jim Crow era, and actively fought against discrimination against Mexicans who had served in the military in World War II. Henry preferred to remain in this neighborhood because of his friendships. Members of his family lived close by, his local businesses served mostly Mexican origin clients, the Catholic Church offered Spanish language mass, and institutions in the neighborhood offered convenient access to Mexican cultural events and commodities.

Case #2: Younger-Generation Mexican American

Georgiana, seventeen, also born in San Antonio's Westside neighborhood, has lived there all her life. When describing the community, she says, "Everybody is Hispanic. Everybody, everybody is Hispanic." Her mother was born in Chicago and her father was born in Durango, Mexico. He came to the United States at age twenty-two or twenty-three because Georgiana says, "Like any other Mexican would want to come to get a job. Basically a job, to find a new life here." He worked both as a cook at a restaurant and had an ice cream truck business. He is now a U.S. citizen. Georgiana refers to herself as a "Hispanic Mexican American." Georgiana lives with her mother, four step siblings from her mother's previous marriage, and her three brothers and sisters, a total of eight children in the family. Although Georgiana now has a little boy, she has returned to school to complete her high school diploma. She told me that most of her friends were Hispanic and added, "It's not important, but that's the only race I grew up with." She has few interactions with African Americans or Anglos. Her father maintains contacts with family members in Mexico by phone and letters and sends his elderly mother money every month. He sometimes takes medicines to family members in Mexico. He inherited land and a house in Mexico from his father, but Georgiana has never seen it or met her grandmother on her father's side. Although she writes letters to her grandmother, she would like to go to Mexico to visit her before she dies.

The family continues Mexican celebrations in San Antonio. They have organized quinceñeras for the girls. Georgiana attends Catholic mass regularly in Spanish. Her mother maintains a religious altar in the home. Georgiana is teaching her son Spanish because "That's his culture, his mom's culture, his grandfather's culture, his whole family's culture." She speaks Spanish with her friends, "mostly every day, sometimes not in a whole conversation, but, you know, little parts here in English and little parts here in Spanish." The family watches Spanish language

TV, especially telenovelas, and listens to Mexican music. Her parents know both Spanish and English. Georgiana noted, "There's some Hispanics in our neighborhood that can't speak Spanish, they can only speak English. In order to understand each other we have to speak English or speak Spanish or both." Georgiana took Spanish classes in school but felt like she knew more Spanish than her teachers did. In her current school "Everybody is Hispanic. Everybody talks Spanish." Georgiana has not experienced discrimination directly, but she observed, "I think mostly Hispanics are doing construction, you know, stuff like that. You rarely see anybody in an office that's Hispanic or like a doctor that's Hispanic."

Georgiana's aunts and uncles live in the same neighborhood and they see one another almost every day. They are involved in her life emotionally and financially. Her aunt helped her get the job she currently holds at a front desk of a hotel. Her younger sister often takes care of her son. Georgiana was in gifted and talented classes in middle school and high school, but got into fights with other girls and was expelled from high school. She hung out with friends and smoked marijuana. She was also disruptive in elementary school and was held back a year in third grade because of behavioral problems. No one in her family has graduated from high school; Georgiana hopes to be the first. Her older sister completed a GED and took one course in college, but Georgiana doesn't know anyone else who has attended college. Georgiana believes that family is what makes people successful. Her parents have taught her that "it doesn't matter what you have or what you don't have, as long as you have your family . . . without family, without any support, there is nothing."

Both Henry and Georgiana are second-generation Mexican Americans. Both have lived in the predominantly Mexican American San Antonio Westside neighborhood. Their parents maintained links with communities of origin in Mexico, but they themselves have had little contact with Mexico. Henry experienced overt discrimination against Mexicans that Georgiana has been spared. The majority of social contacts of both the younger generation and the older generation continue to be Mexican or Mexican American. Extended family relations are important and family members live within the immediate neighborhood.

Mexican food, media, and cultural traditions are maintained in the homes. Spanish is spoken in both households, although a mixture of English and Spanish is common. Henry sees improved images of Mexicans and Mexican Americans in leadership positions, but Georgiana sees few professional Mexican Americans in her daily interactions in the Mexican community.

Life stage and length of time in the United States contribute to how individuals and family members participate in transnational activities. Demands of school, jobs, and families have lessened the second generation's ability to continue transnational ties maintained by their parents. As family networks are established in U.S. communities and older family members die, personal relationships with Mexican family members lessen. Henry's family often vacationed in Mexico and Georgiana's family will inherit the house owned by her grandmother. Both Henry and Georgiana continue to live in Mexican neighborhoods and socialize among predominantly Mexican Americans. Henry primarily hired Mexican workers in his business and Georgiana's classmates at school are Mexican or Mexican American. Cultural values and the Spanish language are maintained, although they are influenced by assimilation experiences in San Antonio.

WORK SHAPES TRANSNATIONAL LIVES

To say that second-generation Mexican Americans no longer go back and forth to home communities in Mexico does not mean that they have fewer contacts with Mexico. In San Antonio, work sites are often transnational, maintaining personal relationships with Mexican nationals, establishing networks of colleagues, and promoting Spanish language interactions. Many work positions require professional skills and demand that the workers read, write, and speak Spanish well.

Case #1: Transnational Banker and Investor

Gerardo is forty-four years old and has lived in San Antonio for ten years. He was born in a Mexican city near the Texas border but lived most of his adolescent and young adult years in Mexico City. He attended private schools in Mexico and has a bachelor's degree from a Mexican university. He is married and has three children, all of whom were born in Mexico. The two younger children, however, have grown up mostly in the United States. Gerardo's grandmother was born in the United States but grew up in Mexico and his mother is in the process of becoming an American citizen. His father was also born in the United States in a border town on the U.S. side of the border, but grew up on the Mexican side. Gerardo was very familiar with San Antonio even before moving to the city because his family during the first thirteen years of his life spent the summers in San Antonio and went back and forth from Mexico to San Antonio frequently. His parents held a special visa or "border crossing permit" that allowed them to go back and forth from their border town to the United States almost every other day because they did business on both sides of the border. His parents and his wife's parents still live in Mexico as do the majority of their siblings and extended family members. Gerardo and his family members in Mexico communicate by telephone at least once a week and more frequently by email.

Gerardo's wife is also Mexican. Many of their closest friends and long-time friends are Mexican but they do have close American friends they met through their children's friends at school. They interact socially primarily with persons from Mexico and attend events sponsored by Mexican organizations to meet people to help with his business which involves international investing. Gerardo feels comfortable interacting with Americans, especially those with similar educational levels, and commented that it is helpful to his business to have friends across different groups.

Gerardo had worked in the Mexican government and came to San Antonio because of a job opportunity in investments. Initially, the family planned to stay in the United States for two years and return to Mexico, but Gerardo had an opportunity to start his own firm with several Mexican colleagues. His work in Mexico had involved travel to the United States so he was very familiar with business in the United States as he had lived for fifteen years in a border town with constant contact with U.S. culture. The biggest transition for all family members was leaving friends and family in Mexico. They continue to maintain contacts in Mexico by returning eight to ten times a year. Gerardo's investment clients are predominantly Mexican. He explained, "I'm a financial advisor, so all my clients are from Mexico, so I have to be in contact with Mexico on a daily basis. I'll say that I'll have to speak English probably 20 percent of the day and 80 percent of the day I will have to speak Spanish. I write in Spanish and I write emails and all my communication is basically in Spanish. And so, I keep contact on a daily basis based on my job."

Gerardo explained that many of their friends and relatives from Mexico visited their home in San Antonio and often asked them to bring things from the United States to Mexico, "They buy online and I keep getting golf clubs, all kinds of things, books or whatever. My clients sometimes order things to my office, so I take a lot of things. Every time I go to Mexico, I have to take something to somebody."

Gerardo and his family still own the house that they lived in in Mexico and rent it. They maintain bank accounts in Mexico and have financial investments and some businesses in Mexico, but their plans have changed and now they are hoping to obtain permanent residency and remain in San Antonio. His company is owned by him, a Mexican who is an American citizen who previously worked in Mexico, and two Mexican partners who live in Mexico. All of the partners are very aware of the differences in doing business in the United States and Mexico and the laws and regulations in their business in each country. When the company needs service providers they often choose Mexican institutions or businesses. Gerardo explained, "Not just for the sake of being Mexicans. I think that if there is the service and the service they provide are the same, oh, definitely I will say that I will choose the Mexican. If they bring the same service and the same results that I need for my clients, I will definitely in the equality of circumstances, I will choose the Mexican."

Gerardo explained that the family has maintained Spanish in the home and many cultural traditions: "We've maintained our language, our food, our way of thinking. I think pretty much our behavior is like Mexicans right now, especially in this town, it is easier to keep your Mexican traditions, you know? But I think sometimes I feel like I haven't changed my way of approaching life or seeing life. I feel that I'm a Mexican in the United States, that's how I see it, you know. So it's fun, I think it's a great combination."

Gerardo and his family are first-generation migrants, although his family has a long history of transnational experiences, particularly on the border. His work experiences continue to promote daily contacts with Mexican clients and associates, so his work life remains closely connected with Mexico. The family has made American friends through the children's school activities and school friendships. Culturally, the family maintains the Spanish language and Mexican traditions in the home, but Gerardo was familiar with American culture prior to coming to the United States because of childhood vacations in San Antonio and border living. Both he and his wife are very bilingual and speak, read, and write well in English and Spanish. Although they have lived in San Antonio for ten years and the youngest children know the United States better than Mexico and sometimes struggle in their Spanish, the close family and work relationships in Mexico help maintain the family ties with the country of origin. The children have attended summer camp in Mexico with their Mexican cousins to strengthen their Spanish and the family visits one another regularly. Work and family help maintain transnational ties.

Case #2: Transnational Media

Another example, also at the high socioeconomic level, is a family that lives in San Antonio although the head of household, Jose, works as a journalist in Mexico. Both Jose and his wife, Lucia, come from well-educated Mexican families. One of Lucia's sisters went to Guadalajara to study and is now a dentist. Jose is the second generation of his family to study communication in Mexico. He has been in the communications industry for more than twenty years, working as a TV news anchor for a Spanish language television company before his children were born. For many years, after finishing the Friday U.S. 6:30 pm newscast, he caught a plane to his family's Mexico City residence. Many family members, including his grandfather and grandmother on the father's side and his brother, still live in Mexico City. Eventually, however, Jose and his wife sold their house in Mexico—traveling back and forth became too hectic and they wanted the girls to attend school in the United States. The family has lived in San Antonio about ten years and they now maintain two homes in Mexico, one in a small town and another on the coast. The oldest daughter, Carina, age fifteen, was born in Miami and the youngest daughter, age eleven, was born in San Antonio. Both girls attend school in one of the wealthiest public school districts in San Antonio. Jose's mother is a U.S. citizen. His father, from Chiapas, Mexico, was a prominent surgeon in Mexico City. Jose was raised speaking English in his home in Mexico City and still speaks English with his mother. He speaks Spanish with his brother, who is also a physician in Mexico City, and with his wife, who is from a Mexican border city.

Jose writes a political column every day for a major Mexican newspaper and is the editor of the newspaper's section of political commentary on Sundays. He gets information for his articles from the Internet and through a network of Mexican journalists in all states of Mexico. He constantly uses his cell phone, television, and email to communicate with friends and colleagues throughout Mexico; while working on a story, he often goes back and forth between Mexico City and Cuernavaca—a trip that often takes longer than flying from San Antonio to Mexico City.

Lucia, Jose's wife, is proud of her Mexican heritage. Born in Sonora, a small town in Baja California along the border of the United States, Lucia grew up familiar with U.S. culture. Her father worked as a Bracero and used his earnings to buy his own farm in Mexico. In San Antonio, Lucia is active on the boards of museums and is a fund-raiser for social events with Mexican themes.

The girls value being together as a family, have respect for their parents, and exhibit a Mexican formality of manners, greeting parents or their parents' friends with kisses and embraces. Despite adapting well to their U.S. school and friends, the girls love the Spanish language (the eldest is fluent although the youngest struggles) and Mexican art. The family has books in Spanish from Mexico throughout the house. In addition, the family often hosts Mexican artists and intellectuals who come to San Antonio for shows, talks, or business. Despite their love of the culture and their strong familial ties, the family does not envision the girls' permanent return to Mexico. The girls fear kidnappings of friends or family members, and they also have strong ties to the people and culture in the United States; the majority of their school (approximately 80 percent) consists of Anglo students who speak English.

Both of these families interact in Mexican and Anglo settings in San Antonio. Gerardo and his wife and Jose and Lucia have the education, language, and job skills to function in multiple settings. They have the cultural capital, manners, and physical appearance to handle themselves with presidents of corporations, intellectuals, and high-level administrators. As a result of their transnational experiences they can choose from a wide range of opportunities to get ahead. They have considerable financial resources to maintain regular, frequent contact with family members still in Mexico. They are in daily contact with Mexican nationals in their work and must deal on a regular basis with Mexican culture, institutions, and agencies. While both families are firmly rooted in San Antonio, the transnational context of San Antonio as an international center of business, media, trade, and cultural and intellectual activities between the United States and Mexico contributes to the transnational fields in which both families interact in their work and professional lives. Additionally, their socioeconomic status encourages contact with the non-Mexican, Anglo elite population of San Antonio, a dimension of transnational experiences not available to Henry or Georgiana.

INSTITUTIONS FOSTER TRANSNATIONAL CULTURAL FIELDS IN SAN ANTONIO

A number of prominent Mexican institutions create political, economic, and social fields and shape transnational life in San Antonio. The Mexican consulate office, the Office of Mexican Cultural Affairs, and UNAM (the major public university in Mexico) are important institutions in San Antonio.

Organizations such as the Empresarios Mexicanos, a group of wealthy Mexican entrepreneurs, play an important economic, civic, and intellectual role in San Antonio. This organization that has incorporated as a non-profit has a membership of over 200 Mexican-owned businesses. The group raised over $600,000 to bring the Mexican artist, Sebastian, to San Antonio and install his controversial Torch of Friendship sculpture in the downtown area. These Mexican nationals succeeded over the objections of the Anglo-dominated San Antonio Conservation Society, part of the traditional "white mainstream," whose members argued that the statue was too modern to fit into the historic downtown section of San Antonio.

Other similar institutions bring Mexican intellectuals, political figures, and artists to San Antonio on a regular basis. The Mexican Cultural Center brought author and intellectual, Carlos Fuentes, to San Antonio; the San Antonio Museum of Art featured the work and words of artist Jose Cuevas; and UNAM sponsored exhibits of Mexican photographers.

San Fernando Cathedral promotes ethnic culture, holding several masses in Spanish in the heart of downtown San Antonio; in addition, they televise a bilingual mariachi mass weekly to Mexico and Central and South America. UNIVISION, a Spanish-language television station in San Antonio, films various important religious events to promote Mexican indigenous traditions, including a *Seranata,* the Posada, and the Virgin of Guadalupe Procession in December, as well as the Holy Passion Play on Good Friday. The bishop serving the San Antonio area and the priest at the Cathedral are Mexican American. The priest at the Cathedral, a Tejano, explained that at one point after the Mexican Revolution, half of the Mexican bishops lived in San Antonio. San Antonio provided a refuge because the city was bilingual and close to the border. Today, of the one hundred diocesan priests, about twenty-five are Mexican American. In addition, Catholic social service agencies and other informal Catholic institutions shape the Mexican character of life in San Antonio.

The Mexican Consulate Office provides many services to Mexicans and promotes Mexican culture in San Antonio, serving essentially to formalize aspects of transnational lives. Most Consulate employees are members of the Mexican Foreign Service serving under the Mexican Ministry of Foreign Affairs; many others are U.S. citizens who are of

Mexican descent. Staff at the office handle the necessary paperwork for a wide variety of services: providing and processing passports; registration papers for children born in the United States of Mexican parents; visas for persons traveling to Mexico; identification cards for check cashing; bankcards for the transmission of money from U.S. residents to Mexico; documentation of household goods and materials transported from the United States to Mexico; and applications for dual nationality. In addition, the office provides the power of attorney for purchase of property in Mexico and assists the transportation of bodies when Mexicans die in the United States. The Consulate will also provide protection when Mexican citizens need help to return to Mexico, have legal problems, or experience fraud or robbery.

The Consulate provides educational programs for adults who want to earn a Mexican GED and tries to help Mexican citizens and Mexican Americans maintain their Spanish by providing Spanish language textbooks and sponsoring essay contests for children. Their Office of Community Affairs promotes programs related to education and health awareness and health fairs with free testing for diabetes. The office also sponsors sports teams of Mexican and Mexican American youth in the United States (those with parents or grandparents from Mexico) to compete against teams in Mexico. This Office brings Mexican cultural events to San Antonio, including a large September 16 music festival to celebrate Mexican Independence Day. The Consulate has played a major role in helping social organizations and clubs that represent each Mexican state, such as the twelve Clubes de Mexico, organize members from their states of origin in Mexico in San Antonio. Eight clubs are members of a Federation and the Consulate serves as their administrative agency.

The Consulate works closely with the Mexican Ministry of Education on educational programs and with the Mexican Office of Exterior Affairs on other issues. Of course, many Mexican nationals living in San Antonio never have contact with the Consulate. Undocumented workers live their transnational lives often without formalizing their relationships with employers, institutions, or their communities. Nonetheless, the Consulate's office contributes to the ability of Mexican nationals to live transnational lives in San Antonio and facilitates the transnational experiences of families in San Antonio.

THE AMERICANIZATION OF MEXICAN COMMUNITIES

While transnationalism has an impact on the communities of origin in Mexico as a result of the cultural, social, and economic exchanges promoted by Mexican residents in San Antonio, the effects of Anglos and others visiting, living, and retiring in Mexico have additionally influenced the experience of transnationalism. Mexican communities have not remained static. In some small communities, the American retired population outnumbers the native Mexican population. In the Sunday markets of smaller towns, it is often not the Mexican indigenous population who sell their crafts, but American retirees selling their watercolors and hand-sewn articles. In large Mexican urban markets, the majority of the goods for sale may be Adidas backpacks, dishes made in Taiwan, or other Americanized or global products, as also present are doughnut shops and Starbucks Coffee.

Monterrey, Nuevo Leon, Mexico, the largest city on the Mexican northern frontier, is considered one of the most Americanized of Mexican cities. Many residents of San Antonio have business relationships in Monterrey or maintain residences there as well as in San Antonio. San Miguel Allende, a colonial city in the Mexican state of Guanajuato, has several neighborhoods developed by American realtors and contractors. Former residents of San Antonio run many of the craft and tourist shops in San Miguel. San Antonians go there regularly during the hot summer months, rent homes and maintain active social lives among other Texans from Houston, Austin, and Dallas. Life in these Mexican cities has taken on many American influences as a result of transnational experiences.

Residents and planners consider cities such as Laredo, Texas, and Nuevo Laredo, Mexico, both border cities at the Texas-Mexico border and only a few hours drive from San Antonio, a single metropolis. People cross the international border daily to conduct routine business, buy groceries, shop for clothes, attend school, or visit friends and relatives. The malls of San Antonio give special tax rebates to shoppers from Mexico and at Easter holidays hire extra staff to handle the crowds of Mexican shoppers. It is common to find Mexican shoppers in prominent furniture, home furnishing, and clothing stores anywhere in the city on any given day. Wealthy families from the Mexican border towns often own apartments or homes in San Antonio as well as homes in Mexico. Entrepreneurs conduct their businesses on both sides of the border, and workers cross back and forth or live for long periods in each nation state on a regular basis.

The intermingling of Mexican, Mexican American, and Texan cultures in San Antonio has resulted in a context that emphasizes transnationalism without physically traveling from one nation state to the other. The older generation of Mexican Americans in San Antonio experienced the discriminatory laws in Texas schools that forbade the speaking of Spanish in the classroom or on the playground. Some vowed to teach their children to speak only English so they would not experience similar discrimination. Still, many "old timers" maintained their Spanish skills. They watch Spanish language TV, read *La Prensa*— a long-time Spanish language newspaper in the community—or listen to Spanish language radio.

The younger generation of high school students finds it more difficult to read, write, and speak Spanish, an important part of their Mexican identity (Alba, Logan, Lutz, and Stults 2002), even though today's San Antonio accepts and even welcomes Spanish—as bilingualism is understood to enhance economic and social situations. Most parents interviewed did not have rules about speaking Spanish or English in the home. They encouraged English as a way of facilitating upward economic mobility for their children and English became dominant among peers. Youths with first-generation relatives in their homes, such as the children of Gerardo and Jose, maintain more Spanish than third- and fourth-generation Mexican American peers, such as Georgiana, who may speak a blend of Spanish and English, but they too struggle to read and write in Spanish (Hurtado and Vega 2004).

The experiences documented in San Antonio suggest that transnational lives do not have to be lived only by links between the Mexican "sending" community and the U.S. "receiving" community. In a major metropolitan area like San Antonio, where the Mexican American population is the majority and variations of Mexican culture permeate all areas of life, transnationalism is an essential element of the experience of the city. Many residents of San Antonio, such as those interviewed in this study, extend their families, their households, their economic enterprises, and their cultural roots across the U.S.-Mexico border, even if they do not travel to Mexico regularly. A far-reaching Mexican influence in San Antonio is driven by a Mexican American and Mexican immigrant population that is increasing ten times faster than the Anglo population. New immigrants, especially those with strong Spanish skills and economic resources, replenish Mexican cultural identity and practices (Jimenez 2010). The presence of recent immigrants, particularly business owners and middle- and upper-class families, and the continued existence of segregated Mexican origin communities in San Antonio blur the line between assimilation and transnationalism. The San Antonio political structure is changing (Wolff 1997). With two former Mexican American mayors, a current Mexican American mayor, a majority of Mexican American councilmen, and a large Mexican American representation from San Antonio in the state legislature, persons of Mexican heritage are becoming part of the "elite stakeholders" and as a result, an association with Mexican identities and culture is encouraged.

The significant number of residents of San Antonio, both Anglo and Mexican, who continue to maintain physical transnational links with family members and communities in Mexico reinforce cultural, social, economic, political, and family transnationalism. The economic ties between communities are significant in both countries, but there is not just one community-to-community transnational link. A strong policy interest in U.S.-Mexico economic relations in San Antonio may also continue to promote governmental transnational networks and relations. Thus, based on the definitions emerging for the concept of transnationalism (Levitt and Waters 2002; Guarnizo and Portes 2001, 3), this study has illustrated how a number of economic, political, and cultural fields that involve individuals and institutions located both in Mexico and San Antonio are prominent in San Antonio. A significant portion of the people of San Antonio engage regularly in activities in these fields guaranteeing that transnational experiences are an integral part of the habitual life of the community. Moreover, these activities and institutions play a significant role in the construction of identities of immigrants, their second-generation children, and third- and fourth-generation Mexican Americans.

NOTES

1. Georges Fouron and Nina Glick-Schiller define transnational social fields as "an ideology of belonging that extends across the territorial boundaries of states, as well as across generational divides" (see Levitt and Waters 2002, 170). They also emphasize social relationships of persons who remain connected with their country of origin creating a form of "long distance nationalism" (in Levitt and Waters, 173). This concept encompasses broader social, economic and political processes through which migrants and their children are embedded in more than one society even if they do not move back and forth physically. The concept of "transnational fields" focuses on human interactions and personal social relationships rather than physical presence in a home and receiving community. Persons living in San Antonio have many such interactions and relationships with various communities in Mexico.

2. Research for this chapter was part of a larger study, "Knowledge, Culture, and the Construction of Identity in a Transnational Community: San Antonio, Texas" that was funded by a grant from the Rockefeller Foundation, Arts and Humanities Division. The author would like to acknowledge the work on interviewing, transcribing, and coding on the part of the staff and students of the University of Texas San Antonio, particularly Marcela Becker, Tamera Casso, Carina Hurtado, Olivia Lopez, Sophia Ortiz, Carmen Rivas, Maria Rodriguez, Crissy Rivas and Martha Stiles. The interview guide used in the study was adapted with permission from one used by Mary Waters in her study of transnational identity with valuable input from Raquel Marquez and Ellen Clark, professors at UTSA. This chapter is based on interviews conducted by the author.

REFERENCES

Alba, Richard D. 1999. "Immigration and the American Realities of Assimilation and Multiculturalism." *Sociological Forum* 14 (1): 3–25.

Alba, Richard D., John. R. Logan, Amy Lutz, and Brian J. Stults. 2002. "Only English by the Third Generation? Mother-Tongue Loss and Preservation among the Grandchildren of Contemporary Immigrants." *Demography* 39 (3): 467–84.

Alba, Richard D., and Victor Nee. 1997. "Rethinking Assimilation Theory for a New Era of Immigration." *International Migration Review* 31 (1): 826–74.

Arreola, Daniel D. 2004. *Hispanic Spaces, Latino Places: Community and Cultural Diversity in Contemporary America.* Austin: University of Texas Press.

Clavita, Kitty. 1992. *Inside the State: The Bracero Program, Immigration, and the I.N.S.* New York: Routledge.

Cohen, Robin. 1997. *Global Diasporas: An Introduction.* Seattle: University of Washington Press.

Cordero-Guzman, Hector, Robert C. Smith, and Ramon Grosfoguel, eds. 2001. *Migration, Transnationalization, and Race in a Changing New York.* Philadelphia: Temple University Press.

De La Teja, Jesus F. 1996. *San Antonio de Bexar.* Albuquerque: University of New Mexico Press.

De Leon, Arnoldo. 1982. *The Tejano Community, 1836–1900.* Albuquerque: University of New Mexico Press.

———. 1993. *Mexican Americans in Texas: A Brief History.* Arlington Heights: Harlan Davidson.

Diehl, Kemper, and Jan Jarboe. 1985. *Cisneros: Portrait of a New American.* San Antonio: Corona Publishing.

Durand, Jorge, Douglas S. Massey, and Fernando Charvet. 2000. "The Changing Geography of Mexican Immigration to the United States: 1910–1996." *Social Science Quarterly* 81 (1): 1–15.

Durand, Jorge, Douglas S. Massey, and Emilio A. Parrado. 1999. "The New Era of Mexican Migration to the United States." *Journal of American History* 86 (2): 518–36.

Eckstein, Susan E. 2002. "On Deconstructing and Reconstructing the Meaning of Immigrant Generations." In *The Changing Face of Home,* edited by Peggy Levitt and Mary C. Waters, 211–41. New York: Russell Sage Foundation.

Fouron, Georges E., and Nina Glick-Schiller. 2002. "The Generation of Identity: Redefining the Second Generation within a Transnational Social Field." In *The Changing Face of Home,* edited by Peggy Levitt and Mary C. Waters, 168–208. New York: Russell Sage Foundation.

Galarza, Ernesto. 1978. *Merchants of Labor: The Mexican Bracero Story—An Account of the Managed Migration of Mexican Farm Workers in California, 1942–1960.* 3rd ed. Charlotte: McNally.

Garcia, Richard A. 1991. *Rise of the Mexican American Middle Class: San Antonio 1929–1941.* San Antonio: Texas A&M University Press.

Gibson, Margaret A. 1989. *Accommodation without Assimilation.* Ithaca: Cornell University Press.

Glick Schiller, Nina, Linda Basch, and Cristina Szanton Blanc. 1995. "From Immigrant to Transmigrant: Theorizing Transnational Migration." *Anthropological Quarterly* 68 (1): 48–63.

Gordon, Milton. 1964. *Assimilation in American Life: The Role of Race, Religion, and National Origins.* New York: Oxford University Press.

Guarnizo, Luis E., and Alejandro Portes. 2001. "From Assimilation to Transnationalism: Determinants of Transnational Political Action among Contemporary Immigrants." Working Paper Series. Princeton: Center for Migration and Development, Princeton University. (Cited in chapter by Philip Kasinitz, Mary C. Waters, John H. Mollenkopf, and Merih Anil in the volume *The Changing Face of Home,* edited by Mary C. Waters and Peggy Levitt.)

Gutiérrez, David G. 1995. *Walls and Mirrors: Mexican Americans, Mexican Immigrants, and the Politics of Identity.* Berkeley: University of California Press.

Hagan, Jacqueline, and Nestor Rodriguez. 2009. "Resurrecting Exclusion: The Effects of 1996 U.S. Immigration Reform on Communities and Families in Texas, El Salvador, and Mexico." In *Latinos Remaking America,* edited by Marcelo M. Suarez Orozco and Mariela M. Paez, 190–201. Berkeley: University of California Press.

Hernandez-Leon, Ruben. 2008. *Metropolitan Migrants: The Migration of Urban Mexicans to the United States.* Berkeley: University of California Press.

Hirshman, Charles. 1983. "The Melting Pot Reconsidered." *Annual Review of Sociology* 9: 397–423.

Hoffman, Abraham. 1974. *Unwanted Mexican Americans in the Great Depression: Repatriation Pressures 1929–1939.* Tucson: University of Arizona Press.

Hurtado, Aida, and Luis A. Vega. 2004. "Shift Happens: Spanish and English Transmission between Parents and their Children." *Journal of Social Issues* 60 (1): 137–55.

Jimenez, Tomas R. 2010. *Replenished Ethnicity: Mexican Americans, Immigration, and Identity.* Berkeley: University of California Press.

Kasinitz, Philip, Mary C. Waters, John H. Mollenkopf, and Merih Anil. 2002. "Transnationalism and the Children of Immigrants in Contemporary New York." In *The Changing Face of Home,* edited by Peggy Levitt and Mary C. Waters, 96–122. New York: Russell Sage Foundation.

Levitt, Peggy. 2001. *The Transnational Villagers.* Berkeley: University of California Press.

———. 2002. "The Ties That Change: Relations to the Ancestral Home over the Life Cycle." In *The Changing Face of Home,* edited by Peggy Levitt and Mary C. Waters, 123–44. New York: Russell Sage Foundation.

Levitt, Peggy, and Mary C. Waters, eds. 2002. *The Changing Face of Home: The Transnational Lives of the Second Generation.* New York: Russell Sage Foundation.

Lieberson, Stanley. 1980. *A Piece of the Pie.* Berkeley: University of California Press.

Lieberson, Stanley, and Mary C. Waters. 1988. *From Many Strands: Ethnic and Racial Groups in Contemporary America.* New York: Russell Sage Foundation.

Lopez, David E., and Ricardo D. Stanton-Salazar. 2001. "Mexican Americans: A Second Generation at Risk." In *Ethnicities: Children of Immigrants in America,* edited by Rubén G. Rumbaut and Alejandro Portes, 57–90. Berkeley: University of California Press.

Márquez, Raquel R., and Harriett D. Romo, eds. 2008. *Transformations of La Familia on the U.S.-Mexico Border.* Notre Dame: University of Notre Dame Press.

Massey, Douglas S., Jorge Durand, and Nolan J. Malone. 2003. *Beyond Smoke and Mirrors: Mexican Immigration in an Era of Economic Integration.* New York: Russell Sage Foundation.

McLemore, S. Dale, and Harriett D. Romo. 2005. *Racial and Ethnic Relations in America.* Boston: Pearson.

Menchaca, Martha. 2001. *Recovering History, Constructing Race: The Indian, Black, and White Roots of Mexican Americans.* Austin: University of Texas Press.

Montejano, David. 1987. *Anglos and Mexicans in the Making of Texas: 1836–1986.* Austin: University of Texas Press.

———. 2010. *Quixote's Soldiers: A Local History of the Chicano Movement, 1966–1981.* Austin: University of Texas Press.

Mora-Torres, Juan. 2001. *The Making of the Mexican Border.* Austin: University of Texas Press.

O'Brien, Eileen. 2008. *The Racial Middle: Latinos and Asian Americans Living Beyond the Racial Divide.* New York: New York University Press.

Perlmann. Joel. 1988. *Ethnic Differences: Schooling and Social Structure Among the Irish, Italians, Jews, and Blacks in an American City, 1880–1935.* New York: Cambridge University Press.

Perlmann, Joel, and Roger Waldinger. 1997. "Second Generation Decline? Children of Immigrants. Past and Present—A Reconsideration." *International Migration Review* 31 (4): 893–922.

Portes, Alejandro, ed. 1996. *The New Second Generation.* New York: Russell Sage Foundation.

Portes, Alejandro, and Min Zhou. 1993. "The New Second Generation: Segmented Assimilation and Its Variants." *The Annals of the American Academy of Political and Social Sciences* 530 (1): 74–96.

Poyo, Gerald E., and Gilberto M. Hinojosa. 1991. *Tejano Origins in Eighteenth-Century San Antonio.* San Antonio: Institute of Texan Cultures.

Pycior, Julie Leininger. 1997. *LBJ and Mexican Americans: The Paradox of Power.* Austin: University of Texas Press.

Romo, Harriett D. 2008. "The Extended Border: A Case Study of San Antonio as a Transnational Community." In *Transformation of La Familia on the Texas-Mexican Border,* edited by Raquel R. Márquez and Harriett D. Romo, 77–104. Notre Dame: University of Notre Dame Press.

Romo, Ricardo. 1983. *East Los Angeles: History of a Barrio.* Austin: University of Texas Press.

———. 1993. "Responses to Mexican Immigration, 1910–1930." In *Beyond 1848: Readings in the Modern Chicano Historical Experience,* edited by Michael Raúl Ornelas, 179–203. Dubuque: Kendall Hunt Publishing.

Rumbaut, Rubén G., and Alejandro Portes, eds. 2001. *Ethnicities: Children of Immigrants in America.* Berkeley: University of California Press.

Smith, Robert C. 2002. "Life Course, Generation, and Social Location as Factors Shaping Second-Generation Transnational Life." In *The Changing Face of Home,* edited by Peggy Levitt and Mary C. Waters, 145–67. New York: Russell Sage Foundation.

———. 2006. *Mexican New York: Transnational Lives on New Immigrants.* Berkeley: University of California Press.

Smith, Michael P., and Matt Bakker. 2008. *Citizenship Across Borders: The Political Transnationalism of El Migrante.* Ithaca: Cornell University Press.

Stephen, Lynn. 2007. *Transborder Lives: Indigenous Oaxacans in Mexico, California, and Oregon.* Durham: Duke University Press.

Stepick, Alex, and Carol Dutton Stepick. 2009. "Power and Identity: Miami Cubans." In *Latinos: Remaking America,* edited by Marcelo M. Suarez-Orozco and Mariela M. Paez, 75–92. Harvard University: David Rockefeller Center for Latin American Studies.

Telles, Edward E., and Vilma Ortiz. 2008. *Generations of Exclusion: Mexican Americans, Assimilation, and Race.* New York: Russell Sage Foundation.

U.S. Census. 2000. "Redistricting Data (Public Law 94–171) Summary File. Matrices PL1, PL2, PL3, and PL4." http://quickfacts.census.gov/qfd/states/48/48029.html.

———. 2010. "Hispanic or Latino by Specific Origin." American Fact Finder. http://www.census.gov.prod/cen2010/doc/sf1.pdf.

———. 2010. "San Antonio (city), Texas." http://quickfacts.census.gov/qfd/states/48/4865000.html.

U.S. Immigration and Naturalization Service. 1991. Statistical Yearbook of the Immigration and Naturalization Service. Washington, DC: U.S. Government Printing Office.

Valle, Victor M., and Rodolfo D. Torre. 2000. *Latino Metropolis: Globalization and Community.* Vol. 7. Minneapolis: University of Minnesota Press.

Vigil, James Diego. 1998. *From Indians to Chicanos: The Dynamics of Mexican-American Culture.* 2nd ed. Prospect Heights: Waveland Press.

Waldinger, Roger, ed. 2001. *Strangers at the Gates: New Immigrants in Urban America*. Berkeley: University of California Press.

Waters, Mary. 1990. *Ethnic Options: Choosing Identities in America*. Berkeley: University of California Press.

———. 1999a. "Ethnic and Racial Identities of Second-Generation Black Immigrants in New York City." In *Race and Ethnic Relations in the United States: Readings for the Twenty-First Century,* edited by Christopher G. Ellison and W. Allen Martin, 476–85. Los Angeles: Roxbury Publishing.

———. 1999b. *Black Identities: West Indian Immigrant Dreams and American Realities*. Cambridge, MA: Harvard University Press.

Weber, David J. 1982. *The Mexican Frontier 1821–1846: The American Southwest Under Mexico*. Albuquerque: University of New Mexico Press.

Wolff, Nelson W. 1997. *Mayor: An Inside View of San Antonio Politics, 1981–1995*. San Antonio: San Antonio Express News.

Looking North and the Immigrant's Social Imaginary

RICARDO AINSLIE AND DAPHNY
DOMINGUEZ AINSLIE

In an interdisciplinary examination of the impact of immigration on the North American social landscape at the end of the millennium, Marcelo Suárez-Orozco (1998) noted that the phenomenon is likely to have a "momentous" effect on American culture and society. The current climate of debate over national immigration policy makes clear how prescient Suárez-Orozco's views were. And if immigration is having a significant effect upon the United States, the same can be said for its impact on the countries immigrants are leaving behind. The research presented here is primarily interested in this phenomenon in terms of the psychology of immigration in the context of the Mexican experience. This mass migration of Mexicans north of the border is having as profound an impact on Mexico as on the United States. According to the most recent Pew Hispanic Center study on immigration patterns (Passel 2005), one out of every eleven Mexicans now resides in this country—a fact that clearly has equally momentous implications for both Mexico and the United States.

Our interest in the present chapter, however, is not to explore the impact of immigration upon Mexico and Mexicans as such, but rather to explore the ways in which that impact might "live" in the experience of the Mexican immigrant as a kind of imaginary, that is, as a conscious and unconscious "presence" in the psychological experience of the immigrant. This perception is derived from and embedded in an ongoing, explicit, and implicit understanding of how one's fellow countrymen view the current immigration phenomenon and what the immigrant is undergoing.

CULTURE AND IDENTITY

Leaving one's homeland for another land represents a dislocation of varied meanings and implications. In order to understand the psychological impact of that experience, we must first understand the role of culture in identity, since the immigrant's dislocation stirs, in part, internal, psychological dislocations as well. Elsewhere, the first author has written about culture in relation to the development of identity (Ainslie 1995). Others, too, have theorized related points (see Winnicott 1971; Volkan 1997). From the very beginnings of human life the internalization of culture is part of identity. Indeed, Winnicott's implication is that without theorizing culture as a psychological process it is impossible to conceive of relationships more generally. Relatedness between infant and caregiver may be the foundation for identity, but to theorize about relationships as if they stood outside of a cultural embeddedness is meaningless.

Winnicott (1971) argues that each mother-infant dyad relates within a particular idiom of mothering, that is, through the particular ways in which that child is held, spoken to, and engaged, as well as through the kinds of objects that are brought into the child's life. This idiom is obviously embedded within and draws from the culture within which the dyad exists. The flavors, odors, and rituals that accompany the experience of being fed, or the language that governs parent-child interactions, with its specific tones, cadences, and melodies, are created by and in turn form a specific parent-infant culture. In the same moment, the broader culture shapes the dyad. These elements contribute to a specific "aesthetic of being" (Bollas 1987), that is, an aesthetic that becomes indistinguishable from identity itself.

Winnicott underscores the essential role of continuity and stability in creating a familiar "holding environment" for the child: a specific constellation of experiences, rituals, and forms of engagement defined by a measure of predictability, notwithstanding the fact that development is an unfolding process also characterized by moments of spontaneity and novelty. Invoking Winnicott's work, Bollas (1987) notes that it is against this "reciprocally enhancing stillness" that a continuous negotiation of intersubjective experience gains coherence. Key to this formulation is the understanding that in this developmental context, the mothering figure represents an "other" through which the infant's experience of "inside" and "outside" is transformed. This is Winnicott's "environment mother," the person who, to the child, represents the total environment.

The child's experience of being taken care of, of being "mothered," is indistinguishable from the child's still unthought notions about culture. But not being thought does not diminish the impact or power of these cultural elements as they insinuate themselves into the child's understanding of himself and of everything in his surroundings. Never are these experiences of self and culture more tightly bound, more thoroughly fused in an unreflected way, than at this earliest developmental juncture. So it is here that we can begin to appreciate the depth of every person's attachment to cultural elements and how it is that they are so irreducibly paired with all that is life-sustaining in a psychological sense.

In adulthood, significant portions of this still remain unthought, that is to say, implicit and unconscious, but much of it, too, comes to be not only articulated but also something to be sought after and appropriated. We may choose to eat certain foods, to listen to particular music, and to live in communities that share our language and cultural rituals and conventions, for example. We often experience this selection at two levels, notwithstanding the ways in which social class and prejudice frequently truncate options for some or problematize these choices by devaluing them or infusing them with feelings of shame. At a conscious level, we may love and value those things that are from 'our culture,' while at the same time we may not fully understand the deeper unconscious referents contained in these choices, links to the earliest "unthought known" (Bollas 1987) elements of our development which fused them to our identities in profound ways. Thus, when an immigrant leaves home, he or she is not only leaving a familiar place and people who are loved, the immigrant is also dislocated in this deeper sense from essential components that provide meaning and identity.

THE SUPEREGO AND THE SOCIAL IMAGINARY

Freud's construct of the superego may be useful here in order to understand the aspects of this psychic dislocation that we are attempting to describe in this chapter. We are not necessarily referring to the judgmental connotations of the superego, specifically, but rather to the idea of the superego as a psychic "institution" that is derived not solely from familial experience but also from the internalization of societal norms, values, and aesthetics more broadly. Freud (1923) theorized this psychic function as a kind of inner voice against which the individual engages, compares, verifies, or seeks validation for his thoughts, feelings, and actions. In other words, the superego, in this sense, is a psychic process that is deeply embedded in this broader social context within which we exist, a process through which we filter what we do and to which we continually refer what we do. While in common usage we are accustomed to thinking of the superego as the internalization of parental voices and attitudes, Freud's concept also lends itself to this more social-cultural reading.

These are the Freudian roots of the Social Imaginary concept as deployed (if differently) by both Lacan (see 2006) and, later, Castoriadis (1987). Castoriadis views the Social Imaginary as a system of meanings that define the social structure, created out of the interplay of individuals and society. It is not necessarily "real," but is rather constructed out of the imagination of each social subject living within a given social structure. Like Freud's notion that every superego is to some extent highly idiosyncratic (that is, we may be members of the same society but each of us nonetheless possesses a superego that is created out of the particularities of our specific social-familial contexts and out of our imagined readings and constructions of what those elements really mean), Castoriadis's Social Imaginary is equally particularized and idiosyncratic and equally constructed out of the imaginary.

Castoriadis theorizes the individual's identity as more radically embedded within the broader social structure than does Freud, arguing that the tension between the individual and the social is irreducible. Yet, like Freud, he maintains an interest in the psyche as a meaningful, essential component to theorizing about the individual and about the subjective experience of living within any given social structure.

Another, perhaps more explicitly psychological way of stating this is that, from this perspective, we might imagine the human subject as constantly carrying on a kind of implicit internal "dialogue" (experienced at both conscious and unconscious levels) in which all of one's thoughts, feelings, and actions are being referred to the Social Imaginary. That is, we participate in an ever-present and ongoing process—partly reflected, partly unconscious and intruding on us from our interior psychic landscape as well as from society—as we go about living our lives. This dialogue has implications for how we experience what we do, and it shapes our experience of it. It can make us feel proud, affirmed, and validated when we believe that those that matter in our world are pleased with who we are and what we are doing. And it can make us depressed, angry, and even hopeless, when we feel that the world around us disapproves, devalues, or is critical of our efforts. These evaluations, however, are not exclusively familial in origin; they also derive from broader social and cultural frames of reference.

Freud discussed the superego as an internalized psychic agency that by mid-childhood was relatively autonomous of the 'real' world around us. Castoriadis, Lacan, and others have helped us see the shortsightedness of this position. 'Reality,' that is, the socio-cultural context within which we are held, engages us and plays a role in how we understand ourselves continuously and profoundly throughout life. We do not grow increasingly impervious to the world around us, psychologically speaking; rather, we are inseparable from this 'reality' and it has a powerful role in shaping what we do, who we are, and our evaluative notions about each. The psyche and social institutions are thoroughly interpenetrated in an ongoing, fluid way.

REASONS FOR MIGRATION

A recent study, "Unauthorized Migrants: Numbers and Characteristics," found that there are over ten million people of Mexican origin in the United States, the largest share of which are "unauthorized" (Passel 2005). Unlike many other immigrants to the United States, the overwhelming majority of immigrants from Mexico come exclusively for economic reasons. One study (COLEF, CONAPO, and STPS 1994) found that almost 28 percent of Mexican migrants did not have a job prior to coming to the United States. In addition, the gap between Mexican per capita income ($6,230) relative to that of the United States ($37,610), has grown continuously (CIDE, COMEXI, CCFR, 2004, 15). Finally, the Mexican economy has not been producing enough new jobs to keep abreast of population growth (Dussel Peters 1998).

Mexicans who decide to migrate to the United States are doing so primarily because of economic motives. If Mexico could provide for them and their families, most would prefer to stay home. Similarly, a recent study conducted by CIDE, COMEXI, and CCFR (2004) found that only a third of the Mexicans polled said they would go to the United States if they could. Economic necessities are driving this immigration, and this phenomenon is also producing powerful psychological implications because of the profound dislocations that affect individuals, families, and entire communities.

These economic realities, too, are part of the Social Imaginary. That is, the significations that form the Social Imaginary are not created in a vacuum; rather, they are always derived and constructed out of existing conditions. In the context of Mexican immigration, these conditions are the economic circumstances that form the backdrop to the decision to leave, a backdrop that contains a universe of images of self and family and society. These are the building materials for the Social Imaginary, the stuff from which conscious and unconscious dialogues are being formed and taking place; a Social Imaginary, in other words, that the immigrant brings along, as it were, and which is further engaged and constituted by a universe of images derived from the personal encounter with what it means to be in the United States and the various meanings and experiences derived from engagement with American culture. In fact, Castoriadis would perhaps argue that the phenomenon of immigration itself might be understood as a "creative" manifestation of Mexican society, "personified" in the act of many individual crossings to the United States, all part of a simultaneously thought and unthought engagement with the meaning of overwhelmingly complex economic challenges.

A WORLD LEFT BEHIND

In this chapter we argue that part of the immigrant Social Imaginary is the world that has been left behind and their understandings of how this world views them. And this is reflected, in part, in the immigrant's inner experience of the real and imagined understandings of what those who are left behind think and feel about the immigrant's "project." The influence of an implicit collective, namely, a broader set of assumptions about what Mexico and Mexicans more generally think about the immigration phenomenon, are important, but immediate family and friends play perhaps a more salient role. If families back home are grateful for and supportive of the risks and deprivations that are inherent in the immigrant experience, these views are no doubt reassuring to the immigrant. Typically, however, feelings are complex even for families who are benefiting from the immigrant's odyssey, since spouses and children are often left behind and separations are frequently extended. When those left behind do not fully comprehend the travails involved in crossing the border or in finding employment once inside the United States, immigrants may feel additional conflict. Some family members may have idealized or otherwise unrealistic notions about how easy it is to make money or how much money their loved one will be able to send home given the cost of living in the United States. There may also be anxieties and conflicts about what one does with money while in the United States.

These are all potentially important variables in the psychology of an immigrant's experience, but this chapter will explore the fact that in Mexico there are a variety of attitudes toward those who leave for the United States and it is our assumption that these attitudes are in some way conveyed or understood by the immigrant after he or she has left home. In turn, such attitudes may have an impact on the immigrant's adjustment to the myriad challenges of the immigration experience. Per Castoriadis's view that society is an anonymous social dimension (as opposed to the subjectively immediate psyche), our interviews may be seen as an attempt to concretize these otherwise abstracted and anonymous voices.

THE INTERVIEWS

In the summer of 2004 the first author made two trips to Mexico City with a film crew to explore Mexicans' views concerning immigration, a social phenomenon that, as we have noted, has had wide-ranging impact upon the country. Thirty individuals were interviewed. They came from all walks of life and included several salesmen, factory workers, a cab driver, a cashier, security guards, teachers, a shoeshine man, a musician, domestics, and dog trainers, among other occupations. In terms of social class, they ranged from lower working class to middle class. An informal, open-ended set of questions explored their views on immigration, beginning with (after a brief introduction to the project) "Do you have any family members, friends, or neighbors who have immigrated to the United States?" The responses of the interviewees were followed up in whatever direction the process took, but the goal was to understand what they felt about the immigration phenomenon, the forces behind it, and the effect on those who left as well as on those left behind. The interviews were videotaped and a subset of them form part of a thirty-minute documentary film titled "Looking North: Mexican Images of Immigration" (Ainslie 2006).

Every one of the thirty randomly selected individuals interviewed in Mexico City had a family member, a friend, or a neighbor who had migrated north. Some of them knew people in all three categories, and several had made the trip themselves. This alone reflects the impact that migration to the United States is having on Mexico. We have selected several themes from these interviews to illustrate the complexity of attitudes and understandings regarding the migration of so many of their countrymen; following these descriptions, we will discuss their implications for what we are calling "the immigrant's Social Imaginary."

HEROES AND VILLAINS

Many Mexicans view compatriots who have gone to the United States as heroic figures. They are acutely aware of the dangers involved in attempting to cross into this country illegally, for example (and 80–85 percent of migrants from Mexico are undocumented) (Passel 2005). They are also cognizant of the fact that crossing the border represents an enormous sacrifice both financially and in terms of personal relationships.

Heroic Adventurers

This first collection of quotations articulates the narrative of risk and vulnerability that is a salient thread in Mexican understandings of what their compatriots experience.

> From the moment they decide to go over there, they put themselves in the hands of a coyote, they have to walk at night, they're hunted along the way, and if they're caught they club them, and where they cross . . . that's a risk.
>
> Ostrich Goods Salesman

> Mistreatment, that is all. Physical mistreatment. Mistreatment in the way they always have to be hiding. The simple fact that they have to cross over to the other country by way of the rivers, hiding—How many people have died trying to do that? And in what conditions have they died? Sometimes, in the United States, when they encounter an immigrant they have mistreated him, or accosted him. That is what one hears in the news.
>
> School Teacher #2

> Everyone knows the suffering they undergo, the hunger, no home, hiding all the time. They do without so much, and risked so much to go over.
>
> Security Guard

These are powerful narratives that speak to an acute awareness of the real dangers inherent in the immigrant's journey. Many Mexicans, perhaps most, are outraged by these experiences, which are prominent in Mexican media accounts of migrant experiences. Those who decide to come to the United States live, psychologically, within the shadow of this narrative. It forms part of their understanding for what lies ahead, or, once here, the meaning of what they have endured or are enduring. In addition, as the following quotes illustrate, Mexican views are often coupled with a sense of tragedy that what is driving this migration is the fact that Mexico cannot provide for many of its people.

Driven By Need

> Look, if you are in your house and your children are hungry and you are the head of the family, you have to do something, go across the border, expose yourself to death, to being shot down like they did in Arizona.
>
> School Teacher #1

> If you visit Puebla, Oaxaca, there are ghost towns where only old people live, or only women, because the men have gone to work in the United States, to better themselves. They risk everything, leaving the children, the older parents, sometimes even not knowing their children, to bring dollars.
>
> Museum Guide

> That is very complicated, no? I believe it is sad that Mexicans must migrate to be able to find work.
>
> School Teacher #2

These reflections underscore a different dimension of the forces driving the immigrants' experience. Here, what is articulated is the social cost of migration, in terms of family and social networks, for example. What makes the immigrant's experience arduous is not only the life threatening possibilities sometimes inherent in the crossing, but also the very real circumstance of leaving behind so much of what organizes a sense of self and identity. Further, there is the fact that employment and other resources are scarce, leaving some with no other recourse but to migrate.

They're Pursuing an Illusion

However, there are other voices that also form part of the Mexican view of this complex social process, including less positive, even disparaging attitudes toward those who have migrated north and their reasons for doing so.

> When you listen to others and see that they come back with a truck, well, you can get a truck here, too. It's just a matter of wanting it; and if you want it you can get one. . . . And there's work here, this is a rich country, but you can't look for the easy way. You have to work. . . . And then when they are working [in the United States], they work twelve hours, they can't rest, to me it's a form of slavery, of disguised slavery. And I have sons, and I've told them, "Better to study here, prepare yourself here, than to go pursue an illusion somewhere else."
>
> Ostrich Goods Salesman

> I've even said, "Why are you going up there when you're better. . . . At least here you're going to be free in your own country, not hiding or selling your labor for cheap."
>
> First Park Man

> There is work [in Mexico] if you look for it. But they wanted more. So you see that and you say, "No, better to stay here."
>
> Domestic #1

> Well, people are very materialistic and they like good things, expensive things, designer things. For example, here people wear ordinary clothing, but up there what's normal is to wear designer clothing. So that's part of the good life they have up there and that's why they don't come back.
>
> Dog Trainer #1

I thought "You can work in Mexico, too." What I was going to find there I could find it here too.

Butler

Well they go because their own 'paisanos' return and tell them that it's nice and they have lots of comforts, and that makes them go. And since they see that those up there have money, they think that they, too, will go up there and get some money. In other words, it's the illusion of the dollar. . . . And people don't think what they're going to have to go through to attain that. That's the falsity of life.

Cab Driver

These views have a sharp edge, and are perhaps based on the psychodynamics of envy (many of these accounts revolve around assumptions about material excesses, or the quest for expensive things or easy money, for example). They also devalue the immigrant, implying that they could "make it" in Mexico if they really tried.

Mistreatment by Their Own

Surprisingly, several interviewees voiced the view that often it was fellow Latinos who were least supportive, or most likely to mistreat their immigrant compatriots.

The United States is OK; it has something for everyone, but . . . the people who've become residents up there, there is a discrimination against their compatriots. I think the North Americans treat the Mexicans better than the compatriots do, even the immigration people.

Park Man #2

The Americans, well, they treated me well. But there's more envy with your own *paisanos*. . . . I don't know why, like they're afraid we're going to take away their work or something. . . [The] Mexican Americans, who went there and made their lives, they are more rejecting of the new ones who come.

Park Man #1

One sees on television specials of former immigrants who have gone. When others now go as immigrants—what they once were—they humiliate them, they mistreat them. And these are their own people! Do you understand me?

Cashier

Anti-immigrant attitudes are more frequently assumed to come from mainstream "Anglo" sectors, not other Latinos. A subset of the people interviewed suggested that tensions between recent immigrants and Latinos who may have preceded them by several generations have been reported as well.

Impact on Families

Interviewees were also concerned that the act of migrating to the United States often has problematic repercussions for the families and those who are left behind:

They have been sending money and then when they find out from their families how much they have, they will say, "OK, buy a house, buy a car, put up a business." The ones that I know. But there are also people that I have known, that they leave and just forget.

Motorcycle Salesman

The family always asks how they're doing because I don't think they've even written. So they don't know what's happened, if they're alive or not or what. And then sometimes you forget, even about your family, because you see other places, other people, more money, so you even forget your people. They don't even remember them, call them or anything. That's a big change.

Domestic #1

They separate, the children are lost—the education from the father that they should receive. They start drinking, hanging out with bad people, and the family begins to disintegrate. The son is just waiting to grow up to be with the father.

Ostrich Goods Salesman

My husband is a very resentful person, he feels that the United States stole his family away from him! And he says, "But if we'd stayed together here in Mexico we could have made it! And they wouldn't be suffering up there." But *they* see it differently.

Museum Guide

These perspectives are also complex. One theme here revolves around anxieties that the people who have left home, often driven by economic need and often leaving families behind that need their support, end up not meeting the family's expectations. There is the fear that the migrants will lose touch. This may be due to adversity (people finding themselves in circumstances that make communication difficult) but may also be because they begin to make their lives in the United States. The Museum Guide's comment is especially telling in that it voices the often-unarticulated feeling that somehow the United States is to blame for this circumstance.

They Come Back Changed

Perhaps the greatest ambivalence that many Mexicans have about the immigration phenomenon is that it often changes those who migrate to the United States in ways that create tensions and conflict with those who remain.

They forget where they are from. It changes them, I don't know why—if it's a lack of love from family—so I think to forget that feeling, they enter the circle where they are now. And that changes them, makes them forget who they were, their country, it happens to all of them. After a month you start feeling that you are an American, try to talk as they talk up there, immediately. (And when they come back?) They come back as Americans, and they don't talk to you about anything other than dollars, what all they have up there, they think of themselves as Americans.

Security Guard

Well, actually, there is change of every type. Some think that because they have been to Los Angeles, they think the world is too small for them. They think, "Chilangos, poor things." The same Mexican will look down upon another Mexican.

Teacher #1

They come like they want to make us less, like "It's great up there and there are better things, better clothing." Well, yes, there may be better things up there, but it's the same. I don't see a big difference. I had a friend who went up there at sixteen years of age and when he came back he acted like he didn't know what *tacos al pastor* were, like "Oh, what's this?" As if it were a rarity. And he left at sixteen or so. (So some return with an attitude?) Yes, like they want you to feel like you're less, to humiliate. They may have money, because it's what they've saved all year.

Park Man #1

They want to change their roots, and that's impossible, because we have known them all their lives. They come back speaking bad Spanish. But, OK, doubtless, they pick up the accent from over there. . . . They must not forget their roots. And remember that this is their country, not that one.

Motorcycle Salesman

Obviously, when they come to Mexico, they come with a lot more money, because of the exchange rates. And that affects them, too. They start getting into a conflict of feeling superiority, that's not good either.

Dog Trainer #1

I don't like this topic. I'm very Mexican. I love Mexico, so it bothers me that so many people are going up there. And, yes, there are lots of advantages, right? But they've also got them very under foot. The laws here are more "light." Up there they have the Statue of Liberty; here we have real liberty, they've only got the statue.

Dog Trainer #2

The question of how identity is affected by the experience of immigration is very salient in Mexico. There is great anxiety that those who leave will be altered by the experience, that they will lose their identities as they become acculturated to American values and American ways of living. It is evident that these concerns run deep and, not infrequently, carry considerable emotion. The parallel concern, however, is that some indeed return home changed. They may feel themselves empowered by the fact that they now have wealth they did not have in the past, for example, or other tastes and habits may have changed over time. All of these, of course, are tied to questions of identity.

MEXICAN VIEWS

Mexican views of the immigration phenomenon are varied and complex. They range from narratives of mythic struggle and life-threatening adversity to an awareness of the economic realities that are driving millions of Mexicans to pursue a better life for themselves and their families by crossing the U.S.-Mexico border. However, they also include narratives that suggest that, in the eyes of some, those who go north are pursuing the easy way out and grasping at illusions, often at the expense of their families. We make no claims regarding how representative these views are, given that they are drawn from thirty random interviews with individuals in Mexico City. The latter, less flattering, views were clearly the minority among those interviewed, but that they were expressed at all was surprising. They would seem to suggest ambivalence within Mexico with respect to immigration, an ambivalence that is understandable when viewed in relation to the profound impact that this phenomenon is having on every facet of Mexican society.

INNER VOICES PRESENT REALITIES

The immigrant's experience is one of high stress derived from multiple sources: difficulties finding work, difficulties adjusting to an alien cultural context, long hours of toil, constant fear of the immigration authorities, and the emotional toll of being treated as a non-person, as if one is invisible. These are realities that infiltrate the immigrant's emotional life, a constant source of pressure, stress, and anxiety. To these better-known sources of conflict we add another: an awareness that Mexicans back home have varying and sometimes ambivalent attitudes toward the immigration phenomenon.

Every immigrant from Mexico arrives in the United States and lives against a backdrop of these inner voices—voices that continuously reference what he is doing, why she is doing it, and what it means. The extent to which they feel understood and validated in their day-to-day struggles within this country, in the face of employment anxieties and immigration status uncertainties, affects their sense of well-being and the psychological resources that are available to them for managing these challenges. These challenges are also taking place in the context of a deep cultural dislocation that has separated them from family and friends and everything that they know, that is, the collection of feelings that the first author has termed *cultural mourning* (Ainslie 1998).

Perhaps to an extent not fully acknowledged, a portion of the stress that immigrants experience is related to their thoughts and feelings about the opinions of the compatriots they left behind. As we have seen, those views are as complex as they are mixed. Some fellow Mexicans view them as heroic figures, facing severe challenges, even life-threatening challenges, in order to bring something to their families. Most Mexicans are aware, too, that individuals who have migrated to the United States represent the third leading source of income, after oil exports, and foreign investments for their country (González González 2004). These are not small considerations. Many interviewees noted that the sacrifices made by these migrants translate into vital resources for their families back home, whether in the form of capital to open a business or funds to renovate or purchase a family home.

On the other hand, some have a more disparaging attitude toward their compatriots' activities. They suggest that "where there is a will there is a way," and that, if these men and women really wanted to "make it," they could do so in Mexico. These voices use words such as "chasing an illusion," or "it's the illusion of the dollar," to describe their fellow countrymen's pursuit of a better life via the decision to migrate north. This undercurrent of derision is sometimes linked to nationalistic feelings ("Well, I'm very Mexican, so this idea of migrating to the United States doesn't interest me in the least."), as if migrants were being unpatriotic. This nationalist strain also becomes linked to a broader derision of the United States as a materialistic place, or as a country with a kind of pseudo liberty as compared to Mexico ("Up there they have the Statue of Liberty, but down here we have real liberty"). The theme of Mexico as a kind of failed provider is strong among some of these individuals, and there's a tone of hopelessness in the face of Mexico's enormous social and economic problems. Perhaps envy, too, plays a part in some of the more disparaging attitudes. The accounts of how some immigrants return home changed, more "Americanized" in language and style of dress, flush with cash, and sometimes exuding cosmopolitan airs, all might stir ambivalence.

No doubt the latter, more ambivalent views, are not predominant, but they are views that exist, and they reflect the complexity of a nation's self understanding with respect to the steady flow of immigrants to the United States, a fact that has profoundly transformed Mexico itself, where today nearly every Mexican has a family member, friend, or neighbor (or all three) who has migrated north of the border, or has done so themselves. Our point is that immigrants who find themselves struggling to make a way for themselves here in the United States at some level "carry" these differing voices within themselves. As they reflect on their circumstance, there is a continuous internal dialogue taking place, one in which varying moods and states make reference back to this universe of voices back home, voices that form part of the immigrant's Social Imaginary, which is part of the material from which immigrants draw to make sense of who they are and what they are doing.

REFERENCES

Ainslie, Ricardo. 1995. *No Dancin' in Anson: An American Story of Race and Social Change.* Northvale: Jason Aronson.

———. 1998. "Cultural Mourning, Immigration, and Engagement: Vignettes from the Mexican Experience." In *Crossings: Immigration and the Socio-Cultural Remaking of the North American Space,* edited by Marcelo Suarez-Orozco, 283–300. Cambridge, MA: Harvard University Press.

————, producer, director, writer. 2006. *Looking North: Mexican Images of Immigration*. Documentary Film.

Bollas, Christopher. 1987. *The Shadow of the Object: Psychoanalysis of the Unthought Known*. Northvale: Jason Aronson.

Castoriadis, Cornelius. 1987. *The Imaginary Institution of Society*. Cambridge, MA: MIT Press.

El Colegio de la Frontera Norte (COLEF), Consejo National de Población (CONAPO), and Secretaría del Trabajo y Previsión Social (STPS). 1994. "Encuesta sobre Migración de la Fontera Norte." Tijuana: El Colegio de la Frontera Norte.

Dussel Peters, E. 1998. "Recent Structural Changes in Mexico's Economy: A Preliminary Analysis of Some Sources of Mexican Migration to the United States." In *Crossings: Immigration and the Socio-Cultural Remaking of the North American Space,* edited by Marcelo Suarez-Orozco, 53–74. Cambridge, MA: Harvard University Press.

Freud, Sigmund. 1923. "The Ego and the Super-Ego (Ego Ideal)." In *The Standard Edition of the Complete Psychological Works of Sigmund Freud,* vol. 19, edited by J. Strachey, 28–39. London: Hogarth.

González González, Guadalupe. 2004. "Global Views 2004: Comparing Mexican and American Public Opinion and Foreign Policy." Mexico: CIDE (Centro de Investigación y Docencia Económicas).

Lacan, Jacques. 2006. *Écrits: The First Complete Edition in English*. Translated by Bruce Fink in collaboration with Héloïse Fink and Russell Grigg. New York: Norton.

Passel, Jeffrey. 2005. "Estimates of the Size and Characteristics of the Undocumented Population." Washington, DC: Pew Hispanic Center.

Suarez-Orozco, Marcelo (Ed.). 1998. *Crossings: Immigration and the Socio-Cultural Remaking of the North American Space*. Cambridge, MA: Harvard University Press.

Volkan, Vamik. 1997. *Bloodlines: From Ethnic Pride to Ethnic Terrorism*. Boulder: Westview Press.

Winnicott, Donald Woods. 1971. "The Location of Cultural Experience." In *Playing and Reality,* edited by Donald Woods Winnicott, 95–103. New York: Basic Books.

PART II

Immigrants and Civic Life

THREE

Latino Immigrants

Transnationalism, Patterns of Multiple Citizenships,
and Social Capital

JOHN A. GARCIA

Studies of immigration have centered on the flows, nature, impact, and adaptation of immigrants on the economic, sociocultural, and political life of the receiving countries. In addition, the formation of immigrant communities and the social networks they utilize serve to facilitate economic, political, and sociocultural transactions. More recently, the concept of transnationalism has received greater attention as to the patterns, extensiveness, and impact of binational connections among immigrants with their home country/communities and residence in the United States (Alger 1997). One of the potential consequences of this phenomenon is the creation of multiple citizenships and attachments. For example, individuals can be engaged in the civic affairs of both their countries of origin as well as their current country of residence.

This chapter explores the major components of the concept of transnationalism with emphasis on the political connections and ramifications of exercising these sustained activities in both countries (Foner 1997). More specifically, this study focuses on the consequences of transnational interactions on the civic life of Mexican immigrants residing in the Chicago metropolitan area. Our use of the concept of *transnationalism* indicates a sustained range of interactions and exchanges that transcends national boundaries and is maintained by a system of social networks and institutional structures (Portes et al. 1999). These transactions occur between individuals and communities, capital flows, trade, citizenship affiliations and activities, political incorporation, inter-governmental organizations, social movements, familial ties, identities, and policy influence.

For our purposes here, this chapter examines Chicago Latino immigrants and their transnational activities. We look specifically at the civic and political engagement of Mexican immigrants who maintain transnational ties with their country of origin. We then examine the extent and nature of their transnational networks that have relevance for community civic involvement in both the countries of residence and origin.

By doing so, we are introducing the idea of multiple citizenships as our transnational participants are engaging in civic and political activities on both sides of the border. This deviates from an emphasis on economic and sociocultural exchanges usually associated with transnationalism (Garcia 2012; Brubaker 1996). Our exploration of the effects of transnational involvement among Mexican immigrants looks at forms of civic engagement, political activities and influencing, and the development of social capital skills in the United States (see Glick Schiller 1996; DeWind and Kasinitz 1997). In addition, we will profile what types of Mexicanos engage in transnational activities and to what extent. For the most part, the extant research has examined primarily the transnational relationship between immigrants and their country of origin and "hometown" and familial ties. The objective of this study is to identify, measure, and relate transnationalism among Latino immigrants to indicators of civic engagement in their U.S. communities.

TRANSNATIONALISM, MIGRATION, AND POLITICAL CITIZENSHIP

The study of transnationalism has included the regular contacts or interactions with one's country of origin in a variety of different economic, political, and sociocultural exchanges. Some necessary conditions would include: (1) a significant portion of the immigrant and national origin community members are involved in the exchanges; (2) the activities are not fleeting, but are relatively stable; and (3) the content of interactions are not captured by preexisting concepts (Levitt 2001; Morawska 2001).

Using this definition, the transnational phenomenon could include activities related to an immigrant's occupation and activities that require regular contact that are sustained over time across national boundaries. For example, immigrant entrepreneurs rely on transnational ties for goods, products, and other materials from their home country to conduct their business. Other businesses provide services such as travel planning and tickets and custom brokerage services that are dependent on ongoing transnational connections. The majority of these transactions occur with familial networks such that remittances and other means of economic assistance take place from the United States to family members in one's country of origin (Goldring 1996; Hannerz 1996). Resultant activities of transnationalism include the idea of a trade diaspora, circular migration, multiple identities, and mechanisms for immigrant adaptation, expanding the asset base for U.S. residence and in country of origin, as well as developing social capital skills (Eckstein and Barberia 2002).

The creation of hometown associations facilitates and directs a wide range of transnational interactions. In addition to direct familial assistance, group sponsored public projects (that is, infrastructure and public works projects, creation of libraries and acquisition of books, community activities, and so on) are also part of hometown association activities (Fitzgerald 2000). The rise of hometown associations can be found wherever immigrants reside and, generally, are organized based on geographical subregions in the country of origin, such as the city, town, or state.

The examination and discussion of transnationalism directs some attention toward the appropriate unit of analysis (Portes et al. 1999; Glick Schiller et al. 1995). Various levels and units of interest include individuals, organizations, sociopolitical structures, and the network of social relations that result from that contact, as well as political parties, communities, economic enterprises, and the state. For purposes of this research, the unit of analysis is the individual. The individual is the primary initiator of actions and triggers the nexus of transnational engagements. At the same time, the other contexts or frames of reference impact the nature, extent, and manner of transnational interactions (Vertovec 1999). For example, with our focus on Mexican immigrants, the State has become an important part of the transnational equation as their actions have promoted linkages, identities, policy/financial support, and electoral involvement of their citizens now living in the United States (Massey et al. 1994; Guarnizo 1998).

What are the necessary conditions that facilitate or impede transnationalism among immigrant populations? Although transnationalism has existed among immigrants prior to the contemporary waves of America's immigrants, technological advances have enabled them to maintain contacts and engage in exchanges, and to do so in a relatively short period of time. Air transport, electronic mail, cell phones, and other time compressing technologies have facilitated ties and transferring important economic, political, and sociocultural interchanges. For this reason, the recent interest in contemporary transnationalism may overstate the presence of interactions in relation to previous periods of immigrant settlement in the United States.

My particular interest in transnationalism lies with the sites of engagement—that is, global and public space (Kenney and Roundnetof 2002; Mahler 1998). Again, more attention has been directed toward homeland politics. Immigrants in the United States can still affect political outcomes, and political parties have reached out to them for support, votes, and campaign contributions. Government agencies in Mexico were established specifically to interact and sustain homeland ties motivated by emotive and economic attachments (Goldring 2002; Goldring 1988). The data on remittances demonstrate their growing contribution as part of gross national product (GNP). In addition, the status of dual citizenship enables immigrants to be potentially relevant political actors in the home country. They can exercise the vote, run for office, and support political parties.

At the same time, Mexican immigrants can obtain citizenship in the United States to participate in this country politically. For example, in addition to expanding the size of the Latino electorate, they can become advocates for better foreign and trade relations with their country of origin. The home country may encourage dual citizenship (Baubock 1994; Faust 2002). A product of global citizenship is the presence of multiple identities, loyalties, and global contact and communication (Issac 1997; Pessar and Graham 2002). These types of consciousness—from both country of origin and residence—have implications for introducing modes of cultural reproduction (that is, constructed styles that incorporate realities of economic and spatial arrangements) and establishing behaviors in both locations. Social institutions like hometown associations, cultural events, and economic exchanges become the vehicles for being a global citizen. Communications media like newspapers and television help to sustain these relationships (Munch 2001; Portes 1996).

Until this point, our discussion of transnationalism has focused upon the nature and extent of transactions that can occur among immigrants. The concept of capital accumulation is equally pertinent in this discussion. Most of the research that focuses on capital accumulation is economically centered by examining supply, production, marketing, investment, information transfer, and management of capital flows from immigrants to familial and community destinations and purposes. Assisting the homeland economy through remittances, funding local projects, and meeting family members' living expenses and consumer demands are the more common basis for capital accumulation (Jacobson 1996). The next section links transnationalism with the accumulation of social capital and its political ramifications for political engagement in immigrants' area of residence.

THE POLITICAL DIMENSION OF TRANSNATIONALISM: SOCIAL CAPITAL

Social capital is an important phenomenon that intersects the concept of transnationalism (Coleman 1988; Hanifan 1916). The processes that cultivate good will, congenial fellowship, affinity, and social interaction, serve to build community and involve its residents, are essential elements of social capital. We examine the political participation and civic engagement of immigrants who maintain transnational ties, the extent and nature of their networks, and relate these to levels of community involvement in both the countries of residence and origin.

For the most part, research has focused upon the sociological, familial, and economic forms of social capital. In contrast, this chapter examines whether and to what extent transnational immigrants may forsake political incorporation in their country of residence in exchange for continuous involvement in their country of origin. Our perspective is that this does not have to be an either/or arrangement. The effect of immigrants' continued involvement in their country of origin may influence their residentially based activities in the United States. Many countries now encourage their citizenry to naturalize in their country of residence, which may additionally impact their political behavior.

Before 1991 only four Latin American countries (Uruguay, Panama, Peru, and El Salvador) allowed dual nationality. Jones-Correa (2001) suggests that the post-1990's passage of dual nationality was the result of a "bottom-up" effort by Latino nationals living in the United States. That is, organized lobbying directed at the respective Latino immigrants' legislatures and political parties was initiated to extend dual citizenship. Issues of property rights, electoral representation, and other legal statuses were at the core of these efforts. Similarly, their countries of origin had a vested interest in maintaining good relations with their nationals because remittances, privately financed public works projects by hometown associations, and political party donations are an integral part of this symbiotic relationship.

For example, Colombians, Ecuadorians, and Dominicans created formal organizations to lobby their nation's respective legislatures to pass enabling legislation. Ecuadorian efforts began in 1967 and continued until passage in 1995 (Jones-Correa 2001, 162–63). Part of the rationale and motivation was not to forfeit their rights in their "home" country. By obtaining the dual citizenship option, these Latino immigrants could participate (economically and politically) in both nations. Economic considerations have also been a contributing factor (especially property ownership and transfers) to Latino immigrant efforts to obtain dual citizenships. Another consequence of dual citizenship for Latino non-U.S. citizens was a marked increase in U.S. naturalizations (Jones-Correa 2001).

While dual citizenship has become more prevalent (that is, recent actions by Mexico, Colombia, and the Dominican Republic), the issues of which national citizenship has primacy, the question of possible foreign influences on domestic issues, and requirements to relinquish other citizenships have been the center of our national discussions. Some believe that dual nationality is a legitimate link and reality for these "global citizens" and can reduce the disadvantages that can follow the acquisition of a new nationality, including inheritance rights, property ownership, and other entitlements (Martin 1999, 30). Yet others see this as a question of loyalty and allegiance to the country you live in.

A requisite component in this discussion of dual citizenship is that the "immigrant" has completed the naturalization process in the United States. The status of dual citizenship reinforces the realities of multiple attachments, interests, connections/involvements, and impacts of several governments. The question surfaces whether a representative government can function without the political participation of significant portions of constituents (Hammar 1985, 442–45). Even among the Latino transnationals who do not become dual citizens, there is less difference of rights between citizens and non-citizens; and the political incorporation of both "types" has connections in both democratic principles and praxis.

For example, the European experience has evidenced the role of governmental institutions playing a consultative role in order to involve non-citizens in local decision-making. Twenty-two democracies allow non-citizen voting. New Zealand allows all non-citizens voting rights after one year residency. Sweden, Denmark, Norway, Ireland, Hungary, and the Netherlands allow non-citizens to participate in local elections (Layton-Henry 1990, 189–91). Thus, our brief discussion of dual citizenship introduces, hopefully, the notion that multiple attachments among Latinos across national boundaries have implications politically for both their home country and country of residence. Secondly, their participation in both spheres has interactive and cumulative effects. It is these linkages that serve as the focus and attempt to understand these dynamics.

Transnational connections can create a submerged national sovereignty under a myriad of transnational practices. People are linked to their fellow nationals, hometown communities and regions, and political and social agencies, introducing the idea of multiple citizenships. Local and transnational interests and involvements can and usually do coexist (Roberts et al. 1999; Rodriguez 1996).

I believe that the principles of social capital apply to transnationals. Attachment and interaction within community and focused activities operate through social structures and processes including organizations, communication systems, information, leadership, strategies, participatory/organizational experiences, and so on. Using the individual as the unit of analysis, the development of knowledge, skills, and experiences has utility in both territorial contexts. James Coleman (1988) contends that social capital is constituted by the obligations and expectations produced from individuals' involvement in social organizations. The later works of Robert Putnam (Putnam et al. 1993; 1995; 2000) examine the link between the social behavior of individuals and the quality of social/political institutions. Putnam (2000) places social capital in the context of democracies by identifying the keys to a successful democracy. They include the individual's relationships and involvement in community activities leading to diminished isolation and increased social networks, friendship ties, and other social connections. He describes the creation of social capital through formal and informal social networks, such as ordinary socializing, relationships with neighbors, personal support networks, and social behaviors at the workplace.

The political implications of transnationalism are often overlooked without the inclusion of the accumulation of social capital in the context of the immigrants' country of residence. That is, the acts of conducting transnational interactions usually require social networks, knowledge, and interactions with social, economic, and political institutions in both countries (Itzigsohn et al. 1999). These activities allow the individual to accumulate and use social capital both in the country of residence as well as the country of origin (Cano 2004; Guarnizo 2001). This can effect political incorporation, civic engagement, political participation, and intergenerational transfer.

The application of the social capital concept to Mexican immigrants living in the United States serves to link transnational activities with social capital accumulation and its use in a U.S. political context (Rouse 1992). In this situation, individuals develop social capital through the process of learning how to conduct and negotiate transnational dealings while maneuvering within the frameworks of hometown associations and resident country institutions. The individual and collective behaviors related to social capital, however, have been relatively unexplored as to how they impact on immigrant political involvement, civic engagement, and organizational activities in a U.S. environment (Smith 1994). In reality, this research represents an exploratory attempt to operationalize both transnational activities and social capital and link the two to their American political behaviors.

TRANSNATIONALISM, MIGRANTS, AND U.S. POLITICAL CONTEXTS

Given this discussion, I propose the following set of relationships between transnationalism, social capital, and civic engagement. Hypotheses:

1. Latino migrants closest to the immigration experience will be engaged in a greater number of transnational interactions.
2. Latino immigrants with both the lowest and highest levels of human capital resources are higher on transnational activities.
3. Transnational Latino immigrants are more likely to be civically engaged than their lesser-involved transnational counterparts in the U.S. Civic engagement will include both activities and attitudinal orientations.
4. Transnational involvement will have a positive effect on levels of civic engagement in a U.S. political context, even when controlling for sociodemographic characteristics.

THE CHICAGO AREA STUDY

The recent Chicago Area Study (CAS), conducted by the Institute for Latino Studies at the University of Notre Dame, provides the data for this study. The primary objective of the Chicago area study was to interview 1500 Latinos in the Chicago metropolitan area, covering a six county region, which included Cook, Kane, Lake, DuPage, Will and McHenry counties. The total sample of Latino interviews consisted of five hundred interviews from the Berwyn/Cicero area, five hundred from the other neighborhoods in the city of Chicago, and five hundred from the remaining suburban counties surrounding the city of Chicago. The Latino interviews were conducted using a face-to-face setting; each interview was designed to last an average of sixty minutes in English or Spanish, depending on the respondent's language preference. The questionnaires were administered using a PDA on which three questionnaires (long Spanish, long English, and short English) were programmed.

Fieldwork began on July 7, 2004, and continued until mid-October. The content of the survey included a wide range of social science topics, such as political participation, health care, labor market participation and experiences, education policies and school experiences, economic resources and their sources, transnational activities, culture and language, religion, and public policies. The Institute for Latino Studies conducted the study, which involved a number of scholars from various social science disciplines. A total number of 1,614 Latinos completed the interview schedule. For purposes of this research, the Latinos selected were those born outside of the United States (N=765). While the second generation and beyond can also engage in transnational activities, this exploratory analysis was restricted to the foreign-born segment.

ANALYSIS

We begin our analysis with a presentation of the sociodemographic characteristics of the CAS sample (see Table 3.1). Females represented almost three-fifths of the sample, somewhat greater than the gender distribution in the general population. Over one-half of the respondents are in the labor force (43.5 percent working full time and 9.2 percent working part time). The median age of the respondents was 39.2 years with a range of 18 to 80 years of age. It is an overwhelmingly Catholic population as 87.7 percent fall into that category.

Homeowners and renters are nearly evenly distributed in the sample. Spanish language use in the home predominates as 68.2 percent are

Table 3.1. Sociodemographic Characteristics of Latino Immigrants in Chicago Area Study

Sociodemographic Characteristics	*Observations*	*Percentage*
Gender		
Male	321	42.0%
Female	444	58.0
Employment Status:		
Working full-time	330	43.5
Working part-time	70	9.2
Not in labor force	358	47.2
Marital Status:		
Single	124	17.2
Married	483	67.1
Other	113	15.7
Language Spoken at Home:		
Primarily Spanish	514	68.2
Primarily English	44	5.8
Both English/Spanish	195	25.9
Homeowner Status:		
Homeowner	389	54.3
Renter	328	46.7
Religious Affiliation:		
Catholic	641	87.7
Protestant	32	4.4
Other	17	2.3
No Religion	40	5.5
United States Citizens:		
Yes	291	42.5
No	393	57.5
Age:	Mean=39.2 yrs.	Range=18–80
	N=765	

primarily Spanish speakers and 25.9 percent speak both languages, while only 5.8 percent are monolingual English speakers. Over two-thirds of the respondents indicated that they were married. Finally, over two-fifths of the respondents are U.S. citizens.

The CAS instrument included a number of elements that represent the operational measures of transnationalism. A composite index indicates the cumulative range of activities in which respondents participated. Table 3.2 illustrates the distribution of the Latino respondents along the specific questions that determine transnational composite index. Seven items used in the additive index included the following: (1) formal membership in an organization; (2) land ownership in country of origin; (3) sending money to home country; (4) frequency of sending money to home country; (5) father and/or mother still living in country of origin; (6) interest in political matters in home country; and (7) moving to the Chicago area due to presence of family and friends. In terms of specific items in the index, the greatest number of respondents sends money to their home country (66.5 percent); 43.4 percent send money on a weekly basis. The second highest affirmative response was rejoining family in Chicago (64.4 percent).

The use of a composite index incorporates the idea of a broad range of exchanges and does not discern the relative weight of any one item. Given our earlier discussion of transnationalism, this range of activities represents social networks that serve a variety of purposes. Clearly, most Latino immigrants in this sample engage in some transnational activities (Table 3.3). Only 7.8 percent *do not* engage in any of these activities. The largest category, the mid-point of the index, represents almost one-fourth of the sample; less than one-third affirmatively answered two or fewer items.

The responses in Table 3.3 illustrate the range of transnational activities in the CAS survey. Two items directly asked the respondent if he or she belonged to a hometown association or an ethnically based group that works on projects in the country of origin. The first figure represents a combination of those two questions in which only 3.9 percent indicated any formal affiliation. Given the extent of transnational activities, it was surprising to find such a low response rate. At the same time, research is being conducted to see how individuals differentiate between formal association and less formal involvement. In some cases,

Table 3.2. Transnational Interactions among Latino Immigrants in
Chicago Area Study
(Specific items used to determine index in Table 3.3)

Transnational Interaction	Observations	Percentage
Formal Member of organization		
Yes	30	3.9%
No	735	96.1
Own or Expect to Own Land in Country of Origin		
Yes	60	9.9
No	626	91.1
Send Money to Country of Origin		
Yes	458	66.5
No	231	33.5
How Often Money Sent to Country of Origin		
Weekly	199	43.4
2–4 times/month	36	7.9
Once a month	109	23.8
Several times/yr.	17	3.7
1–2 times/yr	97	21.1
Parents Residing in Mexico		
Yes	410	63.0
No	241	37.0
Interest in Politics of Home Country		
A lot	56	10.1
Some	81	14.6
A Little	108	19.5
None	309	55.8
Moved to Chicago to be w/ Family		
Yes	458	64.4
No	253	35.6

persons may not identify their collective involvement as part of a formal
organizational affiliation. More effective measures and questions to pursue this inquiry are beyond the scope of this chapter.

Another connection is that of family, especially parents, and if they
still resided in their country of origin or if they lived in Chicago. Almost two-thirds of the respondents' parents still live in their country of

Table 3.3. Composite Transnational Index and Range of Responses among Latino Immigrants

Transnational Composite Index	Observations	Percentage
None	50	7.8%
One	71	11.1
Two	85	13.3
Three	149	23.4
Four	91	14.3
Five	88	13.8
Six	56	8.8
Seven	47	7.4

Note: Range of activities included: sending money; how often sent money; came to Chicago because of family/friends; mother still living in home country; father living in home country; home country awareness.

origin. In addition, respondents were asked if they moved to the Chicago area to join family and friends; almost two-thirds did so on that basis.

Based on these statistics, it is clear that remittances to Mexico and family ties to Chicago are the primary transnational connections, indicating that respondents connect through economic and familial aspects.

Table 3.4 correlates the transnational index with the key sociodemographic variables commonly associated with behavior and attitudes, including: age, gender, workforce status, homeowner status, citizenship status, home language, educational level, and religious affiliation. All of these variables have proven to be key factors in differentiating those who engage in transnational actions from those who do not.

Four were significant in this study: age, working status, homeownership status, and citizenship status. Those Latinos who are younger, in the work force, and renters are more likely to score higher with the index. Looking at the composite variable as a whole, citizenship status shows the strongest correlation, indicating that the respondents closest to the immigration experience are the ones maintaining the transnational connection.

Table 3.4. Correlation Coefficients among Latino Migrants and Sociodemographic Characteristics

Sociodemographic Characteristics	Transnational Composite Variable	Transnational Component Remittances	Transnational Component: Home Country Awareness
Age of Respondent	-.1515*	-.1999*	-.1606*
Respondent's Gender	.0313	.0542	.0439
Workforce Status	.1355*	.1460*	.0812*
Homeowner Status	-.1060*	-.0164	-.2029*
Citizenship Status	-.4771*	-.1928*	-.5466*
Home Language	-.0296	-.0034	-.0891*
Educational Level	-.0447	.0531	-.0137
Religious Affiliation	.0034	-.0267	.0466

* Significant at the <. 05 level.

Several correlations between sociodemographic factors and the individual measures of transnationalism—specifically, sending money and remaining aware of home country political affairs—were also significant. The act of sending money proved to be significantly correlated with younger immigrants, those in the work force, and non-U.S. citizens. In contrast, home country awareness produced five significant correlations; in order of strength, they are citizenship status, homeowner status, age, workforce status, and home language. The first four are in the same direction and are of similar magnitude as the composite variable. Spanish use in the home was additionally associated with home country awareness. Differentiating transnationals based on this range of activities will provide the information necessary to construct demographic profiles.

The types and extent of transnationalism is the focus of this research, but the political connection is equally salient. Table 3.5 presents the correlations and levels of significance between civic engagement and participation orientation variables. Based on the composite transnational index, only two variables were significant—both were related to working together with neighbors. Correlations with sending money

Table 3.5. Correlation Coefficients among Latino Migrants and U.S. Participatory Variables

Participatory Variables	Transnational Composite Variable	Transnational Component Remittances	Transnational Component: Home Country Awareness
Working w/ neighbors in last two years	.1092*	.044	.0530
Perceived impact of neighborhood involvement	.0378	-.0035	.03
Membership in group working on social/political issues	-.0215	-.0045	-.0313
When faced w/ problem, probability work w/ neighbors	.1361*	.1060*	.1285*
Have become more involved in community in past few years	.0625	.0393	.0105
How much do you think public officials care?	.0110	-.0122	-.0581
Language source of political information	.0010	.0095	.0543
How much say so do you have in what government does?	-.0012	.0252	-.0275
Amount of interest one's friends have in politics	.0404	-.0588	-.0040
Amount of interest R has in politics	.0424	-.0677*	.0125

* Significant at the <.05 level.

were significant for (1) working with neighbors to deal with a community problem, and (2) having less interest in politics. On the other hand, home country awareness proved to be significant only in the case of having worked with neighbors on community problems.

The final stage of our analysis places our transnational variables along with sociodemographic ones and explores, in a multivariate context, the relative contribution of each of these variables (see Table 3.6). The dependent variable is whether the immigrant has been involved in neighborhood matters (that is, our measure of civic engagement in the

Table 3.6. Logistic Regression Analysis of Neighborhood Involvement among Latino Immigrants by Sociodemographic, Attitudinal, and Transnational Variables

Independent Variables (Y)	Model 1	Model 2	Model 3
Homeownership	-.3109*	-.3477*	-3292*
	(.1542)	(.1476)	(.1489)
Respondent's Age (<37 yrs.)	1.252	1.186	1.19
	(4.24)	(4.224)	(4.13)
Age (>37 yrs.)	1.701	1.675	1.69
	(4.23)	(4.221)	(4.219)
Employment Status	.3653*	.3448*	.2848*
	(.1536)	(.1483)	(.1445)
Gender	-.3203*	-.2772*	-.3053*
	(151.)	(.1448)	(.1428)
Extent that Political Officials Care	-.0033	-.0035	-.0055
	(.0102)	(.0101)	(.0107)
Extent of Say So People have in	-.004	-.0071	-.007
Government	(.0138)	(.0137)	(.0146)
Religious Affiliation (Catholic)	-.046	.0198	.059
	(.2217)	(.2066)	(.1972)
Citizenship Status	-.316	-.1528	-.1596
	(.1683)	(.1429)	(.1656)
Home Language	.0957	.1068	.1153
	(.1543)	(.147)	(.1465)
Transactional Composite	.1909*		
	(.0866)		
Trans: Awareness of Home Politics		.6628*	
		(.2872)	
Trans: Remittances			-.0192
			(.2259)
Classification Table: % Correctly			
Classified	87.79%	88.93%	88.47%
Constant	-4.2845	-3.8399	-3.542

Note: Model one used the composite transaction composite index. Model two uses the specific variable of sending money to country of origin. Model three uses the specific variable of extent of interest in political matters of home country. Standard error in parentheses.

United States). The independent variables are: homeownership; age; employment status; gender; political efficacy measures (that is, whether public officials care, and extent of say so in government); religious affiliation; citizenship status; home language; and the transnational variables. The use of logistic regression served to test three models. *Model one* uses the composite transnational index while *models two and three* use the variables of sending money (remittances) and home country awareness respectively as the dependent variables.

Three of the sociodemographic variables and the composite index proved to be significant. Renters, those in the work force, and women are much more likely to be involved in neighborhood matters. This was also the case for those immigrants who score higher on the transnational index. There is support for the benefits of transnationalism in producing dual, active citizens. In *model two,* these same sociodemographic variables were significant along with one of the individual measures of transnationalism—sending money to one's country of origin. Those who send money are more likely to engage in neighborhood activities. Finally, in *model three,* the sociodemographic variables are similarly significant, but home country awareness is not. The percentage of cases correctly classified with the variables in each of these equations exceeds 87 percent. Again, examining transnational activities and connections is key to understanding immigrants in a global society. In particular, transnational involvement can affect matters of incorporation and civic/ political engagement in the United States positively. While these are modest results, exploring the linkage between transnational activities and forms of civic engagement among Mexican immigrants and their U.S. communities of residence shows promise.

■ ■ ■

While researchers have acknowledged the breadth of economic, sociocultural, and political exchanges, applying transnationalism to the political world of an immigrant's country of residence is a relatively unexplored dimension. Economic exchange, capital formation, trade, job creation, and the like have been the mainstay of economists and sociologists, and immigrant efforts in cultural reproduction and adaptation have inspired many anthropological and sociological case studies. To the extent that researchers have examined the political aspects of transnationalism and immigrant social capital, they have generally sought to explain the actions of the home country institutions (especially the government) in their bid to foster and maintain home country affinity and attachment, to study immigrants' continued political involvement in their home country, or to investigate economic ties to and assistance from the country of origin.

This exploratory research attempts to capture the multi-faceted aspects of transnationalism and relate them to the immigrant's political world in their country of residence. More attention has been directed toward immigrant political involvement in their home countries. I am proposing that this is not an either/or proposition, as a sense of dual citizenship/membership can be present. Pragmatically, living in the United States creates many situations and opportunities in which there are intersections between the immigrant and socio-political institutions. As taxpayers, renters, workers, parents of school children, and participants in other community activities, transnationals are engaged in both geographical contexts. One of the challenges for further research is to represent the nature and extent of these transnational relationships such that respondents can respond fully and accurately; the realities of place require some degree of civic interaction, which deserve further examination. Including social capital warrants exploring its relevance for immigrants and their political involvement in the United States.

Using sociodemographic variables to differentiate immigrants, a composite index of transnationalism showed some significant correlates, including age, employment status, and citizenship status. Those closest to the immigration experience appear to be more involved in transnational activities. In addition, participation in transnational activities was correlated with higher levels of engagement in community matters in their country of residence. Sending money and home country awareness, the primary components of transnationalism, were treated as separate factors as well; in conjunction with sociodemographic factors, transnationalism can play an important role in the development of a dual citizenship and civic involvement.

At the same time, future research into transnationalism will require continued refinement and better specification and measurement of indicators of transnationalism. For example, the CAS survey includes items measuring the amount of money sent and its use; although preliminary indications suggest that most remittances go toward living expenses for family members and financial assistance for community based projects, the low response rate meant that this information was not useful in this analysis.

Studies on transnationalism must include attitudinal variables as well as sociodemographic variables, and social structures. This study captures some important dynamics regarding immigrants' civic involvement in the United States through attitudinal and sociodemographic measures, but social structures will need to be incorporated into later analysis as well.

The nature of our global society has blurred the demarcation of national boundaries and spatial relations. Technology, economic growth and development, a global labor market, intercultural exchanges and influences, and political inter-connectedness places this period of migration in a different historical context from previous eras. The influence of transnationalism on the political development of immigrants in their country of residence can enhance skills, knowledge, organizational mechanisms, and experiences that promote civic engagement in their communities. Such communities may be immediate, across states, and across national boundaries. The work on transnationalism and its political ramifications requires sustained scrutiny in terms of its conceptualization and variable operationalization. This chapter represents a beginning.

REFERENCES

Alger, Chadwick. 1997. "Transnational Social Movements, World Politics, and Global Governance." In *Transnational Social Movements and Global Politics,* edited by Jackie Smith, C. Chatfield, and R. Pagocco, 260–78. Syracuse: Syracuse University Press.

Baubock, Rainer. 1994. *Transnational Citizenship: Membership and Rights in International Migration.* Aldershot: Edward Elgar.

Brubaker, Rogers. 1996. *Nationalism Reframed: Nationhood and the National Question in the New Europe.* New York: Cambridge University Press.

Cano, Gustavo. 2004. "The Virgin, the Priest, and the Flag: Political Mobilization of Mexican Immigrants in Chicago, Houston, and New York." San Diego: Center for U.S.-Mexico Studies, University of California, San Diego.

Coleman, James. 1988. "Social Capital in the Creation of Human Capital." *American Journal of Sociology* 94: S95–S120.

DeWind, Josh, and Philip Kasinitz. 1997. "Everything Old Is New Again: Processes and Themes of Immigrant Incorporation." *International Migration Review* 31 (4): 1090–1111.

Eckstein, Susan, and Lorena Barberia. 2002. "Grounding Immigrant Generation in History: Cuban Americans and their Transnational Ties." *International Migration Review* 36 (3): 799–837.

Faust, Thomas. 2000. "Transnationalization in International Migration: Implications for the Study of Citizenship and Culture." *Ethnic and Racial Studies* 23 (2): 189–222.

Fitzgerald, David. 2000. "Navigating Extra-Territorial Citizenship: Mexican Migration and the Transnational Politics of Community." La Jolla: Center for the Comparative Study of Immigration Studies.

———. 2004. "Beyond Transnationalism: Mexican Hometown Politics at an American Labor Union." *Ethnic and Racial Studies* 27 (2): 228–47.

Foner, Nancy. 1997. "What Is New about Transnationalism: New York Immigration Today and at the Turn of the Century." *Diaspora* 6 (3): 355–75.

Garcia, John A. 2012. "Immigrants and Suffrage: Adding to the Discourse by Integrating State Versus National Citizenship, Dual Domestic Residency, and Dual Citizenship." *Harvard Journal of Hispanic Policy* 24.

Glick Schiller, Nina. 1996. "Transmigrants and Nation States: Something Old and Something New in the U.S. Immigrant Experience." In *Handbook of International Migration: The American Experience,* edited by Charles Hirschman, Philip Kasinitz, and Josh DeWind, 93–119. New York: Russell Sage Foundation.

Glick Schiller, Nina, Linda Basch, and Cristina Szanton Blanc. 1995. "From Immigrant to Transmigrant: Theorizing Transnational Migration." *Anthropological Quarterly* 68 (1): 48–63.

Goldring, Luin. 1988. "The Power of States in Transnational Social Fields." In *Transnationalism from Below,* edited by Michael Smith and Luis Guarnizo, 165–95. New Brunswick: Transaction Books.

———. 1996. "Blurring Borders: Constructing Transnational Communities in the Process of Mexico-U.S. Immigration." *Research in Community Sociology* 6: 69–104.

———. 2002. "The Mexican State and Immigrant Organizations: Negotiating the Boundaries of Membership and Participation." *Latin American Research Review* 37 (3): 55–79.

Guarnizo, Luis. 1998. "The Rise of Transnational Social Formation: Mexican and Dominican State Responses to Transnational Migration." *Political Power and Sociological Theory* 12: 45–94.

———. 2001. "On the Political Participation of Transnational Migrants: Old Practices and New Trends." In *E Pluribus Unum? Contemporary and Historical Perspectives on Immigrant Political Incorporation,* edited by Gary Gerstle and John H. Mollenkopf, 213–63. New York: Russell Sage Foundation.

Hammar, Tomas. 1985. "Dual Citizenship and Political Integration." *International Migration Review* 19 (3): 438–50.

Hanifan, L. J. 1916. "The Rural School Community Center." *Annals of the American Academy of Political and Social Science* 67: 130–38.

Hannerz, Ulf. 1996. *Transnational Connections: Culture, People, Places.* London: Routledge.

Issac, Larry. 1997. "Transforming Localities: Reflections on Time, Causality, and Narratives in Contemporary Historical Sociology." *Historical Methods* 30 (1): 4–13.

Itzigsohn, Jose, Carlos Dore Cabral, Esther Hernandez Medina, and Obed Vazquez. 1999. "Mapping Dominican Transnationals: Narrow and Broad Transnational Practice." *Ethnic and Racial Studies* 22 (2): 316–39.

Jacobson, David. 1996. *Rights across the Border: Immigration and the Decline of Citizenship.* Baltimore: Johns Hopkins University Press.

Jones-Correa, Michael A. 2001. "Under Two Flags: Dual Nationality in Latin America and Its Consequences for the United States." *International Migration Review* 35 (4): 997–1029.

Kenney, Michael, and Victor Roundnetof, eds. 2002. *Communities across Borders: New Immigrants and Transnationalism.* New York: Routledge.

Layton-Henry, Zig. 1990. "Citizenship or Denizenship for Migrant Workers." In *The Political Rights of Migrant Workers in Western Europe,* edited by Zig Layton-Henry, 186–95. London: Sage Publications.

Levitt, Peggy. 2001. *The Transnational Villagers.* Berkeley: University of California Press.

Mahler, Sarah. 1998. "Theoretical and Empirical Contributions toward a Research Agenda for Transnationalism." In *Transnationalism from Below,* edited by Michael Smith and Luis Guarnizo, 64–100. New Brunswick: Transaction Books.

Martin, David. 1999. "New Rules on Dual Nationality for a Democraticizing Globe: Between Rejection and Embrace." *Georgetown Law Review* 14 (1): 9–30.

Massey, Douglas, Luin Goldring, and Jorge Durand. 1994. "Continuities in Transnational Migration: An Analysis of Nineteen Mexican Communities." *American Journal of Sociology* 99 (6): 1492–1533.

Morawska, Ewa. 2001. "Immigrants, Transnationalism and Ethnicization: A Comparison of this Great Wave and the Last." In *E Pluribus Unum? Contemporary and Historical Perspectives on Immigrant Political Incorporation,* edited by Gary Gerstle and John H. Mollenkopf, 175–212. New York: Russell Sage Foundation.

Munch, Richard. 2001. *National Citizenship in a Global Age: From National to Transnational Ties and Identities.* New York: Palgrave Macmillan.

Pessar, Patricia, and Pamela Graham. 2002. "Dominican Transnational Identity and Local Politics." In *New Immigrants in New York,* edited by Nancy Foner, 251–74. New York: Columbia University Press.

Portes, Alejandro. 1996. "Transnational Communities: Their Experiences and Significance in the Contemporary World System." In *Latin America in the World Economy,* edited by Roberto Patricio Korzeniewicz and William C. Smith, 151–68. Westport; Greenwood Press.

Portes, Alejandro, Luis Guarnizo, and Patricia Landolt. 1999. "The Study of Transnationalism: Pitfalls and Promises of an Emergent Research Field." *Racial and Ethnic Studies* 22 (2): 217–37.

Putnam, Robert D. 1995. "Bowling Alone: America's Declining Social Capital." *Journal of Democracy* 6 (1): 65–78.

———. 2000. *Bowling Alone: The Collapse and Revival of American Community.* New York: Simon and Schuster.

Putnam, Robert D., Robert Leonardi, and Raffaella Y. Nanetti. 1993. *Making Democracy Work.* Princeton: Princeton University Press.

Roberts, Bryan, Reanne Frank, and Fernando Lozano-Ascencio. 1999. "Transnational Migrant Communities and Mexican Migration to the U.S." *Racial and Ethnic Studies* 22 (2): 238–66.

Rodriguez, Nestor. 1996. "The Battle for the Border: Notes on the Autonomous Migration, Transnational Communities, and the State." *Social Justice* 23 (3): 21–38.

Rouse, Roger. 1992. "Making Sense of Settlement: Class Transformation, Cultural Struggle, and Transnationalism among Mexican Migrants in the U.S." *Annals of New York Academy of Science* 645 (July): 117–29.

Smith, M. Peter. 1994. "Can You Imagine? Transnational Migration and Globalization of Grassroots Politics." *Social Text* 39: 15–33.

Vertovec, Steve. 1999. "Conceiving and Researching Transnationalism." *Racial and Ethnic Studies* 22 (2): 447–62.

FOUR

The Political Consequences of Latino Immigrant Transnational Ties

ADRIAN D. PANTOJA, RAFAEL A. JIMENO,
AND JAVIER M. RODRIGUEZ

The manner by which immigrants incorporate themselves into the American political system has generated much scholarly attention in recent years (Rogers 2006; Wong 2006; Ramakrishnan 2005; Barreto and Muñoz 2003). Although research on immigrant political incorporation is not new (Grebler 1966; Glazer and Moynihan 1963; Dahl 1961), recent scholarship has turned to examining how transnational ties shape the incorporation process (Staton, Jackson, and Canache forthcoming; DeSipio 2006; Cain and Doherty 2006; Pantoja 2005; Jones-Correa 1998).

An ambiguous concept, immigrant transnational ties are typically defined as "the process by which transmigrants, through their daily activities, forge and sustain multi-stranded social, economic, and political relations that link together their societies of origin and settlement, and through which they create transnational social fields that cross national borders" (Basch et al. 1994, 6). While the ability of some immigrants to maintain a foothold in two countries is not a new phenomenon

(Morawska 2001; Foner 2000), it is argued that advances in technology facilitating communication and travel, increased economic and political ties between the United States and immigrant-sending countries, and intense outreach efforts by ancestral homelands have enabled immigrants to forge and sustain transnational links to a greater degree than immigrants from earlier waves (Foner 2001; Guarnizo 2001).

There is little controversy surrounding the existence of immigrant transnational ties, as they have become an intrinsic feature of the migration process (Itzigsohn 2000; Levitt 2001; Glick Schiller et al. 1992). Yet there is much debate over their political consequences. In particular, the field is divided into three competing camps: some argue transnational ties are an impediment to immigrant political incorporation (Huntington 2004; Stanton, Jackson, and Canache forthcoming; Cain and Doherty 2006); others argue they spur political incorporation (Ramakrishnan 2005; Jones-Correa 2001, 1998); still others take a middle position, suggesting its impact is negligible or can be both positive and negative, depending on the nature of the transnational activity (DeSipio 2006; Pantoja 2005; Barreto and Muñoz 2003).

This study seeks to enter this debate by examining Latino immigrants, the largest immigrant group in the United States; they constitute 53 percent of the 33.5 million foreign-born persons in the country (Larsen 2004). We draw on the 2002 "National Survey of Latinos" conducted by the Pew Hispanic Center and Kaiser Family Foundation. The survey is one of the largest on the Latino population with a representative sample of 2,929 adult Latinos, 1,852 of whom are foreign-born. The 2002 survey is used for several reasons. First, the survey includes a plethora of questions tapping immigrant transnational ties beyond dual citizenship, a widely used measure of transnational networks. Second, as one of the more recent national surveys on Latinos, the data offers a more contemporary portrait of this population beyond that offered by the Latino National Political Survey (LNPS) or the National Latino Immigrant Survey (NLIS), which were carried out over fifteen years ago. Third, unlike the LNPS or NLIS, the 2002 survey includes representative samples of Latin American ancestry groups beyond Mexicans, Puerto Ricans, and Cubans. Finally, as a national survey, the 2002 Latino survey is preferable to more parochial surveys since its conclusions are far-reaching rather than regional in scope (Barreto and Muñoz 2003). Before analyzing the data, we provide a brief overview of the literature examining the political consequences of immigrant transnational ties.

LITERATURE REVIEW

The meaning and significance of transnational ties is an emerging field across various disciplines (Itzigsohn 2000; Jones-Correa 1998; Basch et al. 1994). This research has transformed our understanding of the immigrant experience by challenging the assumption that migration is a unidirectional process whereby uprooted immigrants travel to a new country and begin a process of severing ties with the old country while developing ties with the new homeland. Although much of the existent literature on immigrant transnational ties analyzes them along an economic (Menjivar 2000; Portes, Haller, and Guarnizo 2002; Grasmuck and Pessar 1991) or sociocultural dimension (Menjivar 2000; Levitt 1998; 2001), political scientists have started to analyze their effects on immigrant political participation (Pantoja 2005; Jones-Correa 1998).

Michael Jones-Correa (2001 and 1998) was among the first to systematically explore the political consequences of immigrant transnational ties. He found that naturalization rates among Latin American immigrants in New York City were dismally low because many possessed a "myth of return ideology," or a strong desire to return to the home country. In addition, becoming a U.S. citizen often meant a loss of citizenship in their countries of origin or other forms of severing of formal ties, further discouraging immigrants from seeking naturalization. The end result was that most Latino immigrants prolonged their decision to naturalize and thus remained in a liminal political status for decades.

To break this impasse, Jones-Correa argued that Latin American governments should recognize and extend dual-citizenship to promote naturalization by enabling immigrants to sustain formal ties to the home country while incorporating themselves into the American polity. He found empirical evidence supporting this proposition, noting that

Latin American immigrants from countries recognizing dual citizenship naturalized at higher rates than those from countries that did not recognize dual citizenship (Jones-Correa 2001). In short, transnational ties are a facilitator of immigrant political incorporation, a finding Ramakrishnan (2005) echoed.

The proposition noted above has recently come under challenge (Staton, Jackson, and Canache forthcoming; Cain and Doherty 2006). Drawing on the 1999 Washington Post/Kaiser Family Foundation/ Harvard University "Latino Survey," Cain and Doherty (2006) found that naturalized Latinos from countries that allow for dual citizenship are less likely to register to vote and vote in the United States than similarly situated Latinos from countries that do not permit dual citizenship. The same relationship holds true for naturalized Latinos who have formally acquired dual citizenship. Staton, Jackson, and Canache (forthcoming) reported similar results, finding that Latino immigrants who are dual citizens are less politically connected than are immigrants who are not dual citizens. Their measure of political connectedness included language use, self-identity, civic duty, voter registration, and voting. Hence, for these scholars transnational ties *via* dual citizenship were an impediment to Latino immigrant political incorporation.

Pantoja (2005), Barreto and Muñoz (2003), and DeSipio (2006) put forth an alternative perspective to these two propositions. Pantoja (2005) drew on a unique survey specifically designed to measure a wide-range of transnational activities among Dominicans in New York City. He found that the degree to which transnational ties foster or impede political incorporation was largely the result of how one defines and operationalizes political incorporation and transnational ties. When political incorporation is defined and measured by naturalization, two forms of transnational ties depressed its pursuit: (1) participation in the politics of the home country and (2) having family abroad. When incorporation is defined and measured by non-electoral political participation, two forms acted as catalysts: (1) participation in the politics of the home country and (2) participation in hometown associations. Moreover, there is no evidence that the so-called "myth of return ideology" exerts a powerful influence on immigrants' decision to naturalize or become politically engaged. Barreto and Muñoz (2003) also presented findings that could be grouped into this camp—they observed that (1) Mexican immigrants are more likely to be civically engaged than native-born Mexicans, and (2) transnational ties (as measured by the sending of remittances) had no discernible impact on civic engagement. DeSipio (2006) also noted that transnational ties had a negligible effect on Latino immigrant political incorporation, but when they did, it was in a positive direction. Thus, transnational ties can impede, foster, and/or have no effect on immigrant political incorporation depending on the measures used to capture them.

In short, political scientists do not agree about the political consequences of immigrant transnational ties. For some, the effects are positive (Ramakrishnan 2005; Jones-Correa 2001, 1998), for others they are negative (Staton, Jackson, and Canache forthcoming; Cain and Doherty 2006), and for others the relationship is more complex (DeSipio 2006; Pantoja 2005; Barreto and Muñoz 2003). This study revisits these debates by examining the political consequences of transnational ties among Latino immigrants through data drawn from the 2002 Latino National Survey.

THE ARGUMENT

The task at hand is to sort out these competing propositions on the political consequences of transnational ties. Political incorporation is a value-laden concept whose meaning and measurement is subject to contestation. Various political attitudes, beliefs, orientations, and behaviors have been used as measures of political incorporation. What is clear is that the degree to which individuals or groups are politically incorporated is largely based on whether one employs an expansive or narrow definition of politics (Jones-Correa 2002). This study uses two popular behavioral measures of political incorporation: (1) naturalization and (2) political participation.

In addition, transnational ties encompass a wide-range of diverse practices that are not solely limited to the acquisition of dual citizenship. While dual citizenship is among the most politically controversial of these activities, many others, such as voting in country of origin elections, are not without controversy. This chapter analyzes five measures of transnational ties: (1) dual citizenship; (2) voting in home country elections; (3) sending remittances; (4) affective attachments toward the homeland; and (5) the myth of return ideology.

The ties immigrants maintain with their countries of origin are wide-ranging. Some of these linkages require greater resources to develop and sustain such as voting abroad, while others require little effort, such as maintaining psychological attachments to the country of origin. Since individual costs are associated with naturalization and voting in the United States, it follows that immigrants who are engaged in costly transnational political projects are less likely to naturalize and vote in the United States since migrants possess finite resources (Cain and Doherty 2006). Hence, voting abroad and being a dual citizen are likely to depress naturalization and voter participation in the United States.

What makes these transnational activities costly relative to the others is that immigrants must not only possess psychological attachments to their respective countries of origin, but they must take an additional step and act on those attachments by actively maintaining their citizenship with the home-country and voting in home-country elections. In each case, immigrants must also spend time gathering and processing information about the legal requirements for maintaining their citizenship status and about the candidates/policies in the country of ancestry before casting a vote abroad. Of course, additional bureaucratic hurdles must be overcome to accomplish both tasks, and these are likely to vary across country. Given similar hurdles in the United States, it is unlikely that an individual will have the time and resources to effectively be engaged/incorporated here and abroad.

Adopting a myth of return ideology, or seeing the country of ancestry as the "real homeland," may deter some from involvement in U.S. citizenship and its politics, but for many others these feelings and activities can coexist, since affective attachments abroad are easily maintained with minimal costs, even among second-generation children of immigrants whose socialization has largely occurred in the United States (Kasinitz et al. 2002). If affective ties to the country of ancestry are significant, however, they will likely impact naturalization, as the acquisition of U.S. citizenship is typically seen as a public renouncement of old allegiances. For immigrants with strong affective ties to the ancestral homeland, the possibility of being considered a *vendepatrias* (someone who sold out the country) by fellow immigrants is likely to deter them from naturalization (Jones-Correa 1998). I expect that affective ties to the ancestral homeland are unlikely to impact voting once naturalization occurs since the decision to participate in politics is unlikely to be considered a betrayal of the ancestral homeland.

Finally, it is anticipated that the effects of sending of remittances on immigrant naturalization and voting will be nonexistent. Of course, the costs associated with sending money abroad may be significant, depending on the amount sent. Unfortunately, this survey merely asked whether the individual "regularly" sent money back to the country of origin, but did not ask to specify a dollar amount or calculate the percentage of earned income to amount sent abroad. Nonetheless, even with a more refined measure of remittance costs at the individual level, it is unlikely that they would impact voting since there is no additional monetary cost associated with this activity. On the other hand, remittance behavior could impact other political activities such as donations, and to some degree naturalization due to the processing fees involved. However, given the available measure of remittance behavior, we anticipate its effects will be negligible on naturalization and non-existent for voting.

DATA AND ANALYSIS

In order to understand the effects of transnational ties on Latino immigrant political incorporation as measured by naturalization and voter participation, multivariate analysis is used to isolate the relevant predictors and assess their relative causal importance. The analysis in Model I (naturalization), is limited to immigrant Latinos (Puerto Ricans excluded) who are eligible for naturalization, or have been residing in the country at least five years. In Model II (examining voter participation), the analysis is limited to immigrant Latinos who are U.S. citizens.

The main concern is with the effects of the five independent transnational variables. The first, *dual citizenship,* is a dichotomous measure, with "1" for respondents who claim to be a legal citizen of their country of origin. In our sample, 80.2 percent (1,151) claimed to possess citizenship from their ancestral homelands. The second variable, *Voting Abroad,* is dichotomous with "1" for respondents who answered yes to the question, "Since you moved to the United States, have you voted in your country of origin or not?" In our sample, 13 percent (187) claimed to have participated in the politics of the home country since moving to the United States. The third variable, *Remittances,* is dichotomous with 1 for respondents who claim to "regularly send money back to [their] country of origin." Remittances were regularly sent by 44.9 percent of the sample. The fourth variable, *Real Homeland* captures identification with the country of origin and, therefore, affective attachment. The question asked, "Which country do you consider your real homeland?" Among the respondents, 53.7 percent (770) noted "the country where I was born" as their real homeland. The final variable captures Jones-Correa's (1998) "myth of return ideology." The variable, *Myth of Return* is dichotomous, with 1 for respondents who noted that they planned to someday move back to the country where they were from. Over a quarter (29.9 percent) possessed this ideology of return. Taken as a whole, it is clear that a large percentage of Latin immigrants have developed transnational ties and identities. Of course, the concern here is not with their existence but their political consequences.

Most of the demographic control variables included in the models are traditional predictors of naturalization and voter participation and do not need much explanation. These include controls for age, education, gender (female), income (homeowner), English language ability, length of residency, and dummies isolating Mexican, Central American (includes Dominicans), and South American respondents from Cuban respondents (see Appendix for coding). In addition to these variables, others merit some discussion. Two variables, *Credit Card* and *Bank Account* can be used as proxies for income, but can also reflect immigrants' financial establishment and acculturation in the United States (Hondagneu-Sotelo 1994). A variable measuring perceptions of discrimination is included. The variable *Discrimination* is dichotomous with 1 for respondents who believed discrimination against (Hispanics/ Latinos) was a major problem. Experience or perceptions of discrimination has been found to foster naturalization and civic engagement among Latinos (DeSipio 1998). Specific to naturalization, discrimination may foster a sense of vulnerability, leading immigrants to seek out citizenship in order to enhance their legal rights and social standing (Pantoja and Gershon 2006).

The variable, *Life Better in the U.S.*, was based on four questions which asked immigrants to compare their experiences in the United States with their ancestral homeland on the following items: treatment of the poor, moral values of the society, strength of the family, and opportunities to get ahead. Each question is dichotomous with 1 for "better in the U.S." and 0 for better in the country of origin. The questions are combined to create a four-point scale ranging from 0 to 3. Two measures of political orientation found to influence civic engagement, *political alienation* and *political trust,* are included. Immigrants who possess positive civic orientations are anticipated to be more likely to seek out naturalization and participate in politics (Pantoja and Gershon 2006). Finally, the voter participation model includes the variables, *Registered Voter* and *Party Identification.*

The two dependent variables are naturalization and voted in a U.S. election. Both are dichotomous variables. The naturalization variable captures Latino immigrants who are naturalized U.S. citizens. Among the respondents, 43.1 percent (619) were naturalized U.S. citizens. The second dependent variable is based on a question asking if they have "ever voted in an election in the U.S.?" In the sample, 33.2 percent (477) of naturalized Latinos stated that they have voted in a U.S. election. Table 4.1 reports the results of the multivariate estimates. Since the dependent variables are dichotomous, logistic regression analyses are used to estimate the impact of the predictors. Because logistic coefficients are not directly interpretable, the second column reports the changes in predicted probabilities, which essentially provides the probability of a change in the dependent variable as a result of the minimum to maximum change in the independent variable (Long 1997).

Model I (Latino naturalization) correctly predicts 80.2 percent of the cases and has a proportional reduction of error (PRE, Lambda-p) of .539. The variables *Dual Citizen, Registered Voter,* and *Party identification*

Table 4.1. Determinants of Naturalization and Political Participation among Latino Immigrants

	Model I Naturalization ß (S.E.)	*Predicted probabilities min>max*	*Model II Voter Participation* ß (S.E.)	*Predicted probabilities min>max*
Dual citizen	--	--	-.875 (.320)**	-.093
Voted Abroad	-.249 (.214)	-.059	-.815 (.404)*	-.115
Remittances	-.057 (.148)	-.014	.036 (.291)	.004
Homeland	-.346 (.149)*	-.084	-.220 (.291)	-.025
Myth of Return	-.001 (.170)	-.000	.185 (.349)	.020
Age	.029 (.007)***	.479	.055 (.014)***	.413
Education	.094 (.038)*	.162	.225 (.078)***	.176
Female	.340 (.145)*	.092	-.187 (.302)	.020
Homeowner	.147 (.154)	.036	-.239 (.295)	-.021
Credit Card	.341 (.165)*	.082	.702 (.327)*	.089
Bank Account	.256 (.180)	.062	-.492 (.368)	-.049
English Language	.270 (.045)***	.371	.090 (.096)	.066
Length of Residency	.087 (.010)***	.813	.024 (.016)	.169
Discrimination	.063 (.143)	.015	.164 (.275)	.018
Life Better in the US	-.000 (.045)	.000	.011 (.087)	.010
Political Alienation	-.113 (.144)	-.027	.023 (.276)	.002
Political Trust	.252 (.144)†	.061	-.245 (.276)	-.027
Registered Voter	--	--	2.917 (.336)***	.549
Party Identification	--	--	1.122 (.273)***	.151
Mexican	-.740 (.226)**	-.175	-.150 (.418)	-.017
Central American	-.422 (.218)*	-.100	.074 (.408)	.008
South American	-.401 (.238)	-.095	-.509 (.424)	-.064
Constant	-4.370 (.483)***		-5.078 (1.055)***	
Chi-Square	630.37		270.31	
Significance	.000		.000	
PPC	80.21		87.20	
PRE	.539		.833	
Sample Size	1400		602	

Significance levels: † p<=.075, * p<=.05, ** p<=.01, ***p<=.001, two-tailed.

are excluded from this model. Obviously, immigrants who have not naturalized are not eligible to vote or become affiliated with a party. In addition, the variable *Dual Citizen* is excluded for three main reasons. First, immigrants who have yet to naturalize remain citizens of their country by default and therefore are not really dual citizens. Second, selecting dual citizens alone is problematic since they have already gone through the naturalization process. Third, using aggregate immigration statistics is questionable since dual citizenship may simply be a proxy for national origin (Yang 1994) or may be capturing a particular time period unrelated to the recognition of dual citizenship within a single country or set of countries (Jones-Correa 2001).

Given these methodological problems, the effects of dual citizenship on immigrant naturalization cannot easily be determined. Nonetheless, the results clearly show that respondents who see the country of origin as their real homeland are less likely to naturalize *ceteris paribus*. While other variables have a larger effect on naturalization, the variable does highlight the negative consequences of affective ties to the homeland on immigrant naturalization (Jones-Correa 1998). Clearly, for immigrants who possess strong orientations toward the country of origin, the psychological costs associated with naturalization as defined as transferring one's loyalty to the new homeland remain formidable.

Consistent with other findings, naturalization is strongly tied to the acculturation and settlement process (Pantoja and Gershon 2006; Yang 1994; DeSipio 1998; Portes and Curtis 1987). Length of residency exerted the strongest impact on Latino naturalization. Knowledge of the English language and having a credit card also had significant and positive effects (Pantoja and Gershon 2006), and the sociodemographic resources immigrants possess (Yang 1994; DeSipio 1998) had significant and positive effects, playing important roles in the decision to naturalize. Naturalization increases with age and education. Women are more likely to naturalize than men (Pantoja and Gershon 2006). Finally, being a Mexican or Central American immigrant significantly lowers rates of naturalization.

Model II examines the determinants of Latino immigrant voter participation. Model II includes three variables excluded in the first model, *Dual Citizen, Registered Voter,* and *Party identification.* In Model II, 87.2 percent of the cases are correctly predicted and the PRE (Proportional Reduction of Error) is .833. Of the five transnational variables, two are significant and negatively related to voter participation: *Dual Citizenship* and *Voter Participation Abroad,* as hypothesized. Being a dual citizen decreased the probability of voting in the United States by .09 and participation in elections in the country of origin decreased electoral participation in the United States by .12. The finding that dual citizenship is an impediment to immigrant political incorporation is similar to those of Staton, Jackson, and Canache (forthcoming) and Cain and Doherty (2006). However, the model also highlights that other transnational activities (sending remittances and affective attachments to the country of origin), as anticipated, have no impact on Latino immigrant voter participation.

The socioeconomic resources immigrants possess, such as age, education, and income (credit card as proxy) also shape participation in voting (Barreto and Muñoz 2003; Highton and Burris 2002; Leal 2002; Ramakrishnan and Espenshade 2001; Tam Cho 1999). Beyond the impact of these variables, partisanship (Barreto and Muñoz 2003) and voter registration (DeSipio 1998) were significant predictors of voter participation. Model II's insignificant predictors are also noteworthy. We find no evidence that the following factors shape voter participation among Latino immigrants: (1) length of residency (Ramakrishnan and Espenshade 2001; Leal 2002), (2) increased knowledge of the English language (Barreto and Muñoz 2003; Johnson, Stein, and Wrinkle 2003), (3) perceptions of discrimination (DeSipio 1998), and (4) having positive political orientations. While several studies highlight the negligible effects of sociodemographic factors in shaping political participation among foreign-born populations (Ramakrishnan 2001; Tam Cho 1999), this study also observes that immigrant-specific predictors such as knowledge of the English language (Johnson, Stein, and Wrinkle 2003) and length of residency (Leal 2002), as well as traditional predictors such as political efficacy and trust (Michelson 2000), may not be as significant either.

■ ■ ■

Contemporary immigrants are developing and sustaining ties with their countries of origin to a greater degree than previous immigrant groups.

Their ability to do so has led a number of political elites and academics to view such ties with suspicion and use them as evidence to claim that contemporary immigrants have dual loyalties and are less inclined to embrace the United States as the new homeland (Huntington 2004). These concerns are not without merit. Although this study finds that most transnational activities have no impact on Latin American immigrant naturalization or voter participation, we also observe that certain ties exerted a negative influence.

The findings that affective attachments to the country of ancestry are an impediment to naturalization parallel Jones-Correa's (1998) study of Latino immigrants in New York City. The in-depth interviews he carried out with community leaders and other participants revealed that many felt pressured from fellow immigrants not to naturalize because it was considered an act of betrayal to the homeland. Some subjects recounted a rumor that one of the requirements during the Oath of Citizenship ceremony was the stepping on the flag from the ancestral homeland; a symbolic renouncement or rejection of the homeland. Immigrants felt conflicted about choosing a single homeland and in the end maintained their allegiances with the homeland by not becoming U.S. citizens. To break this impasse, Jones-Correa contends that dual citizenship provisions would allow immigrants to pursue U.S. citizenship without feeling they were turning their backs on the ancestral homeland. Nonetheless, even if the country of ancestry offers dual citizenship provisions, immigrants continue to feel conflicted about acquiring U.S. citizenship. In our sample, over half claimed that the ancestral homeland was their real homeland and this feeling dampened the pursuit of naturalization.

Dual citizenship may potentially act as a catalyst for naturalization; yet our data reveal that its effects on voter participation are negative. In addition, we find that participation in the politics of the homeland also depresses voter participation in the United States. These findings mirror those by Cain and Doherty (2006), who argue that the limited resources immigrants have can be spent on participating in U.S. politics *or* participating in the politics of the homeland, but not both. Participation in one naturally comes at the expense of the other. Hence, immigrants who use their limited resources abroad will participate in U.S. politics sparingly. The converse is true of immigrants who allocate their scarce resources for U.S. political participation. Our findings seem to support the zero-sum perspective on transnational political engagement.

Although our findings are rather pessimistic when it comes to the effect of transnational ties on immigrant political incorporations; it should be noted that we merely explored two indicators of incorporation, naturalization and voter participation. Moreover, the transnational ties we considered are by no means the only forms of connections immigrants maintain abroad. Hence, it remains to be seen whether other transnational practices have similar effects on these or other measures of political incorporation. Finally, much of the research on transnationalism and immigration incorporation centers on the experiences of Latin American immigrants. Few researchers have undertaken empirical work examining the political consequences of transnational ties among other immigrant groups. Thus, it is unclear whether these findings apply to immigrants from other regions. While this study has sought to advance the literature on the political consequences of transnational ties, it is clear that any definitive conclusions can only be made as a result of additional research.

APPENDIX

Dependent Variables
Naturalization Q68. Now we would like to ask you about U.S. Citizenship. Are you . . . (1 U.S. citizen; 0 other responses)
Voted in U.S. Q78. Have you ever voted in an election in the U.S.? (1 yes; 0 no)

Independent Variables
Dual Citizen Q83. As you know, some countries allow people to be legal citizens of their country even if they are also U.S. citizens. Are you a legal citizen of your country of origin? (1 yes; 0 other responses)
Voted Abroad Q84. Since you moved to the U.S., have you voted in your country of origin or not? (1 yes; 0 other responses)
Remittances Q85. Do you regularly send money back to your country of origin? (1 yes; 0 other responses)

Homeland Q88. Which country do you consider your real homeland? (1 the country where I was born; 0 the United States)

Myth of Return Do you plan someday to move back to the country you are from, or not? (1 yes; 0 other responses)

Age Q 105. What is your age (continuous variable from 18 years +)

Education Q101. What is the last grade you completed (scale ranging from 0 none, or grade 1–8 to 7 post graduate)

Female Q 114. Gender (1 female; 0 male)

Homeowner Q103. Do you own the place where you live or do you pay rent? (1 own; 0 pay rent)

Credit Card Q102. Do you happen to have any credit cards, or not? (1 yes; 0 other responses)

Bank Account Q104. Do you have an account with a bank or not? (1 yes; 0 no)

English Language Q50. Would you say you can carry on a conversation in English, both understanding and speaking (3 very well; 2 pretty well; 1 just a little; 0 not at all); and Q51. Would you say you can read a newspaper or book in English (3 very well; 2 pretty well; 1 just a little; 0 not at all)

Length of Residency Q67. How many years have you lived in the United States (continuous from 5 years +)

Discrimination Q57d In general, do you think discrimination against Latinos/Hispanics is a major problem, minor problem, or not a problem in preventing Latinos/Hispanics in general from succeeding in America (1 major problem; 0 other responses)

Life Better in the U.S. Q22a,b,c,d. Overall would you say (a) treatment of the poor; (b) the moral values of the society; (c) the strength of family; (d) opportunity to get ahead) is better in the United States, better in the country where you came from, or about the same? (1 better in the US; 0 other responses)

Political Alienation Q13. Based on your experience, do you think political leaders are interested in the problems of particular concern to Hispanics/Latinos living here or not? (1 yes; 0 no)

Political Trust Q8. How much of the time do you trust the government in Washington to do what is right (1 just about always and most of the time; 0 other responses)

Registered Voter Q77. Some people are registered to vote and others are not. Are you currently registered to vote at your present address? (1 yes; 0 no)

Party Identification Q90. In politics today, do you consider yourself a Republican, a Democrat, an Independent, or something else? (1 for Republican and Democrat; 0 other responses)

Mexican, Central American, and *South American* (Dummies used to isolate these groups)

REFERENCES

Barreto, Matt A., and José A. Muñoz. 2003. "Reexamining the 'Politics of In-Between': Political Participation among Mexican Immigrants in the United States." *Hispanic Journal of Behavioral Sciences* 4 (25): 427–47

Basch, Linda, Nina Glick Schiller, and Cristina Szanton-Blanc. 1994. *Nations Unbound: Transnational Projects, Postcolonial Predicaments, and the Deterritorialized Nation-State.* New York: Gordon and Breach.

Cain, Bruce, and Brendan Doherty. 2006. "The Impact of Dual Nationality on Political Participation." In *Transforming Politics, Transforming America: The Political and Civic Incorporation of Immigrants in the United States,* edited by Taeku Lee, S. Karthick Ramakrishnan, and Ricardo Ramírez, 89–105. Charlottesville: University of Virginia Press.

Dahl, Robert A. 1961. *Who Governs? Democracy and Power in an American City.* New Haven: Yale University Press.

DeSipio, Louis. 1998. *Counting on the Latino Vote: Latinos as a New Electorate.* Charlottesville: University of Virginia Press.

———. 2006. "Transnational Politics and Civic Engagement: Do Home-Country Political Ties Limit Latino Immigrant Pursuit of U.S. Civic Engagement and Citizenship?" In *Transforming Politics, Transforming America: The Political and Civic Incorporation of Immigrants in the United States,* edited by Taeku Lee, S. Karthick Ramakrishnan, and Ricardo Ramírez, 106–26. Charlottesville: University of Virginia Press.

Foner, Nancy. 2000. *From Ellis Island to JFK: New York's Two Great Waves of Immigration.* New Haven: Yale University Press.

———. 2001. "Transnationalism Then and Now: New York Immigrants Today and at the Turn of the Twentieth Century." In *Migration, Transnationalism, and Race in a Changing New York,* edited by Hector Codero-Guzman, Robert Smith, and Ramon Grosfoguel, 35–57. Philadelphia: Temple University Press.

Glazer, Nathan, and Daniel P. Moynihan. 1963. *Beyond the Melting Pot: The Negroes, Puerto Ricans, Jews, Italians, and Irish of New York City.* Cambridge, MA: Harvard University Press.

Glick Schiller, Nina, Linda Basch, and Cristina Szanton Blanc, eds. 1992. *Toward a Transnational Perspective on Migration: Race, Class, Ethnicity, and Nationalism Reconsidered.* New York: Annals of the New York Academy of Sciences.

Grasmuck, Sherri, and Patricia Pessar. 1991. *Between Two Islands: Dominican International Migration.* Berkeley: University of California Press.

Grebler, Leo. 1966. "The Naturalization of Mexican Immigrants in the United States." *International Migration Review* 1(1): 17–32.

Guarnizo, Luis Eduardo. 2001. "On the Political Participation of Transnational Migrants: Old Practices and New Trends." In *E Pluribus Unum? Contemporary and Historical Perspectives on Immigrant Political Incorporation,* edited by Gary Gerstle and John Mollenkopf, 213–63. New York: Russell Sage Foundation.

Highton, Benjamin, and Arthur L. Burris. 2002. "New Perspectives on Latino Voter Turnout in the United States." *American Politics Research* 3 (3): 285–306.

Hondagneu-Sotelo, Pierrette. 1994. *Gendered Transitions, Mexican Experiences of Immigration.* Los Angeles: University of California Press.

Huntington, Samuel P. 2004. *Who Are We? The Challenges to American National Identity.* New York: Simon and Schuster.

Itzigsohn, Jose. 2000. "Immigration and the Boundaries of Citizenship: The Institutions of Immigrants Political Transnationalism." *International Migration Review* 34 (4): 1126–54.

Johnson, Martin, Robert M. Stein, and Robert Wrinkle. 2003. "Language Choice, Residential Stability, and Voting among Latino Americans." *Social Science Quarterly* 84 (2): 412–24.

Jones-Correa, Michael. 1998. *Between Two Nations: The Political Predicament of Latinos in New York City.* Ithaca: Cornell University Press.

———. 2001. "Under Two Flags: Dual Nationality in Latin America and Its Consequences for Naturalization in the United States." *International Migration Review* 35 (4): 997–1029.

———. 2002. "Bringing Outsiders In: Questions of Immigrant Incorporation." Paper prepared for the Conference on the Politics of Democratic Inclusion. University of Notre Dame, October 17–19.

Kasinitz, Philip, Mary C. Waters, John H. Mollenkopf, and Merih Anil. 2002. "Transnationalism and the Children of Immigrants in Contemporary New York." In *The Changing Face of Home: The Transnational Lives of the Second Generation,* edited by Peggy Levitt and Mary C. Waters, 96–122. New York: Russell Sage Foundation.

Larsen, Luke J. 2004. "The Foreign-Born Population in the United States, 2003" (Report P20-551). Washington, DC: United States Census Bureau.

Leal, David L. 2002. "Political Participation by Latino Non-Citizens in the United States." *British Journal of Political Science* 32 (2): 353–70.

Levitt, Peggy. 1998. "Social Remittances: Migration Driven Local-Level Forms of Cultural Diffusion." *International Migration Review* 32 (4): 926–48.

———. 2001. *The Transnational Villagers*. Berkeley: University of California Press.

Long, Jay Scott. 1997. "Regression Models for Categorical and Limited Dependent Variables." In *Advanced Quantitative Techniques in the Social Sciences,* vol. 7. Thousand Oaks: Sage.

Menjivar, Cecilia. 2000. *Fragmented Ties, Salvadoran Immigrant Networks in America*. Los Angeles: University of California Press.

Michelson, Melissa R. 2000. "Political Efficacy and Electoral Participation of Chicago Latinos." *Social Science Quarterly* 81 (1): 136–50.

Morawska, Ewa. 2001. "Immigrants, Transnationalism, and Ethnicization: A Comparison of This Great Wave and the Last." In *E Pluribus Unum? Contemporary and Historical Perspectives on Immigrant Political Incorporation,* edited by Gary Gerstle and John Mollenkopf, 175–212. New York: Russell Sage Foundation.

Pantoja, Adrian D. 2005. "Transnational Ties and Immigrant Political Incorporation: The Case of Dominicans in Washington Heights, New York." *International Migration* 43 (4): 123–44.

Pantoja, Adrian D., and Sarah Allen Gershon. 2006. "Political Orientations and Naturalization among Latino and Latina Immigrants." *Social Science Quarterly* 87 (5): 1171–87.

Portes, Alejandro, and John Curtis. 1987. "Changing Flags: Naturalization and Its Determinants among Mexican Immigrants." *International Migration Review* 21 (2): 352–71.

Portes, Alejandro, William Haller, and Luis Guarnizo. 2002. "Transnational Entrepreneurs: An Alternative Form of Immigrant Economic Adaptation." *American Sociological Review* 67 (2): 278–98.

Ramakrishnan, Karthick S. 2005. *Democracy in Immigrant America: Changing Demographics and Political Participation*. Palo Alto: Stanford University Press.

Ramakrishnan, Karthick S., and Thomas J. Espenshade. 2001. "Immigrant Incorporation and Political Participation in the United States." *International Migration Review* 35 (3): 870–909.

Rogers, Reuel R. 2006. *Afro-Caribbean Immigrants and the Politics of Incorporation: Ethnicity, Exception, or Exit*. New York: Cambridge University Press.

Staton, Jeffrey K., Robert A. Jackson, and Damarys Canache. Forthcoming. "Dual Nationality Among Latinos: What Are the Implications for Political-Connectedness?" *Journal of Politics.*

Tam Cho, Wendy K. 1999. "Naturalization, Socialization, Participation: Immigrants and (Non-)Voting." *Journal of Politics* 61 (4): 1140–55.

Wong, Janelle. 2006. *Democracy's Promise, Immigrants and American Civic Institutions.* Ann Arbor: University of Michigan Press.

Yang, Philip Q. 1994. "Explaining Immigrant Naturalization." *International Migration Review* 28 (3): 449–77.

From Naturalized Citizen to Voter

*The Context of Naturalization and Electoral Participation
in Latino Communities*

LOUIS DESIPIO

In the 1990s, naturalization surged to levels unprecedented in the history of its federal regulation since 1907 (see Table 5.1). The more than five million immigrants who naturalized as U.S. citizens in the 1990s exceeded the number of naturalizees in the previous three decades combined. Naturalization in the first decade of the twenty-first century increased further. More than 6.5 million immigrants naturalized as U.S. citizens between 2001 and 2010. The large number of newly naturalized citizens—most of whom are adults[1]—will likely influence U.S. electoral politics for many years to come simply based on their numbers and their concentration in a few states, but they also raise a dilemma for democratic institutions in the United States. Specifically, they test whether existing incorporative mechanisms are successful at making these new, voluntary citizens into regular participants in electoral politics.

Numbers alone, of course, do not guarantee regular electoral participation. For these newly naturalized citizens to have a distinct voice

Table 5.1. Naturalizations by Decade

Decade	*Naturalizations*
1907–1910	111,738
1911–1920	1,128,972
1921–1930	1,773,185
1931–1940	1,518,464
1941–1950	1,987,028
1951–1960	1,189,949
1961–1970	1,120,263
1971–1980	1,464,772
1981–1990	2,214,265
1991–2000	5,597,105
1991	307,394
1992	239,664
1993	313,590
1994	429,123
1995	485,720
1996	1,040,991
1997	596,010
1998	461,169
1999	837,418
2000	886,026
2001–2010	6,556,004
2001	606,259
2002	572,646
2003	462,435
2004	537,151
2005	604,280
2006	702,589
2007	660,477
2008	1,046,539
2009	743,715
2010	619,913

Source: U.S. Department of Homeland Security. 2011. *Yearbook of Immigration Statistics 2010.* Washington, DC: U.S. Department of Homeland Security, Office of Immigration Statistics. http://www.dhs.gov/xlibrary/assets/statistics/yearbook/2010/ois_yb_ 2010.pdf. Accessed May 3, 2012.

in politics, they need to participate regularly and, ideally, at higher levels than do their U.S.-born co-ethnics who tend to participate at lower levels than non-Hispanic whites (Anglos) and African Americans (U.S. Bureau of the Census 2005; DeSipio 1996a; Lien, Conway, and Wong 2004). Naturalized citizens may be at a particular disadvantage. A series of studies conducted in the 1990s demonstrate that naturalized citizens participate in elections, as well as other forms of community political activity, at rates lower than comparably situated U.S.-born citizens (Bass and Casper 1999; DeSipio 1996c, 2001; Levitt and Olson 1996; Minnite, Holdaway, and Hayduk 1999; Mollenkopf, Olson, and Ross 2001).[2]

Several of these studies, however, note that the naturalized citizens in their analyses include immigrants who became U.S. citizens exclusively or primarily before the surge in naturalization in the mid-1990s, a period in which more of the naturalizees arguably naturalized for political reasons than had immigrants in previous eras. Thus, this previous scholarship would suggest that it might be valuable to disaggregate 1990s naturalizees and/or immigrants who naturalized for political reasons to ascertain a cohort effect that distinguishes them in terms of their political behavior from earlier naturalizees or from naturalizees who did not naturalize for political reasons.

The post-1992 naturalizees also include a subgroup that may have a claim on electoral participation that is unique from other naturalizees. Specifically, one of the reasons for the surge in naturalization in the 1990s (a topic discussed in more depth later) is the large number of Immigration Reform and Control Act (IRCA) legalizees who became eligible to naturalize in the 1990s (Rytina 2002; Baker 2010). United States residency since at least 1981 was required of this group—many had been resident for much longer—and they had to demonstrate either a facility in English and civics at the time of legalization (in other words, in the late 1980s) or the taking of classes to gain this knowledge. Thus, IRCA recipients should on average have been ahead of other naturalizees in gaining the formal civics skills necessary to participate in U.S. politics.

Finally, previous scholarship has not been able to assess whether the broader context of naturalization, regardless of when it took place, shapes the likelihood of electoral participation. More specifically, I am interested in whether immigrants who naturalized for political reasons—or at least recall that they naturalized for political reasons—are more likely to participate in politics than other naturalized citizens. Some of the historical literature on 1920s/1930s era naturalizees would suggest that this is the case, but this theory has not been tested rigorously.

In this chapter, I test two sets of hypotheses using a survey of Latino[3] voting patterns in the 2000 presidential election. First, I examine whether period of naturalization matters. My null hypothesis is that the longer an immigrant is naturalized, the higher the likelihood that s/he will participate in politics. This assumes that political skills and interests are learned and that, controlling for factors known to shape political behavior in the population as a whole, longer periods of citizenship will increase the likelihood of voting. I counter this null hypothesis with the two cohort measures of specific periods of immigration and naturalization that might prove more important to determining political behaviors than simple duration of naturalized citizenship—IRCA beneficiaries and naturalizees from the period of political contestation of immigration, immigrant status, and naturalization in the mid- to late-1990s (between 1994 and 2000 in my analysis).

Second, I test a mobilization model in which the reasons for naturalization matter for civic and political engagement. I hypothesize that immigrants who naturalized for political reasons are more likely to participate than those who naturalized for other reasons and immigrants who naturalized in order to obtain or maintain access to government services would be less likely to vote. I should note at the outset that the evaluations of reasons for naturalizing are offered *retrospectively* and thus may be shaded by feelings about politics or political institutions in the period between naturalization and the 2000 election. These models are discussed in greater depth later in the chapter.

DATA

My analysis is based on a post-election telephone survey of Latino[4] registered voters in five states conducted by the Tomás Rivera Policy Institute (TRPI) after the 2000 presidential elections. This survey and the data that I analyze are unique for two reasons. First, this is a survey of *registered voters* (whose voter registration status was verified by the sample vendor—Aristotle of Washington, DC). As a result, I analyze the voting behavior among the registered, those who are most targeted by candidates and campaigns in the weeks leading up to the election. Second, the survey includes a battery of eight questions about the respondents' retrospective evaluations of why they naturalized for a subsample of respondents. The questions are asked of the more recent naturalizees, those who naturalized between 1992 and 2000. Although it would have allowed for a richer analysis to have these questions asked of all naturalized respondents, I would have serious concerns about the accuracy of naturalization-related memories for respondents who naturalized in earlier periods. These questions, and the frequencies of responses, appear in Table 5.2.

The survey includes 2,132 Latino registered voter respondents in California, Texas, New York, Florida, and Illinois. The survey included a minimum of 400 respondents from each of these states. Of these respondents, 834 were naturalized U.S. citizens. The survey included an elaborate screen to exclude individuals born abroad as U.S. citizens from the naturalized category (usually because one or both parents were U.S. citizens). So, unlike other surveys that incorrectly specify some foreign-born U.S. citizen respondents as naturalized, the naturalized respondents discussed here have made the voluntary transition to U.S. citizenship. Of the 834 naturalized respondents, 375 naturalized in 1992 or later and were asked for their assessments of why they naturalized.

As is the case with most surveys, a higher share of survey respondents reported that they voted compared to national data on voter turnout. While no single authoritative source provides the share of naturalized Latino voters who vote, the Current Population Survey is the most widely used source, even though it likely misreports citizenship status, registration status, and voting for some individuals (Shaw, de la Garza, and Lee 2000; DeSipio and de la Garza 2005, 49–50). According to this survey, 78.6 percent of Latino registered voters turned out to vote in 2000 (U.S. Bureau of the Census 2002, Table 2). In the five states TRPI surveyed, Latino turnout was approximately 81 percent of registered Latino voters (U.S. Bureau of the Census 2002, Table 4a). Respondents to the TRPI survey reported turnout at the rate of 89

Table 5.2. Importance of Reasons for Naturalizing among Latinos who Naturalized in 1992 or Later

---

Government Services

"I wanted to ensure that my family and I would continue to have access to U.S. government programs and services in the future."

Very important	54.5%
Somewhat important	16.8%
Somewhat unimportant	7.2%
Not at all important	21.4%

"I wanted to immigrate my relatives living abroad more rapidly."

Very important	37.5%
Somewhat important	9.0%
Somewhat unimportant	9.0%
Not at all important	44.5%

"I needed to replace my Green Card which was going to expire."

Very important	28.0%
Somewhat important	9.0%
Somewhat unimportant	7.2%
Not at all important	55.8%

Civic and Political Attitudes and Connections to the United States

"I realized that I had more ties to the U.S. than to my country of origin."

Very important	64.2%
Somewhat important	19.4%
Somewhat unimportant	5.8%
Not at all important	10.7%

"I wanted to vote."

Very important	85.6%
Somewhat important	10.7%
Somewhat unimportant	0.6%
Not at all important	3.2%

"I wanted to protect my children's rights in the United States."

Very important	69.3%
Somewhat important	9.6%
Somewhat unimportant	2.6%
Not at all important	18.6%

"I feared for my status in the United States."

Very important	32.6%
Somewhat important	11.7%
Somewhat unimportant	10.3%
Not at all important	45.5%

"I was concerned that the United States was turning against immigrants."

Very important	41.7%
Somewhat important	17.8%
Somewhat unimportant	6.2%
Not at all important	34.3%

Source: Tomás Rivera Policy Institute Post-Election Survey, 2001.

percent. This gap likely reflects over-reporting of voter turnout in the wake of the many controversies surrounding the 2000 presidential race. Unfortunately, the data do not allow for these over-reporters to be distinguished in the analysis. Thus, the dependent variable—voting in the 2000 election—must be understood as including both voters (the vast majority) and some respondents who think they should have voted or who are offering the more socially acceptable answer.

NATURALIZATION AND ELECTORAL PARTICIPATION

Contrary to popular assumptions, many immigrants never naturalize. In 1990, for example, just eight million of the 19.8 million foreign-born residents of the United States were U.S. citizens (U.S. Bureau of the Census 1993). By 2003, the number of foreign-born residents of the United States increased to 33.5 million and the number naturalized to 12.8 million (U.S. Bureau of the Census 2004). The share of naturalized immigrants declined slightly during the 1990s.

Not all of the non-naturalized immigrants are eligible for citizenship. Approximately four million have immigrated in the previous five years and, thus, are not yet eligible to naturalize (and some of these immigrants have emigrated elsewhere, returned to their home countries, or died prior to achieving naturalization eligibility). In addition, the foreign-born population includes many unauthorized immigrants, although their exact number is somewhat disputed (U.S. Immigration and Naturalization Service 2003, Table Q; Bean, Van Hook, and Woodrow-Lafield 2001; Bean et al. 2001; Passel 2005). A 2004 estimate finds that 4.2 million Latino legal permanent residents and 3.5 million non-Latino legal permanent residents were eligible for naturalization (NALEO Educational Fund 2004). In addition, between 600,000 and 700,000 legal permanent resident adults achieve eligibility for naturalization each year. The overall pool is reduced by the 650,000 who naturalize each year. These numbers are imprecise because there are no comprehensive data sources on the emigration or death of non-naturalized immigrants in the United States.

A long-standing assumption is that the naturalized engage in politics at higher levels than do comparably situated U.S.-born citizens. There is a logic behind this assumption as well as a specific historical circumstance that may explain its origin. Among contemporary immigrants, however, only limited and regionally specific data support these claims and a wealth of data contradict them.

The claims of high levels of political activity and commensurate influence among the naturalized have their roots in the last period of higher-than-routine immigrant interest in naturalization—the 1910s through the early 1930s.[5] Scholarly work from this era speaks of the energetic involvement of naturalized citizens in politics, particularly in local politics, and of their influence in some elections. These claims are for the most part not empirically substantiated in the scholarly analysis of this era, but the assertion is made widely enough to be a truism (some more recent studies have attempted to look at the political behaviors of the naturalized and their children from this era with greater methodological rigor, see Tuckel and Maisel 1994; Andersen 1979; Gamm 1986; Cohen 1990).

When the analysts from this period sought to examine the question of why naturalized citizens would be disproportionately active, they used the following logic, again without any proof: naturalizing citizens developed a more complete understanding of U.S. politics through the requirements of the naturalization process. With this greater knowledge, they took the responsibilities of democracy more seriously and they participated more. Their added participation was spurred by the ethnically charged nature of the 1928 presidential election because of Democrat Al Smith's Catholicism, by support for a repeal of Prohibition, and by the Depression and the beginnings of the New Deal in the 1932 and 1936 elections. The experiences of this period generate the hypothesis that naturalization for political reasons might increase the likelihood of subsequent political participation. This unique historical period—the three national elections between 1928 and 1936— created an environment in which the naturalized (and their children) did have a particularly strong and cohesive political voice. The economic difficulties of the day were important to them and they were able to develop alliances with other disaffected groups to form the coalition that would later support President Roosevelt and the Democrats for a political generation.

Whether or not the naturalized participated in politics at high levels in the 1920s and 1930s, the same assertions are made about today's immigrants. Again, however, few facts substantiate these claims. Instead, anecdotal evidence from specific elections is offered, but such anecdotes do not distinguish between the political behaviors of the naturalized and their U.S.-born co-ethnics. Further, they do not measure the combined impact of the immigrant-ethnic vote.

An example of this sort of claim is the 1996 Orange County, California, congressional race between Loretta Sánchez and Bob Dornan. Many commentators attributed Sánchez's victory to the votes of Latino immigrants. Implicitly, Dornan made this claim with his charge that Sánchez (and a Latino community-based organization, Hermandad Mexicana) "stole" the election by manipulating the votes of naturalizing (but not yet naturalized) Latinos. Undeniably, many people in the district are Latino, as it was drawn under the provisions of the Voting Rights Act to create a majority-minority district. Equally certainly, many of the district's Latino residents were not U.S. citizens. The claim that Latinos influenced the outcome of this race has two major problems, however. First, Latinos—regardless of nativity—made up no more than 30 percent of the *voters* in the district (and probably closer to 25 percent) in 1996. Thus, while they may well have overwhelmingly supported Sánchez, they alone are not responsible for her victory. Second, at least 60 percent of these Latino voters had voted in previous congressional elections. It follows that, if they were naturalized voters, they were not recent entrants into electoral politics. In sum, these anecdotal claims often collapse upon even the simplest investigation.

Several recent studies have tapped survey data (often collected for other purposes) to compare the political behaviors of the U.S.-born and the foreign-born. I, for example, measured four forms of political activity—involvement in community organizations, parental involvement in the schools, voter registration, and voting—to compare the political behavior of naturalized and native-born Mexican Americans and Cuban Americans (DeSipio 1996c). Across each of these four types of political activity, bivariate comparisons indicated that the U.S.-born and the naturalized had comparable levels of activity. When variations did appear, the U.S.-born usually had higher levels of participation.

When I examined these differences using multivariate models that looked not just at the source of citizenship, but also at standard socio-demographic predictors of participation, I found that when naturalization status proved to be statistically significant, it was a *negative* predictor of political activity. The two political activities for which naturalization proved to be a significant, negative predictor of political activity in the multivariate models were the two that related to voting: voter registration and voting in one of the four elections prior to the survey (including both presidential and local elections). In both of these models, the standard sociodemographic measures that predict political activity broadly among American adults (years of education and degrees earned, income, labor force participation, and age) had a greater effect on the dependent variable than did source of citizenship. In addition, the model included two variables unique to immigrant-ethnic populations—national origin and language used at home (neither of which proved to be significant). Source of citizenship proved not to be significant for two other types of political activity—membership in community-based organizations and parental involvement in the schools.

Analysis of the Current Population Survey of registration and voting in the 1996 elections largely tells the same story (Bass and Casper 1999).[6] Controlling for sociodemographic characteristics, foreign-born citizens were one-third less likely to register and one-quarter less likely to vote than the U.S.-born. Interestingly, naturalized citizens from Latin America were somewhat more likely to report registration or voting than immigrants from other parts of the world, though these national-origin differences were not statistically significant.

There is no similar multivariate analysis of the CPS election data from subsequent elections (see DeSipio, Masuoka, and Stout 2008 for analysis of immigrant generation and Asian-American voters in the 2000 and 2004 elections). The bivariate results look quite similar to those from 1996. Overall, the naturalized were less likely to register or vote in both 2000 and 2004. Naturalized Latinos, however, were more likely to register and vote than native-born Latinos in both years (U.S.

Bureau of the Census 2002, Table 13, 2005, Table 13). It is my expectation that these results for the Latino community would disappear in multivariate analysis as they did for the 1996 CPS data.

These national findings are largely reinforced by four studies of immigrant-ethnic populations in specific cities—New York, Los Angeles, and Miami—that rely on both survey data and ecological inference. The first of these city-level studies measures voting among six immigrant-ethnic populations in New York City elections (Levitt and Olson 1996). This study examines electoral districts with high concentrations of Dominicans, Jamaicans, Chinese, Italian, Soviet, and Ecuadorian immigrants in five elections in the early 1990s. The authors find that the high concentration districts for five of the ethnic populations (all but Soviets) turn out at rates lower than the citywide average. Chinese-dominated electoral districts turn out at the lowest rates—just 73 percent of the average for the city. While this study does not adequately account for the interaction between sociodemographic characteristics and nationality characteristics, it reinforces the finding that the naturalized participate at lower rates than native-born citizens.

Mollenkopf, Ross, and Olson (2001) extend this study to look at immigrant neighborhoods in New York and Los Angeles, home to both first- and second-generation immigrants. Though they indicate that structural/electoral factors explain some of the variation within each city, their consistent finding is that neighborhoods with high concentrations of immigrants are *less* likely to turn out than neighborhoods with very low concentrations of immigrants. In New York, the predicted turnout for the 1996 presidential election declined by about one percent for each ten percentage point increase in foreign-born population. In Los Angeles, a ten-percentage point increase in foreign-born population decreases turnout by two percent. Mollenkopf et al. (2001) also found variation among ethnic groups. In New York, West Indians and Dominicans are more likely to vote than native-born citizens. Chinese, Italians, and Russians, on the other hand, are less likely to vote. In Los Angeles, Salvadorans, Mexicans, and Filipinos were less likely than native-born neighborhoods to turn out to vote.

Minnite, Holdaway, and Hayduk (1999) reinforce these findings. Their 1997 telephone survey of 1,662 adults living in New York found that self-reported voting varies based on nativity in a statistically significant manner in the 1994 and 1996 elections, controlling for sociodemographic and institutional factors. As with the other studies, they find that U.S.-born citizens are more likely to participate than the foreign-born. Their contribution comes from their examination of both a presidential and non-presidential election. The gap between the U.S.- and foreign-born is greater in the non-presidential election year under study.

Hill and Moreno (1996) analyze the Cuban respondents to the Latino National Political Survey, most of whom reside in Florida. They examine three subsets of this population—immigrants who migrated before they were ten years of age, immigrants who migrated after they had turned ten, and U.S.-born Cubans (who are almost all second generation). They test which of these three subsets of the Cuban American population are most likely to participate in seven political non-electoral political activities. Overall, second-generation individuals are less likely to undertake these activities than are the migrants who arrived after the age of ten. In a regression model, however, the percentage of life spent in the United States proves a significant and positive predictor of undertaking these activities, suggesting that the relative youth of the second generation may dampen their political activity relative to their immigrant parents.

These studies and others document a pattern of lower levels of registration and voting among naturalized citizens; in contrast, several studies of Latino voter turnout among registered voters in Southern California provide contradictory evidence (Pantoja, Ramirez, and Segura 2001; Barreto and Muñoz 2003; Barreto 2005). Clearly, this work—which relies primarily on lists of registered voters—can only tell half the story. Like the survey data analyzed in this chapter, it begins with a pool of registered voters and cannot speak to whether there are nativity differences in propensity to register; it does, however, raise the question whether the political environment of California in the late 1990s/early 2000s created different incentives from the rest of the country for immigrants, specifically for Latino immigrants, to vote (Fraga, Ramírez, and Segura 2005; Pachon, Barreto, and Marquez 2005). In this chapter, I analyze both period and state-specific effects to see if the Californian experience distinctly predicts higher levels of turnout among naturalized Latinos or among Latinos who naturalized in the 1990s.

Without a national immigrant voting survey that is broadly inclusive in terms of immigrant-ethnic populations and verifies self-reported registration and voting, the results of these disparate studies must suffice in terms of answering the question of the likelihood of voting among immigrants. To the extent that these populations are representative of the naturalized citizen population broadly, however, the data indicate that the naturalized will not have a disproportionate political voice. In fact, they will have *less* of a voice than comparably situated U.S.-born citizens.

CHANGING INCENTIVES TO NATURALIZE IN THE 1990S

Beginning in 1993, the costs of denizenship began to increase and the psychic costs of naturalization for immigrants from some countries began to decline (for a more detailed discussion of these factors, see DeSipio 1996b). The consequence was a dramatic increase in immigrant pursuit of naturalization (see Table 5.1). I trace this surge in interest to 1993, although, due to administrative processing delays, it may appear not to have occurred until 1995 or even 1996. Beginning in 1993, demand for naturalization began to increase (U.S. Department of Homeland Security 2006: Table 31). By 1996, the number of naturalizations roughly tripled the average levels prior to the surge in demand. Naturalizations at this level are unprecedented in the nearly one-hundred-year history of federal administration of naturalization.

Why did immigrants suddenly seek naturalization at such high levels? First, the United States as a whole and at least one of the states— California—began to change a long-standing pattern in the treatment of denizens (DeSipio 1996b). Before 1994, permanent residents, and particularly permanent residents who met the five year residency requirement to make them eligible for U.S. citizenship, had most of the rights and eligibility for programmatic benefits as did citizens. Beginning with California's Proposition 187 and then with the 1996 Welfare

Reform Bill, legislatures began to deny immigrants and their households social welfare benefits (DeSipio and de la Garza 1998, chapter 4). While relatively few immigrants use these benefit programs (at least relative to their economic status), many heard the anti-immigrant message of these legislative changes and more actively pursued naturalization.

A second change also altered the incentive structure of naturalization. Several immigrant-sending countries have sought to reduce the psychic costs of émigrés seeking to become U.S. citizens (Aleinikoff 2000; Jones-Correa 2000). This new approach takes a variety of forms, but all seek to reshape the relationship between the sending country and the émigré; the ultimate goal is to create an interest group in the United States that is sensitive to the needs of the sending country. Colombia, for example, encourages dual-citizenship and seeks to maintain an ongoing relationship with the U.S.-born children of its U.S.-naturalized émigrés. For many years, Mexico promised easy re-naturalization for Mexican nationals who become U.S. citizens but later decide to return to live permanently in Mexico and promoted a dual-nationality that allowed for full economic, but not political rights (González-Gutiérrez 1999); in 2005, Mexico added voting from abroad in presidential elections to the pallet of rights available to Mexican émigrés. The Mexican case is particularly important both because of the numbers of its émigrés in the United States and because its attitude had been traditionally one of disdain when its émigrés sought U.S. citizenship (de la Garza 1997).

A third change in the incentive structure is less instrumental than procedural. Beginning in 1993, the INS required that immigrants replace aging immigrant identification cards ("green cards"). For many long-term residents (who had developed English-language skills), the procedure and cost of replacing the aging cards was not significantly less complicated or expensive than naturalizing. Because these new green cards would have to be replaced every ten years, the utility of naturalization increased (Tomás Rivera Policy Institute 2001).

A fourth change in the mid-1990s affected the pool of eligible immigrants. One of the three components of the Immigration Reform and Control Act (IRCA) of 1986 was the program to legalize long-term undocumented residents of the United States. Approximately two million immigrants who had resided in the United States in an undocumented status since before 1982 earned permanent resident status through this program. Another one million agricultural laborers with generally shorter periods of undocumented residence also earned legalized status. They began to be eligible for naturalization in late 1993. Thus, at the same time that the incentive structure of naturalization was changing and the INS created a bureaucratic incentive to naturalize, the pool of eligible immigrants was growing quite dramatically, by as many as three million.

This increase was notable for two reasons. First, it was much larger than any comparable annual increase. In the average year, between 550,000 and 750,000 immigrants attain naturalization eligibility (some of these are children and can only naturalize if their parents do; children who naturalize as part of their parents naturalization are, for the most part, not counted here). Second, immigrants awaiting legalized status through the IRCA had resided in the United States for long periods of time—at least ten years. Further, in order to obtain legalized status, they had to demonstrate that they knew English, U.S. history, and civics comparable to what is asked of naturalizing citizens, or they needed to take classes to meet these objectives. Thus, they are further along in the process of adapting to U.S. life and better prepared than most newly naturalization-eligible immigrants. They, of course, joined the annual figure of 550,000 to 750,000 immigrants who begin to become eligible for naturalization after living in the U.S. for five years.

A fifth change in the incentive structure to naturalize was a byproduct of the 1996 Antiterrorism and Effective Death Penalty Act. Among other provisions, this federal crime bill raised the likelihood that permanent residents who had committed crimes in the United States would be deported and, for those not deported, would not be able to reenter the United States after a voluntary departure. Anecdotal evidence indicates that some permanent resident parents fearing for the possible application of these provisions against their minor children naturalized to protect their children should they become involved in gang activity. Both before and after the passage of the law, permanent residents convicted of felonies were ineligible to naturalize.

Finally, INS periodically spurred a surge in demand by raising or threatening to raise the fee for naturalization. In January 1999, the fee increased from \$95 to \$225 (the fee is currently \$595, plus \$85 for fingerprints and an additional fee for photographs). Data show that applications increased dramatically in the months preceding the increase or proposed increase.

It is important to note that, even with higher numbers of immigrants becoming U.S. citizens in the late 1990s, no more than half of the eligible pool of long-term immigrants had become citizens since 1993. Their numbers are reinforced by the 550,000 to 750,000 immigrants who reach their fifth year of permanent residence each year. Immigrant naturalizations in the early twenty-first century are well below these levels. In other words, a large untapped pool of citizenship-eligible immigrants has not yet pursued naturalization and that number grows each year.

MODELS AND ANALYSIS

In this chapter, I test a series of logistic regression models that substitute cohort measures or retrospective evaluations for time elapsed since naturalization in a standard model of electoral participation in Latino communities. The models control for factors that have long been shown to shape the likelihood of voting in the U.S. electorate as a whole including sociodemographic characteristics of individuals, mobilization during the campaign, and—in the Latino community more specifically—a measure of acculturation.

The analysis begins with two preliminary steps. First, I analyze *all* respondents to the TRPI survey, regardless of nativity, to assess whether these data follow the general pattern identified above: lower levels of participation among *naturalized* citizens than U.S.-born citizens, controlling for other predictors of voting (see Table 5.3). I limit the subsequent analysis to naturalized respondents to the TRPI survey. First, I present a model that tests my null hypothesis that among naturalized citizens, controlling for other factors, registered voters who naturalized earlier will be more likely to vote than those who naturalized later (see

Table 5.4). I then compare three models testing period of naturalization (see Table 5.5) and reasons for naturalizing (see Table 5.6) to this model in which duration of U.S. citizenship is the key naturalization-related factor explaining what differentiates Latino naturalized registered voters who turn out from those who do not.

Each of these models controls for several factors that reliably predict voter turnout in Latino and Latino immigrant communities (and, in many cases, in the population as a whole). In each of the models, I include five standard demographic characteristics as independent control variables: age, education, household income, gender, and state of residence. Generally, older citizens are more likely to vote, as are more educated citizens. I would expect that these patterns would also appear in these data. Although the impact of income is more erratic in Latino communities than in the population as a whole, higher income respondents are more likely to participate. As with many surveys, a sizeable share of the respondents to the TRPI survey (slightly less than one-quarter) did not report their incomes. In order to avoid excluding these respondents from the analysis, I report income categorically and treat "refused" as a category. I have no expectations for the likelihood of political behavior for the refused category. In the population as a whole, women are somewhat more likely to vote than men, but this pattern does not repeat itself among Latinos. Again, I predict whether Latina or Latino naturalized citizens will be more likely to participate. Finally among demographic predictors, I include state of residence as a control. Its impact varies from election to election; in 2000, for example, the election in Texas, New York, and Illinois was of a lower intensity than in Florida (DeSipio and de la Garza 2005). Because of the more intense scholarly focus on political behaviors of Latinos in California in recent elections, however, I use it as the excluded category and compare voting patterns in each of the other four states to those of Latinos in California. I would expect Florida Latinos to have higher turnout rates and Texas Latinos to have lower turnout rates than those of their California co-ethnics.

I also include a political measure and an acculturation measure as controls. I expect respondents who have been contacted to vote to be more likely to turn out than those who have not (Shaw, de la Garza, and

Lee 2000). Likelihood of such contacts varies by state, so this variable may capture some of the variation in turnout by state. Finally, I include home language use (Spanish, English, or both) as a proxy for acculturation.[7] I should note that past study of Latino communities has found that language spoken at home does not distinguish the behaviors of registered Latinos who vote from those who do not (DeSipio 1996a, chapter 4). It does prove to be a significant predictor distinguishing Latino adult citizens who do not register from those who vote, but once this barrier is overcome, it has less predictive value.

Depending on the specification, I include one of five measures of period or context of naturalization. The simplest is years since naturalization. The second and third are one of two periods of immigration or naturalization—recipients of legalization under the Immigration Reform and Control Act (IRCA) or respondents who naturalized in 1994 or after. Although these categories overlap somewhat since most IRCA recipients who have naturalized did so in 1994 or after, the distinction measures different aspects of the immigration/naturalization experience (Rytina 2002). Finally, I create two scales to measure retrospective evaluations of reasons for naturalizing: a "political access scale" using the five questions related to retrospective evaluations regarding establishing or maintaining political access, and a "government services scale" using the three questions relating to the desire to obtain government services (these questions are listed in Table 5.2). For each question, I assign a value of -2 to "not at all important" answers, -1 to "somewhat unimportant," 0 to no answer/refused, +1 to "somewhat important" and +2 to "very important" and sum the answers. This creates a scale of -10 to +10 for the political access scale and -6 to +6 for the government services scale. The mean respondent scored a +4 on the political access scale (with respondents at both -10 and +10) and a 0 on the government services scale (again, with some respondents at both extremes).

RESULTS

In 2000, naturalized Latino registered voters were less likely to vote than were U.S.-born citizens (see Table 5.3). Controlling for the other factors associated with Latino political participation, naturalized citizens were approximately 29 percent less likely to vote than U.S.-born voters. Source of citizenship was not the only variable that proved to be significant in predicting voting likelihood, however. Older and more educated respondents had higher likelihoods of voting, as did some of the higher income categories relative to the lowest. Only Texas proved to have different voting patterns than California, in the predicted (lower) direction. Gender and language(s) spoken at home were not significant. In sum, these data confirm the relatively consistent finding that the naturalized participate at lower rates than U.S.-born citizens and raise some doubt about the possibility that California is an exception to this pattern.[8]

Among naturalized respondents to the TRPI survey, year of naturalization proved to be a statistically significant negative predictor of voting—in other words, immigrants who naturalized more recently were less likely to vote than those who naturalized several years ago (see Table 5.4). Every year, the likelihood of voting was reduced by approximately 4 percent as the "year since naturalization" approached the present. Neither naturalization during the period of more intense interest in immigration and naturalization after 1994 nor naturalization after receiving legalization under IRCA proved to have a positive effect on the likelihood of voting substantial enough to overcome the general pattern of longer periods of naturalization leading to higher levels of voting (see Table 5.5). Immigrants who naturalized in 1994 or after were approximately 40 percent less likely to vote than those who naturalized earlier, controlling for the other variables in the model. IRCA recipients who could not naturalize before 1993 and, in most cases, did so several years later were approximately 43 percent less likely to vote than non-IRCA recipients who had naturalized, again controlling for the other variables in the model. Thus, these data do not offer evidence that these cohort effects overcame the more general need for political learning and political socialization among naturalized citizens. Without more focused political education for naturalized citizens in the United States, time is the factor that offers the richest likelihood of gaining the skills, knowledge, and confidence to vote, even among the naturalized.

Table 5.3. Predictors of Voter Turnout Among Latino Registered Voters, 2000

Independent Variable	B	SE
Demographic Characteristics		
Age	0.039***	0.005
Education	0.064***	0.021
Household Income ($15,000 or less)		
$15,000–$24,999	0.323	0.284
$25,000–$34,999	0.301	0.299
$35,000–$49,999	0.111	0.286
$50,000–$64,999	0.613*	0.352
$65,000–$74,999	1.066**	0.453
$80,000–$99,999	2.049***	0.754
$100,000+	0.933*	0.486
Don't know/refused	-0.128	0.245
Gender (Men)		
Women	-0.126	0.150
State of Residence (California)		
Florida	-0.035	0.249
Illinois	0.342	0.241
New York	0.154	0.236
Texas	-0.453**	0.222
Political Characteristics		
Contacted to register or vote (No)		
Yes	0.347**	0.174
Immigration and Acculturation Characteristics		
Language spoken at home (Spanish)		
Both equally	0.011	0.186
English	-0.180	0.215
Nativity (U.S. Born/Born to a U.S. Citizen Abroad)		
Naturalized	-0.343**	0.174
Constant	-0.499	0.467
-2 log likelihood	1306.767	
Total cases	2,107	
Predicted correctly	89.5%	

*** $p < 0.01$, ** $p < 0.05$; * $p < 0.10$.

Source: Tomás Rivera Policy Institute 2000 election Post-Election Survey, 2001. Sample drawn from California, Texas, New York, Florida, and Illinois.

Table 5.4. Predictors of Voter Turnout among Naturalized Latino Registered Voters, 2000 (Basic Model)

Independent Variable	B	SE
Demographic Characteristics		
Age	0.023**	0.010
Education	0.028	0.030
Household Income ($15,000 or less)		
$15,000–$24,999	0.521	0.466
$25,000–$34,999	0.985	0.575
$35,000–$49,999	0.182	0.483
$50,000–$64,999	1.048	0.678
$65,000–$74,999	0.792	0.675
$80,000–$99,999	1.751	1.128
$100,000+	1.664*	1.115
Don't know/refused	0.017	0.403
Gender (Men)		
Women	-0.038	0.250
State of Residence (California)		
Florida	-0.178	0.390
Illinois	-0.020	0.387
New York	0.903*	0.491
Texas	-0.967**	0.389
Political Characteristics		
Contacted to register or vote (No)		
Yes	0.126	0.305
Immigration and Acculturation Characteristics		
Language spoken at home (Spanish)		
Both equally	-0.281	0.274
English	-0.839**	0.411
Year of naturalization	-0.049***	0.016
Constant	97.503***	32.357
-2 log likelihood	479.594	
Total cases	772	
Predicted correctly	89.1%	

*** $p < 0.01$, ** $p < 0.05$; * $p < 0.10$.

Source: Tomás Rivera Policy Institute 2000 election Post-Election Survey, 2001. Sample drawn from California, Texas, New York, Florida, and Illinois.

Table 5.5. Predictors of Voter Turnout among Naturalized Latino Registered Voters, 2000 (Period and Cohort Effects)

Independent Variable	Post-1994 Naturalizees		IRCA Recipients	
	B	*SE*	*B*	*SE*
Demographic Characteristics				
Age	0.028***	0.010	0.031***	0.009
Education	0.032	0.030	0.016	0.028
Household Income ($15,000 or less)				
$15,000–$24,999	0.487	0.465	0.154	0.438
$25,000–$34,999	0.985	0.574	0.942*	0.564
$35,000–$49,999	0.151	0.481	-0.089	0.462
$50,000–$64,999	1.072	0.674	0.975	0.659
$65,000–$74,999	0.791	0.672	0.794	0.657
$80,000–$99,999	1.790	1.123	1.894*	1.118
$100,000+	1.673	1.109	1.646	1.101
Don't know/refused	0.020	0.401	-0.322	0.380
Gender (Men)				
Women	-0.015	0.250	-0.135	0.232
State of Residence (California)				
Florida	-0.089	0.390	0.001	0.370
Illinois	-0.019	0.387	-0.026	0.367
New York	0.893*	0.491	0.630	0.437
Texas	-0.885**	0.388	-0.946***	0.361
Political Characteristics				
Contacted to register or vote (No)				
Yes	0.135	0.303	0.224	0.282
Immigration and Acculturation Characteristics				
Language spoken at home (Spanish)				
Both equally	-0.256	0.274	-0.005	0.255
English	-0.675*	0.405	-0.475	0.370
Cohort and Period Effects				
Naturalized in 1994 or after	-0.525*	0.271		
Legalized under IRCA			-0.568*	0.321
Constant	0.438	0.860	0.358	0.757
-2 log likelihood	486.446		558.579	
Total cases	771		841	
Predicted correctly	89.1%		88.1%	

*** $p < 0.01$, ** $p < 0.05$; * $p < 0.10$.

Source: Tomás Rivera Policy Institute 2000 election Post-Election Survey, 2001. Sample drawn from California, Texas, New York, Florida, and Illinois.

In each of these models testing length of naturalized citizenship or cohort effects, age also proved to be a positive predictor of voting as did a couple of the higher income categories (though most did not). Naturalized Tejanos were less likely to turn out than were naturalized California Latinos. The other states did not prove to be statistically different from the California Latinos. Gender, GOTV contact, and education were not significant predictors of voting among naturalized Latinos registered to vote. In both the basic model (the one testing duration of citizenship) and the model testing the "post-1994" cohort effect, language spoken at home proved to be significant. Respondents who spoke English at home were *less* likely to vote than respondents who spoke Spanish at home. While somewhat counterintuitive, I interpret this to mean that immigrant households that are able to maintain Spanish dominance, controlling for each of the other characteristics in the model, particularly education and income, can use linguistic difference as a resource compared to more acculturated naturalized Latinos. I am cautious in this interpretation and would note that the bilingual respondents, who at some level would seem to have the best of both worlds, do not prove to be different than the respondents who speak Spanish at home.

Finally, one's memory of why one naturalized does have predictive power over the likelihood of voting, at least for respondents who remember naturalizing for political reasons (see Table 5.6). Controlling for the other variables in the model, each increment along the twenty-point scale of political reasons for naturalizing increases the likelihood of voting by about 9 percent. Retrospective evaluation of naturalizing to gain or maintain access to government services, on the other hand, does not have a statistically significant effect on the likelihood of voting. These effects are found over and above the expected positive effects of age and higher income categories and the negative effects of residence in Texas (relative to residence in California). In this specification, education, gender, contact, and language spoken at home do not prove to be significant predictors of voting. The positive impact on voting of recalling having naturalized for political reasons remains even if the year of naturalization variable is added to the model. In the specification where it is added, year of naturalization does not achieve significance.

Table 5.6. Predictors of Voter Turnout among Naturalized Latino Registered Voters 2000 (Retrospective Evaluations of Reasons for Naturalizing among Latinos who Naturalized 1992 or After)

Independent Variable	Without Year of Naturalization B	SE	With Year of Naturalization B	SE
Demographic Characteristics				
Age	0.024*	0.014	0.025*	0.014
Education	-0.033	0.044	-0.032	0.045
Household Income ($15,000 or less)				
$15,000–$24,999	1.158**	0.587	1.134*	0.594
$25,000–$34,999	1.736**	0.787	1.747**	0.788
$35,000–$49,999	0.707	0.643	0.692	0.606
$50,000 or above	1.930**	0.795	1.906**	0.799
Don't know/refused	0.445	0.507	0.438	0.508
Gender (Men)				
Women	0.165	0.341	0.156	0.343
State of Residence (California)				
Florida	-0.590	0.518	-0.582	0.519
Illinois	-0.503	0.517	-0.489	0.520
New York	0.948	0.662	0.942	0.662
Texas	-0.923*	0.577	-0.932	0.579
Political Characteristics				
Contacted to register or vote (No)				
Yes	0.190	0.443	0.205	0.446
Immigration and Acculturation Characteristics				
Language spoken at home (Spanish)				
Both equally	-0.065	0.374	-0.051	0.378
English	-0.799	0.696	-0.794	0.697
Retrospective evaluations of reasons for naturalizing				
To receive government services	-0.052	0.059	-0.054	0.060
To establish or maintain political access	0.088**	0.042	0.090**	0.042
Years since naturalization			0.023	0.088
Constant	0.067	1.099	-46.746	176.15
-2 log likelihood	253.269		253.198	
Total cases	347		347	
Predicted correctly	85.6%		85.6%	

*** $p < 0.01$, ** $p < 0.05$; * $p < 0.10$.

Source: Tomás Rivera Policy Institute 2000 election Post-Election Survey, 2001. Sample drawn from California, Texas, New York, Florida, and Illinois.

LINKING PERIOD AND RETROSPECTIVE EVALUATIONS FOR NATURALIZING

I sought to bring these two sets of analysis, cohort and retrospective evaluations for naturalizing, together in a single model by looking at naturalizees in the 1993 to 2000 period and merging their year of naturalization with their evaluations of their reasons for naturalizing. Arguably, in the early period of this window—roughly 1993 to 1996—the primary focus of the national discussion about immigrants and naturalization focused on their political status. Growing out of California's debates about Proposition 187 (which did not directly challenge the rights of legal permanent residents or U.S. citizens), many sought to naturalize in order to gain political rights and challenge the nativist rhetoric that dominated the Proposition 187 debate. Later in the period, beginning roughly in 1996 with the congressional debate over the welfare reform legislation, many sought to naturalize to protect economic and legal rights and benefits. In an effort to test the combined impact of cohort and retrospective evaluations for reasons to naturalize, I disaggregated the respondents who naturalized between 1993 and 1996 *and* had a positive score of the scale of civic and political reasons for naturalizing. I hypothesized that these respondents were particularly political in their approach to naturalization and would be more likely to vote. I also identified respondents who naturalized between 1996 and 2000 *and* had a positive score on the scale of government services as reasons for naturalizing. I would expect these respondents to be less political and less likely to vote.

Ultimately, the interactions that sought to unify period effects and evaluation for reasons for naturalizing did not prove to be significant predictors of voting (models not reported here). While this could easily be dismissed as an interesting idea that did not prove fruitful, I think that it is worth mentioning briefly as an avenue for future research when more precise data become available. Unfortunately, I believe that my results may be confounded by the fact that the measurement of year is not as precise as would be necessary to absolutely dismiss the validity of this form of analysis. First, it is confounded by people's memories and the fact that naturalization could be awarded in one year and the ceremony could take place in another. More importantly, naturalization application processing delays in this period extended from the usual nine to twelve months to as long as thirty-six months in 1997 and 1998. Thus, the year of naturalization may not accurately reflect when an applicant was motivated to complete the application requirements, a better measure of the period that I am seeking to measure. So, while period or cohort effects are not amplified here by knowing why an immigrant believes that s/he sought to naturalize, I would encourage others to pursue this line in inquiry in the future.

■ ■ ■

At the beginning of the chapter, I asked the question of whether incorporative mechanisms are ensuring that the Latinos today who choose to become U.S. citizens are moving toward electoral participation. Many are, but this movement is far from universal, and the naturalized see many of the same barriers to their political participation and empowerment that U.S.-born citizens do. I come to this conclusion for two reasons. First, the demographic barriers that exclude all Americans from electoral participation appear to explain non-participation among Latino naturalized citizens as well. This finding should not be much of a surprise, but it suggests that naturalized citizens do not have a political socialization experience that differentiates their preparation for politics from the U.S. born. Although many naturalized citizens are older and, hence, benefit from the advantage of age in predicting voting, they generally tend to be less educated and have lower incomes, which works to their disadvantage. The composition of the Latino naturalized population will, then, be a continuing barrier to the political empowerment of the Latino community. Naturalization does not overcome these compositional effects.

Perhaps of greater concern is the second broad finding of this chapter, which speaks more directly to the question of incorporative mechanisms that reach out to immigrants and naturalized citizens. Duration of naturalization, rather than unique immigration/naturalization experiences, explains a great deal about the likelihood of voting in U.S. elections. The shared experiences and training of IRCA legalizees (moving from unauthorized to legal status and having to prepare for some of naturalization requirements well before naturalization) did not move those who chose citizenship closer to electoral participation. Nor did naturalization in an era where the political rights of immigrants were in the national debate. Instead, the evidence presented here would suggest that some key element of political learning begins with naturalization and takes a while to take effect. Thus, the somewhat atrophied mechanisms of political socialization that have slowly ebbed participation in the electorate as a whole would seem to also be present, or absent, among naturalized citizens. Instead, political knowledge is acquired slowly, and the confidence to participate in electoral (and other) politics only comes with time. Since many of the naturalized begin this process later than U.S.-born citizens, they will have fewer years of political engagement and their political voice will be more muted.

Only one exception to this pattern appears and that is among the Latino naturalized citizen registered voters who recall that they naturalized for political reasons. I am somewhat cautious about this finding because the retrospective evaluations may well reflect more about survey respondents' current feeling about politics rather than what they were thinking at the time of naturalization. Nevertheless, the political access scale does suggest that the evaluations of the importance of the series of political connections do distinguish some naturalized citizens from others in terms of the likelihood of voting. To the extent that this funding does actually reflect characteristics that were true at the time of naturalization, it would suggest the appropriate target for efforts to incorporate immigrants into U.S. politics. These efforts should focus on immigrants who have not yet naturalized and they should, in addition to offering them assistance with the bureaucracy of the naturalization application, ensure that immigrants clearly see their connections to U.S. politics, to the rights of citizenship, and to their own roles in ensuring that they and their families can exercise these rights. To the extent that naturalizing citizens understand that naturalization confers these rights as well as certain protections, it would appear that they are more likely to exercise the right to vote.

NOTES

I would like to express my appreciation to the Tomás Rivera Policy Institute for use of the data analyzed here. I would also like to thank Frank Bean for comments on an earlier draft of this chapter.

1. Although immigrant children can naturalize as part of their parents' naturalization, immigrants under the age of eighteen do not need to naturalize. Instead, they can become citizens administratively after their parents' naturalization. Instead of formally applying for a Certificate of Citizenship for minor children after naturalization, a recently naturalized parent can apply for a passport in the name of the minor child and that child will have become a U.S. citizen for all intents and purposes. This is cheaper and is often recommended by the Immigration and Naturalization Service/Bureau of Citizenship and Immigration Services. It does, however, create the potential that some immigrants who think that they naturalized as part of their parents' naturalization have not or cannot prove that they are U.S. citizens (Chardy 2006).

2. Several other studies analyzing registered voters in Southern California find higher rates of participation among the naturalized than the native-born. I discuss these studies—and my suspicions about why their findings differ from the national patterns—later in this chapter.

3. I use the terms Latino and Hispanic interchangeably to identify individuals residing in the United States who trace their origin or ancestry to the Spanish-speaking countries of Latin America or the Caribbean.

4. This analysis can only speak to the Latino experience. I am not aware of any data that would allow for a discussion of the political behaviors of non-Latino immigrants who naturalized in the mid- to late-1990s. Latinos make up about 40 percent of immigrants to permanent residence and approximately 35 percent of naturalizing citizens. Jasso and Rosenzweig (1990) find that immigrants from Mexico are less likely than average to naturalize than nationals of other large immigrant-sending countries, controlling for other immigration-related factors. Portes and Mozo (1985) find that immigrants from Canada and Mexico are less likely to naturalize than nationals of other countries, controlling for sociodemographic factors. Finally, controlling for sociodemographic, associational, and immigration-related factors, DeSipio (1996a) finds that among Latinos, Cubans and Dominicans are more likely than Mexicans to begin the naturalization process and, once they began the process, to become U.S. citizens.

5. The experiences from the 1920s and early 1930s are not the only historical examples of the political influence of the naturalized. Thomas Jefferson's 1800 victory in New York State is attributed to the immigrant vote (Muller 1993, 21). Erie finds that the urban machines relied on naturalization to swell

voter roles and win several elections: the 1868 New York gubernatorial race and mayoral races in the 1870s and early 1880s (1988, 51–53).

6. While the Current Population Survey is always subject to over-reporting (as, for that matter, are all surveys that rely on self-reporting of registration and voting), the 1996 election might have triggered higher than average rates of over-reporting, particularly among Latino respondents (Shaw, de la Garza, and Lee 2000).

7. The TRPI survey does not offer other measures that could be used to measure acculturation. Traditionally, a gap such as this can be overcome by using years of U.S. residence or share of life spent in the United States as controls. Unfortunately, both of these measures are highly correlated with "years since naturalization" and the two period measures this chapter tests. As a result, I include language spoken at home as my primary acculturation measure.

8. To further test this question, I ran a specification of the model with state/source of citizenship interaction terms, so that naturalized respondents in California (and in each of the other states) were compared to all other respondents. This model offers substantively similar results to the model presented here with Texas naturalized citizens less likely to vote, but none of the other states' naturalized citizens achieving statistical significance.

REFERENCES

Aleinikoff, T. Alexander. 2000. "Between Principles and Politics: U.S. Citizenship Policy." In *From Migrants to Citizens: Membership in a Changing World,* edited by T. Alexander Aleinikoff and Douglas Klusmeyer, 119–74. Washington, DC: Brookings Institution Press.

Andersen, Kristi. 1979. *The Creation of a Democratic Majority, 1928–1936.* Chicago: University of Chicago Press.

Baker, Bryan C. 2010. *Naturalization Rates Among IRCA Immigrants: A 2009 Update.* Washington, DC: Department of Homeland Security, Office of Immigration Statistics.

Barreto, Matt A. 2005. "Latino Immigrants at the Polls: Foreign-Born Voter Turnout in the 2002 Election." *Political Research Quarterly* 58 (1): 79–86.

Barreto, Matt A., and José Muñoz. 2003. "Reexamining the Politics of In-Between: Political Participation among Mexican Immigrants in the United States." *Hispanic Journal of the Behavioral Sciences* 25 (4): 427–47.

Bass, Loretta E., and Lynne M. Casper. 1999. "Are There Differences in Registration and Voting Behavior between Naturalized and Native-born Americans?" U.S. Census Bureau, Population Division Working Paper 28.

http://www.census.gov/population/www/documentation/twps0028/
twps0028.html. Last accessed February 22, 2006.

Bean, Frank, Rodolfo Corona, Rodolfo Tuiran, Karen Woodrow-Lafield, and
Jennifer Van Hook. 2001. "Circular, Invisible, and Ambiguous Migrants:
Components of Difference in Estimates of the Number of Unauthorized
Mexican Migrants in the United States." *Demography* 38 (3): 411–22.

Bean, Frank, Jennifer Van Hook, and Karen Woodrow-Lafield. 2001. "Estimates of Unauthorized Migrants Residing in the United States: The Total,
Mexican, and Non-Mexican Central American Unauthorized Populations
in Mid-2001." Washington, DC: Pew Hispanic Center. http://www
.pewhispanic.org/site/docs/pdf/study_-_frank_bean.pdf. Last accessed
August 21, 2002.

Chardy, Alfonso. 2006. "Citizenship Claims are Questioned: U.S. Residents
Claim to Derive Citizenship from Naturalized Parents are Detained Because they Lack Papers to Prove their Status." *Miami Herald,* February 22.

Cohen, Lizabeth. 1990. *Making a New Deal: Industrial Workers in Chicago,
1919–1939.* New York: Cambridge University Press.

de la Garza, Rodolfo O. 1997. "Foreign Policy Comes Home: The Domestic
Consequences of The Program for Mexican Communities Living in Foreign Countries." In *Bridging the Border: Transforming Mexico-U.S. Relations,* edited by Rodolfo O. de la Garza and Jesus Velasco, 69–88. Boulder:
Rowman and Littlefield.

DeSipio, Louis. 1996a. *Counting on the Latino Vote: Latinos as a New Electorate.* Charlottesville: University Press of Virginia.

———. 1996b. "After Proposition 187 the Deluge: Reforming Naturalization
Administration while Making Good Citizens." *Harvard Journal of Hispanic Policy* 9: 7–24.

———. 1996c. "Making Citizens or Good Citizens? Naturalization as a Predictor of Organizational and Electoral Behavior among Latino Immigrants." *Hispanic Journal of Behavioral Sciences* 18 (2): 194–213.

———. 2001. "Building America, One Person at a Time: Naturalization and
Political Behavior of the Naturalized in Contemporary U.S. Politics." In
E Pluribus Unum? Immigrant, Civic Life, and Political Incorporation, edited
by John Mollenkopf and Gary Gerstle, 67–106. New York: Russell Sage
Foundation.

DeSipio, Louis, and Rodolfo O. de la Garza. 1998. *Making Americans Remaking America: Immigration and Immigrant Policy.* Boulder: Westview Press.

———. 2005. "Between Symbolism and Influence: Latinos and the 2000
Election." In *Muted Voices: Latinos and the 2000 Elections,* edited by Ro-
dolfo de la Garza and Louis DeSipio, 13–60. Lanham: Rowman and
Littlefield.

DeSipio, Louis, Natalie Masuoka, and Christopher Stout. 2008. "Asian
American Immigrants as the New Electorate: Exploring Turnout and Reg-

istration of a Growing Community." *Asian American Policy Review* 17: 51–71.

Erie, Steven P. 1988. *Rainbow's End: Irish Americans and the Dilemmas of Urban Machine Politics, 1840–1985*. Berkeley: University of California Press.

Fraga, Luis, Ricardo Ramírez, and Gary Segura. 2005. "Unquestioned Influence: Latinos and the 2000 Elections in California." In *Muted Voices: Latinos and the 2000 Elections,* edited by Rodolfo de la Garza and Louis DeSipio, 173–93. Lanham: Rowman and Littlefield.

Gamm, Gerald H. 1986. *The Making of New Deal Democrats: Voting Behavior and Realignment in Boston, 1920–1940*. Chicago: University of Chicago Press.

González-Gutiérrez, Carlos. 1999. "Fostering Identities: Mexico's Relations with Its Diaspora." *Journal of American History* 86 (2): 545–67.

Hill, Kevin, and Dario Moreno. 1996. "Second-Generation Cubans." *Hispanic Journal of Behavioral Sciences* 18 (2): 175–93.

Jasso, Guillermina, and Mark R. Rosenzweig. 1990. *The New Chosen People: Immigrants in the United States*. New York: Russell Sage Foundation.

Jones-Correa, Michael. 2000. "Under Two Flags: Dual Nationality in Latin America and Its Consequences for the United States." Cambridge, MA: David Rockefeller Center for Latin American Studies.

Levitt, Melissa, and David Olson. 1996. "Immigration and Political Incorporation: But Do They Vote?" Paper prepared for presentation at the 1996 Northeastern Political Science Association Meeting. Boston, November.

Lien, Pei-te, M. Margaret Conway, and Janelle Wong. 2004. *The Politics of Asian Americans: Diversity and Community*. New York: Routledge.

Minnite, Lorraine C., Jennifer Holdaway, and Ronald Hayduk. 1999. "Political Incorporation of Immigrants in New York." Paper prepared for delivery at the 1999 Annual Meeting of the American Political Science Association. Atlanta, September.

Mollenkopf, John, David Olson, and Tim Ross. 2001. "Immigrant Political Participation in New York and Los Angeles." In *Governing Cities,* edited by Michael Jones-Correa, 17–70. New York: Russell Sage Foundation.

Muller, Thomas. 1993. *Immigrants and the American City*. New York: New York University Press.

NALEO Educational Fund. 2004. "Four Million Latino Legal Permanent Residents Eligible for U.S. Citizenship as Exorbitant Fee Hike Takes Effect." Press Release. Los Angeles: NALEO Educational Fund. April 30.

Pachon, Harry, Matt Barreto, and Frances Marquez. 2005. "Latino Politics Comes of Age: Latino Politics in the Golden State." In *Muted Voices: Latinos and the 2000 Elections,* edited by Rodolfo de la Garza and Louis DeSipio, 84–100. Lanham: Rowman and Littlefield.

Pantoja, Adrian, Ricardo Ramírez, and Gary M. Segura. 2001. "Citizens by Choice, Voters by Necessity: Patterns in Political Mobilization by Naturalized Latinos." *Political Research Quarterly* 54 (4): 729–50.

Passel, Jeffrey. 2005. *Estimates of the Size and Characteristics of the Undocumented Population.* Washington, DC: Pew Hispanic Center.

Portes, Alejandro, and Rafael Mozo. 1985. "Naturalization, Registration, and Voting Patterns of Cubans and Other Ethnic Minorities: A Preliminary Analysis." In *Proceedings of the First National Conference on Citizenship and the Hispanic Community,* edited by the NALEO Educational Fund. Washington, DC: NALEO Educational Fund.

Rytina, Nancy. 2002. "IRCA Legalization Effects: Lawful Permanent Residence and Naturalization through 2001." Paper presented at conference entitled: The Effects of Immigrant Legalization Programs on the United States: Scientific Evidence on Immigrant Adaptation and Impacts on the U.S. Economy and Society. National Institutes of Health. October 25.

Shaw, Daron, Rodolfo O. de la Garza, and Jongho Lee. 2000. "Examining Latino Turnout in 1996: A Three-State Validated Survey Approach." *American Journal of Political Science* 44 (2): 332–40.

Tomás Rivera Policy Institute. 2001. *Reinventing the Naturalization Process at INS: For Better or Worse.* Claremont: Tomás Rivera Policy Institute.

Tuckel, Peter, and Richard Maisel. 1994. "Voter Turnout among European Immigrants to the United States." *Journal of Interdisciplinary History* 24 (3): 407–30.

U.S. Bureau of the Census. 1993. "The Foreign-Born Population by Race, Hispanic Origin, and Citizenship for the United States and States." CPH-L-134. Washington, DC: U.S. Bureau of the Census.

———. 2002. "Voting and Registration in the Election of November 2000: Detailed Tables." Washington, DC: U.S. Bureau of the Census. http://www.census.gov/population/www/socdemo/voting/p20-542.html. Last accessed February 22, 2006.

———. 2003. "The Foreign-Born Population: 2000: Census 2000 Brief. C2KBR–34." Washington, DC: U.S. Bureau of the Census. http://www.census.gov/prod/2003pubs/c2kbr-34.pdf. Last accessed February 22, 2006.

———. 2004. "Foreign-Born Population of the United States Current Population Survey–March 2003: Detailed Tables (PPL-174)." Washington, DC: U.S. Bureau of the Census. http://www.census.gov/population/www/socdemo/foreign/ppl-174.html. Last accessed July 15, 2010.

———. 2005. "Voting and Registration in the Election of November 2004: Detailed Tables." Washington, DC: U.S. Bureau of the Census. http://www.census.gov/population/www/socdemo/voting/cps2004.html. Last accessed February 22, 2006.

U.S. Department of Homeland Security. 2006. *Yearbook of Immigration Statistics 2004*. Washington, DC: U.S. Department of Homeland Security, Office of Immigration Statistics.

U.S. Immigration and Naturalization Service. 1999. *1997 Statistical Yearbook of the Immigration and Naturalization Service*. Springfield: National Technical Information Service.

———. 2003. *2002 Statistical Yearbook of the Immigration and Naturalization Service*. Springfield: National Technical Information Service.

S I X

At Home Abroad?

The Dominican Diaspora in New York City
as a Transnational Political Actor

A D R I A N   D .   P A N T O J A

Although American diplomatic history is replete with examples of ethnic minorities shaping American foreign policy, the participation of Latinos as transnational political actors has not received serious scholarly attention. This may be due in part to the belief that aside from Cuban Americans (Fernández 1987), most other Latinos are preoccupied with domestic issues and lack the organizations and resources necessary to shape American foreign policy or be involved in the politics of their home countries (Rendón 1981; Cohen 2000). However, in the past two decades the expansion of the Congressional Hispanic Caucus, a new wave of Latin American immigrants, and intense outreach efforts by Latin American countries toward their diasporas have provided Latinos with a greater opportunity to participate in the politics of their home countries (Jones-Correa 2001, 1998; Shain 1999, 2000).

This study explores the emergence of Latinos as transnational political actors by analyzing the Dominican diaspora in New York City. Dominicans are one of the fastest growing Latino ethnic groups in the

182

United States and have long been noted for having vigorous ties to the ancestral homeland. The Dominican population dramatically grew from 170,817 in 1980 to 1,041,910 in 2000. By 2010, they were projected to overtake the Cuban population to become the third largest Latino group in the United States, below Mexicans and Puerto Ricans (Hernández and Rivera-Batiz 2003), although they ultimately did not. Although studies on Dominicans characterize the diaspora as one that has sustained intense transnational networks with the homeland (De-Sipio and Pantoja 2007; Duany 2002, 1994; Levitt 2001; Pessar 1995; Hendricks 1974), these ties are largely analyzed along an economic (Portes and Guarnizo 1991; Grasmuck and Pessar 1991) or socialcultural dimension (Levitt 1998; Duany 1994), with little attention paid to their transnational political networks (Itzigsohn 2000). Indeed, political scientists and other social scientists have not paid sufficient attention to Dominican political participation in the United States and abroad. Without question, this diaspora has become an important agent of economic and social change in the Dominican Republic (Levitt 1998; Grasmuck and Pessar 1991). To what extent are they likely to become agents of political change? This study considers the prospect of the Dominican diaspora as an agent of political change in the Dominican Republic by examining the factors that foster or mitigate their political participation in the politics of the Dominican Republic.

The analysis for this study is based on a unique survey of 413 Dominicans residing in Washington Heights, New York City. Unlike previous works on Dominicans and other diasporas which have largely been based on participant observation or interviews with a limited number of individuals, surveys with randomly selected samples have the advantage of allowing researchers to make more concrete generalizations about the population. While Dominicans are settling in states throughout the East Coast, the heart of the diaspora in the United States remains in New York City (see Table 6.1). New York City is home to 53 percent of the diaspora in the United States or 552,212 Dominicans. The city has the second largest concentration of Dominicans outside of the Dominican capital of Santo Domingo. Within New York City, the largest settlement is in a neighborhood in upper Manhattan known as Washington Heights or *Quisqueya Heights* (Quisqueya being the indigenous name of the Dominican Republic).

Table 6.1. Geographical Distribution of Dominicans by State

Total	1,041,910	100%
New York State	617,901	59.3%
(New York City)	(554,638)	(53.2%)
New Jersey	136,529	13.1%
Florida	98,410	9.4%
Massachusetts	69,502	6.7%
Rhode Island	24,588	2.4%
Pennsylvania	13,667	1.3%
Connecticut	12,830	1.2%
Other States	68,483	6.6%

Source: 2000 U.S. Bureau of the Census.

LATIN AMERICAN DIASPORAS: INFLUENTIAL TRANSNATIONAL POLITICAL ACTORS?

The failure of policymakers to develop and articulate an international grand strategy for the post-Cold War era led some scholars to argue that diasporas or "ethnic lobbies" were playing an influential role in shaping American foreign policy and were in part responsible for its lack of coherence (Clough 1994; Smith 2000). One of the most prominent opponents of ethnic involvement in international affairs is Samuel Huntington. Writing in 1997 in the journal *Foreign Affairs,* Huntington argued that several overlapping forces were leading contemporary diasporas to place their homelands' interests above those of the United States. Foremost among them were the rise in diasporas from non-European countries, challenges to the assimilationist paradigm in favor of one that embraced multiculturalism, and growing transnational ties between contemporary diasporas and their home countries. Most recently, Huntington proffered that Latin American diasporas, in particular those from Mexico, pose the greatest threat to American national identity, a precursor for having a cohesive foreign policy (Huntington 2004a, 2004b).

Whether foreign attachments and ethnic participation in the foreign policy-making process are a threat to U.S. interests has long concerned scholars and policymakers (Smith 2000). Huntington was not the first to raise concerns over ethnic involvement in foreign affairs. However, his writings were a departure from previous research on Latin American diasporas that generally emphasized their lack of interest and influence in foreign affairs, Cuban Americans being the exception (Rendón 1981). Latin America's ambivalence and at times outright hostility toward its expatriates further reinforced the belief that transnational networks in the hemisphere remained underdeveloped. However, several factors in the past two decades have led to the development and expansion of transnational ties between Latin American nations and their respective diasporas in the United States. These trends are most visible among the Mexican diaspora (Shain 1999, 2000; de la Garza 1980; Bustamante 1986).

The Mexican Diaspora

For decades Mexico viewed its diaspora north of the border as an inconsequential actor in American politics. As a result, few if any formal ties existed between the diaspora and Mexican state (Bustamante 1986). Beginning in the late 1970s under President Luis Echeverria Alvarez, Mexico began a policy of *acercamiento* or rapprochement as a result of the growing political influence of Mexican Americans in American politics and, more importantly, Mexico's dependence on immigrant remittances (Shain 1999, 2000). In 2003, Mexicans in the United States remitted $12 billion to families back home. Remittances constitute the largest source of foreign income, surpassing tourism, foreign investment, and exported oil.

The importance of the Mexican diaspora as a foreign policy actor and to Mexico's economic security was noted in the early 1990s when Mexican officials lobbied the Congressional Hispanic Caucus (CHC) and other Latino organizations to support the North American Free Trade Agreement (NAFTA). In addition, Mexico began institutionalizing a variety of economic, social, and cultural programs aimed at strengthening relations with their diaspora. These programs were administered through the Program for Mexican Communities Abroad

(PCME), an office out of the Secretary of Foreign Affairs (Figueroa-Aramoni 1999). The ultimate sign that relations between Mexico and Mexican Americans were entering a new era came in 1998 when Mexico extended the rights of dual nationality to its compatriots in the United States, affording many Mexican Americans the rights of Mexican citizenship and a greater voice in the affairs of Mexico.

Economic necessity is behind Mexico's rapprochement with its diaspora in the United States. While the diaspora is an important economic actor in Mexico, it remains to be seen whether it will be an important political actor. Mexico's outreach efforts have not been entirely rebuffed, but neither have they been entirely embraced; less than 67,000 Mexicans applied for dual nationality in the years immediately after its inception (Associated Press 2003). This ambivalence may be largely a result of decades of neglect by Mexican officials. Nonetheless, Mexico is not unique in its efforts. In the last two decades, other Latin American countries have undertaken similar outreach efforts toward their diasporas. Perhaps no other U.S.-based Latin American diaspora has responded as positively to these initiatives as Dominicans.

The Dominican Diaspora

The extant research on Dominicans suggests that ties between the Dominican Republic and their diaspora parallel those of Mexico and Mexican Americans. Until the 1980s, Dominican transnational political networks were virtually nonexistent. However, as the volume and value of remittances boomed during a period of economic stagnation, the Dominican government became more interested and active in the affairs of the diaspora. For the Dominican Republic, remittances from abroad, which average close to 2 billion annually, constitute the second largest source of foreign exchange behind tourism (Duany 2002). According to Lizardo (2001), about 19.4 percent of all Dominican households receive remittances from abroad.

The election of Salvador Jorge Blanco in 1982 signaled a shift in policy toward the diaspora. Since the 1970s, Dominicans in the United States wanted the Dominican Republic to recognize dual nationality and secure the right of immigrants to vote by absentee ballot in Dominican elections. The Dominican constitution stipulated that any national who obtained another nationality would lose their Dominican nationality. Recognizing the economic and growing political importance of its émigrés, Blanco was sympathetic to their request for an amendment recognizing dual nationality, as well as expatriate voting. The diaspora had also become an important source of campaign contributions to candidates and parties in the Dominican Republic. Some accounts suggest that as much as 10 to 15 percent of overall party fundraising came from abroad (Graham 1997). To varying degrees, each of the three major political parties—the PRD (Partido Revolucionario Dominicano), PLD (Partido de la Liberación Dominicana), and PRSC (Partido Reformista Social Cristiano)—have established offices in Washington Heights and other Dominican enclaves in the East Coast.

President Blanco's attempts to have the legislature change the constitution failed. Nonetheless, his efforts signaled the beginning of a new attitude and policy toward the diaspora. In 1990, the Senate formed the non-partisan Committee on the Affairs of Dominicans Living Abroad. Its principle aim was to explore the issue of dual nationality. Exchanges between this and other entities on the island and within the diaspora continued throughout the 1990s, and in 1994 the constitution was re-formed to recognize dual nationality (Graham 1997). A year later, Congress passed a bill allowing émigrés to participate in Dominican elections and hold elective office (Levitt 2001). In addition, some Dominican officials have proposed creating a seat in the Dominican Congress that would represent the diaspora in New York City (Levitt 2001). This idea is widely popular among the diaspora; the survey used in this study found that 80 percent of respondents favored this proposal.

Latin American Transnational Ties

The need for remittances and having a voice in American politics has led other Latin American countries to forge closer ties with their diasporas. Recognition of dual nationality is among the most visible signs by an immigrant-sending country that it wishes to maintain ties with their diasporas. In the last two decades, Peru (1980), El Salvador (1983), Colombia (1991), the Dominican Republic (1994), Costa Rica (1995),

Ecuador (1995), Mexico (1996), and Brazil (1996) have extended dual nationality to their émigrés (Jones-Correa 2001). Some Latin American countries have considered extending dual nationality to children of émigrés born in the United States to ensure transnational ties continue into the second generation and beyond. While Huntington views the ascendance of Latin American transnationalism with alarm, others take a more optimistic position by arguing that diasporas can use transnational networks to transmit American values and interests abroad (Shain 1999). Yet, the reality remains that aside from anecdotal accounts little is known about the nature and strength of contemporary Latino transnational political ties (Guarnizo, Portes, and Haller 2003). In fact, some continue to portray the Latino diaspora as an inactive transnational political actor (Lindsay 2002; Cohen 2000). For example, James Lindsay in 2002 wrote regarding Latinos:

> Economic hardship, together with the lack of either an exile mentality or a threat, explains why, Cuban Americans aside, Latino organizations usually sit on the sidelines of foreign policy. Groups such as the National Council of La Raza and the Mexican American Legal Defense and Educational Fund have concentrated their focus on the economy, civil rights, and immigration because those are the issues that matter most to their members. Given the economic challenges facing the Hispanic community today and the relative security that most Latin American countries enjoy, foreign policy is not likely to galvanise Latinos any time soon (2002, 3–4).

To proffer a more systematic analysis of Latino political ties with their home countries, some political scientists have recently opted to use surveys with large randomly drawn samples (Barreto and Muñoz 2003; DeSipio 2003; DeSipio and Pantoja 2007). In a 1997 survey of 454 Latino elites, respondents were asked to rank a series of policy issues according to importance. Five of the top six were domestic issues, supporting the contention that Latinos' priorities are domestically rather than internationally oriented (de la Garza, Pachon, and Pantoja 2000). A 2002 survey on Mexican, Salvadoran, Puerto Rican, and

Cuban migrants also found that most were not engaged in transnational political projects (DeSipio 2003; DeSipio and Pantoja 2007). Nonetheless, among the four Latino migrant groups analyzed, it was Dominicans who had developed stronger transnational political networks. Unfortunately, these studies did not consider the reasons why Dominicans have developed more intense transnational connections. Dominicans' strong ties to the homeland, coupled with high levels of immigration warrant a closer examination of this population since their experiences can provide insights into the evolution of transnational political ties in the Western Hemisphere.

Changing Flags? The Role of U.S. Citizenship

One of the most important factors for understanding the evolution of transnational political networks is the acquisition of U.S. citizenship. U.S. citizenship is a precursor for participation in U.S. electoral politics and having a meaningful voice in shaping American foreign policy. As Mathias (1981, 979) notes, "None of the ethnic groups that have wielded significant influence on American foreign policy acquired political clout on the day its members disembarked even when they disembarked in considerable numbers." Immigrants acquired a meaningful voice in foreign affairs by "first forming themselves into voting blocs to be cultivated by those in the existing power structures, then joining the power structure themselves." Although Latino naturalization rates have lagged significantly behind other immigrant groups, in the 1990s these rates dramatically grew as a result of changes in U.S. immigration law and a general rise in anti-immigrant rhetoric and policies (Jones-Correa 1998). This rise in Latino naturalization rates coincides with the extension of dual nationality provisions by Latin American governments.

Dual citizenship was designed to encourage diasporas to become influential actors in American politics while maintaining their ties with the homeland (Jones-Correa 1998, 2001). In an often-quoted speech on the benefits of dual nationality, Dominican President Lionel Fernandez urged the diaspora to pursue U.S. citizenship "with a peaceful conscience, for you will continue being Dominicans, and we will welcome you as such when you set foot on the soil of our republic"

(Rohter 1996). Yet, U.S. citizenship may have contradictory effects on transnational political ties. On the one hand, U.S. citizenship enables immigrants to have a greater voice in American politics and the direction of U.S. foreign policy toward the homeland. On the other hand, U.S. citizenship, typically acquired by socially and economically assimilated immigrants, may dampen ties with the country of ancestry. Hence, diasporas with U.S. citizenship will have a greater opportunity to influence U.S. foreign policy, yet because citizenship acquisition historically signifies a shift in immigrants' allegiance and commitment to the receiving country, naturalized diasporas may have little interest in the affairs of the ancestral homeland. Most studies on Latino transnational ties are largely based on samples of immigrants who have yet to become U.S. citizens, thus it remains unclear whether U.S. citizenship fosters or depresses transnational political ties. To address this limitation, the survey used in this study includes a quota to ensure that half of the respondents were U.S. citizens.

DATA AND ANALYSES

In the winter of 2003, a survey tapping transnational political ties was randomly administered by telephone to 413 Dominicans residing in Washington Heights, New York City. As noted before, Washington Heights is the largest Dominican enclave in the United States and is an area of intense transnational activity (Duany 1994). The survey included a quota to ensure that half of the respondents were U.S. citizens. Out of the 213 U.S. citizens, 169 (79 percent) are naturalized citizens and 44 (21 percent) are U.S.-born citizens.

Transmigration research is noted for its theoretical and conceptual ambiguity. The degree to which migrants are transnationally involved is dependent on whether one employs a narrow or broad definition of "transnational" (Jones-Correa 2002). Within the political sphere, transnational ties typically take on three forms: (1) participation in home-country associations or clubs, (2) direct participation in the politics of the home-country, and (3) indirect political involvement through lobbying U.S. foreign policymakers. Because Dominicans are largely immigrants and have yet to acquire a meaningful voice in American politics, the survey did not include questions asking whether individuals had engaged in lobbying and other political activities designed to influence American foreign policy. Nonetheless, the survey captures *direct* involvement in the two transnational political activities. Specifically, respondents were asked whether they had engaged in any of the following activities in the past three years:

1. Have you been a member of an organization or club that is mostly concerned with issues in the Dominican Republic?
2. Have you ever tried to help out a candidate or political party win office in the Dominican Republic either by donating money, campaigning, voting, or through some other political activity?

Table 6.2 reports the frequency of respondent engagement in each of these activities. Responses are divided by citizenship status.

Contrary to scholars who argue that transnational ties among Latinos remain underdeveloped, the table reveals that a significant portion of Dominicans in Washington Heights are involved in transnational political projects. About 17 percent participate in associations or clubs concerned with events in the Dominican Republic, 21 percent have tried to help candidates or political parties win office in the Dominican Republic, and 10 percent were active in both types of transnational political activities. These percentages may not seem large, but they clearly surpass Latino rates of non-electoral participation in U.S. politics (Hero and Campbell 1996; see also Leal 2002).

Clearly, being a U.S. citizen has a significant impact on transnational political ties. In each instance, U.S. citizens were less likely to be politically involved abroad. Although the differences between citizens and non-citizens are not statistically significant when it comes to participation in home-country organizations (F 0.66, prob>.4174), the differences are significant when it comes to helping a candidate or party win office in the Dominican Republic and participating in the two activities (F 8.44, prob>.0039; F 3.98, prob>.0466).

There is preliminary evidence indicating that the acquisition of U.S. citizenship by naturalization, or simply being born in the United

Table 6.2. Transnational Political Ties among Dominicans in Washington Heights, New York City

Belong to an organization concerned with issues in the Dominican Republic		
Citizens	Non-Citizens	All respondents
N = 213	N = 200	N = 413
16.0%	19.0%	17.4%
(34)	(38)	(72)
Help a candidate or party win office in the Dominican Republic		
Citizens	Non-Citizens	All respondents
15.0%	26.5%	20.6%
(32)	(53)	(85)
Participate in Both Activities		
Citizens	Non-Citizens	All respondents
7.5%	13.5%	10.4%
(16)	(27)	(43)

Source: 2003 Dominican/NYC Survey.

States, has a depressing effect on transnational political ties among Dominicans. Of course, being a U.S. citizen alone does not explain the involvement, or lack thereof, of disaporas in transnational political projects. Any number of individual sociodemographic and political factors may also have significant influences on the forging of transnational political ties. In order to understand the correlates of Dominicans transnational political participation, multivariate analysis is used to isolate the relevant predictors and assess their relative causal importance. While no study can claim to provide a comprehensive treatment of all the factors associated with transnational political practices, an attempt is made to include predictors commonly identified as significant by qualitative scholarship.

The multivariate models include fourteen predictors. Four predictors fall under the category of individual demographic characteristics. These include a respondent's age, education, gender (female), and length of U.S. residency. The variable *Age* is a continuous variable ranging from 18 to 86 years. *Education* is a categorical variable with 0 for "No schooling to Grade 8," (1) for "Some high school (grade 9–12)," (2) "High school graduate," (3) "Some college/vocational (technical) school," (4) "College graduate (BA, BS)," and (5) for "Graduate degree (MA, MS, Ph.D., MD, JD, and so on)." *Gender* is a dichotomous measure with 1 for "female" and 0 for "male." *Length of U.S. Residency* measures the length in years of continuous residency in the United States. Latinos with greater socioeconomic resources (age and education) tend to participate in politics at high rates (Pantoja, Ramirez, and Segura 2001; Barreto and Muñoz 2003; Barreto 2004). It follows that these same resources are likely to contribute to higher levels of transnational political engagement. I am agnostic as to the effects being a female or length of U.S. residency will have on transnational political engagement.

A variable measuring discrimination toward Dominicans is included. Responses range from 0 "not at all" to 3 "a lot." Diasporas experiencing widespread ethnic or racial discrimination are likely to view the environment in the host country as alien and hostile, leading them to feel more at home abroad than in the United States. Consequently, scholars argue that experiences with discrimination contribute to the creation and strengthening of transnational networks (Pessar 1995). Among the sample, 51 percent indicated there was "some" to "a lot" of discrimination against Dominicans. The variable *Discrimination* is hypothesized to have a positive effect on transnational political ties.

The models include two factors traditionally associated with participation in U.S. electoral politics—internal political efficacy and external political efficacy. Internal political efficacy can be defined as "a sense of personal competence in one's ability to understand politics," while external political efficacy can be defined as "a sense that one's political activities can influence what the government actually does" (Rosenstone and Hansen 1993, 15). The survey includes two questions capturing feelings of internal and external political efficacy toward government and politics in the Dominican Republic. Specifically, respondents were asked whether they agreed or disagreed with the following statements: "Sometimes the politics and government of the Dominican Republic seem to be so complicated that a person like me can't really understand what's going on" and "People like me don't have any say about what the government in the Dominican Republic does." Both are coded on a five-point scale, capturing the inefficacious response, or 0 for "strongly disagree" to 4 for "strongly agree." Having inefficacious feelings toward government and politics in the Dominican Republic is hypothesized to have a negative effect on transnational political participation.

Four factors drawn from qualitative research on immigrant transnationalism are included: the so-called "myth of return" ideology; affective feelings toward the home country; frequent visits to the country of origin; and having a transnational family. The variable *Myth of Return* is drawn from the work of Jones-Correa (1998), who contends that the desire to return to the country of origin is a powerful belief shaping immigrant political behavior. In the survey respondents were asked: "How likely is it that you will return to the Dominican Republic to live." The variable takes on a four-point range with (0) for "Not at all likely," (1) "Not very likely," (2) "Somewhat likely," and (3) for "Very likely." Affective feelings toward the home country are captured by the variable *Love the DR*. Respondents were asked, "How strong is your love for the Dominican Republic?" The measure ranges from 0 "not very strong" to 3 "extremely strong." The variable *Visits Abroad* is a measure of the number of times a respondent has traveled to the Dominican Republic. The variable is a categorical variable, with 0 for "never," (1) "less than once a year," (2) "once a year," (3) "twice a year," (4) "three times a year," and (5) for "more than three times a year." Finally, I include a variable measuring the presence of a transnational family. Specifically, I ask whether most of their family resides in the United States or the Dominican Republic. The variable *Family in U.S.* is dichotomous, 1 for respondents whose families mostly reside in the United States and 0 for families who mostly reside in the Dominican Republic. Individuals who desire to return to the home country, have a strong affective connection with the home country, or make frequent visits to the Dominican Republic are more likely to participate in the politics of the Dominica Republic. Having most of one's family in the United States is likely to have the converse effect.

As noted earlier some Dominican officials have proposed creating a seat in the Dominican Congress that would represent the diaspora in New York City (Levitt 2001). The survey asked respondents "Would you be in favor or opposed to the creation of a legislative seat in the Dominican Congress that would represent Dominicans in New York City?" This idea is popular among the diaspora, with 80 percent of the survey's respondents favoring the proposal. The model includes the variable *Dominican Legislative Seat* to capture the effect of this attitude on fostering participation in the politics of the Dominican Republic. It is anticipated that individuals who are in favor of transnational political representation will also be more politically engaged abroad.

There is interest among scholars in examining the nexus between transnational political ties and immigrant incorporation in U.S. politics (Jones-Correa 1998). The model examines the reciprocal effect, whether civic engagement in the United States depresses or fosters transnational political participation. The variable *U.S. Civic Engagement* is a five-point scale based on six questions asking respondents whether they had engaged in any of these activities in the past three years: (1) signed a petition regarding an issue or problem that concerns you; (2) written or called a New York City public official or United States public official about a concern or problem; (3) worn a campaign button, put a political sticker on your car or a sign in your window or in front of your house on behalf of a New York City candidate or United States candidate; (4) gone to any political meetings, rallies, or speeches over a political issue, a New York City candidate, or a United States candidate; (5) contributed money to a New York City candidate, United States candidate or political party and (6) worked with others to try to solve some problem affecting the city or neighborhood? Although Guarnizo (2001, 214) argues that "participation in more than one nation-state is a chief characteristic of contemporary transnational practices," researchers have yet to empirically demonstrate whether participation in U.S. politics coexists or competes with political participation in the country of origin.

Finally, the multivariate model includes a measure of citizenship status—*U.S. Citizens*. What effect does U.S. citizenship have in shaping transnational political behaviors? The evidence presented here suggests that it has a dampening effect across the two transnational political activities investigated by this study. Does this relationship hold true under multivariate scrutiny? If it does, how are Dominican transnational political ties likely to change over time as more immigrants come to acquire U.S. citizenship? In order to reach more definitive answers on the effects of U.S. citizenship and other factors in structuring Dominican transnational political ties, this chapter will now discuss the results of the multivariate models.

The transnational political activities listed in Table 6.2 serve as dependent variables in the analyses. Since the dependent variables are dichotomous, logistic regression analysis is used to estimate the effects of the 14 selected independent variables on participation in hometown associations (Model I); direct participation in the politics of the Dominican Republic (Model II); and participation in both transnational political activities (Model III). Table 6.3 reports two sets of results; (1) the logistic coefficients with the standard errors in parenthesis and (2) the estimated changes in predicted probabilities given a fixed change in the independent variable from its minimum to its maximum value, holding all others constant at their mean (Long 1997).

In the three models, four factors stand out as consistent and robust predictors of Dominican transnational political ties; *Age, Family in U.S., U.S. Civic Engagement,* and *U.S. Citizen.* A change in the variable *Age* from its minimum to maximum value increases belonging to a home-country association by 43 percent (Model I); increases the probability of participating in the politics of the Dominican Republic by 13 percent (Model II); and increases the probability of being active in both activities by 36 percent (Model III). As anticipated, having one's family in the United States depresses participation in transnational political projects.

By far the strongest predictor of transnational political participation is being active in U.S. politics, *U.S. Civic Engagement.* Individuals who are active in U.S. politics were 60 percent more likely to be involved in a home country association, 50 percent more likely to participate in Dominican politics, and 46 percent more likely to be active in both activities. The strong correlation between participating in U.S. politics and the politics of the Dominican Republic is not surprising considering that politically active individuals possess resources and skills conducive to general political activism and are usually well embedded within their communities (Putnam 2001). Being embedded in Washington Heights, "a transnational community" (Duany 2002, 1994), invariably leads individuals to participate in organizations and activities that are also transnationally oriented. These results unequivocally demonstrate that participation in the politics of the host country and home country are not mutually exclusive activities (Duany 2002; Graham 1997, 2001; Guarnizo 2001).

In each of the three models, U.S. citizens were significantly less likely to participate in transnational political activities, *ceteris paribus*. In Model I, U.S. citizens were 10 percent less likely to belong to a home-country association. In Model II, they were 19 percent less likely to be involved politically abroad. In Model III, there was an average decline of 7 percent in the likelihood of being active in both political activities. As noted earlier, the extension of dual nationality by many Latin American governments was designed to keep their émigrés transnationally active as they become integrated in the United States through the acquisition of U.S. citizenship. Counter to this expectation, individuals who are U.S. citizens are less transnationally active than non-U.S. citizens, suggesting that as migrants become integrated in the host country *via* naturalization, transnational ties are likely to weaken over time. Although U.S. citizenship leads to a decline in "direct" political participation abroad, it remains to be seen whether it leads to "indirect" transnational political engagement through lobbying U.S. foreign policymaking institutions.

Aside from the four predictors previously discussed, the three transnational activities were shaped by different sets of predictors, *Education, Gender, Discrimination, Love the DR,* and *Visits Abroad.* Most of the selected predictors are both significant and have signs in the theoretically expected direction. However, it remains unclear why some are significant in certain models but not in others, aside from the obvious speculation that the three types of transnational political activities are distinct and rely on differing individual-level characteristics. In some cases the interpretation behind the differential impact of particular variables is much more straightforward. For example, the negative effects of

Table 6.3. Determinants of Dominican Transnational Political Participation

	Model I DR Hometown Organization		Model II Help Candidate or Party in the DR		Model III Participation in Both Transnational Activities	
	Logit	Predicted probabilities Min>Max	Logit	Predicted probabilities Min>Max	Logit	Predicted probabilities Min>Max
Age	.044** (.014)	.431	.011*** (.013)	.125	.056*** (.018)	.355
Education	.303** (.148)	.165	.179† (.130)	.142	.177 (.167)	.041
Gender (Female)	.249 (.3930	.024	-.502* (.330)	-.078	-.141 (.471)	-.006
Length of U.S. Residency	-.009 (.016)	-.055	-.002 (.016)	-.026	.001 (.020)	.005
Discrimination	.060 (.171)	.018	.431** (.158)	.188	.437** (.215)	.055
Internal Efficacy	-.054 (.117)	-.022	-.038 (.118)	-.023	-.120 (.145)	-.021
External Efficacy	.085 (.127)	.033	.032 (.107)	.019	.068 (.154)	.012
Myth of Return	-.041 (.175)	-.012	-.004 (.152)	-.002	-.114 (.214)	-.061

Love the DR	.463**	.119	.136	.061	.327	.038
	(.215)		(.176)		(.267)	
Visits Abroad	.097	.052	.294**	.262	.239†	.069
	(.148)		(.121)		(.167)	
Family in U.S.	-.763*	-.068	-1.209***	-.162	-1.719***	-.061
	(.437)		(.424)		(.647)	
Dominican Legislative Seat	2.236**	.131	.281	.040	1.307	.039
	(1.080)		(.481)		(1.077)	
Political Participation	.596***	.598	.426***	.504	.657***	.462
	(.108)		(.095)		(.133)	
U.S. Citizen	-.954**	-.098	-1.213***	-.190	-1.531***	-.073
	(.437)		(.387)		(.553)	
Constant	-7.830***	--	-3.357***	--	-8.063***	--
	(1.552)		(.950)		(1.739)	
Chi-square	85.58	--	71.26	--	74.39	--
Significance	.000	--	.000	--	.000	--
PPC	85.5	--	79.77	--	89.5	--
PRE	.5638	--	.4681	--	.5011	--
Sample Size	298		298	--	298	--

Two tailed probabilities: † p <= .075, * p <= .05, ** p<=.01, *** p<=.001
Source: 2003 Dominican/NYC Survey.

gender (female) are likely driven by the nature of politics in the Dominican Republic. In the Dominican Republic, as in other Latin American countries, politics remains a male-dominated activity. Consequently, home country politicians and political parties campaigning in Washington Heights are likely to target male émigrés to a greater degree than women. The fact that men tend to monopolize leadership positions within the community also decreases the likelihood that women will be solicited by Dominican candidates or political parties (Jones-Correa 1998; Hardy-Fanta 1993). Hence, it makes sense that women are less directly active in the politics of the Dominican Republic (Model II), but are no more or less engaged in home-country clubs (Model I) or active in both activities (Model III), *ceteris paribus.*

Contrary to theoretical expectations, the political determinants, internal political efficacy, and external political efficacy appear to have little measurable effect on Dominican transnational political ties. None were statistically significant across the three models. In addition, the "myth of return" ideology that plays a prominent role in the work of Jones-Correa (1998) has no impact on Dominican transnational political activities.

▓   ▓   ▓

The development of transnational political networks between Latin American governments and their diasporas has accelerated in the last two decades. Regrettably, the scholarship on Latin American transnational political ties pales in comparison to that written on transnational economic and sociocultural ties. Part of this is due to the fact that political scientists continue to examine political participation among Latinos as one that occurs largely within the territorial boundaries of the United States. The few works on Latino political participation abroad primarily examine Latino participation through the rubric of diasporic politics, namely ethnic group involvement in shaping U.S. foreign policy. Historically, diasporas need to wield enormous economic or political resources in order to shape U.S. foreign policy toward their home countries (Shain 1999). It comes as no surprise that non-Cuban Latinos are often seen as inconsequential foreign policy actors.

Nonetheless, when examining "direct" involvement in the politics of their countries of origin or "transnationalism from below" a different picture emerges. It appears that different Latino diasporas are beginning to take a greater interest and become more involved in the politics of their countries of origin. However, the scholarship on Latinos as transnational political actors is a recent development and little is known about the degree to which different Latino groups are politically engaged abroad or the factors that foster or mitigate that involvement.

The aim of this study was to systematically explore transnational political participation among Dominicans in New York City through a randomly administered survey of 413 residents in the enclave of Washington Heights. What are the conclusions that can be drawn from the results of the survey and statistical analyses? First, the disapora is clearly active in the politics of the Dominican Republic. About one-quarter of respondents claim to be directly involved in the politics of the Dominican Republic, either through a home-country association or by helping candidates and/or political parties from the Dominican Republic. Also, about 10 percent of respondents simultaneously participated in both transnational political activities. Second, differences in transnational political involvement are noted among Dominicans who are U.S. citizens and those who have yet to undergo naturalization, with the latter being more politically involved abroad. Third, in the multivariate models, the most consistent predictors of transnational political engagement were age, participation in U.S. politics, having one's family in the U.S., and U.S. citizenship. The first two factors fostered political involvement abroad and the latter two depressed political participation abroad. Finally, some of the explanatory variables considered here were found to have varying effects across the three transnational political activities.

As Latin American immigration to the United States rose in the mid-twentieth century, a great deal of scholarship was devoted to examining the factors associated with Latino participation in U.S. politics. If Latin American immigration continues to rise and if home-country governments continue to intensify ties with their diasporas in the twenty-first century, scholarship is likely to turn to examining the factors driving Latino transnational political engagement. Clearly, the theoretical insights generated by the former scholarship are likely to inform much of this emerging research field. Likewise, I anticipate that the study of transnational political behavior will provide important insights into understanding Latino participation and incorporation in U.S. politics.

REFERENCES

Associated Press. 2003. "Mexico's Congress Approves Dual Nationality." October 23.

Barreto, Matt. 2004. "Latino Immigrants at the Polls: Foreign-Born Voter Turnout in the 2002 Election." *Political Research Quarterly* 58 (1): 79–86.

Barreto, Matt, and José Muñoz. 2003. "Reexamining the 'Politics of In-Between': Political Participation among Mexican Immigrants in the United States." *Hispanic Journal of Behavioral Sciences* 25 (4): 427–47.

Bustamante, Jorge. 1986. "Chicano-Mexicano Relations: From Practice to Theory." In *Chicano-Mexicano Relations,* edited by Tatcho Mindiola and Max Martinez, 8–19. Mexican American Studies Monograph 4. Houston: University of Houston.

Clough, Michael. 1994. "Grass-Roots Policymaking: Say Good-Bye to the Wise Men." *Foreign Affairs* 73 (1): 2–7.

Cohen, Isaac. 2000. "Hispanics and Foreign Policy." *International Journal of Public Administration* 23 (4): 1311–39.

de la Garza, Rodolfo. 1980. "Chicanos and U.S. Foreign Policy: The Future of Chicano-Mexican Relations." *Western Political Quarterly* 33 (4): 571–82.

de la Garza, Rodolfo, Harry Pachon, and Adrián Pantoja. 2000. "Foreign Policy Perspectives of Hispanic Elites." In *Latinos and U.S. Foreign Policy,* edited by Rodolfo de la Garza and Harry Pachon, 21–42. New York: Rowman and Littlefield.

DeSipio, Louis, 2003. "Learning There and Doing Here: Transnational Politics and Civic Engagement among Latino Migrants." Paper presented at the Annual Meeting of the American Political Science Association. Philadelphia.

DeSipio, Louis, and Adrián Pantoja. 2007. "Puerto Rican Exceptionalism? A Comparative Analysis of Puerto Rican, Mexican, Salvadoran, and Dominican Transnational Civic and Political Ties." In *Latino Politics: Identity, Mobilization, and Representation,* edited by Rodolfo Espino, David L. Leal, and Kenneth J. Meier, 104–22. Charlottesville: University of Virginia Press.

Duany, Jorge. 1994. *Quisqueya on the Hudson: The Transnational Identity of Dominicans in Washington Heights*. Dominican Research Monographs. New York: CUNY Dominican Studies Institute.

———. 2002. "'Los Paises': Transnational Migration from the Dominican Republic to the United States." Paper presented at the seminar on Migration and Development: Focus on the Dominican Republic, sponsored by the Migration Dialogue. Santo Domingo, DR.

Fernández, Damián. 1987. "From Little Havana to Washington DC: Cuban-Americans and U.S. Foreign Policy." In *Ethnic Groups and U.S. Foreign Policy*, edited by Mohammed Ahari, 115–34. Westport: Greenwood Press.

Figueroa-Aramoni, Rodulfo. 1999. "A Nation beyond Its Borders: The Program for Mexican Communities Abroad." *Journal of American History* 86(2): 537–44.

Graham, Pamela M. 1997. "Reimagining the Nation and Defining the District, Dominican Migration and Transnational Politics." In *Caribbean Circuits, New Directions in the Study of Caribbean Migration*, edited by Patricia Pessar, 91–125. New York: Center for Immigration Studies.

———. 2001. "Political Incorporation and Re-Incorporation: Simultaneity in the Dominican Migrant Experience." In *Migration, Transnationalization, and Race in a Changing New York*, edited by Hector Cordero-Guzman, Robert Smith, and Ramon Grosfoguel, 87–108. Philadelphia: Temple University Press.

Grasmuck, Sherri, and Patricia Pessar. 1991. *Between Two Islands: Dominican International Migration*. Berkeley: University of California Press.

Guarnizo, Luis Eduardo. 2001. "On the Political Participation of Transnational Migrants: Old Practices and New Trends." In *E Pluribus Unum? Contemporary and Historical Perspectives on Immigrant Political Incorporation*, edited by Gary Gerstle and John H. Mollenkopf, 213–63. New York: Russell Sage Foundation.

Guarnizo, Luis, Alejandro Portes, and William Haller. 2003. "Assimilation and Transnationalism: Determinants of Transnational Political Action among Contemporary Migrants." *American Journal of Sociology* 6 (5): 1211–48.

Hardy-Fanta, Carol. 1993. *Latina Politics, Latino Politics*. Philadelphia: Temple University Press.

Hendricks, Glenn. 1974. *The Dominican Diaspora: From the Dominican Republic to New York City—Villagers in Transition*. New York: Teachers College Press.

Hernández, Ramona. and Francisco L. Rivera-Batiz. 2003. "Dominicans in the United States: A Socioeconomic Profile, 2000." New York: CUNY Dominican Studies Institute, Dominican Research Monographs

Hero, Rodney, and Anne Campbell. 1996. "Understanding Latino Political Participation: Exploring the Evidence From the Latino National Political Survey." *Hispanic Journal of Behavioral Sciences* 18 (2): 129–41.

Huntington, Samuel. 1997. "The Erosion of American Interests." *Foreign Affairs* 76 (1): 28–49.

———. 2004a. "The Hispanic Challenge." *Foreign Policy*. http://www.foreign policy.com/story/cms/php?story_id=2495.

———. 2004b. *Who Are We? The Challenges to American National Identity.* New York: Simon and Schuster.

Itzigsohn, Jose. 2000. "Immigration and the Boundaries of Citizenship: The Institutions of Immigrants Political Transnationalism." *International Migration Review* 34 (4): 1126–54.

Jones-Correa, Michael. 1998. *Between Two Nations: The Political Predicament of Latinos in New York City.* Ithaca: Cornell University Press.

———. 2001. "Under Two Flags: Dual Nationality in Latin America and Its Consequences for Naturalization in the United States." *International Migration Review* 35 (4): 997–1029.

Leal, David L. 2002. "Political Participation by Latino Non-Citizens in the United States." *British Journal of Political Science* 32 (2): 353–70.

Levitt, Peggy. 1998. "Social Remittances: Migration Driven Local-Level Forms of Cultural Diffusion." *International Migration Review* 32 (4): 926–48.

———. 2001. *The Transnational Villagers.* Berkeley: University of California Press.

Lindsay, James M. 2002. "Getting Uncle Sam's Ear: Will Ethnic Lobbies Cramp America's Foreign Policy Style." *Brookings Review* 20 (1): 37–45.

Lizardo, Freddy. 2001. "Altas Remesas En Los Ultimos Años." http://www .intec.edu.do/~indes.

Long, J. Scott. 1997. *Regression Models for Categorical and Limited Dependent Variables.* Advanced Quantitative Techniques in the Social Sciences, vol. 7. Thousand Oaks: Sage.

Mathias, Charles, Jr. 1981. "Ethnic Groups and Foreign Policy." *Foreign Affairs* 59 (4): 975–98.

Pantoja, Adrian, Ricardo Ramirez, and Gary Segura. 2001. "Citizens by Choice Voters by Necessity: Patterns in Political Mobilization by Naturalized Latinos." *Political Research Quarterly* 54 (4): 729–50.

Pessar, Patricia. 1995. *A Visa for a Dream: Dominicans in the United States.* Boston: Allyn and Bacon.

Portes, Alejandro, and Luis E. Guarnizo. 1991. "Tropical Capitalists: U.S.-Bound Immigration and Small-Enterprise Development in the Dominican Republic." In *Migration, Remittances, and Small Business Development, Mexico and Caribbean Basin Countries,* edited by Sergio Diaz-Briquets and Sidney Weintraub, 103–31. Boulder: Westview Press.

Putnam, Robert. 2001. *Bowling Alone: The Collapse and Revival of American Community*. New York: Simon and Schuster.

Rendón, Armando. 1981. "Latinos: Breaking the Cycle of Survival to Tackle Global Affairs." In *Ethnicity and U.S. Foreign Policy*, edited by Abdul Aziz Said, 163–85. New York: Preager.

Rohter, Larry. 1996. "U.S. Benefits Go: Allure to Dominicans Doesn't." *New York Times*, October 12. http://www.nytimes.com/1996/10/12/us/us-benefits-go-allure-to-dominicans-doesn-t.html?pagewanted=all &src=pm.

Rosenstone, Steven J., and John Mark Hansen. 1993. *Mobilization, Participation, and Democracy in America*. New York: Macmillan.

Shain, Yossi. 1999. *Marketing the American Creed Abroad, Diasporas in the U.S. Homeland*. Cambridge: Cambridge University Press.

———. 2000. "The Mexican-American Diaspora." *Political Science Quarterly* 114 (4): 661–91.

Smith, Tony. 2000. *Foreign Attachments, The Power of Ethnic Groups in the Making of American Foreign Policy*. Cambridge, MA: Harvard University Press.

Immigration and Public Policy

S E V E N

U.S. and Mexican Schools as Regulators of Dropout Rates for Chicano Students

R A Y M O N D   V .   P A D I L L A

This chapter focuses on the education of Mexican immigrant and Mexican-American students. While these two populations often need to be distinguished, at other times they need to be combined to gain a larger picture; the combined populations will be referred to as Chicano students.[1] In their study of immigrants and U.S. education, Vernez, Abrahamse, and Quigley (1996, 67) reached an important conclusion about Mexican immigrant students and U.S. schools: "these youths are not just drop-outs from U.S. schools; rather, they are failing to "drop in" to the school system in the first place." This failure to "drop in" is not typical of all immigrant students, however. Most characteristic of Mexican immigrant students, it can be placed in a broader context if we examine additional information as provided by Vernez and Abrahamse and in the related research literature. Putting the various pieces together, the overall pattern may be described boldly as follows:

1. Immigrant status itself has no significant influence on high school graduation or college matriculation rates.

2. Race and ethnicity do have a significant influence on high school graduation and college matriculation rates.

3. Therefore, Mexican immigrant students tend to do poorly in U.S. schools not because they are immigrants but because they are Mexicans.

4. However, being Mexican per se is not what leads to doing poorly in U.S. schools. Rather, U.S. schools historically have not provided equitable educational opportunities for Mexicans.

5. This inequity is driven by racialized attitudes of Americans toward Mexicans and by the economic self-interests of Americans, both of which have deep historical roots.

6. On the other hand, Mexican schools also seem to be implicated because they structurally produce an undereducated class for which there are few opportunities in Mexico for economic and social advancement.

7. The Mexican undereducated class then becomes commodified as a labor "product" for export from Mexico to the United States. The commodification of Mexican labor serves the economic and political interests of the Mexican elite classes.

8. The combination of Mexican immigrant students and U.S.-born Mexican American students in U.S. schools then exhibits the typical pattern of high school dropout rates for Chicanos that is consistently and persistently reported in the research literature.

A major theme emerges when these and related points are woven together: the two independent national educational systems in Mexico and the United States together shape educational achievement for Chicano students. In each nation, the educational system reflects abiding and deeply rooted social attitudes, political and economic interests, and school policies and practices that together modulate and regulate the academic achievement of Chicano students.[2] The rest of this chapter will elaborate further this theme of binational regulation of Chicano educational achievement. After the theme is explored more fully, some suggestions will be made for improving the educational attainment of Chicano students.

THE FAILURE TO "DROP IN" TO THE SCHOOLS

With respect to in-school participation rates, Vernez and Abrahamse (1996) found that the biggest gap is in the 15 to 17 year old population (Table 7.1).

When the data are disaggregated by ethnicity, however, it is clear that Mexicans and other Hispanics account for most of the gap in in-school participation rates (Table 7.2).

Table 7.1. In-School Participation Rates (%) in the U.S. by Age and Immigration Status, 1990

Age	*Native*	*Immigrant*
5–7	74	7
8–11	96	94
12–14	97	94
15–17	93	87

Source: Vernez and Abrahamse 1996, 20.

Table 7.2. In-School Participation Rates (%) in the U.S. by Immigration Status and Race/Ethnicity for High School Youths, Age 15–17, 1990

Race/Ethnicity	*Native*	*Immigrant*
Asian	95	94
Chinese, Japanese, Korean, Filipino	96	95
Other Asian	95	94
Black	91	91
Hispanic	91	83
Mexican	91	74
Other Hispanic	90	88
White	93	92

Source: Vernez, Abrahamse, & Quigley 1996, 21.

There is a 17 percentage point difference in in-school participation rates between Mexican immigrant students and native Mexican American students for the 15 to 17 year old group. When compared to White students, the gap in the in-school participation rate of Mexican immigrant students becomes even wider, amounting to 19 percentage points. Indeed, it does appear that many Mexican immigrant students, particularly those of high school age, simply do not make it to school in the first place; if they do, they leave very quickly, as discussed below.

THE CHICANO DROPOUTS FROM U.S. SCHOOLS

Calculated dropout rates can be markedly different depending on who is doing the counting. Official dropout statistics from the Texas Education Agency are notoriously understated (*Education Week* 2003). The calculations of the Intercultural Development Research Association (IDRA) are presented here because they are likely to be more accurate than the figures of state agencies and "education politicians," who go out of their way to deflate dropout rates.[3]

Table 7.3 shows dropout rates for the state of Texas from 1994–1995 to 2002–2003 disaggregated by race and ethnicity. Chicano students have higher dropout rates compared to all other racial/ethnic groups during any given year studied. Hispanic dropout rates for the state of Texas over this nine-year period show a consistent level hovering around the 50 percent mark. There is little evidence here of a "Texas miracle" that has drastically reduced Chicano dropout rates.

As shown in Table 7.3, the percentage of dropouts from Texas schools is high for all groups, including White students. When translated into actual counts of dropouts, these percentages reflect a school system in a dire situation. IDRA (2003) reported that between 1985–1986 and 2002–2003, almost two million (1,922,391) students dropped out of the Texas school system. Hispanics accounted for about half of the total dropouts for this period, totaling almost one million (942,034) students. Starting from a base of 33,583 dropouts in 1985–1986, the number of Hispanic dropouts has increased steadily every year; in 2002–2003, the number of Hispanic dropouts reached 79,219. These impressive figures inevitably lead to certain questions, such as:

le 7.3. Trend Data on Dropout Rates (%) in Texas Public Schools by Race and Ethnicity, 4–1995 to 2002–2003

el nicity	*1994– 95*	*1995– 96*	*1996– 97*	*1997– 98*	*1998– 99*	*1999– 00*	*2000– 01*	*2001– 02*	*2002– 03*
ive Am. ian/Pacific	42	44	43	42	25	43	42	29	39
nder	18	18	20	21	19	20	20	14	17
:k	50	51	51	49	48	47	46	46	45
ite	30	31	32	31	31	28	27	26	24
panic	51	53	54	53	53	52	52	51	50

ce: Intercultural Development Research Association 2003, 8.

1. How do Chicano students actually experience the schools?
2. How do schools engage Chicano students?
3. How might schools engage Chicano students to serve them better?
4. What is the role of the Mexican school system in improving Chicano education?

These and related questions will be addressed in the following sections.

THE CHICANO EXPERIENCE IN U.S. SCHOOLS

In recent years, researchers using qualitative research methods have begun to shed light on how Chicana/o students actually experience school. Although there are some subtle differences between the school experiences of Mexican immigrant and U.S.-born Mexican American students, both groups also have many common experiences. According to Valenzuela (1999), who conducted research in the Houston public schools, Chicano students often perceive that teachers, counselors, and other school personnel do not care about them. The teachers see them in stereotypical ways, as if the Chicano students and their parents did not value education. This lack of caring by the schools expresses itself concretely in many ways, including lowered expectations for Chicano students and an uninspiring curriculum, which often emphasizes rote or below grade level English language instruction. More recently, accountability driven curricula that are tightly aligned with high stakes testing schemes offer little for any remotely curious student, and are especially onerous for Chicano students (Padilla 2004).

Valenzuela contends that Chicano students also undergo a process of "subtractive schooling." In other words, U.S. schools often see Chicano students as possessing traits or behaviors that are not only different, but also inferior to mainstream U.S. culture. Schools, therefore, take it upon themselves to eliminate such traits and behaviors from the students as a first priority. Most often their efforts are focused on eliminating non-English language use and rejecting actual or presumed cultural values that are at variance with U.S. culture. Although this subtractive process can cause rifts between students, schools, and parents, schools persist in subtractive schooling because their strategy is not merely to eliminate inferior traits and behaviors but to replace them with presumably superior ones that represent more "acceptable" American norms.

Curiously, when Chicano students resist the imposition of subtractive schooling by maintaining their cultural or linguistic repertoire, school personnel, especially teachers, often see these students and their parents as "not caring" about their educational and social advancement. A vicious circle therefore closes as students and teachers mutually see each other as "not caring." It is ironic that schools, which by definition are supposed to be "caring" institutions, devolve into "uncaring" institutions under the sway of subtractive schooling (Zanger 1993).

Seen more broadly, subtractive schooling is often experienced by Hispanic students as a marginalizing experience. Frau-Ramos and Nieto (1993), who studied Puerto Rican dropouts from a Massachusetts high school, reported that when a dropout student was asked what could be done to keep students in school he replied, "*Hacer algo para que los boricuas no se sientan aparte* (161)." (Do something so that the Puerto Ricans would not feel isolated.) Another student noted that he had graduated from high school because he kept to himself ("*yo no me meto con nadie*"). Students undergoing subtractive schooling can therefore experience social isolation *porque los apartan o porque se apartan ellos mismos* (because the school environment isolates them or they isolate themselves).

Such isolation of Chicano and Hispanic students can lead to the invisibility of these students (Montero-Sieburth and Villarruel 2000; Zanger 1993). From such invisibility, neglect (Carter 1970) and lack of adequate services and resources can result. The dropout potential for Chicano students is high under these circumstances; when they do graduate from high school, scores on standardized tests, grade point averages, and college matriculation rates reveal their lack of preparation (American Council on Education 2003).

In addition, Chicano students can experience invidious treatment in schools in more prosaic ways that are tied to the bureaucratic organization of U.S. schools. Based on research in Texas public schools, Romo and Falbo (1996) recount how difficult it was for Romo to help a dropout student to return to school given the plethora of bureaucratic obstacles that were placed along the way. Even with the help of a high status Anglo like Romo, it was a major chore to reinstate the student. Without this help, it would have been virtually impossible for the student to continue in school.

Similar bureaucratic rules and obstacles can increase dropout rates in the first place. According to Montero-Sieburth (1993),

Students are presented with the rules and regulations in early September detailing the expectations of the school, the transgressions that are not acceptable, and the consequences for inappropriate behaviors and actions. The carrying out of such rules implies the existence of collective understanding of these laws—an understanding of the way that the rules function, how they are monitored and supervised at every level of the school through the principal, two assistant principals, the registrar, two disciplinary officers, guidance counselors, and teachers . . . these rules are presented in English and the interpretation of these rules is left to individual teachers and other school personnel (231).

Individual interpretation of the rules can result in inconsistencies in their application and in their use for purposes that may suit teachers and school officials but which do not help the students and their parents. During the study of dropouts from a major urban school system in the Southwest, Wong, Padilla, and Montiel (1985) pointed out how bureaucratic rules and procedures were implicated in the regulation of the dropout rate for the school district in question. In particular, the role of student tardiness and absences in driving dropout rates (see Figure 7.1) was clearly shown.[4]

Since the interpretation of tardiness policy was left to individual teachers, teachers could use this policy to promote disciplinary and other controlling actions in their classrooms. Because tardiness levels directly impacted absence levels, and these in turn affected which students would be dropped from school through administrative action, teachers' decisions as to how they would handle tardiness by students was a crucial factor in determining which students could stay in school and which students would be dropped automatically from the system if they ran afoul of attendance rules. Keeping track of student tardiness was far more than a mere bureaucratic exercise in student accounting. It directly impacted both the chances that a student would be dropped from school and the student's opportunity to learn in the classroom. The latter point becomes clear in the details of how individual teachers handled tardiness. At the discretion of teachers, they could withhold class participation from a tardy student. In some cases, teachers actually had a tardy student stand in the corner for the duration of the class even if the student was tardy for only a few minutes or even seconds (after the bell rang). In such cases, students lost all benefit of instruction for the time they would be counted as absent from the class even though they were in class standing in the corner. Such practices are emblematic of "not caring" and reflect teachers' concern for eradicating what they see as loathsome traits and behaviors through the stern means of subtractive schooling.

Yet, it is not always the case that teachers are hard-hearted or that schools do not have the best interests of students in mind. Educational institutions are embedded in a complex school-social matrix that strongly affects how schools function and perform. As Rong and Preissle

Figure 7.1. The Influence of Tardiness and Absence Policies on Student Dropout Rates

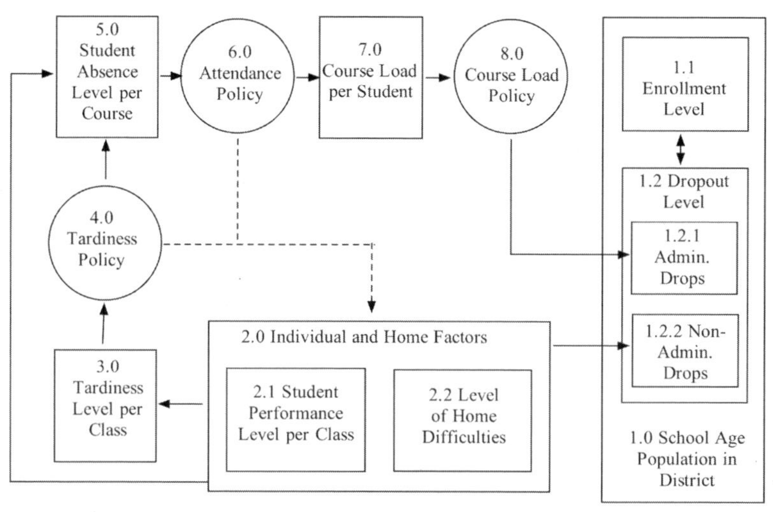

Source: Wong, Padilla, and Montiel, 1985.

(1998) pointed out, in addition to immigrant status, other factors in the school-social matrix include: "race, ethnicity, nationality, gender, social class, and residential location" (xi). Dentler and Hafner (1997) additionally point to society's structural dominance (whereby some groups hold greater power and wealth than others), the availability of social and health services associated with schools, and whether the local cultures welcome or disparage immigrant and minority students. Rong and Preissle (1998) add that student language proficiency and school ability to handle language issues help determine school performance and student educational outcomes.

The effects of the school-social matrix on Chicano educational opportunities are illustrated by two case studies of school districts that attempted to meet student language needs through bilingual education. In both cases, it appears that the schools aimed to substantially improve the education of Chicano students through their initial efforts. Once the full impact of the school-social matrix was brought to bear, however, the initial vision was discarded and the Chicano students were offered an inferior education that essentially followed the more typical subtractive schooling formula.

The first case is reported by Hamann (2002), who examined a school district in Georgia, which had many available jobs in the local carpet mills. These jobs attracted Mexican immigrants to the area, and their children had a great effect on the school district. Within a very short time, it became clear that Mexican immigrant students, most of whom had a low level of English proficiency, were having great difficulty in the local public schools, which taught only in English. Spurred by a local influential Anglo community, the school district agreed to deliver more appropriate instruction to the immigrant students premised on a "maintenance" type of bilingual program and the school district entered into a collaborative arrangement with a prestigious Mexican university[5] to provide technical support. Everything was in place for the school district to provide effective educational services to immigrant students of limited English proficiency (LEP), but it was not to be. Strong community pressures at local and state levels conspired to constrain the school district into a far more traditional model of instruction premised on subtractive schooling. The influence of the school-social matrix can be seen clearly in this case both in terms of the initial effort to move the school district into bilingual instruction and in the ensuing retrenchment that aligned the school district once again with the typical model of subtractive schooling.

The second case (Martinez 2002) illustrates the importance of both ethnicity and social class in the dynamics of the school-social matrix. A small, wealthy community in a Colorado mountain valley experienced the influx of Mexican immigrant students because their parents had been attracted by the jobs available in the service sector tied to the recreational facilities available in the area. Because real estate in this affluent area is at a premium, the Mexican workers became concentrated in trailer park communities in the vicinity of their employment. Consequently, the children of these immigrant workers became concentrated in certain schools. It soon became apparent to school officials that the students, many of whom were LEP, were having difficulty performing well in school. With the help of a consultant from the nearby state university, the school district first decided to offer maintenance bilingual instruction to these students with the help of a federal grant.

Like the Georgia school district, the good intentions of the school district soon ran afoul of local public opinion, which favored the more traditional model of subtractive schooling. In addition, the more affluent community sought the eradication of the trailer park communities because the trailer homes were considered unsightly, offensive, and obstructed mountain vistas. Responding to community pressures, this school district very quickly went from a maintenance model of bilingual education to a very modest and inadequate language program premised on subtractive schooling. In the racialized climate that led to this transition, both the school district and the immigrant workers were intimidated by the powerful dynamics of the school-social matrix. The school district retrenched to the traditional model of subtractive schooling, and with fewer places to park their trailers (as the trailer parks were redeveloped), many immigrant workers simply decided to leave the area.

These two cases show how powerful community forces can be unleashed on school districts to rechannel them into modes of behavior that are consistent with the prevailing values and norms of the larger society or the local community. The majority individuals are not the only retrenchment agents, however. In the Georgia case, for example, the role played by a Hispanic individual holding a high-level position in the state educational bureaucracy was important to language retrenchment by the schools (Beck and Allexsaht-Snider 2002). Likewise, a Texas school district totally controlled by Chicanos saw rebellion against the maintenance and culturally nationalistic bilingual education program initially established in the schools (Navarro 1998). These and other examples illustrate the great complexity of the school-social matrix.

THEORIZING THE CHICANO EXPERIENCE IN U.S. SCHOOLS

The school experience and achievement of Chicano students has been theorized from a number of disciplinary perspectives. Sociological perspectives emphasize the role of schools in producing and reproducing the social hierarchies evident in most modern societies (Bourdieu and

Passeron 1990). From this perspective, schools are seen not so much as engines for social mobility but as engines for sorting individuals into their proper niche in the social hierarchy. In this view, those who start out with a lot of social advantages end up with a lot of social advantages when they leave school, and vice versa. Psychologically oriented theories tend to characterize Chicano students as possessing debilitating deficits whose origin is attributed to mental or cultural deficiencies, and even to inferior genes (see Valencia 1997 for a detailed description and critique of the "deficit model" of Chicano students). From an anthropological perspective, the Chicano educational experience is connected to the notions of "territorial minorities" and "involuntary immigrants" whom the larger society assigns a caste-like low status (Ogbu 1978). Students who resist this ascriptive low social status do so by internalizing the deficit model and behaving accordingly in school. Doing poorly in school and expecting others like them to do poorly as well is an act of rebellion against the discriminatory practices and lack of opportunity, which they experience and cannot overcome.

More recently, the experience of Chicanos in U.S. schools has been theorized from a historical and binational perspective (González 2004). This important new approach places the United States schooling experience of Chicanos squarely within a framework of U.S. expansionist ambitions dating back to the nineteenth century, and in particular to the unique relationship that has developed between the U.S. and Mexico vis à vis the imperial ambitions of the United States (see also Menchaca 1997, 1999). As maintained by González, the U.S. opted for a "peaceful conquest" of Mexico during the latter part of the nineteenth century and the beginning of the twentieth century. The key features of this peaceful conquest included the exploitation of Mexican natural resources and labor under an assumed superiority of American know-how, entrepreneurship, and culture (not to mention an alliance with divine will and manifest destiny). Under American control and tutelage, Mexican wealth could be extracted from the country with the help of a docile but trainable (under supervision) Mexican peon workforce. Peon labor thus became a central feature of the American understanding of the Mexican people. Good only for strenuous labor under tight supervision, peons otherwise were seen as apathetic and congenitally inferior to Anglo Americans.

From this perspective, it is readily apparent how peon Mexican labor, once it had been transplanted into the U.S. proper, would be viewed as a "problem" to be dealt with by American schools and other social institutions. The historical perspective thus provides a context for understanding the persistence of the deficit model that has been applied to Chicano students by U.S. schools for more than a century now. From a schooling perspective, the children of Mexican peons are to be cleansed of their inferior traits and behaviors and infused with superior ones from Anglo American culture. This cleansing and infusing process may take a while, perhaps encompassing several generations. In the meantime, second- and third-generation peon labor (the high school dropouts) can be exploited within the U.S. in segments of the economy where domestic labor is reluctant to participate (Cammarota 2003).

Collectively, these and other theoretical perspectives provide many insights into the school experiences of Chicanos in the U.S. When focused into a single overarching theme, these perspectives seem to point to a distinct orienting framework that prevails in American culture: The belief that all "newcomers" to the U.S. must assimilate into the dominant Anglo American language and culture (Garcia 2001). This "deep value" (Ricento 2003), which is applied to all "newcomers" whether they voluntarily immigrate to the United States or the United States comes to them, has been remarkably resistant to all challenges, including the challenge of multiculturalism that gained strength during and after the 1960s. As a result, no real changes have come about in schools—which necessarily must operate within the school-social matrix already discussed—in their treatment of Chicanos and other minority students as long as they have operated under the sway of assimilationist thinking. In other words, before the school experience of Chicano students can change substantially for the better, the underlying assimilationist model of U.S. schools must be abandoned and replaced by a more democratic view of socialization and enculturation into American society.

SOME PROPOSALS FOR IMPROVING CHICANO EDUCATION

The foregoing analysis of the Chicano educational experience in U.S. schools leads directly to new approaches for the improvement of

Chicano education. Because of space limitations, only three proposals for improvement are summarized here (see Padilla 2001 for additional options). The proposals include: (1) replacing the antiquated assimilationist model with a new model: *multicultural diversity with transcultural unity* (MDTU); (2) developing an advocacy model to promote individual student success in school; and (3) reforming the Mexican educational system to reflect the realities of labor commodification and export.

The MDTU Model

For almost one hundred years, American schools have operated under the sway of assimilationist thinking. If Chicano educational achievement is to be improved substantially, it will be necessary to abandon melting pots, salad bowls, and other gustatory metaphors of American civil society. We need a model of U.S. society that accounts for its ethnomorphic[6] (that is, multiethnic) character and that promotes cultural democracy as well (Ramirez and Castañeda 1974).

Figure 7.2 shows a concept model of *multicultural diversity with transcultural unity* (MDTU). The model shows that the bridge between cultural diversity and social unity is a transcultural foundation of ideas that is agreed to by all members of society. This transcultural foundation includes the three pivotal ideas of freedom, democracy, and justice. These fundamental ideas are seen as transcultural because they encompass and transcend all of the various subcultures existing in the society. The transcultural foundation can thus be seen as a social compact that everyone can agree is an essential part of civil society.

The existence of the transcultural foundation makes it possible to have both multicultural diversity and transcultural unity. The latter is expressed as the suppositions, values, institutions, and practices in society that directly result from the transcultural foundation and that promote its continued existence. The elements of transcultural unity are shown in brackets to indicate that these transcultural expressions have enduring qualities that transcend any particular cultural group and that change only slowly as a result of cultural and social evolution. As such, transcultural unity represents stability and schools should be the en-

Figure 7.2. A Model of Multicultural Diversity with Transcultural Unity (MDTU)

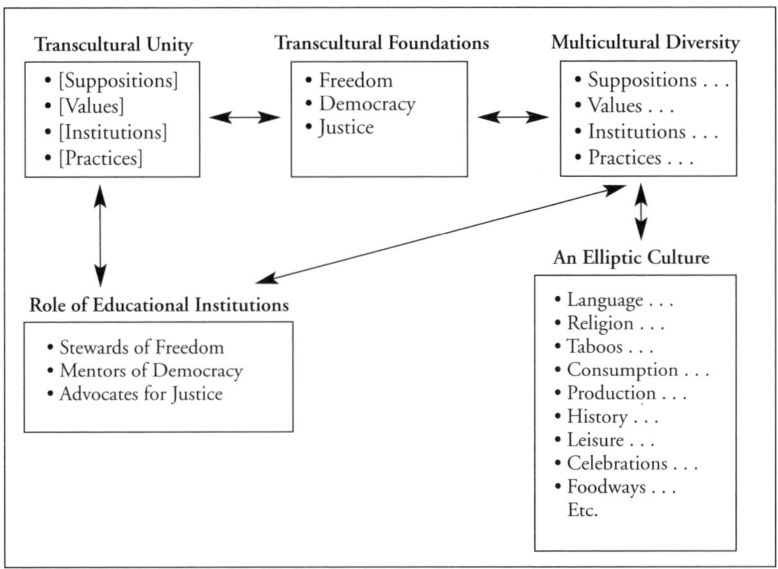

gines that shape students into citizens who are cognizant of the transcultural common ground that binds the society. Specifically, the school curriculum and the extracurriculum are the indicated vehicles for inculcating awareness and appreciation of the transcultural foundation central to social unity.

Multicultural diversity, on the other hand, expresses elliptic (. . .) culture. Elliptic suppositions, values, institutions, and practices can vary considerably from one cultural group to another so long as they are not in conflict with the transcultural foundation. Hence, under multiculturalism, suppositions, values, institutions, and practices are followed by ellipses in order to show that these cultural expressions are open-ended and variable across the society. As such, multicultural diversity has the quality of experimentation, innovation, change, and exchange; it is dynamic and generative. In the school context, multicultural diversity implies a recognition, appreciation, and critical assessment of the elliptic cultural elements that make up the mosaic of society. The theories, principles, and practices developed to promote multicultural education during the twentieth century can be used as a starting point for integrating elliptic cultural elements into the school curriculum and the extracurriculum.

The MDTU model includes additional implications for educational institutions. The transcultural foundation, multicultural diversity, and transcultural unity can be maintained only if educational institutions are designed and operated as the guarantors of the social compact. In this role, educational institutions must function as the stewards of freedom, the mentors of democracy, and the advocates for justice.[7] When functioning in this manner, educational institutions will advocate consistently for students and opt for their success.

The MDTU model can help to clarify difficult and troubling issues that went unresolved during the twentieth century. For example, the assimilationists properly argued for national unity but they incorrectly attributed the transcultural foundation exclusively to the Euro-Anglo cultural group. The bracketed expressions of transcultural unity were equated with Euro-Anglo elliptic cultural expressions, thus creating the hegemony of the Euro-Anglo cultural group over all the other groups. By improperly claiming to be the sole possessor of the transcultural foundation and transcultural unity, the hegemonic group could privilege its elliptic cultural expressions over the elliptic cultural expressions of all other groups. The MDTU shows that this hegemonic behavior is antithetical to both transcultural unity and multicultural diversity, as well as to civil society itself. In the United States, the civil rights movement of the 1960s and beyond represents the most intense effort of the twentieth century to dislodge cultural hegemony by one group and to give voice, vote, and expression to all cultural groups in American society.

As another example, the MDTU model helps to explain why multiculturalists have done poorly in dealing with the issue of unity. Social unity cannot be found in multicultural diversity itself. According to the model, social unity is a transcendent feature of multicultural diversity. In other words, multicultural diversity points to transcultural unity as something that exists beyond multicultural diversity itself. Transcultural unity is necessary if multicultural diversity is to exist in any coherent way. What makes multicultural diversity viable is its transcendent unity. On the other hand, social unity that extinguishes multicultural diversity is a vacuous unity, a unity that extinguishes free cultural expression—hence the wisdom of *E Pluribus Unum.*

Developing the Pedagogy of Advocacy

Ultimately, it may be the case that community activists, educators, and policymakers spent too much time during the latter part of the twentieth century trying to fix every fault in the schools at the expense of *advocating* for each and every individual student. The fact of the matter is that all kinds of students—rich and poor, minority and non-minority, males and females, and so on—have problems and difficulties with the schools. The students who succeed in schools with significant organizational deficits are those students who have had adults behind them who advocated on their behalf. When parents, teachers, and administrators are effective advocates for the children under their care, it is very likely that these children will succeed in school. When such advocacy is absent or marginal, then the student truly will be at risk of not succeeding in school.

Figure 7.3 shows one conceptualization of a *pedagogy* of advocacy. As shown in Figure 7.3, the point of departure for improving the education of Chicano students is the understanding that Chicano students must experience school success even under deficit organizational resources (SUDOR). Chicano success in school cannot wait until the schools are perfectly functioning organizations; instead Chicano educational success must be achieved with schools as they operate at any given time and context. Success is possible under deficit organizational conditions because some students will always experience success in any school (Garcia 2001; González, Huerta-Macias, and Villamil Tinajero 1998); Padilla 1999; Reyes, Scribner, and Paredes Scribner 1999). The idea then is to shift all students in the direction of success regardless of the school that they attend. How can this be done?

As the model shows, success can be achieved if students as learners have the motivation to garner academic knowledge and skills (GANAS) and if they are supported in their learning through advocacy. Advocacy is the responsibility of the family, school, community, and society. Key elements include admiring, democratizing, valuing, organizing, caring, advocating, and challenging youth.

Older people need to admire young people and young people need to feel that older people admire them (Bly 1990; Freire 1995). It is on the basis of this admiration that older people take younger people "under their wing" and advocate for their success; student GANAS to learn will increase as they find older mentors who believe in them.

Advocacy must be based on a profound commitment to the greater democratization of society. Immigrants often come to the United States seeking improved economic futures, but they just as often desire the benefits of a democratic society. By implementing cultural democracy in schools (Ibarra 2001; Ramirez and Castañeda 1974), we become advocates of both native and immigrant students who see that they are appreciated and that they have a positive role to play in the larger society. The school experience itself thus prepares students to participate effectively in civil society.

Students need to feel valued and validated (Rendón 2002). They need to be valued for who they are and their life experiences need to be validated if further learning is to occur (Jalomo 1995; Rendón 1994). An important part of advocacy, therefore, is to show in many ways and throughout the school years that students are valuable. The obscene notion of "throw away kids" is the antithesis of valuing students. The younger generation always represents the future and valuing youth is an essential part of advocacy.

Advocacy implies organization; effective advocacy always requires organization at some level. The COPS organization (Communities Organized for Public Service) in San Antonio, Texas, is a good example of a community-level organization aimed at advocating for students and the community at large (see http://en.wikipedia.org/wiki/Communities _Organized_for_Public_Service). Organization is also required when advocacy is done on an individual basis. Each student is an individual with particular needs that are expressed dynamically in the vicissitudes of life. When a student does not show up for class on a given morning, someone must advocate for that student by taking the time to find out why the student is not in school. If the student's problem can be re-

Figure 7.3. A Model for Developing a Pedagogy of Advocacy

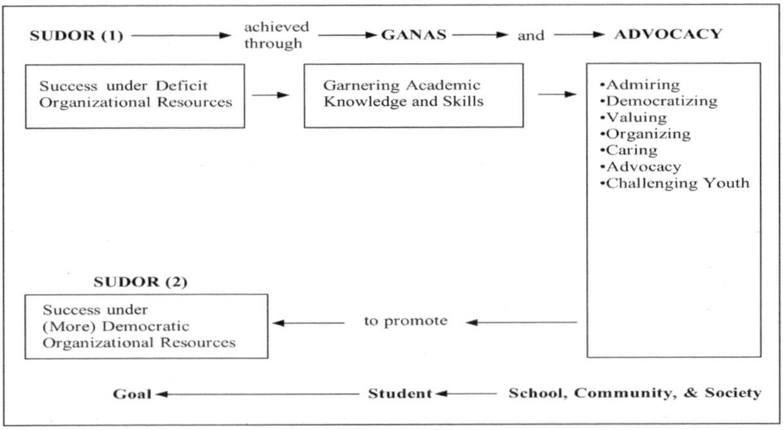

SUDOR (1) ──────▶ achieved through ────▶ **GANAS** ────▶ and ────▶ **ADVOCACY**		

| **SUDOR (1)** → achieved through → **GANAS** → and → **ADVOCACY** |

Success under Deficit Organizational Resources → Garnering Academic Knowledge and Skills → •Admiring •Democratizing •Valuing •Organizing •Caring •Advocacy •Challenging Youth

SUDOR (2)

Success under (More) Democratic Organizational Resources ◀──── to promote ◀────

Goal ◀──────── Student ◀──── School, Community, & Society

solved in real time, then the student can be brought back to school. This type of real-time advocacy requires organization both of schools and communities, or the resources needed to overcome problems will not be available. To the extent that today's schools are not organized to promote advocacy, school reform efforts should be refocused to pursue this goal.

Those who advocate do so because they care about students. The shocking lack of caring expressed by some school personnel when it comes to Chicano and other minority students shows that such individuals have abandoned their obligations as teachers and educators (Romo and Falbo 1996; Valenzuela 1999, 2002). Caring means that the welfare of students is always the highest priority of educational systems. Caring means doing right by students and giving every student a genuine opportunity to learn. Caring means to read between the lines and to help students even when they have not expressed the needs that they have. Advocacy often results from caring, and without caring advocacy seems unlikely.

Advocates also challenge. Youths need to be challenged if they are to apply their copious energy to constructive purposes. Boring curricula and boring schools cannot satisfy the eagerness and curiosity of young people. Spending inordinate amounts of time preparing students for high stakes tests is not a good way to challenge students (McNeil 2000; McNeil and Valenzuela 2000). Students are challenged when they have to reach a little bit farther then what they know they can already do (Moll 1990). They are challenged when novel possibilities are brought before them. They are challenged and inspired when they know that their performance and achievement will result in admiration from peers and adults alike. They are challenged when they see that a better future is possible for themselves and their families. The Chicano community is richly involved in the arts, including music, art, dance, theater, sculpture, muralism, and other arts genres. Educational curriculum and extracurricular activities should challenge Chicano youth in the plastic and performing arts—including traditional forms as well as newer film, video, multimedia, performance art, and so on—alongside a challenging curriculum in science, math, and technology.

Advocacy involves many parallel activities. If students are to garner significant amounts of academic knowledge and skills, advocacy must be deployed on many levels and in many different ways. With proper advocacy, students can succeed even in schools that are less than perfect. In addition, advocacy can be used to improve deficient schools, especially if such improvement is based on the lessons learned from advocating for individual student success. When advocacy shifts its focus from helping individual students to improving particular schools, schools may deploy learning resources more democratically, which enhances the potential for academic achievement for Chicano students as well as all other students in that school. In this sense, school improvement can be measured by the extent to which organizational resources under a school's control are allocated democratically and sufficiently to meet student needs. When resources are allocated to schools democratically, justly, and sufficiently, and schools in turn do likewise with resource allocation to students and teachers, then—if students have GANAS—their achievement potential will be at maximum.

Developing Human Capital through Bilingual Programs in Mexico

The third proposal for improving Chicano education focuses on the Mexican educational system. As already indicated, the Mexican educational system structurally produces an undereducated class for which there are few opportunities for social and career advancement in Mexico. This undereducated class is the equivalent of what a century ago was seen as the Mexican peon by the Americans, essentially representing a source of cheap labor. The surplus of such cheap labor puts Mexico in the position to "export" it through the sheer mobility and the desire for self-improvement of the undereducated class rather than through treaties or trade agreements. Mexican workers find their way into the United States, either legally or without proper documentation, where they are absorbed into the low wage sector of the U.S. economy through legal and extralegal means. From the perspective of U.S. schools, the children of this undereducated Mexican work force—the descendents of the earlier Mexican peons—are seen as having problems needing correction within the framework of assimilationism and using the tools of subtractive schooling. In this context, newly arriving Mexican immigrant students are simply added to the existing Mexican American population and processed by the schools accordingly.

When nearly everything is said and done with respect to educating Chicano students, it becomes readily apparent that the central issue revolves around their proficiency in the English language. The bare facts are that Mexican immigrant students, and often first- and second-generation Mexican American students as well, do not have sufficient English proficiency to participate effectively in schools where English is the standard medium of instruction. Schools are generally not equipped to instruct students whose primary language is not English, in large part due to the fact that Americans are notoriously monolingual (and therefore teachers tend to be monolingual), and also because American society demands that all newcomers learn English as part of the assimilation process.

Under these circumstances, the most powerful advantage that could be possessed by Mexican immigrant students in the United States—who typically start their education in Mexico—would be to receive a Spanish-English bilingual education in Mexico. Even if the student only completed a few years of schooling in Mexico, the advantage of having early English language instruction would become evident as they entered U.S. schools, which typically instruct only in English. If Spanish-English bilingual education in Mexico were complemented with English-Spanish bilingual education for the same students in the U.S., then the likelihood that these students would succeed in U.S. schools would be greatly enhanced.

Is bilingual education in Mexico feasible? It could be if innovative ideas were used. For example, there could be many creative ways to develop the necessary teaching resources if the supply of bilingual teachers is seen in a broad binational context. A binational public service program could be constructed that would attract native English speakers from the United States to teach English in Mexico and native Spanish speakers from Mexico to teach Spanish in the United States. The advantages that would accrue to participants in such a binational teacher corps are numerous—for example, learning another language and culture, developing teaching skills, finding business and career opportunities, and so on. The advantages to the Mexican immigrant and Mexican American students, as well as students of other ethnic backgrounds on both sides of the border, would be equally compelling.

Is bilingual education worth it for Mexico? Considering that Mexican workers in the United States remit some 14 billion dollars annually to Mexico, there is a considerable economic advantage for Mexico to raise the earning potential of this population. If these workers were to earn higher wages in the U.S., their remittances to Mexico would rise accordingly. However, the earning potential of these workers cannot rise substantially in the U.S. without higher English language skills and increased educational attainment. This is where early bilingual education in Mexico would enhance the earning potential of Mexican immigrant workers, who would be better equipped to achieve more in American schools and to obtain better paying jobs in the United States.

International competition in the global economy is hurting Mexico's ability to commodify and export cheap undereducated labor. Mexico can no longer rely on the commodification and export of its undereducated class (or its exploitation on domestic soil), due to cheap labor competition from China and elsewhere. For the Mexican economy to thrive, greater investment has to be made in human capital. Yet, since the exportation of Mexican labor to the U.S. is not likely to end soon, enhancing this "product" through higher academic achievement in general and greater English language skills in particular will provide Mexico a better return through increased remittances.

If the commodification of Mexican labor is seen clearly and realistically, then enhancing the value and productivity of this commodity ought to be a worthwhile goal. As long as Mexican immigrants continue to provide substantial remittances to Mexico, there will be a substantial return to Mexico for modest improvements in the quality of this labor force. Moreover, from a social policy perspective, the distribution of remittances to Mexico is almost ideal; they are typically sent to needy families and communities where they can have the greatest impact in improving the quality of life for the average Mexican.

There are many other ways to improve the educational attainment of Chicano students in the U.S. besides those illustrated here. What is amply clear is that the status quo of ongoing educational underachievement for the Chicano population will weaken U.S. competitiveness in the global economy and lead to increased social tensions as the have-nots become a permanent underclass. So everyone is implicated in the problem as well as in finding a timely solution.

NOTES

1. In citing data and quoting from external sources, the designations used in the originals will be used in the text; designations such as Latino and Hispanic will be retained.

2. The concept of regulation is used here not in the sense of controlling according to rules but in the broader sense of running the schools so as to produce the student outcomes that are actually observable.

3. For example, *Education Week* (2003) reported that: "An analysis of state data by *Education Week* found 108 high schools throughout Texas where 70 percent or more of the students are considered at risk of academic failure. Of those schools, about half claimed a dropout rate of 1 percent or less. Further examination shows that at many of the schools, student enrollments dwindled by 30 percent or more from 9th to 12th grade.

Texas as a whole, with 4.1 million public school students, reports an annual dropout rate of 1 percent (page 2)."

For a list of IDRA dropout studies and access to them visit the IDRA web site at: http://www.idra.org/.

4. Montero-Sieburth (1993) also discusses the impact of tardiness and absence policies on Latino high school students.

5. For accounts of this collaboration see Zúñiga, Hernández-León, Shadduck-Hernández, and Villarreal (2002) and Hamann (2002).

6. The term "ethnomorphic" is intended to convey more than a mere description of multiple ethnicities in a society. It also conveys the notion that ethnic groups arise and disappear historically, so that old ethnicities give rise to new ethnicities, and that through interaction ethnic groups mutually affect, and can transform, each other.

7. The implications of equity in education for democracy are discussed by Bensimon and Polkinghorne (2003).

REFERENCES

American Council on Education. 2003. "Twentieth Anniversary Minorities in Higher Education Annual Status Report." Washington, DC: American Council on Education.

Beck, Scott A. L., and Martha Allexsaht-Snider. 2002. "Recent Language Minority Education Policy in Georgia: Appropriation, Assimilation, and Americanization." In *Education in the New Latino Diaspora*, edited by Stanton Wortham, Enrique G. Murillo, and Edmund T. Hamann, 37–66. Westport: Ablex.

Bensimon, Estela Mara, and Donald Polkinghorne. 2003. *Why Equity Matters; Implications for Democracy.* Los Angeles: University of Southern California, Center for Urban Education.

Bly, Robert. 1990. *A Gathering of Men.* With Bill Moyers; Betsy McCarthy, Producer, and Wayne Ewing, Director. New York: Mystic Fire Video.

Bourdieu, Pierre, and Jean Claude Passeron. 1990. *Reproduction in Education, Society, and Culture.* 2nd ed. Thousand Oaks: Sage Publishing.

Cammarota, Julio. 2003. "Channeling Latino Youth into the Low-Wage Trap: Race and Class Polarization in California." *The Arizona Report* 7 (1): 2.

Carter, Thomas P. 1970. "Mexican Americans in School. A History of Educational Neglect." New York: College Entrance Examination Board.

Dentler, Robert A., and Anne L. Hafner. 1997. *Hosting Newcomers. Structuring Educational Opportunities for Immigrant Children.* New York: Teachers College Press.

Education Week. September 24, 2003. http://www.edweek.org.

Frau-Ramos, Manuel, and Sonia Nieto. 1993. "I Was an Outsider: An Exploratory Study of Dropping Out among Puerto Rican Youths in Holyoke, Massachusetts." In *The Education of Latino Students in Massachusetts: Is-*

sues, Research, and Policy Implications,* edited by Ralph Rivera and Sonia Nieto, 147–69. Boston: University of Massachusetts Press.

Freire, Paulo. 1995. *Pedagogy of the Oppressed.* New Revised Twentieth-Anniversary Edition. New York: Continuum.

García, Eugene. 2001. *Hispanic Education in the United States: Raíces y Alas.* New York: Rowman and Littlefield.

González, Gilbert G. 2004. *Culture of Empire: American Writers, Mexico, and Mexican Immigrants, 1880–1930.* Austin: University of Texas Press.

González, Maria Luisa, Ana Huerta-Macias, and Josefina Villamil Tinajero, eds. 1998. *Educating Latino Students: A Guide to Successful Practice.* Lancaster: Technomic Publishing Company.

Hamann, Edmund T. 2002. "¿Un Paso Adelante? The Politics of Bilingual Education, Latino Student Accommodation, and School District Management in Southern Appalachia." In *Education in the New Latino Diaspora,* edited by Stanton Wortham, Enrique G. Murillo, and Edmund T. Hamann, 67–97. Westport: Ablex.

Ibarra, Robert A. 2001. *Beyond Affirmative Action: Reframing the Context of Higher Education.* Madison: University of Wisconsin Press.

Intercultural Development Research Association. 2003. *IDRA Newsletter* 30 (10, November–December).

Jalomo, Romero, Jr. 1995. "Latino Students in Transition: An Analysis of the First-Year Experience in Community College." Unpublished doctoral dissertation, College of Education, Arizona State University, Tempe.

Martinez, Elias. 2002. "Fragmented Community, Fragmented Schools: The Implementation of Educational Policy for Latino Immigrants." In *Education in the New Latino Diaspora,* edited by Stanton Wortham, Enrique G. Murillo, and Edmund T. Hamann, 143–67. Westport: Ablex.

McNeil, Linda M. 2000. *Contradictions of School Reform: Educational Costs of Standardized Testing.* New York: Routledge.

McNeil, Linda M., and Angela Valenzuela. 2000. "The Harmful Impact of the TAAS System of Testing in Texas: Beneath the Accountability Rhetoric." Houston: Rice University Center for Education Occasional Papers 1.

Menchaca, Martha. 1997. "Early Racist Discourses: The Roots of Deficit Thinking." In *The Evolution of Deficit Thinking: Educational Thought and Practice,* edited by Richard Valencia, 13–40. Washington, DC: Falmer Press.

———. 1999. "The Treaty of Guadalupe Hidalgo and the Racialization of the Mexican Population." In *The Elusive Quest for Equality: 150 Years of Chicano/Chicana Education,* edited by Jose S. Moreno, 3–29. Cambridge, MA: Harvard Educational Review.

Moll, Luis C., ed. 1990. *Vygotsky and Education: Instructional Implications and Applications of Sociohistorical Psychology.* New York: Cambridge University Press.

Montero-Sieburth, Martha. 1993. "The Effects of Schooling Processes and Practices on Potential At-Risk Latino High School Students. In *The Education of Latino Students in Massachusetts: Issues, Research, and Policy Implications,* edited by Ralph Rivera and Sonia Nieto, 217–39. Boston: University of Massachusetts Press.

Montero-Sieburth, Martha, and Francisco Villarruel, eds. 2000. *Making Invisible Latino Adolescents Visible: A Critical Approach to Latino Diversity.* New York: Falmer Press.

Navarro, Armando. 1998. *The Cristal Experiment: A Chicano Struggle for Community Control.* Madison: University of Wisconsin Press.

Ogbu, John U. 1978. *Minority Education and Caste: The American System in Cross-Cultural Perspective.* New York: Academic Press.

Padilla, Raymond V. 1999. "College Student Retention: Focus on Success." *Journal of College Student Retention, Research, Theory, and Practice* 1 (2): 131–45.

———. 2001. *Pedagogy of Engagement: Mapping Possibilities for Educational Improvement.* CD ROM. Boerne: Author.

———. 2004. "High Stakes Testing and Educational Accountability as Social Constructions Across Cultures." In *Leaving Children Behind: How "Texas-style" Accountability Fails Latino Youth,* edited by Angela Valenzuela, 249–62. Albany: State University of New York Press.

Ramírez, Manuel, and Alfredo Castañeda. 1974. *Cultural Democracy, Bicognitive Development, and Education.* New York: Academic Press.

Rendón, Laura I. 1994. "Validating Culturally Diverse Students: Toward a New Model of Learning and Student Development." *Innovative Higher Education* 19 (1): 23–32.

———. 2002. "Community College Puente: A Validating Model of Education." *Educational Policy* 16 (4): 642–67.

Reyes, Pedro, Jay D. Scribner, and Alicia Paredes Scribner. 1999. *Lessons from High-Performing Hispanic Schools.* New York: Teachers College Press.

Ricento, Thomas. 2003. "The Discursive Construction of Americanism." *Discourse and Society* 14 (50): 611–37.

Romo, Harriett D., and Toni Falbo. 1996. *Latino High School Graduation: Defying the Odds.* Austin: University of Texas Press.

Rong, Xue Lan, and Judith Preissle. 1998. *Educating Immigrant Students: What We Need to Know to Meet the Challenges.* Thousand Oaks: Corwin Press.

Valencia, Richard, ed. 1997. *"The Evolution of Deficit Thinking: Educational Thought and Practice.* Washington, DC: Falmer Press.

Valenzuela, Angela. 1999. *Subtractive Schooling. U.S.-Mexican Youth and the Politics of Caring.* Albany: State University of New York Press.

———.2002. "High-Stakes Testing and U.S.-Mexican Youth in Texas: The Case for Multiple Compensatory Criteria for Assessment." *Harvard Journal of Hispanic Policy* 14: 97–116.

Vernez, Georges, Allan Abrahamse, and Denise D. Quigley. 1996. *How Immigrants Fare in U.S. Education.* Santa Monica: Rand.

Wong, Paul, Raymond V. Padilla, and Miguel Montiel. 1985. *Staying and Achieving.* Report of the Phoenix Union High School District, Drop-Out Task Force. Tempe: Arizona State University.

Zanger, Virginia Vogel. 1993. "Academic Costs of Social Marginalization: An Analysis of the Perceptions of Latino Students at a Boston High School." In *The Education of Latino Students in Massachusetts: Issues, Research, and Policy Implications,* edited by Ralph Rivera and Sonia Nieto, 170–90. Boston: University of Massachusetts Press.

Zúñiga, Víctor, Rubén Hernández-León, Janna Shadduck-Hernández, and María Olivia Villarreal. 2002. "The New Paths of Mexican Immigrants in the United States: Challenges for Education and the Role Of Mexican Universities." In *Education in the New Latino Diaspora,* edited by Stanton Wortham, Enrique G. Murillo, and Edmund T. Hamann, 99–116. Westport: Ablex.

EIGHT

Eligibility, Enrollment, Utilization

Barriers to Public Insurance Access among Latino Families in the Age of Welfare and Health Care Reform

ADELA DE LA TORRE, JESSICA NUÑEZ
DE YBARRA, MARISOL CORTEZ,
AND EMILY PRIETO

In a study examining the differential impact of Medicaid expansions on the health status of children by race and ethnicity, Lykens and Jargowsky (2002) have pointed out that access to public health insurance programs depends on three distinct realms of action. To benefit from public health insurance programs, such as Medicaid and the State Children's Health Insurance Program (SCHIP), an individual must first qualify for, enroll in, and ultimately take advantage of the care plan available (Lykens and Jargowsky 2002). Although this is a seemingly simple statement of fact, each of these three realms presents a unique set of difficulties for Latinos, especially in terms of their ability to benefit from public insurance programs like Medicaid and SCHIP. Furthermore, Latino immigrants in the United States face increased challenges in securing health care coverage because eligibility restrictions have become even more stringent for them (Kaiser Commission 2006).

This chapter follows the three-part approach to health care access as outlined by Lykens and Jargowsky, examining existing literature in the areas of eligibility, enrollment, and actual care as it relates to Latino citizens and non-citizens. In addition, the next chapter reviews the limited body of literature on culturally innovative interventions, particularly those that have been shown to be effective in reducing rates of under-enrollment among Latinos eligible for public health insurance programs. The goal of these chapters is thus to use existing knowledge as one basis for identifying practices that will best improve Latinos' access to public health insurance programs in an attempt to improve their well-being and quality of life.

BACKGROUND AND HISTORICAL CONTEXT: INSURANCE STATUS OF U.S. LATINOS

According to United States Census 2000 data, Latinos are now the largest minority group in the United States, comprising 12.5 percent of the total population. However, this demographic growth has not led to better health care access or coverage for the population. Numerous studies have documented the various obstacles that both Latino adults and children encounter in obtaining and utilizing health care. Chief among these obstacles is access to health insurance, which is key to an individual receiving health care services (Maida 2001; Angel and Angel 1996; Schur and Feldman 2001). Barriers to acquiring health insurance can significantly lessen the amount and quality of health care received. For example, when compared to children with Medicaid coverage, children without it are 30 percent less likely to receive ambulatory care and have 50 percent fewer visits to health care providers (Marquis and Long 1996; Lykens and Jargowsky 2002). Figures 8.1 and 8.2, shown below, demonstrate the scope of the problem.

As shown above in Figure 8.1, the number of uninsured Latinos increased 60 percent from 1990 to 2000, rising from 7 million to 11.2 million. According to Doty (2003), this increase in rates of uninsured has been proportional to growth in the United States Latino population during this period; so that "throughout the past decade, one-third or more of all non-elderly Hispanics have been uninsured each year—a

Figure 8.1. Number of Uninsured Hispanics, 1990–2000 (Population in Millions)

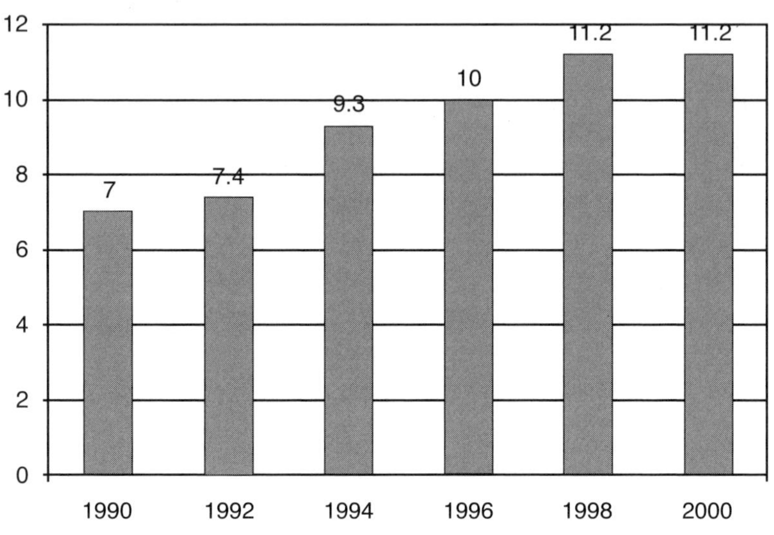

Source: Doty 2003.

rate two to three times that of non-Hispanic whites" (Doty 2003). Figure 8.2 only gives us a snapshot for 2001 of the percentage of uninsured Latinos according to national origin. As is evident here, the most astonishing rates of the uninsured occur within the Mexican- and Central American-origin populations, who at 49 percent and 55 percent, respectively, are uninsured at approximately twice the rate as compared to the total U.S. population. These immense disparities in coverage speak to a health care system that requires change if we are to see parity in health care access across racial and ethnic lines.

Before Medicaid was established in 1965, the likelihood of having health care insurance depended on family income level and access to an employer who offered health benefits. The Medicaid program effectively created a partnership between state and federal levels of govern-

Figure 8.2. Percentage of Uninsured by National Origin, 2001

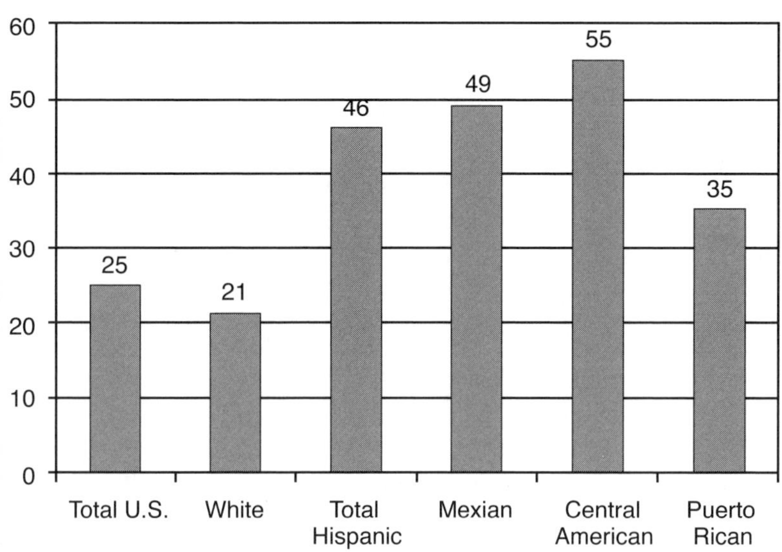

Source: Doty 2003.

ment in order to assure a third source of possible health coverage to the "poorest poor" (Maida 2001). While this created a safety net for the most indigent citizens, Medicaid did not address the needs of the working poor, many of whom continued to be uninsured. To fill this gap, the State Child Health Insurance Program (SCHIP), a federally subsidized health insurance program for children, was established in 1997; it included much broader eligibility criteria than those used for Medicaid (Ross and Hill 2003).

Nonetheless, access to public health programs continues to be a function of race and ethnicity (Shone et al. 2003). For Latinos in particular, one of the factors most directly responsible for race- and ethnicity-based disparities is access to employment-based coverage. If coverage is not provided through an employee's benefits package, his or her remaining options are to purchase private insurance, to rely on a government-funded health program, or to remain uninsured. This first option obviously has its own set of obstacles. According to the March 2002 Current Population Survey (CPS), only about 43 percent of U.S. Latinos received employment-based insurance in 2001, compared to about 63 percent of the total U.S. population. This difference is largely due to the types of industries in which many Latinos work (Levan et al. 1999; Vitullo and Taylor 2002). In California, for example, many Latinos—particularly immigrants—are employed in low-wage industries such as textiles, food processing, and electronics that do not generally offer health insurance (Maida 2001). Schur and Feldman (2001) point out further that Latinos nationwide are disproportionately represented in the construction, agriculture, and service industries, which are also associated with lower levels of job-based health care benefits.

Figure 8.3, shown below, illustrates the extent to which Latinos lag behind non-Latino whites in terms of employment-based health insurance.

Figure 8.3 clearly shows that as of March 2002, employment-based health care is consistently higher for non-Latino whites than it is for Latinos in five states with significant numbers of Latinos. The difference in job-based coverage is especially apparent in New York, in which non-Latino whites are 18 percent more likely to be covered than Latinos.

Low levels of coverage among Latinos are also a result of broader structural changes in the U.S. economy during the past few decades, including a shift from a manufacturing-based economy to a service-based economy, as well as trends toward higher insurance premiums among employers in the 1990s (Berman 1995). Besides these structural changes, the years 1979–1995 saw a marked expansion in the cost of health care relative to personal income, creating an increase in the number of low-wage workers who can no longer afford insurance (Kronick and Gilmer 1999). Moreover, when this trend is viewed in light of Latinos' already higher poverty rates and immigration status as compared to non-Latino whites (see Figure 8.4 below), we can see that adequate health care is financially out of reach for many Latinos, a high percentage of whom earn less than the cutoff established by the federal poverty guidelines.[1]

Figure 8.3. Five-State Comparison of Employment-Based Health Care as Percentage of Population (by Group)

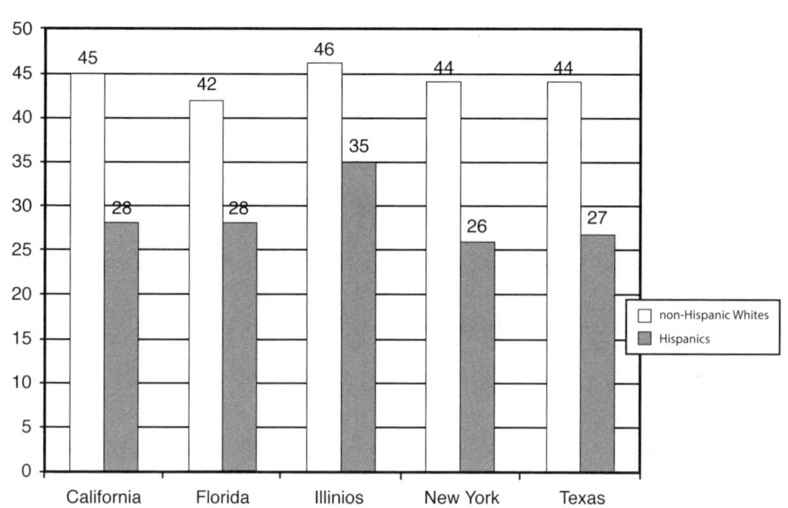

Source: United States Census Bureau 2002.

Figure 8.4 compares the percentage of Hispanics living in poverty to the percentage of non-Hispanic whites living in poverty in each of the five states, indicating the staggering number of Latinos who struggle to afford private health care in comparison to non-Latino whites. Given the economic demographics of Latinos in the United States, the remaining two options for health care are to enroll in a government-funded public insurance program or remain uninsured. However, a number of barriers prevent Latinos from successfully enrolling in and benefiting from public insurance programs. Starting with barriers to eligibility, the following sections survey the literature for those known factors primarily responsible for Latinos' persistent under-enrollment.

BARRIERS TO ELIGIBILITY

Medicaid and SCHIP eligibility requirements are complex and change frequently, which can be one of the greatest barriers in accessing either

Figure 8.4. Five-State Comparison of Percentage Living in Poverty (by Group)

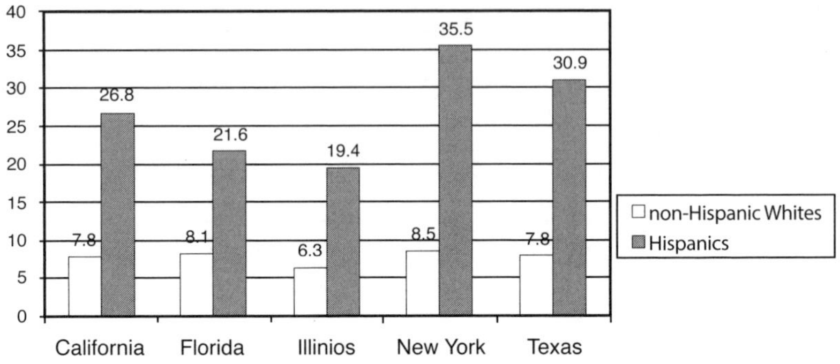

Source: United States Census Bureau. Census 2000.

program, regardless of ethnicity. Before August 22, 1996, for instance, eligibility for Medicaid benefits was closely linked to the receipt of benefits from the federal and state welfare program Aid to Families with Dependent Children (AFDC). The Personal Responsibility and Work Opportunity Reconciliation Act (PRWORA) of 1996 severed that link, creating two independent programs, Medicaid and Temporary Assistance to Needy Families (TANF); the latter is a cash assistance program with strict requirements for eligibility. Although TANF technically replaced AFDC, states nevertheless retained the July 1996 AFDC qualification criteria as their basis for determining Medicaid eligibility (Ku and Coughlin 1997).

In 1997 the Balanced Budget Act established SCHIP, a matching funds program that would provide states with federal dollars to ensure adequate health care coverage to uninsured low-income children who were not otherwise eligible for Medicaid. Depending on the state, this newly created children's health insurance program would function as a supplement to Medicaid, as its own program, or as a composite of these two options (Newacheck et al. 1998; Maida 2001; Lykens and Jargowsky 2002; Byck 2000). States would have flexibility in determining eligibility criteria for SCHIP, a decision that has yielded differences in program implementation across state lines, but which has also allowed states a greater hand in administering to the unique health care needs of their respective uninsured youth populations (Maida 2001; Lykens and Jargowsky 2002).[2]

While PRWORA expanded publicly funded health insurance programs, it also directly placed limits on immigrants' access to both Medicaid and SCHIP, going so far as to allow states the option of barring illegal immigrants from all but emergency and prenatal health care. The most important change effected by PRWORA pertained to legal immigrants entering the United States after August 22, 1996. As stipulated by the legislation, those entering the United States after this cut-off date would be ineligible for government-subsidized health care benefits—including Medicaid and SCHIP—for the first five years of their residency in the United States (Benjamin et al. 2000; Ku and Blaney 2000; Maida 2001). The provision of services to legal immigrant groups was then left to the discretion of the states, a political move that inadvertently jeopardized the eligibility status for many low-income children (Ellwood and Ku 1998). The policy changes between 1995 and 1999 created uncertainty regarding health insurance coverage for low-income immigrant children and parents, and not surprisingly, coverage declined for these groups (Ku and Blaney 2000). However, some states, such as California, have opted to spend their own funds to secure medical coverage for all eligible legal immigrants, irrespective of their entry date (Benjamin et al. 2000).

PRWORA increased restrictions on legal immigrant eligibility, which further complicated an already convoluted system of eligibility and verification procedures. A U.S. General Accounting Office (GAO) report shows that, in the wake of welfare reform, states are attempting to mitigate confusion through the use of a single application and set of qualifying criteria (U.S. General Accounting Office 1998). States have also expanded eligibility requirements for Medicaid and SCHIP to boost the enrollment rate of eligible families. These efforts have met with debatable success, however, given the significant number of state residents and immigrants who continue to lack insurance (Asch, Frayne, and Waitzkin 1995; Halfon et al. 1997; Maida 2001). Despite the leeway of individual states, PRWORA's denial of immigrant access to

Medicaid and SCHIP, when combined with the confusion surrounding the separation of Medicaid eligibility from AFDC, has had the overall effect of lowering Medicaid enrollment in immigrant populations, particularly among non-citizen adults (Ellwood and Ku 1998).

Nonetheless, the overall trend with Medicaid and SCHIP, until recently, has been a relaxation of eligibility criteria.[3] As indicated in the Kaiser Commission's ten year progress report on SCHIP, "as states continued to recover from the effects of the economic downturn, more states implemented positive policy changes that increased outreach and enrollment efforts, simplified enrollment procedures, and expanded eligibility and benefits." At the same time, the report acknowledges that "a few states added more restrictive enrollment requirements and enacted cuts in eligibility that caused many children to lose SCHIP coverage. The restrictive actions that states implemented occurred in relatively few states, but caused significant numbers of children to lose SCHIP coverage and the combined impact was large enough to affect national enrollment trends" (Kaiser Commission 2007).

Nonetheless, for those states with greater eligibility flexibility, it is logical to assume that eligibility expansions would lead to an improvement in health care access and outcomes. Currie and Gruber (1996a) tested this assumption by examining the impact of Medicaid extension of eligibility criteria on low-income children between 1984 and 1992, when the percentage of eligible children doubled. Their first observation was that the resulting "take-up"[4] was far below its potential, which they attributed to the possibility that some of the newly eligible children already had private insurance. Nonetheless, they also found that extending Medicaid eligibility had significant positive effects on the utilization of medical care. Using quantitative data from the National Health Interview Survey (NHIS) and the March Current Population Survey (CPS) from 1985 to 1993, Currie and Gruber created models showing the estimated effect of Medicaid eligibility expansion on the utilization of care. They discovered from these models that it was more efficient to expand eligibility for Medicaid than to raise income cutoffs. This later point could be explained by the fact that higher income families may have access to private health insurance for their children. They also found that Medicaid eligibility expansion efforts significantly increased utilization of care received in physicians' offices, a significant finding given that physician care is a more preventative form of health care and leads to a more efficient use of resources (Currie and Gruber 1996a).

Short and Lefkowitz (1992) similarly discuss the effects of increased eligibility, focusing on well-child visits among poor and near-poor preschool children.[5] Using data culled from the 1987 National Medical Expenditure Survey, they found that among low-income children who would be uninsured without Medicaid, a continuous year of coverage improved the prospect of receiving preventative services by 17 percent; however, their study also points out that eligibility expansion alone cannot ensure that lower-income children will benefit from increased access to preventive visits. Factors other than income level and access to insurance (for example, maternal education level) prevent the gap between lower- and higher-income groups of children from closing, even if Medicaid adopted universal eligibility for children below 200 percent of the federal poverty level (FPL). Short and Lefkowitz's study thus illustrates that a simple increase in eligibility for preventive services is not enough to address disparities in health care access and utilization (Short and Lefkowitz 1992).

Lykens and Jargowsky (2002) have also examined the impact of Medicaid eligibility expansion on different groups of children after the 1986 Omnibus Budget Reconciliation Act (OBRA) was enacted. During the four years following OBRA, states were required to increase the income eligibility threshold to 133 percent of FPL for children under six, with the option of increasing it to 185 percent. The authors ultimately found that these eligibility expansions had less of an impact on Latino children than they did on non-Latino whites, although they state that this result can possibly be attributed to the small sample size of Latinos used in the study. Nevertheless, Lykens and Jargowsky conclude from the disparities in health outcomes between Latinos and non-Latino whites that once providers and communities can reduce the non-financial (that is, linguistic and cultural) barriers that Latinos face, eligibility expansions have the potential to benefit all children equally (Lykens and Jargowsky 2002).

A 2002 brief presented by the Urban Institute analyzed estimates of Medicaid and SCHIP using the eligibility rules in place as of July 2000 for children ages 0–17 using data from the 1999 National Survey of America's Families (NSAF). Among eligible children, 65 percent were eligible for Medicaid and 35 percent were eligible for SCHIP (Dubay et al. 2002). Of uninsured children, 57 percent were eligible for Medicaid and an additional 26 percent were eligible for SCHIP while only 17 percent were not eligible for either Medicaid or SCHIP (Dubay et al. 2002). When ineligibility because of legal status was accounted for, the share of uninsured children who were not eligible for Medicaid or SCHIP coverage increased to 23 percent (Dubay et al. 2002). Among low-income uninsured children, only 8 percent were not eligible for Medicaid or SCHIP when legal status was not accounted for, but this estimate increased to 16 percent when the legal status of children who were not citizens was taken into consideration (Dubay et al. 2002).[6]

The July 2000 eligibility rules qualified more than half of all children and 90 percent of low income children for Medicaid and SCHIP coverage (Dubay et al. 2002). There are substantial opportunities for increasing insurance among children, but significant challenges remain. Policymakers have directed their energy on SCHIP, but 68 percent of uninsured children who qualify for public coverage are actually eligible for Medicaid, not SCHIP (Dubay et al. 2002). Clearly, there should be a significant focus on enrolling children in the Medicaid program to ensure that low-income children have access to health care. Moreover, states should implement policies to facilitate both Medicaid enrollment and SCHIP.

Creating simpler enrollment procedures and incorporating culturally and linguistically sensitive outreach practices without addressing the increasingly restrictive eligibility requirements for Latino families will not address the problem of under-enrollment of Latino children and families in publicly subsidized health programs (Dubay et al. 2002). The most vulnerable of the uninsured population are non-citizen children who do not qualify for Medicaid or SCHIP. This leaves states and particularly local level entities, for example counties, as "providers of last resort" for this underserved population. In stark economic times, this often promotes backlash to immigrant groups receiving services, especially when local budgets are cut and costs of services are apparent.

Thus, the issue of legal status for immigrant children clearly and directly affects eligibility for undocumented children. Families with children that are not legally in the United States are not able to avail themselves of publicly subsidized health insurance. The net impact of this for Latino families is significant as a disproportionate share of Latino families fall within the ranks of the undocumented; their children will no doubt suffer the adverse health consequences from limited access to health care.

More recent policy changes have also impacted eligibility of Latino families of both documented and undocumented legal status. The Deficit Reduction Act (DRA), which passed in 2005, altered many aspects of the Medicaid program, including eligibility determinations. One of the law's provisions, for instance, requires that states obtain proof of citizenship from U.S. citizens, including naturalized citizens, such as birth certificates or passports (Families USA, 2006). Applicants who are unable to provide verification will lose Medicaid coverage. The new regulations place the greatest strain on U.S. citizens who do not have a passport or birth certificate (Families USA 2006).

Even legal immigrants, however, face additional barriers to eligibility for Medicaid. Legal immigrants with sponsors who pledge to support them during their time in the United States are considered *sponsor deeming* (Kaiser Commission 2006). By law, the sponsor's income and resources are required to be disclosed when determining Medicaid eligibility, regardless of whether the sponsor shares their income and resources with the immigrant (Kaiser Commission 2006). Subsequently, an immigrant may be ineligible to receive Medicaid because the sponsor deeming pushes their income and assets over the state's limit for Medicaid (Kaiser Commission 2006).

Creating simpler enrollment procedures and incorporating culturally and linguistically sensitive outreach practices without addressing the increasingly restrictive eligibility requirements for Latino families will not address the problem of under-enrollment of Latino children and families in publicly subsidized health programs (Dubay et al. 2002). Yet as much of the literature also indicates, expanding eligibility does not easily equate to improvements in health outcomes for Latinos, since expansions to public health insurance programs cannot guarantee that beneficiaries will enroll in the programs, nor can they reduce disparities that arise due to cultural, linguistic, or educational factors. Moreover, the disjuncture between eligibility expansions and health outcomes has been found to be more widespread among groups who are unfamiliar with the U.S. health care system or who do not have a history of public assistance, as is the case with many working poor families (Currie and Gruber 1996a; Currie and Gruber 1996b). To the degree that both of these characteristics apply to Latino families of all immigration statuses, it thus becomes necessary to consider enrollment more extensively.

BARRIERS TO ENROLLMENT

Between 1989 and 1995, seven million additional poor and working-poor children received Medicaid due to eligibility expansion efforts (Racine et al. 2001). Racine et al. break down the impact of these expansions according to race and ethnicity, examining their effect on rates of the uninsured, utilization of services, and health outcomes among non-Hispanic white, African American, and Latino children. In order to view the changing impact of expansion over time, the authors use a stratified before-and-after statistical model to compare rates of the uninsured among poor and non-poor groups in 1989 and 1995.[7] Table 8.1 summarizes the results of their study.

Improved enrollment is seen most clearly among Latino populations when eligibility requirements are relaxed. Table 8.1 shows the rates of health insurance coverage of poor and non-poor white, African American, and Latino children. From 1989 to 1995, there was a 19 percent decline in the rate of uninsured poor Latino children, the largest decline among the populations examined. Furthermore, Medicaid rates for Latinos increased by 23 percentage points, which again represents the greatest change among the three groups. The study thus concludes that the changes made to Medicaid eligibility requirements caused significant decreases in the rates of uninsured children among poor Latino and African American populations; between these two groups, Latino children benefited to the greatest degree (Racine et al. 2001).

A 1992 UCLA / Rand Corporation study of 812 Latino families in Los Angeles found, however, that although eligibility expansion efforts

Table 8.1. Children's Uninsured Rates and Medicaid Rates by Income Group and Race/Ethnicity, 1989–1995

Parameter		1989	1995	Change
Uninsured Rates				
Poor	White	0.23	0.19	-0.04
	Af. American	0.25	0.14	-0.11
	Latino	0.46	0.28	-0.19
Non-Poor	White	0.04	0.03	-0.01
	Af. American	0.04	0.03	-0.01
	Latino	0.05	0.09	0.04
Medicaid Rates				
Poor	White	0.17	0.33	0.16
	Af. American	0.40	0.62	0.22
	Latino	0.25	0.48	0.23
Non-Poor	White	0.00	0.01	0.01
	Af. American	0.03	0.07	0.04
	Latino	0.01	0.03	0.02

Source: Racine et al. 2001.

may benefit Latino children, few Medicaid-eligible Latino children are able to obtain full coverage (Shinkman 1997). This study found that despite the fact that 84 percent of the children included in the survey were Medicaid-eligible, 19 percent had never enrolled in the program and an additional 21 percent had irregular coverage. The study pointed to parental non-citizen status as one of the major obstacles preventing full benefit take-up among eligible children.

This UCLA study was conducted before passage of PRWORA in 1996; subsequent studies that have examined the correlation between non-citizen status and enrollment in Medicaid or SCHIP reveal additional concerns. Shortly after the enactment of SCHIP, Ellwood and Ku (1998) predicted that when combined with the immigrant provisions of PRWORA, the focus on expanding coverage for children would result in a disproportionate decrease in coverage for adults. In a more recent study, Carrasquillo et al. (2003) assessed the effects of the immigrant provisions on both uninsured children and parents. Using Current Population Survey (CPS) data, they determined that the primary effect of PRWORA has not been to bar large numbers of immigrants from public insurance programs, but rather to shift costs of covering immigrants to states. By doing so in many states, the cost of covering immigrants is then shifted to local entities.

Similarly, using CPS data from 1995–2001, Borjas (2003) analyzed the impact of welfare restrictions on immigrant access to health insurance. He found, contrary to expectations, that immigrant uninsured rates during this period either remained the same or decreased. Borjas attributed this finding to the fact that, between 1995 and 2001, those immigrants who were potentially most affected by welfare restrictions were able to find employment, and thus increased their probability of having employer-based coverage (Borjas 2003). One possible limitation of these findings, however, is that they do not account for potential effects of PRWORA on immigrant attitudes toward enrolling in public health insurance programs. In other words, while the negative effects of immigrant restrictions were offset by increased rates of employer-based coverage, immigrant populations eligible for public health insurance programs were not necessarily more likely to enroll.

FACTORS CONTRIBUTING TO LATINO UNDER-ENROLLMENT IN MEDICAID AND SCHIP

At every stage of their involvement with the public insurance enrollment process, Latino families face barriers to access. Even before applying, lack of information about available insurance coverage poses a major hurdle. According to a 1998 U.S. General Accounting Office (GAO) report, households may not be aware of their eligibility status;

and since many working immigrant families are not welfare recipients, they may not believe they meet the criteria for public insurance programs. Parents might also believe that insurance coverage is necessary only if their children require immediate medical attention. In addition, the confusing nature of welfare reform, not to mention the lengthy enrollment process, may further discourage families from enrolling in Medicaid (GAO 1998). Access to information may be a factor, either because the program is not well marketed to targeted groups or because potential consumers have difficulty understanding marketing strategies and on that basis are not interested in learning more. Finally, because of immigrant restrictions or cost considerations, some families may be accustomed to using clinics or emergency rooms for all their medical care and opt for these services over enrolling in public insurance programs. Finally, some families may eschew formal health services altogether, relying more on alternative, home-based, or culturally-specific forms of health care (GAO 1998). Given the current economic crisis adversely affecting state budgets during the last few years (2006–2010), cuts to Medicaid budgets have resulted in the following strategies: elimination of optional benefits such as dental and vision services, and substantial reductions in provider payments (Sack and Pear 2010). These strategies intentionally or unintentionally make it more difficult for Medicaid beneficiaries to maintain either continuous enrollment or access to services.

If families do gain access to information about public insurance coverage options, the complexity of Medicaid requirements for enrollment may pose a second barrier. The full list of accepted documents is extensive and complicated (see Table 8.2, below, first published in a Families USA July 2006 brief). The regulations require that states use a four-tier hierarchy of acceptable documentation verifying an individual's citizenship status (Families USA 2006), with documents listed in Tier 1 considered to be the most reliable and documents in Tier 4 least reliable. Tiers 3 and 4 can be used only after an applicant or enrollee shows that he or she cannot obtain any documents from the previous tier (Families USA 2006).

In 1997, SCHIP legislation gave states the option of using Medicaid, a separate state program to help expand coverage for low-income

Table 8.2. Required Documentation for Enrollment in Medicaid

Tier 1 (proves both citizenship and identity)
  U.S. passport
  Certificate of Naturalization
  Certificate of U.S. Citizenship	

Tier 2 (proves citizenship only) • A U.S. public birth record • Certification of Report of Birth • Certification of Birth Abroad • U.S. Citizen Identification Card • Consular Report of Birth Abroad of U.S. Citizen • Final adoption decree • Evidence of U.S. civil service employment before June 1, 1976.	**Proof of Identity** • Any item from Tier 1 Or • U.S. driver's license with either a photo of the individual or other identifying information (e.g., name, age, sex, race, height, weight, or eye color) • School ID card with photo • U.S. Military card or draft record • Government-issued ID with the same information that is included on a driver's license • Native American tribal document • Certificate of Degree of Indian Blood • U.S. Coast Guard Merchant Mariner card • School records for children under sixteen, including nursery school or daycare records • If none of the above documents is available for a child under 16, a parent or guardian can attest to the identity of the child. The affidavit must be signed under penalty of perjury and cannot be used if an affidavit citizenship was provided.
Tier 3 (proves citizenship only and must be established at the time of the person's birth and have been created at least 5 years before application date) • Extract of hospital record on hospital letterhead • Life or health insurance record showing U.S. place of birth.	
Tier 4 (proves citizenship only and must be created at least five years before the application) • Federal or state Census record showing place of birth • BIA tribal census records of Navajo Indians • U.S. state vital statistics official notification of birth • Amended U.S. public birth record • Statement signed by physician/midwife in attendance at birth • Institutional admission papers indicating place of birth • Medical record indicating U.S. place of birth • Written affidavit by at least two individuals.	*Note:* States also have the option of verifying identity by doing a cross match with other agencies that can certify the identity of the person (e.g., food stamps, child support, corrections, motor vehicle, and child protective services agencies).

Source: Families USA 2006.

uninsured children (Dubay et al. 2002). SCHIP legislation, together with the Balanced Budget Act of 1997, provided greater flexibility in the Medicaid and SCHIP eligibility determination for children at the state level. This legislation allowed states to implement presumptive and continuous eligibility for children (Dubay et al. 2002). Despite the expansion of eligibility, many families were unaware that their children were eligible for health care under Medicaid or SCHIP; 9 million children in the United States, a majority of whom were eligible for SCHIP, were uninsured in 2007 (Kaiser Commission 2007).

In addition to barriers posed by access to information and extensive enrollment requirements, language continues to be one of the biggest obstacles to maintaining enrollment for Latino families. A study at the University of Pittsburgh examined over twelve thousand families and determined that difficulties with the English language may have cost five million eligible children their access to Medicaid benefits in 1992. Given that 75 percent of uninsured and Medicaid-eligible Latinos opted to conduct interviews in Spanish, researchers concluded that language difficulties are key to understanding the significantly higher rates of uninsured among Medicaid-eligible Latino children when compared to other racial and ethnic groups (Language Barrier May Keep Children Uninsured 2000).

Research has also shown that educational level greatly affects Latinos' access to and utilization of health care services, since education affects occupational status, which in turn affects the probability of acquiring employment-based insurance. Higher levels of educational attainment are also associated with greater reception to learning about relevant health issues, as well as with increased ability to manage the complexities of any health care system. Research also suggests that higher levels of maternal education lead to greater rates of health care utilization among children (Byck 2000). For the sake of efficient policy implementation, policymakers must take into account clients' differences in educational backgrounds even within the Medicaid- and SCHIP-eligible populations. When advertising the program, for example, program coordinators must clearly identify target groups and address the specific situation of each population.[8]

Yet perhaps the biggest factor contributing to low levels of enrollment in public health insurance programs among Latinos specifically is immigrant status. In addition to the linguistic and cultural barriers that many Latinos encounter, legal immigrants fear that receiving public assistance will threaten their immigrant status (GAO 1998; Maida 2001). This fear has its roots in the United States Immigration and Naturalization Service's (INS) policy for "public charge," which has had harsh effects upon both legal and illegal immigrants in large part due to its ambiguous definition. Prior to 1999, public charge policy essentially gave the INS grounds to deport or to deny entry to any immigrant who relied upon (or who was believed to potentially rely upon) public assistance as his or her main means of support (INS of the U.S. Department of Justice 1999). As Swingle (2000) demonstrated, one effect of public charge policy has been to deter immigrant women from seeking prenatal care and families from using immunization or nutrition programs for their children.

Recognizing the probability of negative health effects such as these, not only for immigrants, but for the larger population as well, in 1999 the INS sought to clearly define public charge as a description applicable only to those immigrants "who ha[ve] become (for deportation purposes) or who [are] likely to become (for admission or adjustment purposes) 'primarily dependent on the government for subsistence, as demonstrated by either the receipt of public cash assistance for income maintenance or institutionalization for long-term care at government expense'" (INS of the U.S. Department of Justice 1999). The Department of Justice created this definition to dispel any confusion regarding the effects of public program participation on immigrant status. The emphasis in the new definition on cash assistance was clearly an attempt to separate public aid programs such as health care from the more long-term and intensive forms of support constitutive of public charge status. Despite these clarifications, the specter of public charge policy as it existed before 1999 may continue unnecessarily to discourage immigrants from using available services. Moreover, it should be stated here that many eligible low-income families, immigrant or not, are also disinclined to participate in public programs for fear of being labeled welfare recipients (GAO 1998). This fear is substantiated given the fact that need-based public programs tend not to remedy racial and economic stratification, often highlighting and maintaining it instead (Meyer 1994). For these reasons, policymakers and administrators should consider these fears when implementing particular programs rather than downplaying or dismissing them.

BARRIERS TO EFFECTIVE UTILIZATION OF CARE

In their study of the impact of Medicaid expansions on low-income children, Currie and Gruber (1996a) found that enrollment in public insurance programs does not necessarily result in health improvements, since it can ensure neither the proper utilization of health care nor the competency and efficacy of providers. In the case of Latinos, unfamiliarity with both the health care system and the importance of preventative care practices can preclude the positive health outcomes associated with eligibility and enrollment in public health insurance programs. In addition, in certain areas health care providers may not offer services at all to publicly insured patients or maintain services at all in poor communities. Logistical and cultural issues can also detract from many providers' abilities to provide necessary or appropriate services, although it is important to point out that such issues may vary widely not only from state to state, but from county to county and community to community. The differences that may exist in access to public health programs and health care services between rural and urban Latino communities are especially relevant.

Although immigrant populations are often aware of services available to them in the event of a medical emergency, they may be unacquainted with the preventative health services available in their community, such as routine medical examinations and childhood vaccinations (Maida 2001). This is problematic, as research has found that when children lack access to preventive services, they tend to rely upon improper and often costly sources of treatment. The current economic recession has further eroded prevention services (Sack and Pear 2010). Lacking early detection of and treatment for medical conditions, these children are then more susceptible to serious illness (Byck 2000).

FACTORS BEHIND BARRIERS TO UTILIZATION OF CARE

Many factors account for this lack of access to primary care and prevention services. Cotler (2001) points to underlying social conditions like poverty. In their study of racial and ethnic differences among pregnant substance abusers eligible for Medicaid, Argeriou and Daley (1997) also found that Latinos place greater emphasis on the family than do other racial/ethnic groups, another factor that can negatively impact utilization of preventative services. As Maida (2001) explains, familial networks serve as the primary caregiving unit for many Latinos, and for Latino immigrants coming from rural areas in particular. This may shape attitudes toward methods of caring for the ill in ways that may not be amenable to regular use of the health care system (Maida 2001). Rural Latinos may also have problems finding health care providers in their area who will treat publicly insured patients, an issue that perhaps stems from the lower reimbursement rates that accompany public health insurance as compared to private insurance (Currie and Gruber 1996a).

The location of primary care providers can also predict access and utilization rates (Halfon et al. 1997). Many studies have documented a direct relationship between the distance individuals must travel to providers and the rate and quality of treatment, particularly among low-income, minority, and Medicaid-eligible populations (Currie and Reagan 1999; Lykens and Jargowsky 2002). Due to disjunctions in location between practitioners and eligible children, some beneficiaries cannot find a provider.

Studies have also shown that disparities in treatment exist even within the Medicaid-enrolled population (Vitullo and Taylor 2002; Lieu et al. 2002). A study by Lieu et al. (2002) investigated health status and use of asthma management techniques among children of different racial and ethnic backgrounds. The authors examined the medical records of children with asthma enrolled in Medicaid through five different Managed Care Organizations (MCOs) and interviewed parents by telephone concerning the asthma status of their children. Though researchers did find that asthma status scores of Latino children were comparable to those of white children, the study also provided evidence that, relative to white children, Latino children had more absences from school due to asthma and tended to use inhaled anti-inflammatory medication less often than needed. Lieu et al. concluded from these findings that, compared to white children, Latino children with asthma had poorer health and higher rates of under-use for preventative asthma treatments.

Finkelstein et al. (2002) demonstrated similar findings, further substantiating the relationship between minority status and under-use of preventative medications. In their study of inhaler usage among children with asthma, the authors concluded that Latinos and African Americans were significantly more likely than non-Latino whites to under-use controller medication for the prevention of asthma symptoms (79 percent and 75 percent vs. 69 percent, respectively). The authors found that these higher rates of under-use could be linked to the lack of a primary care physician—88 percent of all patients with asthma without a regular source of primary care reported under-use, as compared to only 71 percent among those under the care of a primary practitioner. The study also found that the administration of written care plans lowered the likelihood of under-use from 79 percent to 60 percent. Follow-up appointments produced similar effects, reducing under-use of controller medications from 85 percent to 68 percent, provided that the appointment had taken place within the previous six months (Finkelstein et al. 2002).

Thus, even when Latinos are eligible for and utilize Medicaid benefits, there is a repeating history of under-use (Halfon et al. 1997; Shinkman 1997; Barents Group of KPMG Consulting Inc. 2001; Vitullo and Taylor 2002; Maida 2001; Finkelstein et al. 2002; Doty 2003). A study conducted jointly by the Centers for Medicare and Medicaid Services (CMS) with Barents Group of KPMG Consulting Inc. (2001) has attributed these patterns of under-use to the shortage of basic information about public programs within both Latino communities and the Community Based Organizations (CBOs) that work with them (Barents Group of KPMG Consulting Inc. 2001). It may very well be that this unfamiliarity with available options results in Latino beneficiaries' relative lack of concern with the quality of care received. Because much of this informational gap arises from a community-level lack of infrastructure for communicating health-related information, the study recommends that CBOs forge stronger links with federal-level programs such as Medicaid and SCHIP. Such partnerships would provide the requisite resources and tools for the successful transmission of program information to Latino enrollees.

MEDICAID AND MANAGED CARE

A general trend in public health care in certain states has been the move from private providers to Managed Care Organizations (MCOs). In

2002 over half of Medicaid beneficiaries in California and Florida were enrolled in a managed care plan, as shown in the chart below.

Figure 8.5 shows that, excluding Illinois, those states with a significant number of Latinos also contain a large percentage of Medicaid enrollees who participate in managed care plans. When discussing Latinos' utilization of health care services, it is necessary to make this distinction between managed care and traditional providers, because different sets of barriers accompany different forms of health care. While patients typically pay traditional providers according to a fee for service (FFS) schedule, managed care plans receive capitated (or flat) rates per enrollee, appropriating funds to meet the needs of beneficiaries. This can cause problems for Latinos, as well as for other disadvantaged groups, given that "[i]n a managed care or capitated rate environment, delivery of a service to an individual becomes a cost," potentially leading MCOs to "limit costs by limiting services" (Center for Mental Health Services 2001). One drawback to MCOs is that they may have a financial incentive to eschew services that are necessary for delivering culturally specific or culturally competent care (Center for Mental Health Services 2001).

The issue of educational literature is one of the most problematic areas for MCOs with respect to their provision of services. Most MCOs publish instructional literature to inform beneficiaries about available services, program policies, and enrollee rights. Studies have found, however, that managed care plans have had difficulties producing and supplying linguistically appropriate educational materials to beneficiaries (Kominski et al. 2003). This stems in part from enrollees' lower levels of education; in California, for instance, a study conducted by the UCLA Center for Health Policy Research found that 35 percent of adult HMO enrollees ages 18–64, and 45 percent of enrollees ages 65 and older have a high school education or less. The same study found that linguistic barriers may also significantly impede access to and utilization of the services provided by HMOs. The study reports that immigrants constitute more than a quarter of all HMO members in California, that 34 percent of HMO enrollees report that English is not their at-home language, and that in some counties this percentage increases to nearly 50 percent. In addition, 4 percent of all HMO enrollees do not speak English well or at all (Kominski et al. 2003). As

Figure 8.5. Percent of Medicaid Enrollees in Managed Care Plans

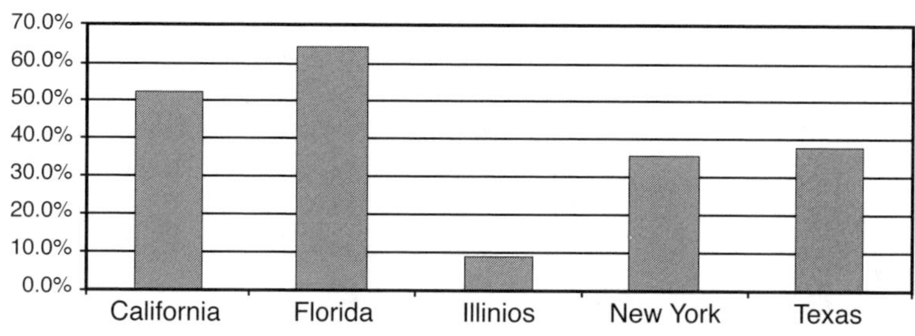

Source: Center for Medicare and Medicaid Services, n.d. State Children's Health Insurance Program 2001 Annual Reports.

suggested below in Figure 8.6, this percentage is much higher for Latinos in each of the five states shown, pointing to the need for MCOs in those states to provide linguistically appropriate health care services to their beneficiaries.

Ideally, linguistically and educationally sensitive services would be a part of broader efforts by MCOs to provide all their beneficiaries with equal access to care. It is an implicit reference to the need for such equitable standards that the idea of cultural competency has gained currency within the literature. In the chapter that follows, we examine at length some of the culturally innovative interventions that have proved effective in overcoming the barriers to eligibility, enrollment, and utilization described above, thereby increasing access to public health insurance programs for Latinos.

LATINO ACCESS TO INSURANCE AND OBAMA'S HEALTH CARE REFORMS

As indicated above, Latinos face numerous barriers to accessing quality health care, and the undocumented population is the group that is most likely to be denied access to publicly financed health services. Under the current health care reform efforts, known as the Patient Protection and

Figure 8.6. Percent of Hispanics Who Speak English "Not Well" or "Not at All"

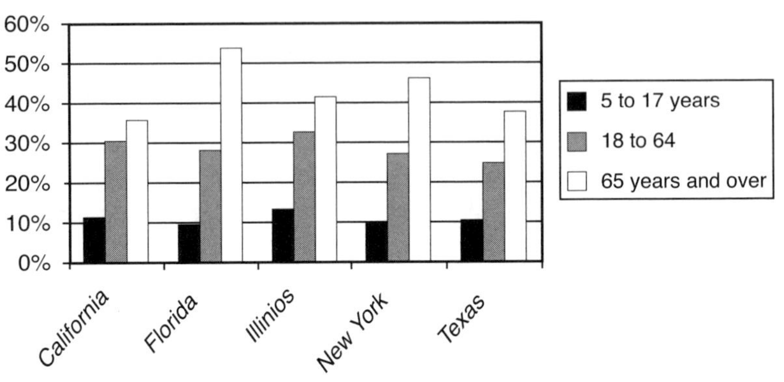

Source: United States Census Bureau 2000.

Affordable Care Act of 2010, the target is to increase health care coverage and access to American citizens with the goal of rolling in these reforms within the next 5 years (HealthCare.gov n.d.). Indeed, some estimates suggest that when fully implemented, almost 95 percent of all U.S. citizens will have some type of health care coverage (Tumulty 2010). Thus, this legislation will have a key impact on Latino citizen families and legal immigrants. Nevertheless, the new health care legislation efforts do not address the needs of the undocumented Latino community, and will further exclude them from access to a mechanism for financing health care, subsequently limiting their access to medical care.

According to the new federal coverage proposal, undocumented individuals, including their children, would not be eligible for Medicare, nonemergency Medicaid, or SCHIP, adding to the already growing numbers of Latinos who lack health insurance (NILC 2010). However, if an individual is eligible for coverage, having an undocumented person in the family would not change that individual's eligibility status (NCLR 2010). Moreover, under the new laws all legal immigrants and U.S. citizens would be required to have insurance, excluding the undocumented population, which due to immigration status are exempt from mandates or requirements to obtain health insurance (NCLR

2010). As a result, many undocumented immigrants will be uninsured, but may be able to waive the penalties against them. While the new laws do have potential to positively impact the legal Latino population, those individuals who lack citizenship will continue to be in a position where they avoid accessing certain public benefits due to the threat of deportation (Berk and Schur 2001).

Thus we see overall that immigration laws, as they affect access to public services and public health insurance differentially, create barriers to eligibility, enrollment, and utilization of Medicaid and SCHIP programs for segments of the Latino population. This final point must be underscored, as the fundamental premise of Medicaid, SCHIP, and the more recently passed Patient Protection and Affordable Care Act is to increase health care access among vulnerable and uninsured individuals who reside in the United States. The exclusion of undocumented immigrants from these measures thus means that these health care financing programs fail in their charge to protect the most vulnerable populations in a comprehensive or humane manner, Latino or otherwise. Undocumented children in particular fall within a very high-risk population. Without access to health care, undocumented children not only lack access to appropriate health screening, but also place themselves, their families, and other community members at risk for various infectious diseases, since the cost of containing infectious diseases and providing regular immunization will rely on the idiosyncratic availability of school-and community-based health clinics. Although targeted funding to community-based health clinics exists for Latino communities, the current state budgetary constraints combined with the issues of immigrant status create significant resource constraints for providing basic services to mixed status families who have both legal and undocumented family members.

NOTES

1. According to data from the U.S. Department of Health and Human Services, the federal poverty level in May 2010 was set at $18,310 for a family of three living in the continental U.S. See http://aspe.hhs.gov/poverty/ for more detailed information on federal poverty guidelines according to family size.

2. Income eligibility cut-offs and general SCHIP facts for California, Florida, Illinois, New York, and Texas can be found in Appendices 1 and 2, respectively.

3. Prior to 2003 many states had increased income cut-off levels and done away with other requirements, such as in- person interviews and quarterly status reports (Ross and Hill 2003).

4. The take-up rate is calculated as a percentage of those who enroll in a program divided by the number of eligible persons. "Take-up" is used in reference to full capacity, or a 100 percent take-up rate.

5. Well-child visits are regular preventative check-ups at a physician's office.

6. In 2004, 30 percent of the 35.2 million immigrants in the United States were undocumented, which accounted for 21 percent of the nation's nearly 46 million uninsured (Kaiser Commission on Key Facts 2006). Studies have shown that the approaches agencies use to determine non-citizen eligibility (e.g., five-year limitations on legal immigrant eligibility) are very challenging for immigrant applicants (Health and Human Services 2002). Furthermore, the new regulations passed in 2006 create more stringent citizenship documentation requirements in Medicaid and present an additional layer of complexity for non-citizen applicants (Families USA 2006).

7. "Poor" indicates family income less than 200 percent of the Federal Poverty Level (FPL). "Non-poor" refers to income levels from 300 percent to 400 percent of the FPL.

8. Research has also examined the difference between the Medicaid-eligible and SCHIP-eligible populations. Byck (2000) attempts to identify characteristics of each group in order to see how uninsured, SCHIP-eligible children compare to children with different sources of insurance coverage including Medicaid and private insurance providers, as well as children that are covered through private insurance but have an income level that qualifies for SCHIP enrollment. Her research determined that both the health status and socioeconomic characteristics of uninsured SCHIP-eligible children varies from those of children with other sources of coverage. When compared to those children enrolled in Medicaid, for example, SCHIP-eligible children were older, healthier, more likely to be white, and to come from a better educated, employed two-parent family. Furthermore, because the higher educational levels among parents of SCHIP-eligible children often translate to increased job opportunities, it may be necessary to employ SCHIP outreach strategies that are different from those used for Medicaid-eligible populations (i.e., disseminating information at the work place). Program coordinators should also take into consideration the differences in employment patterns among groups with divergent sources of coverage, selecting particular industries for worksite outreach depending on the target population.

REFERENCES

Angel, Ronald J., and Jacqueline L. Angel. 1996. "The Extent of Private and Public Health Insurance Coverage among Adult Hispanics." *The Gerontologist* 36 (3): 332–40.

Argeriou, Milton, and Marilyn Daley. 1997. "An Examination of Racial and Ethnic Differences Within a Sample of Hispanic, White (Non-Hispanic), and African American Medicaid-Eligible Pregnant Substance Abusers." *Journal of Substance Abuse Treatment* 14 (5): 489–98.

Asch, Stephen M., Susan Frayne, and Howard Waitzkin. 1995. "To Discharge or Not to Discharge: Ethics for the Care of an Undocumented Immigrant." *Journal of Health Care for the Poor and Underserved* 6 (1): 3–9.

Barents Group of KPMG Consulting Inc. 2001. "Development and Testing of Medicare Health Plan Choice Materials for Hispanic/Latino Beneficiaries and Intermediaries Serving Them." McLean: Health Care Financing Administration (Centers for Medicare and Medicaid Services).

Benjamin, A. E., Steven P. Wallace, Valentine Villa, and Kathy McCarthy. 2000. "California Immigrants Have Mostly Lower Rates of Disability and Use of Disability Services than State's U.S.-Born Residents." Los Angeles: UCLA Center for Health Policy Research. http://www.healthpolicy.ucla.edu/pubs/files/CaliforniaImmigrantsPolicyBrief.pdf. Last accessed February 29, 2004.

Berk, Marc L., and Claudia L. Schur. 2001. "The Effect of Fear on Access Care among Undocumented Latino Immigrants." *Journal of Immigrant Health* 3 (3): 151–56.

Berman, Stephan. 1995. "Uninsured Children: An Unintended Consequence of Health Care System Reform Efforts." *Journal of the American Medical Association* 274 (18): 1472–73.

Borjas, George J. 2003. "Welfare Reform, Labor Supply, and Health Insurance in the Immigrant Population." *Journal of Health Economics* 22 (6): 933–58.

Byck, Gayle R. 2000. "A Comparison of the Socioeconomics and Health Status Characteristics of Uninsured, State Children's Health Insurance Program-Eligible Children in the United States with Those of Other Groups of Insured Children: Implications for Policy." *Pediatrics* 106 (1): 14–21.

Carrasquillo, Olveen, Danielle H. Ferry, Jennifer Edwards, and Sherry Glied. 2003. "Eligibility for Government Insurance if Immigrant Provisions of Welfare Reform Are Repealed." *American Journal of Public Health* 93 (10): 1680–82.

Center for Medicare and Medicaid Services. n.d. "State Children's Health Insurance Program 2001 Annual Reports." http://www.cms.hhs.gov/schip/annual-reports/year-report.asp?year=2001. Last accessed April 9, 2004.

Center for Mental Health Services, with the Substance Abuse and Mental Health Services Administration (SAMHSA). 2001. "Cultural Competence Standards in Managed Care Mental Health Services: Four Underserved/Underrepresented Racial/Ethnic Groups." Washington, DC: U.S. Department of Health and Human Services. http://www.mentalhealth.samhsa.gov/publications/allpubs/SMA00-3457/default.asp. Last accessed March 1, 2004.

Centers for Medicare and Medicaid Services. June 30, 2002. "Medicaid Managed Penetration Rates by State: National Summary Table." *2002 Medicaid Managed Care Enrollment Report.* http://www.cms.gov/medicaid/managedcare/mcsten02.pdf. Last accessed April 5, 2004.

Cotler, Miriam Piven. July 1, 2001. "Background on Health Care Coverage: Equity and Quality." Paper prepared for the Department of Health Services, State of California. http://www.healthcareoptions.ca.gov/csun equity.asp. Last accessed July 16, 2003.

Currie, Janet, and Jonathan Gruber. 1996a. "Health Insurance Eligibility, Utilization of Medical Care, and Child Health." *Quarterly Journal of Economics* 111 (2): 431–66.

———. 1996b. "Saving Babies: The Efficacy and Cost of Recent Changes in the Medicaid Eligibility of Pregnant Women." *Journal of Political Economy* 104 (6): 1263–96.

Currie, Janet, and Patricia B. Reagan. 1999. "Distance to Hospital and Children's Access to Care: Is Being Closer Better, and for Whom?" *UCLA Economics Online Papers* 15. http://www.econ.ucla.edu/people/papers/currie/dist.pdf. Last accessed February 29, 2004.

Doty, Michelle M. 2003. "Hispanic Patients' Double Burden: Lack of Health Insurance and Limited English." New York: Commonwealth Fund. http://www.cmwf.org/programs/insurance/doty_hispanicdoubleburden_592.pdf. Last accessed February 29, 2004.

Dubay, Lisa, Jennifer Haley, and Genevieve Kenney. 2002. "Children's Eligibility for Medicaid and SCHIP: A View from 2000." Washington, DC: Urban Institute.

Ellwood, Marilyn R., and Leighton Ku. 1998. "Welfare and Immigration Reforms: Unintended Side Effects for Medicaid." *Health Affairs* 17 (3): 137–51.

Families USA. 2006. "Medicaid Alert. The Burden of Proof: New Regulations Worsen Citizenship Documentation Requirement in Medicaid." www.familiesusa.org/assets/pdfs/DRA-Citizenship-July-2006.pdf.

Finkelstein, Jonathan A., Paula Lozano, Harold J. Farber, Irina Miroshnik, and Tracy A. Lieu. 2002. "Underuse of Controller Medications Among

Medicaid-Insured Children with Asthma." *Archives of Pediatrics and Adolescent Medicine* 156 (6): 562–67.

Halfon, Neal, David L. Wood, R. Burciaga Valdez, Margaret Pereyra, and Naihua Duan. 1997. "Medicaid Enrollment and Health Services Access by Latino Children in Inner-City Los Angeles." *Journal of the American Medical Association* 277 (8): 636–41.

Health and Human Services. 2002. "The Application Process for TANF, Food Stamps, Medicaid, and SCHIP: Chapter 5. Eligibility Determination Policies and Verification Procedures: Special Issues for Immigrants."

Health Care and Education Reconciliation Act of 2010, Public Law 111-152, 111th Congress, 2nd session. March 30, 2010, §1204.

HealthCare.gov. n.d. "Provisions of the Affordable Care Act, By Year." http://www.healthcare.gov/law/about/legislation/order/byyear.html. Last accessed July 12, 2010.

Immigration and Naturalization Service of the U.S. Department of Justice. 1999. "Inadmissibility and Deportability on Public Charge Grounds; Field Guidance on Deportability and Inadmissibility on Public Charge Grounds; Proposed Rule and Notice." *Federal Register* 49, no. 101 (May 26, 1999): 28676–88.

Kaiser Commission. 2007. "SCHIP Turns 10: An Update on Enrollment and the Outlook on Reauthorization from the Program's Directors." Washington, DC: Henry J. Kaiser Family Foundation.

Kaiser Commission on Key Facts. 2006. "Medicaid and the Uninsured: Medicaid and SCHIP Eligibility for Immigrants." Washington, DC: Henry J. Kaiser Family Foundation.

Kominski, Gerald, Pamela Davidson, Crystal Lynn Keeler, Natasha Razack, Lida Becerra, and Rabeya Sen. 2003. "Profile of California's HMO Enrollees: Findings from the 2001 California Health Interview Survey." Los Angeles: UCLA Center for Health Policy Research, for the California Office of the Patient Advocate. http://www.healthpolicy.ucla.edu/pubs/files/OPA_Report_022003.pdf. Last accessed February 29, 2004.

Kronick, Richard, and Todd Gilmer. 1999. "Explaining the Decline in Health Insurance Coverage, 1979–1995." *Health Affairs* 18 (2): 30–47.

Ku, Leighton, and Shannon Blaney. 2000. "Health Coverage for Legal Immigrant Children: New Census Data Highlight Importance of Restoring Medicaid and SCHIP Coverage." Washington, DC: Center on Budget and Policy Priorities. http://www.cbpp.org/10-4-00health.pdf. Last accessed March 1, 2004.

Ku, Leighton, and Teresa A. Coughlin. 1997. "How the New Welfare Reform Law Affects Medicaid." Washington, DC: Urban Institute Series A, No. A–5.

"Language Barrier May Keep Children Uninsured." 2000. *Alcoholism and Drug Abuse Weekly* 12 (27): 7.

Levan, Rebecka, E. Richard Brown, Nancy Hays, and Roberta Wyn. 1999. "Disparity in Job-Based Coverage Places California's Latinos at Risk of Being Uninsured." Los Angeles: UCLA Center for Health Policy Research.

Lieu, Tracy A., Paula Lozano, Jonathan A. Finkelstein, Felicia W. Chi, Nancy G. Jensvold, Angela M. Capra, Charles P. Quesenberry, Joe V. Selby, and Harold J. Farber. 2002. "Racial/Ethnic Variation in Asthma Status and Management Practices among Children in Managed Medicaid." *Pediatrics* 109 (5): 857–65.

Lykens, Kristine A., and Paul A. Jargowsky. 2002. "Medicaid Matters: Children's Health and Medicaid Eligibility Expansions." *Journal of Policy Analysis and Management* 21 (2): 219–38.

Maida, Carl A. July 1, 2001. "Access to Health Care for California's Immigrants." Paper prepared for the Department of Health Services, State of California. http://www.healthcareoptions.ca.gov/csunimmigrant.asp. Last accessed July 16, 2003.

Marquis, Susan M., and Stephen H. Long. 1996. "Reconsidering the Effect of Medicaid on Health Care Services Use." *Health Services Research* 30 (6): 791–808.

Meyer, Madonna Harrington. 1994. "Gender, Race, and the Distribution of Social Assistance: Medicaid Use among the Frail Elderly." *Gender and Society* 8 (1): 8–28.

National Council of La Raza. 2010. "Critical Things You Should Know about Health Care Reform, Fact Sheet." http://www.nclr.org/content/publications/detail/63138/. Last accessed July 12, 2010.

National Immigration Law Center. 2010. "How Are Immigrants Included in Health Care Reform?" http://www.nilc.org/immspbs/health/immigrant-inclusion-in-HR3590-2010-04-19.pdf. Last accessed July 12, 2010.

Newacheck, Paul W., Jeffrey J. Stoddard, Dana C. Hughes, and Michelle Pearl. 1998. "Health Insurance and Access to Primary Care for Children." *New England Journal of Medicine* 338 (8): 513–19.

Racine, Andrew D., Robert Kaestner, Theodore J. Joyce, and Gregory J. Colman. 2001. "Differential Impact of Recent Medicaid Expansions by Race and Ethnicity." *Pediatrics* 108 (5): 1135–42.

Ross, Donna Cohen, and Ian T. Hill. 2003. "Enrolling Eligible Children and Keeping Them Enrolled." *Future of Children* 13 (1): 81–97.

Sack, Kevin, and Robert Pear. 2010. "States Consider Medicaid Cuts as Use Grows." *New York Times,* February 18. http://www.nytimes.com. Last acessed July 12, 2010.

Schur, Claudia L., and Jacob Feldman. 2001. "Running in Place: How Job Characteristics, Immigrant Status, and Family Structure Keep Hispanics Uninsured." New York: Commonwealth Fund. http://www.cmwf.org/programs/insurance/schur_running_453.pdf. Last accessed March 1, 2004.

Shinkman, Ron. 1997. "Latino Kids Underinsured: L.A. Children Fall through Medicaid Cracks, Study Finds." *Modern Healthcare* 27 (10): 36.

Shone, Laura P., Andrew W. Dick, Cindy Brach, Kim S. Kimminau, Barbara J. LaClair, Elizabeth A. Shenkman, Jana F. Col, Virginia A. Schaffer, Frank Mulvihill, Peter G. Szilagyi, Jonathan D. Klein, Karen VanLandeghem, and Janet Bronstein. 2003. "The Role of Race and Ethnicity in the State Children's Health Insurance Program (SCHIP) in Four States: Are There Baseline Disparities, and What Do They Mean for SCHIP?" *Pediatrics* 112 (6): 521–32.

Short, Pamela Farley, and Doris C. Lefkowitz. 1992. "Encouraging Preventive Services for Low-Income Children: The Effect of Expanding Medicaid." *Medical Care* 30 (9): 766–80.

Swingle, Digna Betancourt. 2000. "Immigrants and August 22, 1996: Will the Public Charge Rule Clarify Program Eligibility." *Families in Society: Journal of Contemporary Human Services* 81 (6): 605–10.

Tumulty, Karen. 2010. "Making History: House Passes Health Care Reform." *Time,* March 23. http//:www.time.com/time. Last accessed July 12, 2010.

United States Census Bureau. 2000. "Census 2000 Gateway." http://www.census.gov/main/www/cen2000.html. Last accessed April 9, 2004.

———. 2002. "Technical Paper. Current Population Survey, March 2002: Annual Demographic Profile (11/19/02)." Washington, DC: U.S. Bureau of Labor Statistics of the U.S. Census Bureau.

U.S. General Accounting Office. 1998. "Medicaid: Demographics of Non-Enrolled Children Suggests State Outreach Strategies." Washington, DC: U.S. General Accounting Office.

Vitullo, Margaret Weigers, and Amy K. Taylor. 2002. "Latino Adults' Health Insurance Coverage: An Examination of Mexican and Puerto Rican Subgroup Differences." *Journal of Health Care for the Poor and Underserved* 13 (4): 504–25.

NINE

Cultural Sensitivity or Cultural Innovation?

A Review of Interventions to Improve Enrollment of Latino Immigrant Children in Public Insurance Programs

ADELA DE LA TORRE, JESSICA NUÑEZ
DE YBARRA, MARISOL CORTEZ,
AND EMILY PRIETO

In their study of the ways in which managed care plans in California have adapted their services to meet the health needs of the state's diverse populations, Coye and Alvarez (1999) introduce the idea of cultural competency by distinguishing it from cultural sensitivity. According to the definitions they provide, cultural sensitivity refers to an awareness on the part of health care providers of the impact that racial, ethnic, and linguistic variations can have on patient health. Coye and Alvarez distinguish this from cultural competency, which they define according to its functionality; cultural competency is "the ability to provide services [to diverse groups] that yield the desired clinical outcomes combined with a high degree of patient satisfaction." Given this emphasis on functionality, cultural competency is less a capacity for relating to others and more a set of practices or interventions that have concrete and measurable implications for health outcomes, cost-effectiveness, and level of patient satisfaction.

Although the ideal measure of cultural competency with respect to Latinos would be an improvement in health outcomes, very little of the existing literature attempts to investigate the effects of culturally competent interventions or practices on Latino health status. Most of the available literature is descriptive, focusing not on the effects of particular practices or interventions, but on the need for providers to adapt services to the particular needs of the populations they serve. In the case of Latinos, this most often amounts to studies that demonstrate the need for linguistic adaptations such as provision of interpreter services (Doty 2003), availability of bilingual and bicultural health workers (Center for Mental Health Services 2001), and Spanish translations of program information (Coye and Alvarez 1999). Other adaptations described in the literature include the establishment of community advisory committees that providers can consult to assess the changing needs of enrollees (Bureau of Primary Health Care 1999) and the inclusion of Latino cultural issues as part of the curriculum of U.S. medical schools (Flores et al. 2002).

However, when referring to increasing health care access to insurance, it might be more useful to define cultural competency here as the interventions or practices that are best able to reduce the gap between the number of Latinos eligible for public insurance and the number actually enrolled and utilizing available services. Thus the question becomes: Why do Latinos remain under-enrolled in Medicaid and SCHIP despite high levels of eligibility, and despite measures such as eligibility expansions and established methods of outreach? In answering this question, it is important to explore how culture influences behavior when an individual accesses health care. Culturally competent practices are those that are able to address and remedy the specifically *cultural* or non-financial reasons for Latino under-enrollment and under-utilization. This chapter will therefore focus on what we term "culturally innovative interventions"—methods shown to effectively reduce the gap between Latinos' eligibility and their enrollment in and utilization of services—by examining recent literature that documents the effects of outreach practices on Latinos specifically, or whose results can be applied to Latinos. However, in order to examine the culturally innovative interventions that have been most successful with Latino populations, it will be useful to first briefly review the general literature on outreach strategies in order to provide some basis for comparison.

OUTREACH LITERATURE: GENERAL OVERVIEW

When lawmakers signed SCHIP into existence in August 1997, federal legislation recognized outreach to be a central part of the newly created program. As defined by SCHIP legislation, outreach entails "activities to inform families of available coverage and to assist them in enrolling" (Westpfahl 1999). Title XXI mandated that states not only include such activities as a central component of their SCHIP program,[1] but that they also submit a description of outreach plans to the federal government for review (Moore 1999). Further recognizing the centrality of outreach to the successful operation of SCHIP, the Health Resources and Services Administration (HRSA) of the United States Department of Health and Human Services (DHHS) created a standard for outreach in identifying four criteria of "model outreach programs:"

1. The program is tailored to serve specific populations;
2. The program collaborates with existing networks and community organizations in order to efficiently use financial and social capital;
3. The program relies on funding from both public and private sources; and
4. The program implements and utilizes systematic data collection in order to track the program's effectiveness over time (Westpfahl 1999).

Most of the literature that describes general outreach practices reflects these four criteria as well as the federal definition of outreach consisting primarily of education and enrollment assistance. To that extent, we can divide general outreach strategies into two broad categories. The first is what might be termed a "call to action" strategy, the purpose of which is to familiarize the general population with the availability of public health insurance programs and services and to elicit inquiries from potential beneficiaries (Orchard Communications 1999). Mass media campaigns, websites, telephone hotlines, local health fairs, and coordination with other government programs (such as school lunch programs) are all forms of a call to action approach. These broad, information-centered campaigns may be carried out through partnerships with county- or community-based organizations or through person-to-person contact, and may take place in innovative settings (that is, malls, day care centers, fast food restaurants) or using innovative methods of information dissemination such as wash-off tattoos and refrigerator magnets (Westpfahl 1999).

The second type of outreach approach uses a strategy of assistance, whereby state- or community-level outreach workers help eligible families to navigate the enrollment process. Different states have tried various types of enrollment assistance, but the two main strategies are fee-based assistance and assistance via Community Based Organizations (CBOs). In fee-based programs, state certified assistants receive a stipend for each successful application submitted. In the case of assistance via CBOs, states or private organizations endow community groups with grants to fund state-certified assistants who then provide application outreach to target groups. It has generally been found that applications submitted with the aid of a certified assistant have a significantly higher application approval rating. For example, between July 1, 1998, and January 31, 2002, California's SCHIP program had a 79 percent approval rating for assisted applications compared to a 63 percent approval rating for non-assisted applications (Managed Risk Medical Insurance Board 2002a).

Most of the general outreach literature stresses the importance of simplifying enrollment and renewal processes as a way of maximizing the effectiveness of application assistance and removing unnecessary "procedural barriers" to the utilization of programs (Ross and Hill 2003). Also, in line with the "model outreach program" criteria defined by the HRSA, much of the literature suggests that alongside efforts to simplify enrollment and renewal processes, data collection must be a central component of outreach programs. In their survey of state outreach practices, for example, Ross and Hill (2003) mention the problems associated with a lack of quantitative data on outreach, stating that their research methods were limited to telephone interviews with program representatives and an examination of case studies due to the fact that "rigorous studies evaluating specific outreach strategies are largely unavailable." As we will see below, while the number of studies examining the effectiveness and cultural appropriateness of specific outreach interventions is on the increase, these studies are largely qualitative measures conducted in localized areas and often admit to limitations in that regard.

The final issue to mention in relation to the literature on federal and state outreach strategies, especially as they pertain to Latinos, is the role of private sponsors in enrolling beneficiaries in public health insurance programs. For example, the Robert Wood Johnson Foundation's "Covering Kids" initiative was a three-year, forty-seven-million-dollar outreach effort implemented in 1997 that operated through state grants to all fifty states plus the District of Columbia (About Covering Kids 2003). The primary goals of Covering Kids overlap considerably with those specified in the general outreach literature; as stated by Judith Moore (1999), Covering Kids was established to "design and conduct outreach programs to assure children's health coverage, simplify enrollment processes, and coordinate existing coverage programs for low-income children."

The Covering Kids initiative is worth mentioning because its broad focus on outreach included a specific focus on Latino families. One of the projects funded by the Covering Kids initiatives, for example, convened public health workers and policy analysts specializing in Latino health in order to formulate a set of practices useful in enrolling Latino families in public health insurance programs. Through a partnership with the communications firm GMMB, the result of this collaboration was a communications kit entitled "Covering Kids: Reaching Latino Families." Printed in both English and Spanish, the contents of the binder included specific information for conducting both community and media outreach, fact sheets on Latino health, template documents, and sample images for posters and fliers. Included among the outreach strategies discussed were the recruitment of *promotoras,* or lay community outreach workers; the use of holidays, cultural festivals, and other "fun" events as occasions for outreach; and relationship-building with existing networks of community organizations, businesses, schools, public programs, and health care facilities (*Covering Kids:* A National Program of the Robert Wood Johnson Foundation). In many ways, this initiative particularizes many of the main features summarized above from the general literature on outreach in that it stresses the dual importance of providing information and enrollment assistance.

In enumerating culturally specific methods of carrying out these two broad functions of outreach, the "Covering Kids: Reaching Latino Families" communications kit provides a good segue from a discussion of general outreach literature to literature that documents culturally innovative interventions. Having first focused on some of the general strategies described by the literature, we are in a better position to see how specific interventions are not only culturally specific and sensitive, but effective in terms of enrolling Latinos in public health insurance programs.

OUTREACH LITERATURE: CULTURALLY INNOVATIVE INNOVATIONS

When the general literature on outreach notes issues related to Latinos and enrollment, this is usually in the context of community-specific outreach procedures that target vulnerable populations (that is, minorities, immigrants, or children with special health care needs). Westpfahl (1999), for example, mentions that the ability to target specific populations is an important aspect of county- or community-based initiatives. Felland and Staiti (2001) elaborate more fully on this idea in their review of a report on local outreach efforts conducted by the Center for Studying Health System Change (HSC). In light of research suggesting that outreach is more effective at increasing enrollment than eligibility expansions, the HSC visited twelve communities around the nation and conducted interviews with outreach workers, county and state officials, health care providers, and SCHIP and Medicaid representatives. The goal was to survey the sorts of effective outreach activities at the local level so as to recommend state- and federal-level public health policies, particularly in a time of budget crisis. According to the study, states partner with a variety of different organizations; the most significant of these in terms of their ability to maximize enrollment of eligible populations are:

- Health care organizations such as hospitals, community clinics, and commercial health plans;
- Schools and school-related programs;
- Community and religious groups such as day care centers, food banks, churches, homeless shelters, and Americorps programs; and
- Employers, including businesses with large numbers of low-wage workers and small businesses that do not offer employment-based insurance (Felland and Staiti 2001).

Offering support for this contention, a study funded by the Texas Department of Health examined the marketing strategies used during the starting phases of the state's SCHIP program, and found that families were much more responsive if SCHIP was portrayed as a non-welfare or Medicaid type of program (Orchard Communications 1999). Some parents who participated in the study, for example, questioned the quality of care and the respect they would receive if the care were free. Barriers such as these stem from a prior history of economic and political disenfranchisement among the target population, which contributes to skepticism about government programs.

Additional barriers to enrollment include logistical deterrents, such as location of enrollment sites, enrollment hours, transportation, and communication problems. With the help of private and grassroots organizations, state agencies generally have been successful at overcoming these logistical barriers to enrollment (Managed Risk Medical Insurance Board 2002b).

In addition to the strategies mentioned in the general literature on outreach, more recent studies outline what we have been calling here culturally innovative interventions, or interventions within Latino communities specifically which address non-financial barriers to enrollment and use of public health insurance programs and improve health outcomes. As described below, some of these include school-based outreach programs; community-based data collection and application assistance efforts; outreach worker competency in key areas (such as intensive personal contact and public communication strategies); and state-specific interventions.

For instance, a study by Howard L. Taras et al. (2002) expands upon the general findings of the HSC by looking specifically at the effectiveness of school-based assistance programs in one predominantly Latino community. In this study, the authors examine the effectiveness of using schools as sites to conduct Medicaid and SCHIP outreach, focusing on the Health-insurance Access Through Schools (HATS) program. HATS was an outreach effort implemented in California's San Diego County in 1999 following the initiation of the state's SCHIP program; the intent of HATS was to use local schools to enroll eligible children that initial program advertisements had failed to reach. In addition to providing information and education about SCHIP and Medicaid, HATS provided application assistance to eligible parents. The schools targeted by the program had large numbers of low-income families (below 250 percent FPL), of whom more than 85 percent were Latino.

Evaluation of the HATS program revealed that schools were particularly effective outreach sites given the access they gave outreach workers to large numbers of eligible children and to information that would otherwise be difficult, if not impossible, to obtain (for example, telephone numbers from school databases). Though the cost per enrolled child was significantly higher than the typical rate that the state pays application assistants ($75 compared to $50), the authors concluded that this extra expense was cost-effective since HATS enabled outreach workers to reach those parents of eligible children who had not responded to broader methods of outreach, such as mailing flyers to parents, sending notes home with students or enrolling children on the basis of their participation in free or reduced-price lunch programs. As measured by the study, some of the effects of the HATS program included a greater utilization of well-child visits among those enrolled through HATS, including increased timeliness of required vaccinations. One year after enrolling their children in public health insurance via HATS, parents were also more likely to recognize the necessity of seeing a health care provider for issues such as obesity, gang involvement, and learning difficulties. From this study it is evident that while traditional mass marketing-based campaigns may fail to reach many parents of eligible children, the strategic use of location and community-based resources can maximize contact between outreach workers and parents and hence increase Latino enrollment.

COMMUNITY-BASED OUTREACH PROGRAMS

Community-based interventions have also proven effective in the realm of data collection on health insurance status among Latinos. By partnering with community members, Manos et al. (2001) were able to gather information on the insurance and health status of Latinos in a predominantly immigrant community. Researchers trained women in Marin County, California, to conduct interviews with Spanish-speaking mothers in their neighborhood concerning their children's health insurance status and access to care. The goals of the study were to develop collaborative relationships between communities and researchers, to utilize these collaborations to assess Latinos' eligibility for and enrollment in public insurance programs, and to use the results of community-based health investigations as the basis for interventions and policy recommendations. Community members interviewed a random sample of 252 mothers, who provided information on 464 children between the ages of 0 and 18. Interviewers collected information on family demographics, medical insurance history, experiences in accessing health care, and mothers' opinions about health insurance.

From their interviews with mothers about their children, academic and community researchers found that 83 percent of neighborhood children were eligible for either Medicaid or Healthy Families (48.4 percent for Medicaid, 35 percent for Healthy Families). Of these, 28 percent were not enrolled in either public health insurance program. Researchers found that unenrolled children were older (median age 7 as compared to median age 4 for enrolled children), more likely to be noncitizens (22.2 percent compared to 4.8 percent for enrolled children), and less likely to have seen a doctor within the past year (58 percent compared to 78.7 percent). Researchers also determined that mothers of unenrolled children had lower levels of education, were more likely to have paid out of pocket for medical expenses, and were more likely to cite difficulties with the enrollment process such as providing documentation and understanding the required forms (Manos et al. 2001).

However, Manos et al. suggest that much of the difficulty in understanding enrollment paperwork resulted not from language barriers but from literacy levels, given the fact that most families received care at a community health care center where bilingual forms and services were available. For example, despite the fact that language was not perceived to be a major barrier, 19 percent of mothers who did not enroll their children said that they had difficulty understanding the translated forms. That many mothers reported barriers to enrollment despite the availability of translated materials points to the difference between cultural sensitivity and the sorts of culturally innovative interventions necessary to reducing the gap between eligibility and enrollment. Often linguistic services such as the translation of forms are cited in the literature as essential to providing culturally competent care (Doty 2003; Coye and Alvarez 1999; Bureau of Primary Health Care 1999). Manos et al. suggest that these services are not enough to boost enrollment of eligible Latino children. Instead, the authors point to the need for extensive community-based outreach and application assistance coupled with the streamlining and simplification of enrollment procedures.

Castañeda et al. (2003) made similar recommendations when they investigated best practices for enrolling eligible low-income children in California's First Things First (FTF) program. FTF was a health care initiative launched in 1998 by the California Health Care Foundation, which funded public and private coalitions in nine California communities to determine the factors preventing eligible children from enrolling in Medicaid and SCHIP. These findings served as the basis for formulating and implementing practices to circumvent these barriers.

Because community outreach workers were understood to be essential to the efforts of FTF, and because "[a] review of other studies reveals that although many broad generalizations are made about the importance of outreach, little specific guidance is provided for defining and conducting 'outreach' in the context of enrolling children in health insurance programs," the authors of the FTF study attempted to identify specific characteristics of successful outreach workers and strategies

(Castañeda et al. 2003). To collect data on these characteristics, Castañeda et al. conducted site-visit interviews with outreach workers and program administrators, arranged monthly conference calls, and engaged in discussion with each of the nine California FTF coalitions at a statewide conference. Using content analysis of the resultant data, the authors determined that successful outreach resulted from a combination of competent outreach workers and effective practices. Outreach worker competency was found to be a composite of personal/relational skills and training in seven key areas. These personal/relational skills include cultural sensitivity and linguistic competency; respect for confidentiality of information given by enrollees; ability to build community standing of organization; commitment to community; capacity for effective communication on both one-on-one and group level; ability to work independently; and flexibility and ability to multitask. From interviews and discussions with program workers and representatives, researchers then determined that to be successful, outreach workers possessing these skills needed training in six different knowledge areas: overall outreach strategy; insurance rules and criteria for eligibility; immigration law pertaining to Medicaid and SCHIP; local organizations and networking strategies; client-centered outreach; and how to keep information confidential (Castañeda et al. 2003).

Yet the appropriate selection and training of outreach workers was found to be only part of successful outreach practices. Castañeda et al. found that effective outreach needed to combine competent outreach workers with three basic avenues for action: (1) Personal contact with clients. In the communities studied, this took the form of home visits and potlucks in rural areas, "street outreach" in urban areas, information sessions at places of employment, and aggressive personal follow-up for both enrollment and renewal processes. (2) Coordination between existing networks and programs. As has been documented in much of the literature on outreach, elementary and middle schools, community health centers, hospitals, churches, union meetings, neighborhood alliances, day cares, and other community organizations were strategically useful locations for conducting outreach. (3) Utilization of public communication strategies. Complementing personal contact, outreach workers would use community-wide events such as fairs and public celebrations to distribute information and advice about insurance programs. Radio programs were also found to be useful vehicles for spreading information, particularly in immigrant communities.

Thus, the best way to enroll all eligible children is to combine informed outreach worker selection and training with the use of specific routes of action. The authors conclude that although this kind of outreach is essential, it must take place alongside an attempt to reduce structural barriers to enrollment at state and federal levels (Castaneda et al. 2003).

These structural limits to effective outreach have also been the subject of recent discussion among public health researchers, particularly as they pertain to racial and ethnic minorities. In December of 2003, the journal *Pediatrics* devoted an entire issue to the current state of SCHIP in regard to giving low-income children access to health care. Among the articles featured in this issue, two in particular have important implications for the issue of increasing Latinos' enrollment in SCHIP and Medicaid.

In one of these studies, Dick et al. (2003) examine demographic shifts in New York SCHIP enrollees between 1994 and 2001.[2] The objectives of the study were threefold: first, to describe the nature of these shifts; second, to ascertain whether changes in the populations eligible for SCHIP were responsible for demographic shifts; and third, to describe programmatic changes with respect to demographic changes in enrollees. The authors found that over the course of seven years, enrollees in SCHIP are more likely to be older, poorer, and more racially diverse; they are also less likely to have access to health care, as measured by longer periods of being uninsured before enrollment and by a decreased likelihood of having a usual source of care.

Based on their findings, Dick et al. see these demographic shifts as less the product of changes in the populations eligible for SCHIP than in greater widespread knowledge of SCHIP as the program has matured. Changes in the program structure itself, a result of increased federal funding for outreach/advertising, and enrollment simplification efforts have also altered the demographics of SCHIP enrollees over time. Enrollment of Latino children in particular has increased significantly relative to enrollment of white children; with 590,000 children enrolled in 2001, 48.1 percent of SCHIP enrollees were Latino, as compared to 16.4 percent of 70,000 children enrolled in 1994. In contrast, white enrollment fell from 74.3 percent in 1994 to 23.2 percent in 2001. By 2001, Latino children were thus the largest racial/ethnic group of enrollees in New York's SCHIP program.

A significant corollary to this dramatic increase in Latino enrollment has been a shift in the ways enrollees first hear about SCHIP. In both 1994 and 2001, more enrollees surveyed originally encountered SCHIP via word of mouth than from other sources, with 38.8 percent of survey respondents replying that they learned about the program from a friend, neighbor, or relative. By 2001 this figure dropped to 28.3 percent, with more enrollees reporting that their first contact with SCHIP was through television advertisements (10.6 percent in 2001 versus 2 percent in 1994), outreach workers (13.1 percent in 2001 versus 2 percent in 1994), and doctor's offices or clinics (28.1 percent in 2001 versus 23.9 percent in 1994). The importance of outreach workers is significant. While these trends may simply reflect greater program maturity and funding of outreach, the authors also suggest that the growth and success of the program itself may indicate that current enrollment demographics more accurately reflect eligible populations as the program has grown from 70,000 to 590,000 children enrolled and the opportunities for "differential selection" have diminished (Dick et al. 2003). In this context, the increase in significance of outreach workers as a source of program information perhaps indicates the degree to which outreach has helped enroll those who, because of the difficulty in reaching them, were previously eligible but unenrolled.

Shonc et al. (2003) have also examined the role of race and ethnicity among recent enrollees to SCHIP. The authors use data from the Child Health Insurance Research Initiative (CHIRI) to investigate differences in health insurance status and health care access between white, black, and Latino enrollees living in four states (Alabama, Florida, Kansas, and New York). These authors are interested in determining whether, after controlling for other factors, race/ethnicity affects health insurance status and access to care prior to enrollment in SCHIP.

Utilizing telephone and mail-in surveys with parents of newly enrolled SCHIP children, the study found that among new enrollees, black and Latino children generally had poorer health status and access to care prior to enrollment, as determined by access and utilization measures such as prior enrollment in Medicaid, prior incidence of a usual source of care (USC), and prior continuity of care. Among socio-economic measures surveyed, researchers found that black and Latino children were also more likely to live in a single-parent household, to have lower socioeconomic status, and to live in households with higher levels of unemployment or part-time employment. After controlling for other possible sources of disparity, researchers found that race and ethnicity at least partially affected health status and access to care among children newly enrolled in SCHIP; other factors possibly contributing to disparities included the type and extent of outreach efforts as well as the level of program maturity in different states of residence (Shone et al. 2003).

Their results have important policy implications. Although SCHIP did reduce racial/ethnic disparities in health care access and health status, the fact that race/ethnicity has some independent impact on health status indicates that the provision of insurance to historically vulnerable groups may not be enough. Reducing these disparities will depend in part on "identifying and reducing nonfinancial barriers to care" (Shone et al. 2003)—that is, cultural barriers. The culturally innovative interventions that other recent studies have elaborated, however nongeneralizable their results, may therefore be necessary to increase enrollment of minority children. In line with much of the other literature on outreach, Shone et al. also strongly recommend the systematic collection of data on race/ethnicity among SCHIP enrollees so as to monitor the effect of program efforts on disparities of access and outcome. Furthermore, because geography influences the degree of racial/ethnic disparity among SCHIP enrollees, the authors state that interventions (including data collection) must be state-specific, a suggestion that resonates with the collaborative, community-based methods of data collection detailed above. Shone et al. conclude by advocating that policymakers carefully consider the potential negative effects of budget cuts on equity, access, use, and outcomes for all racial and ethnic groups.

BEST PRACTICES IN A TIME OF BUDGET CRISIS

A review of the literature on barriers to health insurance among Latinos and on practices useful in overcoming such barriers yields a number of themes that point toward best practices. Among these are the following:

- Because many of the barriers to enrollment that Latinos face are non-financial, eligibility expansions are a necessary, but not sufficient, condition of increasing Latino enrollment in Medicaid and SCHIP;
- Strictly information-based outreach campaigns are not enough; personal contact with community insiders is necessary;
- This personal contact must be intensive;
- Effective, culturally appropriate data collection methods must be devised and implemented; and
- States must continue to combine community-based outreach with efforts to simplify and streamline enrollment and renewal procedures.

In sum, it is important to consider the unique characteristics, both linguistically and culturally, of the growing Latino community in developing strategies to incorporate them within the public health care financing and delivery system. Moreover, public policies that target the Latino community should also recognize the mixed legal status of these communities both across immigrant groups and within these immigrant groups. Developing public policies that acknowledge these differences and that are not punitive with regard to legal status is clearly necessary if our goal is to increase the enrollment of Latino families in health care programs targeted to improve health care access. Without such policy reforms, the highest risk populations within the Latino community will continue to under-enroll in Medicaid and SCHIP despite implementing the best outreach practices.

NOTES

1. Under 42 CFR 457.90.

2. Although SCHIP was not initiated at the federal level until 1997, New York has offered a children's health insurance program, Child Health Plus (CHPlus), since 1991.

REFERENCES

About Covering Kids. 2003. "Covering Kids and Families." http://www .coveringkids.org /pages/index.php?DocID=67. Last accessed March 1, 2004.

Bureau of Primary Health Care. 1999. "Cultural Competence: A Journey." New Orleans: Health Resources and Services Administration, U.S. Department of Health and Human Services.

Castañeda, Xochitl, Zoe Cardoza Clayson, Tom Rundall, Liane Dong, and Margo Sercaz. 2003. "Promising Outreach Practices: Enrolling Low-Income Children in Health Insurance Programs in California." *Health Promotion Practices* 4 (4): 430–38.

Center for Mental Health Services, with the Substance Abuse and Mental Health Services Administration (SAMHSA). 2001. "Cultural Competence Standards in Managed Care Mental Health Services: Four Underserved/Underrepresented Racial/Ethnic Groups. Washington, DC: U.S. Department of Health and Human Services." http://www.mentalhealth .samhsa.gov/publications/allpubs/SMA00-3457/default.asp. Last accessed March 1, 2004.

Covering Kids, with the Southern Institute on Children and Families. 2003. "Communication Kit: Reaching Latino Families." Princeton: Robert Wood Johnson Foundation. http://coveringkidsandfamilies.org/ communications/materials/latino. Last accessed March 1, 2004.

Coye, Molly, and Deborah Alvarez. 1999. " Medicaid Managed Care and Cultural Diversity in California" New York: Commonwealth Fund. http:// www.cmwf.org /programs/minority/coye_medicaid_managed.pdf. Last accessed March 1, 2004.

Dick, Andrew W., Jonathan D. Klein, Laura P. Shone, Jack Zwanziger, Hao Yu, and Peter G. Szilagyi. 2003. "The Evolution of the State Children's Health Insurance Program (SCHIP) in New York: Changing Program Features and Enrollee Characteristics." *Pediatrics* 112 (6): 542–50.

Doty, Michelle M. 2003. "Hispanic Patients' Double Burden: Lack of Health Insurance and Limited English." New York: Commonwealth Fund. http://www.cmwf.org/programs/insurance/doty_hispanicdoubleburden _592.pdf. Last accessed February 29, 2004.

Felland, Laurie E., and Andrea Staiti. 2001. "Communities Play Key Role in Extending Public Health Insurance to Children." Washington, DC: Center for Studying Health System Change. No. 44. http://www.hschange .org/CONTENT/377/?PRINT=1. Last accessed February 29, 2004.

Flores, Glenn, Elena Fuentes-Afflick, Oxiris Barbot, Olivia Carter-Pokras, Luz Claudio, Marielena Lara, Jennie A. McLaurin, Lee Pachter, Francisco Ramos Gomez, Fernando Mendoza, R. Burciaga Valdez, Antonia M.

Villarruel, Ruth E. Zambrana, Robert Greenberg, and Michael Weitzman. 2002. "The Health of Latino Children: Urgent Priorities, Unanswered Questions, and a Research Agenda." *Journal of the American Medical Association,* v288 (1): 82–90.

Managed Risk Medical Insurance Board. 2002a. "Application Assistance Fact Book." http://www.mrmib.ca.gov/MRMIB/HFP/CAAFactBk.pdf. Last accessed February 29, 2004.

———. 2002b. "Rural Health Demonstration Project: 2002 Fact Book." http://www.mrmib.ca.gov/MRMIB/HFP/RHDPFactBk.pdf. Last accessed February 29, 2004.

Manos, M. Michelle, Wendy A. Leyden, Cynthia I. Resendez, Elizabeth G. Klein, Tom L. Wilson, and Heidi M. Bauer. 2001. "A Community-Based Collaboration to Assess and Improve Medical Insurance Status and Access to Health Care of Latino Children." *Public Health Reports* 6 (116): 575–84.

Moore, Judith D. 1999. "CHIP and Medicaid Outreach and Enrollment: A Hands-On Look at Marketing and Applications." No. 748. Washington, DC: National Health Policy Forum. http://www.nhpf.org/pdfs_ib/IB748 %5FSCHIPOutreach%5F10%2D19%2D99%2Epdf. Last accessed February 29, 2004.

Orchard Communications. 1999. "A Marketing Identity for the Texas Children's Health Insurance Program: Executive Summary, Key Findings, and Recommendations." Austin: Texas Department of Health, Bureau of Children's Health Insurance Program. http://www.hhsc.state.tx.us/chip/ cbo/sect1-2.pdf. Last accessed February 29, 2004.

Ross, Donna Cohen, and Ian T. Hill. 2003. "Enrolling Eligible Children and Keeping Them Enrolled." *Future of Children* 13 (1): 81–97.

Shone, Laura P., Andrew W. Dick, Cindy Brach, Kim S. Kimminau, Barbara J. LaClair, Elizabeth A. Shenkman, Jana F. Col, Virginia A. Schaffer, Frank Mulvihill, Peter G. Szilagyi, Jonathan D. Klein, Karen VanLandeghem, and Janet Bronstein. 2003. "The Role of Race and Ethnicity in the State Children's Health Insurance Program (SCHIP) in Four States: Are There Baseline Disparities, and What Do They Mean for SCHIP?" *Pediatrics* 112 (6): 521–32.

Taras, Howard L., Maria Luisa Zuniga de Nuncio, and Elaine Pizzola. 2002. "Assessing an Intensive School-Based Assistance Program to Enroll Uninsured Children." *Journal of School Health* 72 (7): 273–77.

United States Department of Health and Human Services. 2004. "The 2004 HHS Poverty Guidelines." http://aspe.hhs.gov/poverty/04poverty.shtml. Last accessed April 9, 2004.

Westpfahl, Amy E. 1999. "Outreach and Enrollment Challenges: Increasing Participation in *Child Health Plus* in Onondaga County, New York." *Journal of Public Health Management and Practice* 5 (5): 52–65.

Policy Actors and the Immigration Policy Process

LISA MAGAÑA

THE IMMIGRATION POLICY PROCESS

The immigration policy process is as follows: Popular and emotional reactions to undocumented immigration develop at the local and state level. When these sentiments eventually reach politicians at the federal level, Congress responds with a new policy, which only creates more responsibilities for immigration policy actors, agencies, and organizations. When these immigration policies are eventually assigned to policy players, they lack adequate direction for implementation, improvements in the budget, or newly designed organizational infrastructures. Subsequently, immigration policy actors appear inefficient, and new policies are assigned as an attempt to improve performance (Magaña 2003).

It is important to consider the impact that the immigration policy process has on Mexican immigrants, given the large numbers processed every year. For instance, according to the Department of Homeland

Security, Mexican immigrants represent the largest group to be admitted into the United States legally, as well as the largest group to be naturalized. Mexican immigrants also represent the largest group to be apprehended and deported. How an agency carries out policy mandates has much to do with the success or failure of a policy. That is, from a theoretical research perspective, organizational characteristics such as: (1) impossible and multiple tasks; (2) illogical and shifting federal mandates; and (3) the appearance of ineffectiveness and inefficiency merit consideration in immigration reform research. This chapter will highlight the findings of three studies of the policy process and how it influences delivery. Overall, agents carry out immigration policy in environments with shifting federal mandates while being assigned impossible tasks.

POLICY ACTORS

When examining immigration policy implementation, enforcement activities generate a significant amount of attention, however, they are only one part of the overall mission of immigration agencies. One study showed that the public's tendency to believe enforcement activities more important than service activities deters Mexican legal immigrants from going to the agency (Magaña 2003).

In the last decade, a number of new policies have been assigned to the immigration agencies, thereby increasing agency responsibilities and establishing new roles and procedures. These may not be in the best interest of the organization, however. For instance, one study found that policy actors maintain that they are typically not given enough resources to carry out their objectives efficiently. In addition, these mandates have not coincided with sufficient time to formulate clear agency guidelines, and as a result implementation performance has suffered (Magaña 2011).

Other studies examine the environments from which policy actors operate, having much to do with the way policy decisions are made. Theorists find that environments inculcate systems of rewards and values in the minds of policy actors. For example, local policy actors who work within federal agencies have overwhelming and complex duties to perform. The agency's expectations are ambiguous, vague, and often conflicting. Furthermore, since agencies are often large, actors can only see problems narrowly and independently of their connections to other issues. A variety of studies focusing on the organizational constraints show that the agency must carry out complex immigration policies despite inadequate funding (North and Portz 1989), and poor management styles (GAO 1991). One study illustrated the agency's inability to carry out policies effectively based on dysfunctional organizational aspects (GAO 1991).

Immigration bureaucrats, particularly those at the local level, have the most influence over policy decisions. Which is to say, regardless of the political and financial capital dedicated to a given immigration policy and the clarity with which it is defined, its effectiveness ultimately rests with the individuals responsible for its implementation. Because expectations placed on policy actors tend to be ambiguous and their performance is difficult to measure, theorists more often tend to consider the policy process (Lipsky 1980; Romzek and Johnston 1999).

Historically, immigration policy has been implemented by a variety of organizations, institutions, and agencies, like the Border Patrol Agency (BPA). The first immigration office in the federal government was created in 1864. The agency to be formed within the Department of State was to be led by a Commissioner of Immigration and serve a term of four years. During this period, the agency was responsible for interviewing and denying entrance to individuals convicted of political offenses, lunatics, idiots, and persons likely to become public charges.

In 1888, a federal committee was formed, "The Ford Committee," to study the growing immigration problem. This committee found that countries were sending thousands of their "paupers and insane persons to America, immigration through Canada was a problem, immigration laws were being violated, and the 1882 Chinese Exclusion Act was simply too difficult to enforce." On March 3, 1891, Congress codified federal control over immigration, establishing an Office of the Superintendent of Immigration. The immigration agency was moved into the Department of the Treasury.

At the turn of the century, several laws solidified the duties of this newly formed immigration bureau. The Act of 1893, for example, changed the title of the Superintendent of Immigration to the Commissioner-General of Immigration. In 1899, statutes provided for stricter control of immigrants entering the country through maritime ports. In 1900, agency headquarters were set up in Washington, DC, as were inspection centers at important ports of entry. In 1903, the agency was moved again into the Department of Labor.

As the Bureau grew larger and laws more complex, the agency found it more difficult to meet its assigned objectives and annual reports began to document problems in enforcing immigration policies. By 1918, a labor shortage had developed in the United States. Congress and the Immigration Bureau were encouraged by business interests to secure cheap workers to fill labor needs. This program allowed the Immigration Bureau to directly recruit Mexican workers and place them in jobs in both the agriculture and railroad sectors.

When World War I ended, anti-immigrant sentiment surfaced again. Opinion polls indicated that many Americans felt that a large influx of European immigrants coming from war-destroyed areas would result in a decrease in available jobs. Furthermore, anti-immigrant sentiment toward particular types of European immigrants once again escalated. Based on both economic and nativistic motives, in 1921 and 1924 Congress enacted "The Quota Limit Laws," which marked the beginning of specific restrictions of the entry of certain groups into the United States. These included Eastern Europeans, Africans, Australians, and Asians. However, immigration from the Western Hemisphere was not as restrictive. Because sailors had a legal right to go ashore, many European immigrants denied access by quota laws were entering via boat "desertion." As the Mexican borders became a point of entry for Europeans who could not otherwise gain admittance due to a lack of proper documentation or illiteracy laws, the smuggling industry grew. Addressing the problem of border entries, Congress established the first Border Patrol unit; immigration representatives began to patrol both the Mexican and Canadian borders on horseback.

In yet another attempt to improve agency effectiveness, in 1933, the Bureau of Immigration and the Bureau of Naturalization were consolidated, forming what was famously known as the Immigration and Naturalization Service, or the INS. The consolidation of these two agencies was an effort to ensure greater uniformity of immigration procedures. The agency remained the INS under the Justice Department for approximately seventy years.

In 1986 the Immigration Reform and Control Act (IRCA) was enacted. The overall objective of IRCA was to decrease the number of undocumented immigrants in the United States by implementing two provisions: employer sanctions and legalization. The employer sanctions provision intended to end the economic lure for immigrants who come to the United States seeking employment. The legalization provision was to legalize undocumented immigrants already in the United States, thereby reducing the total number of undocumented individuals. Overall, the policy resulted in the processing of over three million immigrants seeking legalized status. In addition, the INS took responsibility for informing over seven million employers of the provisions and penalties of the new law.

In 1996 the Illegal Immigration and Reform and Responsibility Act (IIRA) was passed. A small provision of the Act, 287(g) allowed local police officers, for the first time, to work with the immigration officials in order to carry out immigration policy. However, officers must receive some training, necessary resources, and latitude to pursue investigations relating to violent crimes, human smuggling, gang/organized crime activity, sexual-related offenses, narcotics smuggling and money laundering. Police agencies that participate in the training receive more funding in order to subsidize immigration enforcement activities. In order to carry out 287(g) you must be a U.S. citizen, pass a background investigation, have a minimum of two years experience, and no disciplinary actions pending.

Attacks on the World Trade Center and the Pentagon resulted in dramatic new policy mandates. Indicative of the reactive nature of immigration policy, the Border Patrol was charged with sealing off the nation's borders and deploying agents to airports immediately after the attacks. Popular sentiment then shifted from illegal immigration to visa over-stayers, immigrants who remained in the country after their visas expired. Because several of the terrorists had entered the United States "legally," public sentiment shifted its focus to how this could happen. Politicians, quick to respond to popular sentiment, set the stage for a variety of initiatives, such as making it more difficult to overstay a visa and "getting tougher" on terrorism. Despite the fact that immigration experts had complained about the problem well before the attacks, a new system for reporting the status of foreign and exchange students was implemented in their aftermath.

Attempting to address terrorism, Congress restructured the INS. The agency's two functions, enforcement and service, were separated and placed under the supervision of the Homeland Security Department. The Border Patrol was placed in the Bureau of Customs and Border Protection while the previous service functions of the INS are now in the Bureau of Citizenship and Immigration Services.

METHODOLOGY

Studies that examine immigration policy often use macro evaluations or quantitative approaches, such as assessing the rate of border patrol apprehensions, the number of people processed, or the amount of funding for operations in a given year. While these data are useful, they reflect only part of the picture for the reasons cited above. Therefore, this study relies on both qualitative and qualitative research methodologies as a means to supplement research approaches. Extensive interviews provide insight into the organizational dynamics of the immigration agencies that traditional quantitative approaches are unable to describe fully. These interviews also provide a unique framework for the inner workings of agencies when carrying out policy.[1] I also used policy evaluations and surveys conducted by governmental and non-governmental agencies such as the Justice Department, the General Accounting Office, and another survey conducted by Peter D. Hart Research and Associates.[2] These studies assess agency performance at the federal, regional, and local levels. Newspaper articles and other sources via the LexisNexis News are also examined. What follows are the consistent findings of three major studies, on IRCA, IIRA, and 287(g). The following section highlights some of the consistent attitudes of policy actors while implementing immigration policies.

FINDINGS

It is clear that policy players are assigned policy mandates with little direction, resources, and funding. Some respondents maintain that the general public does not understand how immigration policy is carried out. Unless someone deals with an immigration issue, the role of the policy actors is unclear. One respondent noted, "People want to control immigration when it is faceless, but when someone has a friend who needs immigration help, people have no problem calling us for assistance or asking us to make exceptions."

Respondents also feel that since the public does not understand the agency's duties, the organization is held accountable for unrelated directives. For instance, although undocumented immigration to the United States is the result of geopolitical and international forces outside the agency's control, immigration policy actors are responsible for decreasing the level of "undocumented" immigration. In short, the representatives work in an environment shrouded in public ambiguity and demand for dealing with impossible mandates.

Respondents also insist that public ambiguity and perception of the immigration phenomenon generally, and the agency specifically, has much to do with how policies are carried out. For instance, they explained that if programs are not well understood by the public, the agency might need to use precious resources and time clarifying issues. Conversely, if the agency's objectives are clearly perceived or programs have been relatively consistent, the agency can rely on its reputation and provide more efficient assistance. Since immigration laws rapidly change, particularly so in the last twenty years, the respondents maintain they spend considerable time explaining issues misunderstood by the public.

Respondents overwhelmingly expressed concern that the press selectively magnifies negative events, which makes the agency look insensitive. One respondent said, "Only the bad things get printed; the good stuff never does, but what sells papers?" Recent attention on immigration issues in the press may fuel the public's perception that the agency is ineffective. One respondent maintained that Border Patrol activities generate the most attention and it is perhaps considered the "sexiest" of all immigration activities (Magaña 2003).

The organizational missions of enforcement and service contradict each other when the agency attempts to carry out policy. Representatives maintained that they must work to overcome these opposing missions. For instance, representatives on the service side must make immigrants feel that they are a safe place to visit when they ask for assistance, while representatives on the enforcement side must perpetuate its image that it is tough on undocumented immigration. In order to implement policy effectively, the Department of Homeland Security must consider its contradictory public appeal.

Poor communication styles characterize the agency's working conditions. Although it is particularly important that upper management remain in touch with agents and events in the field, the communication style is described as highly bureaucratic; respondents maintain that it affects their ability to carry out policies. Respondents were asked to describe the communication process from upper management down to the street level; at all levels of the organization, from management to field officers, they typically said it was "out of touch."

In order to thwart public criticism regarding their own records on immigration policy, politicians use the immigration policy actors as a scapegoat, incapable of fulfilling its assigned duties; governmental officials often express their disdain through major media platforms. Undocumented immigration and the long processing time for legal immigrants are typically used as examples of the agency's ineffectiveness.

Respondents criticized the ever-changing organizational directives of newly appointed administrators and leaders of the agency. They maintained that as new elected officials come into office, so do new ideas for the agency. In addition, respondents, particularly those at the federal level, maintain that it is difficult to develop administrative procedures when implementing poorly designed policies. Reorganization efforts and new funding proposals have rarely met the anticipated goals.

Inexperienced agents display much lower levels of discretion than more experienced agents. That is, rookie agents feel that they constantly have to look to their supervisors for input before implementing enforcement policies. Discretion is an indication of an experienced agent, and the level of discretion drastically increases as agents become more experienced (Magaña 2003).

Conversely, in terms of service, representatives expressed that they are not afforded enough discretion when making decisions, and that it is not realistic to work in an environment where such bureaucratic rigidity exits. Immigrants with diverse backgrounds and complex political realities make it difficult to standardize procedures for processing them. Respondents on the service side expressed frustration that they are not allowed to make decisions based on an immigrant's own unique circumstances. For instance, recent laws make any legal immigrant with a felony ineligible for citizenship. Immigrants who may have received a felony for a youthful indiscretion and had paid for their crime were still denied citizenship status. Respondents felt this was unfair and that they should be given more discretion. They also maintained that these types of laws are examples of Congress appeasing constituents and not understanding operations (Magaña 2011).

When Border Patrol respondents were questioned about the agency's new restructuring effort and policy mandates assigned to them, their responses were consistent with those expressed in previous studies. Respondents overwhelmingly maintained that expectations for their services changed with little consideration of their capacity to implement policy. Furthermore, most respondents stated that policy mandates assigned to them have not coincided with enough funding; therefore they appear inadequate or incapable of meeting policy expectations (Hart 2004).

New responsibilities placed on the agency include greater emphasis on improving national security and deterring terrorism, as well as the new mandate to increase focus on foreign visitors, such as checking paperwork for individuals who may overstay their visas. Respondents overwhelmingly maintain a sense of being overworked; in general, the workload has increased, particularly with regard to paperwork, reducing the amount of time they are able to spend in the field (Hart 2004).

Consistent with previous surveys, these agents are not satisfied that they are provided the tools, training, and support needed to be effective. They describe feeling frustrated at being assigned tasks without any input to help them improve effectiveness. They also maintain that field-level operations procedures were out of touch and dated.

Respondents also complained that they lacked the training, equipment, and technology necessary to carry out assigned policy mandates. As a result, respondents felt that morale within the agency could be higher. Clear organizational mandates that are not dictated by external concerns as well as communication style changes would greatly improve morale (Hart 2004).

The Border Patrol respondents believe that the country is safer from terrorism since the September 11 attacks. Although respondents insist that the Department of Homeland Security could be doing more to stop potential terrorists from entering the country, they overwhelmingly noted that restructuring or being placed under the Homeland Security organizational umbrella has not improved their policy objectives or helped them meet policy expectations. These respondents believe that the restructuring effort was yet another attempt based on external, immaterial forces to improve unrealistic agency directives (Hart 2004).

In 2009 the Government Accountability Office (GAO) released a report to Homeland Security on the impact of 287(g), a policy that trains police officers to carry out immigration policy. They found "that immigration officials have failed to develop key internal controls over a controversial program that trains state and local police to identify illegal immigrants involved in crime, so some departments are focusing on minor violations rather than on serious offenses, according to federal investigators" (Aizenman 2009). The report also showed that the program has expanded too rapidly in recent years, "receiving $60 million between 2006 and 2008, training 951 state and local law enforcement officers in 67 agencies and resulting in the arrests of at least 43,000 immigrants, almost 28,000 of whom ultimately were ordered out of the country" (Aizenman 2009). In the report, GAO said that four local law-enforcements agencies were arresting immigrants for minor violations like speeding, contrary to the objective of the program (Aizen-man 2009).

The GAO report noted that ICE failed to provide clearly defined objectives for the program or to create a consistent system for supervision. The authors warned that confusion over the purpose of 287(g) could result in referrals of an "unmanageable number" of low-priority illegal immigrants to ICE as well as "misuse of authority" by local officials. According to the report, one sheriff said that his understanding of his authority was that "287(g)-trained officers to go to people's homes and question individuals regarding their immigration status even if the individual is not suspected of criminal activity." Although it does not appear that any officers used the authority in this manner, the report continued, "it is illustrative of the lack of clarity regarding program objectives and the use of 287(g) authority by participating agencies" (Aizenman 2009).

In another study conducted by the Goldwater Institute, researchers found that the policy is highly ineffective and deters officers from pursuing more important law enforcement activities (Goldwater Institute 2008). They find that before 287(g), police targeted more smugglers or coyotes—those individuals that illegally bring people into the country. In 2006 and 2007, the police arrested only low-level operatives, such as drivers and drop-house guards. More importantly, 287(g) has diverted substantial resources away from other law-enforcement activities. The sweeps have involved a substantial number of deputies that were not trained to implement this policy. Furthermore, the response time to 911 calls has increased (Goldwater Institute 2008).

■ ■ ■

This chapter provides an examination of policy actors and the immigration policy process. It illustrates the critical relationship between bureaucratic structures, laws, agency level behavior, and the impact on Latino immigrants based on the prevailing political economy. The immigration policy process is influenced by a variety of forces, such as politics, popular sentiment, bureaucratic structures, and the economy, to name but a few. This study of implementation over time also points out that geographic location of policy implementation helps to either support or hinder the ease of implementation.

The immigration policy process influences immigration agencies, which in turn influences how immigrants, specifically Mexicans, are treated. If this short chapter teaches anything, it is that these agencies do not implement policy in isolation; they are responsible for multifaceted and sometimes illogical tasks. The agencies are accountable to a variety of interests that are constantly changing, such as popular sentiment, the economy, Congress, and the business sector, to name but a few. Because carrying out immigration policy is complicated, these agencies will continue to confront a variety of immigration interests and may never appear effective as an agency. All three studies illustrated a frustration on the part of policy players with how policies are formulated and assigned. Studies illustrated a lack of insight as to how feasible policies can be carried out.

Popular opinion regarding immigration favors the enactment of more enforcement-type procedures such as stronger border patrol and stricter penalties toward undocumented immigration. Congress has been more active in enacting enforcement policies rather than service policies. The creation of federal immigration policies, according to respondents, only results in backlogs of work and inordinate complex objectives. Consequently, the quality of service on both the enforcement and the service side suffers.

These issues are important to consider for a variety of reasons. First, Mexican immigrants represent the largest group to be admitted into the United States legally, as well as the largest group to be naturalized. Mexican immigrants also represent the largest group to be apprehended and deported. Historically, these agencies will continue to have a profound influence on the lives of Mexican immigrants, both legal and undocumented, as a wide variety of data sources and demographic trends illustrate.

NOTES

1. In the mid-1990s to 2001, I conducted approximately eighty-five in-depth interviews with past and current federal commissioners of the INS, regional commissioners of the INS, district directors and local INS representatives;

sixty-five interviews were ultimately used for this chapter. Usually, the interviews took two to three hours to conduct. Some respondents were revisited. In order to interview some of the representatives within the agency, I had to submit to the public relations person and the district director of Los Angeles written statements describing, "why I wanted to interview INS individuals, my interview questions, what was the point of my research, and who would read these findings." After six weeks of correspondence and several in-person visits, I was authorized interviews with representatives currently employed by the INS. After I interviewed some INS representatives it became much easier to interview others. INS representatives made calls or introduced me to other key respondents. The other INS officials I interviewed were no longer employed with the INS; they provided very candid insights into the INS organizational environment. From the federal down to the street level, my sample responses represent the experiences of INS employees from the numerous organizational levels within the agency. I also interviewed some representatives of immigrant advocacy groups in order to understand some of the constitutional and civil issues at hand. Like most of my INS respondents, many immigrant advocates wished to remain anonymous. Interviews were conducted in Los Angeles, California, Phoenix, Arizona, Santa Ana, California, and Washington, DC, providing insight into local and federal agency operations. Most respondents did not want their names cited in this chapter. Those respondents whose names appear gave me permission.

Approximately fifteen interviews also have been conducted between 2007 and 2011 with police officers and border patrol agents in Arizona on immigration policy implementation.

2. The Hart survey was commissioned by labor organizations and consisted of telephone interviews with 250 Border Patrol agents and 250 Bureau of Customs and Border Protection inspectors.

REFERENCES

Aizenman, N. C. 2009. "GAO Report Says 287(g) Illegal Immigration Program Lacks Key Internal Controls." *Washington Post,* March 4, 2009

Dunn, Timothy J. 1996. *The Militarization of the U.S.-Mexico Border, 1978–1992.* Austin: Center for Mexican-American Studies.

General Accounting Office. 1990. "Immigration Reform: Employer Sanctions and the Question of Discrimination." Report to Congress. Washington, DC: General Accounting Office.

———. 1991. "Immigration Management: Strong Leadership and Management Reforms Needed to Address Serious Problems." Report to Congress. Washington, DC: General Accounting Office.

Goldwater Institute. 2008. *Mission Unaccomplished: The Misplaced Priorities of the Maricopa County Sheriff's Office*. Phoenix, Arizona.

Governmental Accounting Office. 2009. "Immigration Enforcement Better Controls over Programs Authorizing State and Local Enforcement of Federal Laws." http://www.gao.gov/new.items/d09109.pdf.

Immigration Customs and Enforcement. 2009. "Delegation of Immigration Authority Section 287(g): Immigration and Nationality Act The ICE 287(g) Program: A Law Enforcement Partnership." http://www.ice.gov/pi/news/factsheets/section287_g.htm.

Hart, P. July/August, 2004. "Study 7320." NBPC/NHSC/AFGE Survey.

Lipsky, Michael. 1980. *Street-Level Bureaucracy: Dilemmas of the Individual in Public Services*. New York: Russell Sage Foundation.

Magaña, Lisa. 2003. *Straddling the Border: Immigration Policy and the INS*. Austin: University of Texas Press.

———. 2011. "Fear of Calling the Police: Regulation and Resistance." In *Social Welfare Policy: Regulation and Resistance among People of Color*, edited by Jerome H. Schiele. Thousand Oaks, CA: Sage Publications.

North, D. S., and M. Portz. 1989. *Decision Factories: The Role of the Regional Processing Facilities in the Alien Legalization Programs*. Report prepared for the consideration of the Administrative Conference of the United States.

Office of Management and Budget, Executive Office of the President. 2004. "Department of Homeland Security." http://www.whitehouse.gov/omb/budget/fy2004/homeland.html.

Romzek, Barbara S., and Jocelyn M. Johnston. 1999. "Reforming Medicaid through Contracting: The Nexus of Implementation and Organizational Culture." *Journal of Public Administration Research and Theory* 9 (1): 107–39.

PART IV

Political Reactions to Immigration

ELEVEN

Rhetoric and Realities

American Immigration Policy after September 11, 2001

RODOLFO ESPINO AND
RAFAEL A. JIMENO

American immigration policy is based on a mix of fact and fiction. The maintenance and control of a border between nations is as much a function of economic and human resources as it is about rhetoric and symbolism (Massey 1990). The U.S.-Mexico border is a case in point. The border drawn between the United States and Mexico has increased as a national concern for the United States over time (Hero 1992). Shortly after the United States became an independent nation, its physical border quickly pushed west and south. Control of individuals in newly acquired lands presented problems to American politicians long before the Border Patrol was founded in 1924. Early border control responsibilities fell to quasi-militia groups or, on occasion, to the American military. Notable in American historical folklore, blue-coated buffalo soldiers were sent to quell indigenous Americans who were resisting the westward advance of the American state.

Once the majority of Native American populations were moved to tracts of land surrounded by American borders on all sides, control of the southern Mexican border and the northern Canadian border emerged as new policy concerns for American politicians. Smuggling alcohol over the Canadian border during the Prohibition years was the major problem to the north. The southern border arose as a problem due to an influx of immigrants—not Mexican immigrants but rather Chinese immigrants—seeking to bypass restrictions on their entry to the United States due to the Chinese Exclusion Act of 1882.

Due to labor shortages brought on by World War II, U.S. immigration policy changed to accommodate Mexican migrant workers with the implementation of the Bracero program, and Mexicans soon became the largest proportion of immigrants coming to the United States (Hero 1992). The trend continues today, forty years after the end of the Bracero program due to economic, social, and political conditions in both Mexico and the United States (Chavez 1992; Martinez 2001). The White House and leaders in Congress have been constantly altering existing immigration laws and policies since the 1950s in an effort to control the flow of migrants across the Mexican border. This continuous tinkering is, perhaps, the clearest comment on the rarity of successful immigration policies. Shifting policies over time is, perhaps, also indicative of the ways in which immigration as a policy concern gets constructed and redefined over time by policymakers in response to changing events (Newton 2005; Wong and Cho 2006).

The changing political and economic environments have affected immigration policy throughout the twentieth century (as will be demonstrated below), as have the events of September 11, 2001. These events have entered into the calculus of American politicians and influenced their views on immigration and the way they construct policy to control it in both its legal and non-legal variants. The terrorist attacks on New York and Washington introduced two new terms to the American political lexicon: "war on terrorism" and "homeland security." These concepts suggest a perpetual war against an elusive enemy abroad and at home and have made their way into nearly all aspects of American foreign and domestic policymaking. Immigration policy has been no exception. In this environment, a mix of disparate and often contradictory goals may lead policymakers to work toward certain political advantages by focusing their efforts on poorly chosen targets that, when inappropriately framed, could be publicly construed as entirely appropriate.

The United States has long defined itself as a nation of immigrants. Celebrated Horatio Alger stories frame the immigrant experience in the United States, instructing American-born citizens and immigrants that the United States is a land of opportunity in which newcomers are welcome and anyone can move up the American socioeconomic ladder by displaying behavior consistent with the "Protestant work ethic," regardless of their country of origin (Jones-Correa 2007). The realities of the American immigrant experience often do not comport with the constructed, celebrated notions extant in American folklore, however. Empirical evidence marshaled on the subject signals that upward socioeconomic mobility for immigrants is not so easily achieved within a single generation and that upward mobility is even difficult for subsequent generations (Snipp and Tienda 1982; Portes and Zhou 1992; Tienda and Singer 1995). Individual and aggregate socioeconomic factors, levels of segregation, and the paradigmatic forces of discrimination experienced by nonwhites in American society are important factors that explain sluggish immigrant mobility, but are beyond the scope of this chapter.

In this chapter, we seek to briefly identify where American immigration policy fits into studies of political science. We propose some factors that political scientists should be taking into account when studying how the realities of immigration interact with the rhetoric of immigration. We briefly follow that discussion by examining a few of these factors in further detail. Finally, we suggest new avenues of research and how the events of September 11 are indicative of the raw material that policymakers use to further their own career interests—an idea that is not entirely novel—and what future studies can look for.

IMMIGRATION POLICY IN POLITICAL SCIENCE

Every subfield of political science studies immigration policy, though each approaches the subject quite differently. For example, international relations and comparative politics studies place immigration in two different topical areas that rarely speak to each other. The political economy field generally treats immigration as a consequence of the globalization of commerce (Massey 1990), while conflict studies generally treats immigration as a cause of security issues. Recent work, however, has begun to draw these disparate areas more closely together with immigration policy as the conduit (Rudolph 2003).

In American politics, the subject of immigration is often given its most thorough treatment in the field of public policy (Lindblom 1959), especially in the realm of sociopolitical construction of groups and group identities (Schneider and Ingram 1993; Newton 2005). Recent immigration trends have led scholars with an interest in race and ethnicity, particularly those studying Latino politics, to examine the influence of immigration on political behavior, elections, and identity (Jones-Correa 1998; Wong 2000; Hritzuk and Park 2000; Cain and Doherty 2006). With shifting demographic trends in the United States, the fundamental importance of immigration studies will increase to those studying race and politics for it is the process of obtaining citizenship that provides us insight to how the American community seeks to define itself socially and politically.

The scholars who study immigration policy in American politics do not divide it into the aforementioned separate focal points; they have, however, observed the paradox of recent American immigration policy that characterizes the differential focus in other fields of political science (Andreas 1996, 1998–1999; Massey and Espinosa 1997; Sassen 1996; Sierra, Carrillo, DeSipio and Jones-Correa 2000). Notably, American politicians will often preach "open borders" when it comes to capital flows in durable goods but scream "closed borders" with respect to human capital flows. Policymakers have struggled with the appropriate balance between the two in relation to advancing the American economy, but oftentimes this is confounded by the schizophrenic efforts of politicians to please constituent bases, though politically active immigrant populations may also influence politicians to support immigration (Shain 1999). The North American Free Trade Agreement (NAFTA), which was heralded as the appropriate solution to strike a balance between benefiting the American economy and reducing incentives for Mexican migration, has failed to live up to its promises (Rudolph 2003).

Prior to September 11, 2001, the restrictions on human capital flow were largely framed with reference to domestic employment or crime prevention. Domestic employment considerations were framed in terms of the need for unskilled labor that the American labor pool was unwilling to provide, such as agricultural work, or the need for skilled labor that the American employment pool was not deep enough to sustain. At the same time, conflicting claims were made that undocumented workers took jobs away from Americans (Huntington 2004). These opposing arguments have led to contradictory policy. Regarding crime prevention, appeals were made to restrict the influx of illicit drugs into the country.

Prior to September 11, 2001, theoretical constructs seeking to establish immigrants as a problem (like "zero-sum narratives" and "criminal alien narratives") have been well documented by Newton (2005, 151–60), as have the "counter narratives" (160–64) seeking to increase immigrant support networks. In addition, policymakers or interest groups occasionally suggest militarization and near-complete shutdown of the border, but these proposals were few and rarely went very far. It is not surprising that after September 11 much of the discussion about border control has invoked notions of national security even at the expense of any considerations of domestic labor needs and drug trafficking issues. Now, calls to militarize the U.S.-Mexico border—a border that has never been militarized in its history because it was considered largely impractical to do so—have gained significant momentum (Bedolla 2006). This is suggestive of the ways in which policy ideas may exist but only gain support once concrete events can help to substantiate the transformation of ideas into policies (Kingdon 1984).

While the terrorist attacks of September 11 highlighted the need for increased security at America's points of entry, the realities of Mexican migration to the United States did not disappear. We wrote this chapter in order to understand the extent to which the events of September 11 became intertwined, if at all, with the realities and rhetoric of American immigration policy subsequent to the attacks. We do so first by highlighting the ways in which American immigration policy has been or could be examined. We then follow with a brief pursuit of some of these areas to highlight how American immigration policy has been transformed, if at all, by the events of September 11.

METHODOLOGICAL CONSIDERATIONS: LOOKING FOR APPROPRIATE DATA

Data for Latino politics scholars tend to be in short supply (Leal 2007), let alone data examining issues pertinent to the Latino community, such as immigration, with any level of depth. In order to provide insight into American immigration policy, we provide a list of pertinent data areas below. Scholars have utilized some of these areas to a greater extent than others, but those less utilized areas might provide the greatest insight into the construction of American immigration policy. Admittedly, we do not claim to present an exhaustive list of all the avenues by which to examine American immigration policy—rather, this list provides us with a firm grounding in those areas of research already produced on the topic. Appropriate areas to examine include: immigration patterns; financial and physical expenditures by government; variations in laws and policies and organizational structure; mass public opinion; and elite public opinion.

Immigration Patterns

Immigration patterns, defined as the flow of people to the United States categorized by their nation of origin over time, can be used to explain how American immigration policy takes shape (Huntington 2004). The endogenous relationship between immigration flow and immigration policy must not be overlooked, however; while immigration policymaking can be seen as a response to immigration patterns at any point in time, immigration patterns are equally responsive to immigration policies. For example, the Chinese Exclusion Act, driven in large part by xenophobic sentiment against immigration from China in the latter half of the nineteenth century, was enacted when the number of Chinese immigrants peaked. Conversely, it is no surprise that illegal immigration from Mexico and Central America increased dramatically once restrictive quotas were imposed in 1921 (Massey 1990).

A further complication with the use of data on immigration patterns to examine American immigration policy is that the American government is typically its source. Politicians or bureaucrats seeking to frame a particular agenda can change the collection methodology and classification of such data, which can, in turn, alter public perceptions. Two such instances are the federal government's "war on drugs" in the 1980s and 1990s, and the visa classification system in place today. The processes by which classifications are created (for example, "political refugee") and by which individuals are allowed to enter such categories are in continual flux (for example, the definition of "skilled worker" changes over time). Although at present there are forty-five visa classifications, these shifting definitions influence the classification scheme of legal and illegal immigrants and influence deportation patterns as well (Bedolla 2006).

Such efforts trigger shifts in the balance between legal and illegal immigration from particular countries, but immigration flows following nonconventional routes are more difficult to ascertain and, at best, can only be calculated with a minimal level of certainty (Huntington 2004). Nevertheless, the balance over time between legal and illegal immigration patterns in response to policies and vice versa proves to be insightful to any understanding of the construction of immigration policy. Clearly, the status of who is legal or illegal can vary over time even while holding the particular individual as a constant.

Financial and Physical Expenditures by the Government

Resource allocation and expenditure distribution toward immigration issues relative to other items in the budget may signal how politicians view the "problem" and the degree to which they think it is worth solving or not. For example, the proportional allocation of resources toward the southern border versus the northern border, and on air versus sea ports of entry are indicative of how policy seeks to control immigration patterns. U.S. government expenditures on areas related to immigration are naturally a function of laws and policies.

Variations in Laws and Policies and Organizational Structure

While the allocation and distribution of resources provides some insight, more can be gleaned from the laws and policies themselves directly. Laws can raise or lower barriers of entry or direct other entities or organizations to respond in particular ways. Additionally, changes in the bureaucratic structure of organizations tied to immigration can serve to further reveal how the realities and rhetoric of immigration collide. Notably, while the flow of immigration across the southern border has remained constant, in the years preceding and following the September 11 attacks, significant bureaucratic restructuring of the Immigration and Naturalization Service indicated the extent to which bureaucratic agencies were expected not only to bar entry to "traditional" illegal immigrants, but also to participate in efforts to prevent the entry of terrorists.

Mass Public Opinion

While public opinion is an important factor to consider in the construction of American immigration policy, as with the relationship between immigration patterns and immigration policymaking, an endogenous relationship may exist between the ebbs and flows of immigration and public opinion toward immigration. Economic crisis can increase public attention toward immigration (Citrin, Green, Muste, and Wong 1997). The events of September 11 created the linkage in the public's mind between national security and immigration control. A 2002 poll conducted by Harris Interactive on behalf of the Chicago Council on Foreign Relations as part of its continuing "Worldviews" studies found that 77 percent of Americans were in favor of restricting immigration in order to prevent terrorist attacks.

Elite Public Opinion

The case for elite-level opinion may in fact be even stronger than its mass-level counterpart because elites can offer cues to the public (thereby shaping public opinion) as well as be in the position to actually formulate immigration policy. Two ways of measuring elite-level opinion are: (1) to analyze the rhetoric coming from the mass media, and (2) to analyze the rhetoric used by policymakers on Capitol Hill. In what follows, we briefly describe the organizational shifts in border control and the rhetoric recorded in the halls of Congress to provide preliminary insights into how two of the areas we just described can be leveraged to gauge how the terrorist attacks of September 11, 2001, impacted American immigration policy with respect to Mexico.

EVOLUTION OF U.S. BORDER CONTROL

Figure 11.1 presents the annual levels of immigration to the United States from 1820 to 2003. The historical trend illustrates notable periods of American immigration history. An early peak in immigration to the United States is evident, largely a function of political and economic events pushing individuals out of Europe and the need for immigrant labor in the United States because of rapid industrialization. A notable drop-off in immigration to the United States occurred in the period during the worldwide economic depression of the 1930s. This trend began to slowly reverse following World War II when U.S. immigration policies were altered to remove restrictive quotas on immigration to the United States from particular areas of the world. Immigration hit its peak in 1991 when nearly two million immigrants entered the United States. Although there was a drop-off in immigration to the United States following the terrorist attacks of September 11, this downward trend began a decade before those events.

Figure 11.2 presents the number of bills introduced as well as the number of laws passed in Congress from 1942 to 2003—the period in Figure 11.1 where one can see notable increases in immigration from its historical low to its record highs. Figure 11.2 illustrates several important issues. First, the difference in success rates of bill introduction on policies affecting immigration or naturalization to final bill passage. Second, the number of laws passed remains fairly constant, previous to and following the peak of the 1950s, regardless of how many bills are

Figure 11.1. Immigration Trends, United States, 1820–2003

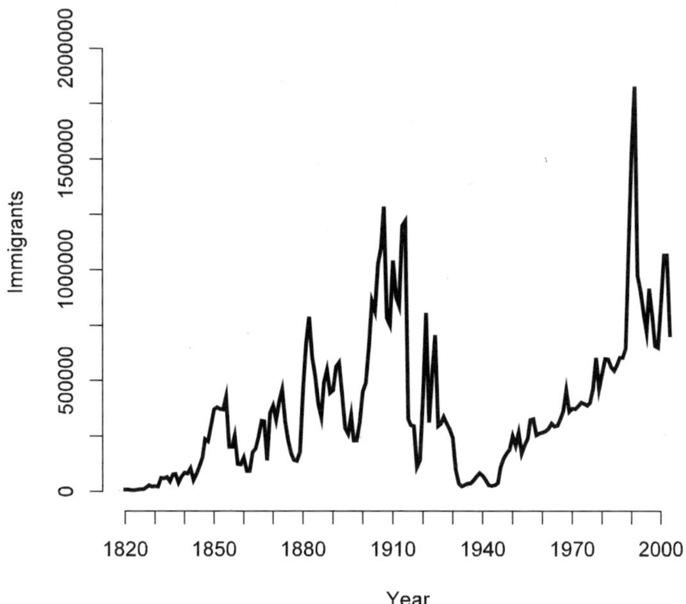

introduced. While the level of congressional concern for immigration fluctuates over the last half-century, these changes do not correspond to the changes in immigration patterns displayed in Figure 11.1, however. This is certainly worth exploring beyond this chapter in order to ascertain whether the changes we see in bill introduction are corresponding to external events related to immigration patterns, or simply to institutional changes in Congress affecting the process of legislation. One such institutional change may be the effort of party leaders to reign in the centrifugal forces in Congress produced by the increasing power over legislation exercised by committee and subcommittee leaders (Deering and Smith 1997; Loomis 2000).

These figures are also important in explaining how the result of such policies, displayed in these historical immigration trends, can influence bureaucratic responses to immigration through changes in orga-

Figure 11.2. Bills and Laws on Immigration in Congress, 1942–2003

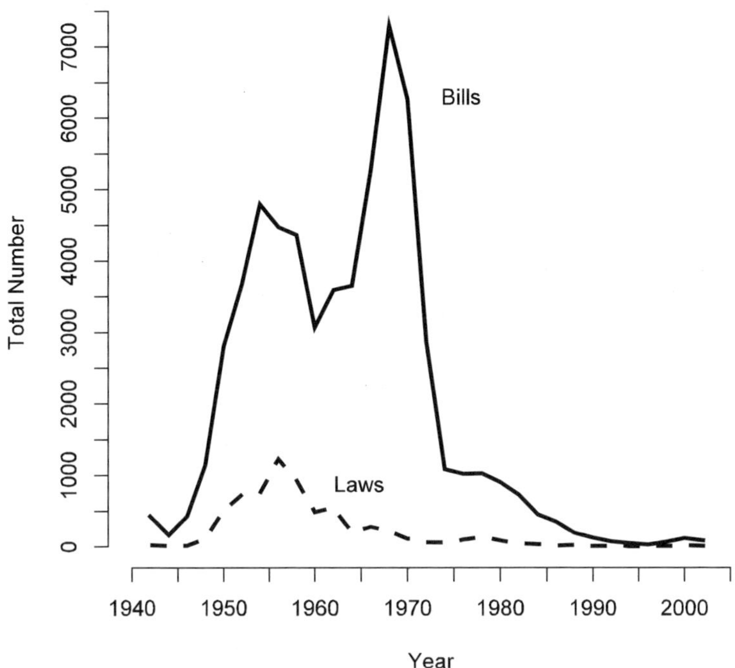

nizational structure. Here, we provide a brief historical account of how the organizations that oversee immigration and, particularly, border control have evolved over time in response to changes in immigration policies and to shifting priorities of legislators in response to immigration trends.

The first precursor to the Immigration and Naturalization Service (INS), the Office of the Superintendent of Immigration, was housed in the Treasury Department and was created in response to the numerous pieces of legislation regulating immigration. In 1895, this office was enhanced to become the Bureau of Immigration, dedicated to better enforce the cumbersome corpus of restrictions. In 1903, the Bureau of Immigration left the Treasury Department and joined the Department of Commerce and Labor in recognition of the fact that the thrust of its activities was aimed at protecting the American worker. The Basic Naturalization Act of 1906 effectively transferred naturalization jurisdiction and activities from the states to the federal courts, transformed the Bureau of Immigration into the Bureau of Immigration and Naturalization, and formed the basis of immigration law today. In 1913, the Bureau split into the Bureau of Immigration and the Bureau of Naturalization, both now under the newly separated Department of Labor.

In the early twentieth century, mass immigration became an issue and Congress began issuing immigration quotas and limited numbers of visas. The result of these restrictions was a dramatic increase in illegal immigration. During these early years, physical border control was parochial and haphazard. The first notable effort by the federal government at physical border control was the formation of the "Mounted Guards" in 1904 as part of an effort to stem the flow of Chinese immigrants across the Mexican border. This was followed by a congressional order in 1915 establishing the "Mounted Inspectors." The base of operations for these groups was largely out of El Paso.

America's entry into the Prohibition era introduced strong incentives for the illegal flow of alcohol across American borders. Congress responded to this crisis by passing the Labor Act of 1924, which created the U.S. Border Patrol (under the Bureau of Immigration) whose charge was to patrol land borders and deport illegal aliens. While main offices were established in El Paso and Detroit to monitor both borders, most of the border patrol resources and manpower were directed at the Canadian border.

In 1933 the Bureau of Immigration and the Bureau of Naturalization merged to form the Immigration and Naturalization Service (INS). With the onset of World War II, immigration ceased to be an economic issue and became a question of security. As such, it was moved from the Department of Labor to the Department of Justice in 1940 (as a side note, the INS operated the internment camps during the war). In the 1950s, the attention again shifted toward the economic impact of illegal aliens residing in the states, as well as to the impact of criminal elements entering the country on the community and the justice system. In 1986 the role of the INS was expanded to include issuing and enforcing penalties against employers who hired illegal aliens as part of the Immigration Reform and Control Act (Newton 2005). In the immediate aftermath of September 11, 2001, and cognizant of the illegal status of the terrorists involved, INS duties became inextricably linked to issues of national security and aimed to bar entry to terrorists. On March 1, 2003, the INS was essentially dissolved and all of its responsibilities were transferred from the Department of Justice to the Department of Homeland Security. Immigration services were placed under U.S. Citizenship and Immigration Services and the U.S. Border Patrol is now a branch of U.S. Customs and Border Protection.

All of the foregoing is to say that the underlying functions of controlling the border and regulating immigration have not remained constant throughout the various institutional changes. The point is that the "mission statement," if you will, has metamorphosed over time. Quite simply, while the main functional purpose of any border patrol agency has always been seemingly to prevent entry of undesirable individuals to this country, the publicly justified reasons for such preventions has shifted over time. All of this can be assessed through an analysis of changes to organizational structure over time. Early on, for instance, the primary justification (albeit, not exclusive justification) for immigrant apprehensions was tied to employment reasons, then to crime prevention reasons, and today it has shifted to a terrorism prevention justification.

IMMIGRATION AND BORDER CONTROL IN CONGRESSIONAL RHETORIC

An analysis of rhetoric is useful for a number of reasons. First, the members of the United States Congress are the instrumental forces in creating and deciding the nature of U.S. immigration policy (Casellas 2007; Espino 2007). Beyond formally crafting bills that are presented to the whole chamber for votes, such as debate over the formation of such policies, their actions are instrumental in framing immigration considerations. Framing allows members of Congress to push other governmental actors (such as the executive branch, interest groups, and the administrative bureaucracy) as well as state or foreign governments in particular desirable directions. It also signals what is possible or not possible in the crafting of immigration policy at any point in time.

To examine the rhetoric, we searched the *Congressional Record* from the 101st Congress to the 108th Congress (1988–2004). A cursory reading of public discourse over immigration to the United States would identify a number of issues that have become associated with immigration policy. Three such notable associations have been made with immigration between trade/economics, drugs/crime, and terrorism. Therefore, for our introductory analysis of the rhetoric of immigration in Congress we grouped discourse into the following categories: trade and immigration; drugs and immigration; terrorism and immigration.

With each of these classifications, we include associations to the two countries bordering the United States—Mexico and Canada. This is not exhaustive of all the levels of association between immigration and other areas of public policy; however, it does provide us the first insight into how members of Congress are framing the public discourse over immigration policy and, in particular, how they associate this framing with our neighbors. In searching the *Congressional Record,* which includes the text of all legislation but more importantly all the spoken and written speeches and debates of members of Congress in both chambers, we utilized a series of word proximity searches and Boolean inclusion/exclusion algorithms. This method of text searching is a technique that can uncover levels of association between various concepts in public discourse from politicians to the media (Jasperson et al. 1998) that gives us an approximate understanding of the rhetoric in the United States Congress surrounding immigration policy. The particular search algorithms we utilized for which we present results here are as follows:

1. Unordered Word Proximity of Trade, Immigration/ Immigrant(s), Mexico/ Mexican(s) excluding Canada/Canadian(s)
2. Unordered Word Proximity of Trade, Immigration/ Immigrant(s), Canada/ Canadian(s) excluding Mexico/Mexican(s)
3. Unordered Word Proximity of Drugs, Immigration/ Immigrant(s), Mexico/ Mexican(s) excluding Canada/Canadian(s)
4. Unordered Word Proximity of Drugs, Immigration/ Immigrant(s), Canada/ Canadian(s) excluding Mexico/Mexican(s)

5.   Unordered Word Proximity of Terrorism/ Terrorist(s), Immigration/ Immigrant(s), Mexico/ Mexican(s) excluding Canada/Canadian(s)
6.   Unordered Word Proximity of Terrorism/ Terrorist(s), Immigration/ Immigrant(s), Canada/ Canadian(s) excluding Mexico/Mexican(s)

Figure 11.3 presents our findings for the first two categories of word searches— the level of association between the mention of trade, immigration/immigrants, and country (that is, Mexico or Canada). In light of the current economic trends (globalization, reduction in barriers between countries, NAFTA-related policies, and so on), this analysis of congressional rhetoric reveals the different associations between two of our largest economic trading partners. Figure 11.3 clearly shows that as members of Congress have discussed and crafted legislation during the fifteen-year study period, they consistently have had higher levels of association between trade and immigration with Canada than with Mexico.

Figure 11.3. Congressional Mentions of Trade, Immigration, and Canada or Mexico, 1988–2004

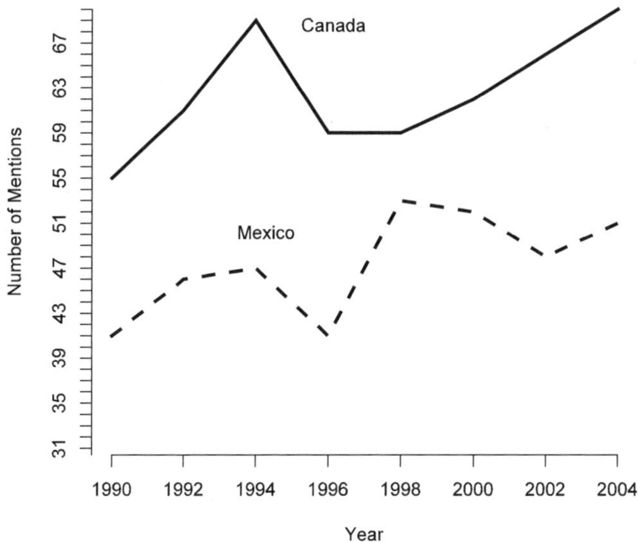

Figure 11.4. Congressional Mentions of Drugs, Immigration, and Canada or Mexico, 1988–2004

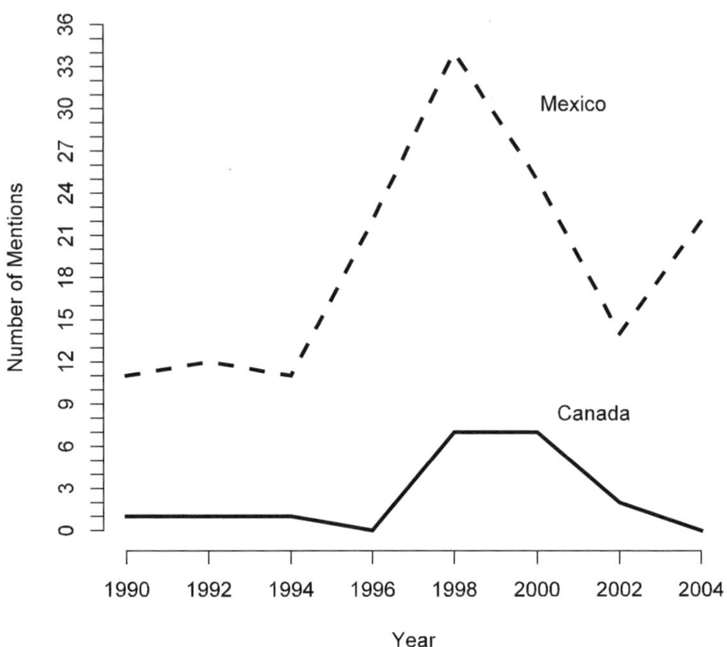

Figure 11.4 presents the level of association between the mention of drugs, immigration/immigrants, and country (that is, Mexico or Canada). In contrast to searching on trade in Figure 11.3, the level of association with drug control and immigration searches shows a nearly complete reversal of the level of association between the United States' neighbors. In both Figures 11.3 and 11.4, we see that while there are slight fluctuations over time in the levels of association, the gaps in the levels of the association between the two countries remains relatively constant across this time period.

Finally, Figure 11.5 presents the level of association between terrorism, immigration, and country (that is, Mexico or Canada). Such associations were minimal and fairly constant prior to the terrorist attacks of September 11, 2001. Following the attacks, it is quite striking how members of Congress instantly associated threats of terrorism and immigration with Mexico and not so with Canada. In 2004, the *Congressional Record* mentions Mexico in relation to terrorism and immigration nearly six times as much as Canada.

▪ ▪ ▪

U.S. immigration policy can be examined in several ways. This chapter highlights two of those ways: examining organizational structure changes over time in bureaucracies tied to immigration as a response to immigration flows and legislative actions taken by Congress; and examining the congressional rhetoric surrounding issues related to immigration.

Changes in organizational structure show that, while the nature of border control remains constant, the logical justifications for border control vary significantly over time (Newton 2005; Bedolla 2006). Perhaps even more telling about the changing nature of American immigration policy over time is the recent variation in the rhetoric of members of Congress on issues concerning immigration. Mexico has a greater association with drugs and terrorism in relation to immigration, and Canada has a greater association with trade in relation to immigration.

This chapter is also suggestive of further avenues of research, particularly when it comes to congressional rhetoric. First, we may want to explain the variation in the rhetoric we described; in other words, do characteristics of congressional districts affect the ways in which they frame such discussions and legislation (Espino 2007)? Such an inquiry should not only consider characteristics within a given district but more importantly characteristics in surrounding districts. Second, an analysis of the rhetoric of political leaders on the other sides of the border would be particularly telling; in other words, how do leaders in Mexico and Canada frame such issues? To what extent is such rhetoric influenced by rhetoric in the United States and vice versa? Finally, while we just examined the levels of association between immigration issues and the United States' neighbors, how do such levels of association compare to other countries, particularly those countries suspected of supporting terrorist networks or labeled as members of the "Axis of Evil?"

Figure 11.5. Congressional Mentions of Terrorism, Immigration, and Canada or Mexico, 1988–2004

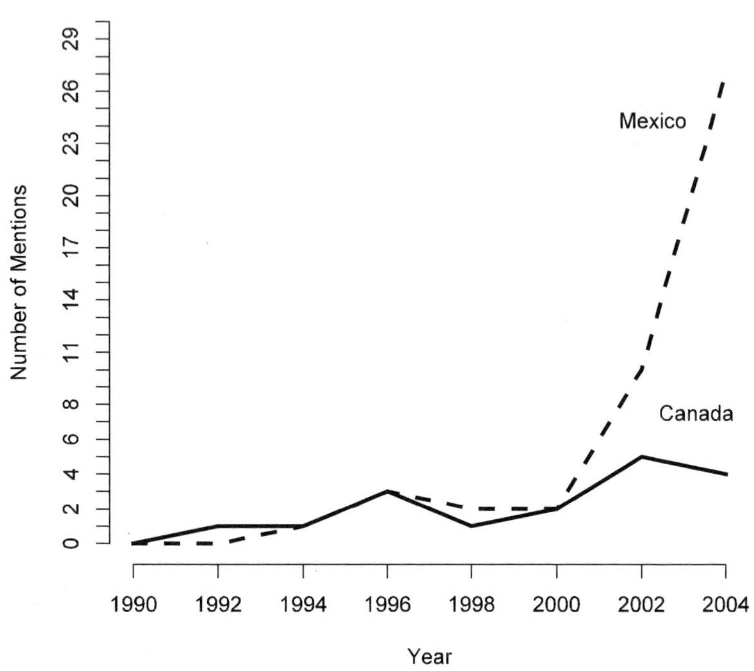

REFERENCES

Andreas, Peter. 1996. "U.S.-Mexico: Open Markets, Closed Border." *Foreign Policy* 103: 51–69.

———. 1998–1999. "The Escalation of U.S. Immigration Control in the Post-NAFTA Era." *Political Science Quarterly* 113 (4): 591–615.

Bedolla, Lisa G. 2006. "Rethinking Citizenship: Noncitizen Voting and Immigrant Political Engagement in the United States." In *Transforming Politics, Transforming America: The Political and Civic Incorporation of Immigrants in the United States,* edited by S. Taeku Lee, Karthick Ramakrishnan, and Ricardo Ramírez, 51–70. Charlottesville: University of Virginia Press.

Cain, Bruce, and Brendan Doherty. 2006. "The Impact of Dual Nationality on Political Participation." In *Transforming Politics, Transforming America: The Political and Civic Incorporation of Immigrants in the United* States, edited by S. Taeku Lee, Karthick Ramakrishnan, and Ricardo Ramírez, 89–105. Charlottesville: University of Virginia Press.

Casellas, Jason P. 2007. "Latino Representation in Congress: To What Extent Are Latinos Substantively Represented?" In *Latino Politics: Identity, Mobilization, and Representation,* edited by Rodolfo Espino, David L. Leal, and Kenneth J. Meier, 19–231. Charlottesville: University of Virginia Press.

Chavez, Leo R. 1992. *Shadowed Lives: Undocumented Immigrants in American Society.* Fort Worth: Harcourt Brace Jovanovich.

Citrin, Jack, Donald P. Green, Christopher Muste, and Cara Wong. 1997. "Public Opinion toward Immigration Reform: The Role of Economic Motivations." *Journal of Politics* 59 (3): 858–81.

Deering, Christopher J., and Steven S. Smith. 1997. *Committees in Congress.* 3rd ed. Washington, DC: Congressional Quarterly Press.

Espino, Rodolfo. 2007. "Is There a Latino Dimension to Voting in Congress?" In *Latino Politics: Identity, Mobilization, and Representation,* edited by Rodolfo Espino, David L. Leal, and Kenneth J. Meier, 197–218. Charlottesville: University of Virginia Press.

Hero, Rodney E. 1992. *Latinos and the U.S. Political System: Two-Tiered Pluralism.* Philadelphia: Temple University Press.

Hritzuk, Natasha, and David K. Park. 2000. "The Question of Latino Participation: From an SES to a Social Structural Explanation." *Social Science Quarterly* 81 (1): 151–65.

Huntington, Samuel. 2004. "The Hispanic Challenge." *Foreign Policy* 141: 30–45.

Jasperson, Amy, Dgavan Shah, Mark Watts, Ronald Faber, and David Fann. 1998. "Framing and the Public Agenda: Media Effects on the Importance of the Federal Budget Deficit." *Political Communication* 15: 205–24.

Jones-Correa, Michael A. 1998. *Between Two Nations: The Political Predicament of Latinos in New York City.* Ithaca: Cornell University Press.

———. 2007. "Fuzzy Distinctions and Blurred Boundaries: Transnational, Ethnic and Immigrant Politics." In *Latino Politics: Identity, Mobilization, and Representation,* edited by Rodolfo Espino, David L. Leal, and Kenneth J. Meier, 44–60. Charlottesville: University of Virginia Press.

Kingdon, John W. 1984. *Agendas, Alternatives, and Public Policies.* Boston: Little, Brown and Company.

Leal, David L. 2007. "Latino Public Opinion: Does It Exist?" In *Latino Politics: Identity, Mobilization, and Representation,* edited by Rodolfo Espino, David L. Leal, and Kenneth J. Meier, 27–43. Charlottesville: University of Virginia Press.

Lindblom, Charles. 1959. "The Science of Muddling Through." *Public Administration Review* 19 (2): 79–88.

Loomis, Burdett A. 2000. *The Contemporary Congress.* 3rd ed. Boston: Bedford/ St. Martin's.

Martinez, Ruben. 2001. *Crossing Over: A Mexican Family on the Migrant Trail.* New York: Metropolitan Books.

Massey, Douglas S. 1990. "The Social and Economic Origins of Immigration." *Annals of the Academy of Political and Social Sciences* 510 (1): 60–72.

Massey, Douglas, and Kristin Espinosa. 1997. "What's Driving Mexico-U.S. Migration? A Theoretical, Empirical, and Policy Analysis." *American Journal of Sociology* 102 (4): 939–99.

Newton, Lina. 2005. "'It Is Not a Question of Being Anti-immigration': Categories of Deservedness in Immigration Policy Making." In *Deserving and Entitled: Social Constructions and Public Policy,* edited by Anne L. Schneider and Helen M. Ingram, 139–67. Albany: State University of New York Press.

Portes, Alejandro, and Min Zhou. 1992. "Gaining the Upper-Hand: Economic Mobility among Immigrant and Domestic Minorities." *Ethnic and Racial Studies* 15 (4): 491–522.

Rudolph, Christopher. 2003. "Security and the Political Economy of International Migration." *American Political Science Review* 97 (4): 603–20.

Sassen, Saskia. 1996. "U.S. Immigration Policy toward Mexico in a Global Economy." In *Between Two Worlds: Mexican Immigrants in the United States,* edited by David G. Gutiérrez, 213–28. Wilmington: Scholarly Resources Press.

Schneider, Anne, and Helen Ingram. 1993. "Social Construction of Target Populations: Implications for Politics and Policy." *American Political Science Review* 87 (2): 334–37.

Shain, Yossi. 1999. *Marketing the American Creed Abroad: Diasporas in the U.S. and Their Homelands.* New York: Cambridge University Press.

Sierra, Christine Marie, Teresa Carrillo, Louis DeSipio, and Michael Jones-Correa. 2000. "Latino Immigration and Citizenship." *PS: Political Science and Politics* 33 (3): 535–40.

Snipp, Matthew C., and Marta Tienda. 1982. "New Perspective on Chicano Intergenerational Occupational Mobility." *Social Science Journal* 19 (2): 37–49.

Tienda, Marta, and Audrey Singer. 1995. "Wage Mobility of Legalized Immigrants." *International Migration Review* 29 (1): 112–38.

Wong, Cara, and Grace Cho. 2006. "Jus Meritum: Citizenship for Service." In *Transforming Politics, Transforming America: The Political and Civic Incorporation of Immigrants in the United States,* edited by S. Taeku Lee, Karthick Ramakrishnan, and Ricardo Ramírez, 71–88. Charlottesville: University of Virginia Press.

Wong, Janelle S. 2000. "The Effects of Age and Political Exposure on the Development of Party Identification among Asian American and Latino Immigrants in the United States." *Political Behavior* 22 (4): 341–71.

TWELVE

Indecent Proposal?

The Rise and Success of Arizona Proposition 200

SYLVIA MANZANO

Long before Arizona SB1070[1] came to symbolize the most stringent anti-immigration policy in the country, Proposition 200[2] placed immigration enforcement at the center of Arizona politics. The 2004 campaign for Prop 200 framed state immigration policy in a manner that blurred the lines between Latino identity, national security, and economic concerns. This was one of the first successful campaigns to incorporate homeland security language in the post–September 11 political context in order to mobilize support for a policy agenda targeting and penalizing Latinos. Unlike 1990's California politics characterized by anti-immigration and anti-minority politics, Arizona Prop 200 was bolstered by national sentiment post–September 11 regarding homeland security and national identity. Today Latino immigration politics often appeals to public fears that tie immigration, Latino identity, and national security (Chavez 2008), but it was novel in the 2004 Arizona setting.

In essence, Prop 200 paved the way for Arizona SB1070, and contributed to the larger national discourse around immigration politics that remains heated and polarized. The rise and success of Prop 200 merits closer analysis for a few reasons. The initiative itself provides a compelling case study in racial threat political dynamics and minority rights in direct democracy venues. Additionally and importantly, examining the context and factors that produced the 2004 law can lend insight into how and why divisively framed immigration politics became a state priority and model for other contests and campaigns around the country.

The majority of Arizona voters, 56%, voted in favor of Proposition 200 in November 2004. The omnibus initiative included several controversial provisions including requiring citizenship validation in order to register and to vote,[3] and to apply for and receive public benefits. The law also placed new burdens on state and local employees to absorb immigration enforcement duties as the new legal requirement compelled them to report immigration law violations found in the course of their new verification procedures to federal immigration authorities. Prop 200 further criminalized non-compliance, such that employees found guilty of failure to document and report violation of federal immigration could be charged with that crime, punishable by up to four months in jail time and fines. The final stipulation in the new law gave the public legal standing to enforce immigration law through lawsuits against individuals and agencies. That is to say, any Arizona citizen can sue an individual state or local employee or larger government entity for inadequate response or failure to report undocumented immigrants whose status was discovered as part of the public benefits verification process. Clearly, the scope of the law reached far beyond penalizing undocumented individuals residing in the state.

The confluence of forces that made such sweeping and severe policies attractive to the Arizona electorate had been brewing for decades. Scholars can correctly point to various historical, contemporary, social, and legal phenomena that contribute to the heated and salient nature of immigration politics in the United States. For the purposes of this chapter, three context-specific factors are considered to explain the emergence and success of Prop 200. First, recent state elections demonstrated ballot initiatives could be a successful mechanism to generate public policy that penalizes cultural differences. Voters approved measures in favor of Official English (Prop 106 in 1988) and repealing bilingual education (Prop 203 in 2000), demonstrating a public willingness to support laws that might otherwise be too controversial for legislative action. Secondly, the flow of immigrants into Arizona dramatically increased during the late 1990's and into the 2000's due to favorable economic conditions coupled with U.S. Border Patrol fortification of the Texas and California borders (Hanson 2007; Cornelius 2001). Finally, the post-September 11 context provided a new way to frame immigration policy, in terms of national security threats, that resonated with public opinion (Chavez 2008; Cornelius 2005). These unique factors (prior punitive ballot initiative success, increased immigration, and post–September 11 context) were simultaneously present, producing a sociopolitical environment favorable to aggressive initiatives from sophisticated and well-funded policy entrepreneurs (Muller 1994; Blumenthal 2004a).

In 2010, nearly six years after Arizona passed Prop 200, the US Ninth Circuit Court of Appeals struck down the registration verification provision on the grounds that it conflicts with federal laws requiring states to remove obstacles to voting and make registration widely available (Hee Lee 2010). It is unclear whether the Supreme Court will weigh in on the matter or if all other Prop 200 provisions will remain intact. No matter the final legal decisions on contentious anti-immigration policies, the practical and symbolic effects associated with these laws will continue to influence Latinos and non-Latinos alike in the broader American political landscape.

PRECEDING INFLUENCE: LANGUAGE POLICY AND BALLOT INITIATIVES

Perhaps the most influential factors contributing to the success of Arizona SB1070[4] are the nativist policies that preceded it; Prop 200 among them but also a product of precedent. Policy and politics have a reinforcing relationship such that policy influences politics which in turn generates more policy (Pierson 1993). Similarly, state-level immigration and ethnic-targeted policy is most likely to be incremental in nature;

whereby policy changes are initially small and gradually increase in scope over time (Hayes 1992). The Arizona legislature did not begin addressing immigration by challenging the Fourteenth-Amendment guarantee of birthright citizenship as some state senators promised to do in the 2011 legislative session (Rau 2010b). Rather, state attention and policy orientation to immigration and related issues became increasingly punitive over time.[5] Prop 200 was a pivotal point on the slippery slope that has made Arizona the national model for polarized Latino and immigration politics. One rationale for the reaching nature of SB1070 is that the state of Arizona had already enacted so much regulation through ballot initiatives and legislative action that lawmakers had few alternatives to advance additional punitive immigration-related laws.

As previously noted, Prop 200 was introduced a few years after official English and a repeal of bilingual education were approved by the Arizona electorate in ballot initiatives. Though these two laws do not regulate immigration, it was logical for anti-immigration proponents to surmise that the same voters supportive of ending bilingual education for schoolchildren and establishing English as the official state language may also have an appetite for immigration restriction policy. Immigration fuels the linguistic differences that Props 203 and 106 sought to diminish. Proponents highlighted immigration concerns related to these language initiatives in advertising and the official campaign arguments provided to voters in official state election information booklets (Wright 2005; Arizona Secretary of State 1988, 2000a, 2000b).

Laws that target cultural differences, like language, are usually unpopular with a wide swath of the Latino American population, regardless of citizenship status or English fluency (Leal 2007). Latinos comprise 31 percent of Arizona's population, and two-thirds are US born American citizens (Pew Hispanic Center 2010a). Despite the fact that the large majority of Arizona Latinos are native-born American citizens, 70 percent use a language other than English in their homes (Pew Hispanic Center 2010b). Thus, it is appropriate to consider immigration-specific laws and culturally pointed policy within the same discussion and framework because Latinos disproportionately absorb the impact of these various rules. It is irrelevant that the formal text of the laws does not single out Latinos; laws regulating immigration violation reporting, requiring proof of citizenship for voter registration, official English, and bilingual education will have a disproportionate impact on Latinos. This fact is not lost on Latinos, there is a strong perception that immigration policy is not actually about immigration at all, but rather a campaign tactic used to scapegoat the entire group to score political points with non-Latinos (Campo Flores 2010). A survey conducted in the weeks after SB1070 was signed into law found an overwhelming 76 percent of Latino voters in Arizona believe the law never would have passed if the state's immigrants were white Europeans (Marrero 2010). Relatedly, experimental research studies indicate whites do feel threatened and anxious specifically in response to Latino immigrants, holding more amenable attitudes toward white European immigrants (Brader, Valentino, and Suhay 2008).

In 1988, Arizona voters narrowly approved Proposition 106 (50.5 percent to 49.5 percent). Proposition 106 not only made English the official language of government entities, but also barred the state from enforcing other state and local laws that had required the use of any language other than English. By 1998 both federal and state courts found the proposition reached too far; the Ninth Circuit Court of Appeals and the Arizona Supreme Court struck down different aspects of Prop 106 on the grounds that it violated the First and Fourteenth Amendments discriminating against non-English speakers. In 2000, Arizona voters overwhelmingly approved Proposition 203 (with 63 percent approval), an anti-bilingual education measure that remains state law and has been upheld in federal and state court challenges. The immediate lesson to candidates and policymakers was that Arizona voters were supportive of culturally-targeted policies; legal proceedings and implementation details became less important once the ballot measures passed.

The success of Propositions 203 and 106 signaled policy entrepreneurs, parties, and candidates that the state electorate was friendly testing ground for ballot initiatives dealing with issues that might otherwise be too politically divisive for legislatures to entertain. Political context and partisan divisions could have stalled or weakened similar proposals had they been initiated within the legislature. For example, in 1988

Arizona state legislators were unlikely to engage yet another high-profile racial policy controversy. The state was in the midst of what became a six-year long battle over whether to observe a holiday honoring Martin Luther King, Jr.[6] Less dramatic but equally important, the 2000 Arizona State Senate was equally divided by party, with fifteen Democrats and fifteen Republicans in the upper chamber. Party composition kept controversial partisan legislation from emerging. Four years later the GOP controlled both chambers, but Democratic Governor Janet Napolitano presented a veto threat to policies perceived as antagonistic to minorities. By the time unauthorized migration into the state was cresting, the state was already primed for the kind of policy demands written in Prop 200. Previously successful ballot initiatives showed electoral support for laws that disproportionately affected Latinos but were framed in the interest of economic efficiency and American assimilation. At this same time the post–September 11 national political discourse regarded a wider range of topics in terms of national identity, patriotism, and security—immigration and ethnic politics were part of the new national issue framing (Hill et al. 2010; Altheide 2009; Chavez 2008). Arizona's history with ballot initiatives, surging immigration population, and national trends produced a political environment that was an obvious setting for social and cultural policy entrepreneurs to fund and stage campaigns to test and advance their policy agenda.

THE PROPOSITION 200 CAMPAIGN

State ballot initiatives commonly originate from well-resourced out-of-state interest groups. Because statewide campaigns are expensive endeavors, wealthy individuals and groups with clear policy agenda goals are well poised to advance their interests via the direct democracy process (Smith and Tolbert 2004). Minority group interests often find themselves outmatched; frequently they do not have comparable organization or mobilization capacity to wage an unexpected campaign to protect their interests (Smith and Tolbert 2004; Ellis 2002; Gamble 1997). In this case, however, the narrow alliance of anti-immigration interests that initiated the Prop 200 measure raised far less money than the broader coalition of business, labor, and minority interest groups that organized in response. Initiative sponsors were outspent by a three-to-one margin, raising just under eight hundred thousand dollars compared to nearly 2.5 million raised by the opposition[7]. Washington, DC, area interest groups and think tanks funded 88 percent of the entire campaign to generate a host of new Arizona immigration enforcement laws. Conversely, Arizona residents and interest groups funded 60 percent of the effort against Prop 200.

The state battle over immigration politics was a fight between well-organized and funded interests groups: national anti-immigration lobbyists and organized interests clashed with national business, labor, and Latino advocacy groups. State and local victories for policy-specific interest groups (as opposed to party- or candidate-oriented lobbies) are important because they build momentum for the cause at hand. Wins and losses in state and local elections add up to either strengthen or weaken the national prospects of a given policy agenda. For these reasons, national lobbies had a vested interest in this outcome. Arizona voters would signal the appeal of this brand of immigration policy to the rest of the country.

Records filed with the Arizona Secretary of State and further detailed by the non-partisan state campaign finance research outfit Follow the Money indicate the Federation for American Immigration Reform (FAIR) contributed half of all Prop 200 campaign funds. Other groups with ties to FAIR including Americans for Immigration Control, Americans for Better Immigration, Population Stop, and Population-Environment Balance funded another larger share of the campaign costs. Established in 1979, FAIR's agenda is dedicated to advancing immigration restriction policy at all levels of government. The group's website outlines a broader nativist agenda aimed at addressing large social, economic, and political problems they attribute to undocumented Latino immigration. For example, FAIR advocates ending birthright citizenship (using the phrase "anchor babies" often), banning bilingual education and implementing official English laws. In the past two decades FAIR has influenced local, state, and federal immigration laws by offering financial, strategic, and organizational support to targeted campaign and legislative efforts around the country (Rau 2010a).

Fueled by Washington interest-group funding, political action committees (PACs) worked to complete bureaucratic formalities associated with the petition process, collect signatures, and execute the on-the-ground campaign for Prop 200 (Judis 2006; Wingett 2004). Republican State Senator Russell Pearce, Phoenix area businessman and GOP party leader Randy Pullen, along with community activist Kathy McKee spearheaded the local logistical and formal Prop 200 effort (Benson and Sherwood 2006; Diaz and Sherwood 2005; Judis 2006). Despite political spats that erupted, Pearce and McKee are credited with authoring the initiative, and all three led PACs ("Protect Arizona Now" and "Yes on 200") that received support from these large out-of-state anti-immigrant organizations (Blumenthal 2004a, 2004b). The campaign did not have to spend as much money advertising and informing the public about the bill because television, print, radio, and online outlets commonly covered the bill as a topical matter of interest. Advocates providing commentary to media became news themselves; it is typical for controversy to generate public interest. Pearce and Pullen in particular developed greater stature in state GOP politics as a result of their local leadership with the initiative. Pearce authored and sponsored several more immigration-related bills, including SB1070. He remains a highly visible anti-immigration policy advocate in and outside of Arizona and has promised to introduce legislation challenging birthright citizenship in the 2011 legislative session (Rau 2010b). Pullen leveraged his role to rise in state party ranks; twice he was elected state GOP chairman, and held several committee appointments with the Republican National Committee as well.

Perhaps more interesting than the Prop 200 organizational structure, is the coalition that developed in opposition. High profile Republican elected officials and traditionally GOP interest groups worked in conjunction with local Arizona Latino activists and traditionally Democratic interest groups to oppose Prop 200. Together, they raised 1.6 million dollars from national lobbies including the US Chamber of Commerce and large union interests like the SEIU. Half of all opposition campaign funding came from in-state sources and half from national or other state groups. Republican Attorney General Grant Woods was among the most visible and vocal leaders in the anti-200 effort.

Senators John McCain and John Kyl made a public showing of their strong opposition to the initiative, culminating in McCain's *Arizona Republic* op-ed that argued the policy would be inefficient, intrusive, and divisive (McCain 2004). The wide-ranging scope of new regulations in the proposition prompted the diverse opposition coalition. Industries that rely heavily on immigrant labor including construction, hospitality, and agriculture opposed the bill. State-employee unions, especially hospital and health care workers viewed the law as an intrusion on their jobs, forcing them to serve in a law enforcement capacity that depleted time and attention from patients.

Despite the fact that the opposition raised and spent more on their effort, several problems were associated with their operation. Although leading Democrats and Republicans unanimously denounced Prop 200, a bipartisan coalition never materialized at the state level. State and local GOP legislators and elected officials were somewhat divided on the issue, with many favoring the law. Among the Democrats, Congressman Raul Grijalva was the only high-profile elected official that actively campaigned against it; he went so far as to include anti-200 literature in his door-to-door mobilization efforts (Bernick 2004). The No on 200 campaign was also relatively slow to get off of the ground. There had not been any formal campaign events, advertisements, or coordinated efforts in opposition to 200 until summer of 2004. By this time, the public had already been exposed to large quantities of pro-200 information via new stories and advertising. The Prop 200 groups had been actively campaigning for almost a year when the opposition started their work.

BEYOND THE CAMPAIGN: ARIZONA BORDER POLICY CONTEXT

The Mexican American population, native-born and foreign-born, has long been a part of the American Southwest landscape (Martinez 1998; Lorey 1999). Recent U.S. Border Patrol policies in the mid-1990's had the unintended consequence of dramatically increasing unauthorized immigration to Arizona, thus this wave of Latino presence in the state was unprecedented in pace and size (Andreas 2000). Two large-scale initiatives in place between 1994–1998 designed to stop unauthorized immigration, Operation Gatekeeper in San Diego and Operation Hold-the-Line in El Paso, effectively pushed the flow of immigrants from those two busy entry points toward Arizona. New technology, more agents, and expanded check-point procedures in these two operations initially led to increased apprehensions, but soon enough, crossings decreased in those locales and picked up where there was less enforcement—the Arizona border. In the small town of Douglas, Arizona, the number of apprehensions jumped from 3,000 a month in 1995 to 27,000 a month in 1999 (Andreas 2000). These patterns became common in the small towns dotting the Arizona-Mexico border. Ultimately, illegal border crossings decreased at the California and Texas borders to the point that Arizona became the primary point of entry for unauthorized immigration from the Southern border. By 2004 Arizona accounted for more than half of all apprehensions made on the U.S.-Mexico border (Winograd 2004). The influx of immigrants was palpable to local residents; Arizona's border towns are significantly smaller than El Paso and San Diego, making it difficult to blend in on the journey to a metro area. An added complication at this crossing-point is that most land along the Arizona-Mexico border is private property, making the presence and impact of unauthorized immigrants more apparent and pressing in these communities. Arizona communities and metro areas were faced with social and political consequences of a new and large migration phenomenon that arose out of Border Patrol operations implemented in other states.

NEW ANTI-IMMIGRANT CONTEXT: RHETORIC AND ORGANIZATIONS LEGITIMIZED

The ever-growing flow of immigrants, stories of would-be criminals, and associated economic pressures played on Arizona residents' extant discomfort with immigrants (Espenshade and Belanger 1998; Gallup Poll 2004; Malone 2004). Growing attention to problems associated with undocumented immigrants along the Arizona border drew the frustration from those that saw the federal government as shirking their responsibility on the matter. Politicians had found a populist selling point when they argued that the federal government was not assisting the states with law enforcement or defraying expenses the state made in an effort to resolve their own problem (Bustos 2003; Cornman 2004). Since the federal government helped create the problem (with afore-mentioned border enforcement policy) and offered no viable resolutions, Arizona was ripe for the efforts of national organized anti-immigrant groups.

Post–September 11 rhetoric added more fuel to the already simmering Arizona climate. Since the terrorist attacks on the United States in 2001, the federal government linked the discussion of terrorism, homeland security, and immigration reform. The Bush Administration moved the Immigration and Naturalization Service (INS) under the Department of Homeland Security (now the Immigration Customs and Enforcement, ICE). There is evidence that increased numbers of Americans and political leaders believe that illegal immigration is in fact a threat to national security (Beck and Camarota 2002; Gallup Poll 2004). The 200 campaign capitalized on this sentiment and blended the language of patriotism and fear of terrorism with domestic policies that regulate social services. Anti-immigration sentiments were punctuated with fears regarding terrorism. Chris Simcox, founder of the border militia group American Border Patrol has repeated his experiences to national reporters. "There was a large group of Middle Eastern men who were captured by the Border Patrol in the Chiricahua Mountains back in June. The men spoke Farsi, the language of Iran. The media and the Border Patrol covered it up by saying that they were a tribe of Huachuca Indians who didn't speak Spanish, and that the Border Patrol agents were confused. A Muslim prayer rug was found right near my house. It shows there's not just Mexicans coming across there, 'cause I don't think there's many Muslims in Mexico" (Seper 2002; Strand 2005).

On May 3, 2000, Arizona ranchers Roger and Donald Barnett employed the assistance of their dogs to apprehend nine immigrants who were resting in the brush on their ranch. After ordering the dogs to attack the immigrants, the Barnetts called the Border Patrol to pick up the trespassers (Moser 2003). Violent stories like this one have been repeated in Arizona for decades (Martinez 1998; Southern Poverty Law Center 2001). The difference now was that these stories were becoming political rallying cries, no longer socially frowned upon. A wide range of media outlets (local, national, television, radio, and online) gave border vigilantes a sympathetic ear and a national platform to make their case in the years and months building up to Prop 200. Mainstream media discourse regularly incorporated rhetoric and points of view that singled out Latino immigrants as a national, social ill. Lou Dobbs on CNN, the epitome of mainstream American news media, famously made Latinos and immigration the focal point of his program several years running. The *Arizona Republic, Tucson Citizen, Arizona Daily Star,* Fox News, and the Christian Broadcast Network News all interviewed militia participants as sources for immigration policy stories.

The political and policy discussions in national politics were now full of Arizona references. The state became a shorthand reference for several policy and security concerns that were at the forefront of American discourse and tense racial politics that seemed to escalate with each election.

ELECTION RESULTS

Proposition 200 passed with 56 percent of the vote in November 2004, mirroring President Bush's margin of victory in the state. Eleven of fifteen counties approved the measure.[8] The victory fueled a claim that there was a public mandate to enforce the law and pursue more of this sort of policy. The Republican partisan advantage in the electorate and presidential election bolstered support for the proposition. Latino majority precincts in Tucson voted heavily for Kerry and overwhelmingly against 200. Suburban, largely white precincts that supported Bush also passed Prop 200 by a similar margin (Bernick 2004). Arizonans are clustered in two metro areas, Maricopa (greater Phoenix area) and Pima (Tucson and suburbs); together the two account for 78 percent of all state residents. The Latino population follows this same pattern, where 59 percent reside in Maricopa and another 19 percent in Pima. This bimodal population distribution means local politics in these two cities has substantial influence on statewide electoral outcomes. Latinos have enjoyed more political incorporation in Tucson relative to Phoenix. In this southern Arizona city, Latinos have a history of political activism,

no regulatory authority over this matter. It is common knowledge among those on both sides of the immigration debate that regulation of immigration and federal social spending are under the purview of the federal government. Prop 200 is comprehensive insomuch as it addresses many aspects of social and public life for not only immigrants, but technically for all Arizonans. Because the policy changes and enforcement effort called for in the proposition are dramatic, it is possible that the motivation was symbolic posturing to move more restrictive policy forward, as opposed to actual reform and decreased immigration rates to the state. A few politicians have suggested this is the case. Mesa-area State Representative Pearce described the symbolic power of the initiative that "sends a message that we have the right to report those people who are in the country illegally, especially when they're attempting fraud" (Carroll and Wingett 2004). Perhaps the authors and political insiders associated with Prop 200 implemented a strategy that asked for many restrictions in one initiative, in the hopes that at least a few would pass the legal threshold. It is likely that the reformers knew that portions of the proposition would not have legal standing. Indeed, when California passed similar legislation in 1994, the federal government struck down Proposition 187 under great scrutiny (Garcia 2003).

Prop 200 supporters claimed the new policy would stop undocumented immigrants from receiving welfare in Arizona. Yet state law already stipulated state and local services are reserved exclusively for its citizens. Pro-200 leaders and literature often state that the policy was needed to make certain that non-citizens were not voting in the state. No single instance of an undocumented immigrant (or groups of them swinging electoral outcomes) voting in an Arizona election has been presented in the media or documented at the county or state level. Despite this fact, Proposition 200 requires submission of proof of citizenship when registering to vote and casting a ballot.

Latinos of different citizenship status voiced concern that Prop 200 would have stinging impact on Latino American citizens and breed ill will toward immigrants and Latinos more broadly. Voting rights have been especially noted in press coverage after 200 passed. The new voting requirements were particularly problematic for many in the state that viewed the range of identification and enforcement as an infringement on voting rights and a threat to enfranchisement. Proposition 200 now requires a birth certificate for voter registration and photo identification for voting in any election. As of the 2000 Census 12.8 percent, or 656,183, of Arizona residents are foreign-born. Among Arizonans who are United State citizens, 3.8 percent, or 193,994, are foreign-born. It is quite possible that these people will encounter difficulty with the voting process because they do not have United States birth certificates. The birth certificate requirement also changes some of the more liberal voting practices that the state had adopted in an effort to increase voter participation. As written, 200 would eliminate voter registrations conducted at college campuses, at shopping malls, door-to-door, and at public fairs. The picture identification requirement also ended Arizona's successful vote-by-mail program.

Despite the state's best efforts to clarify specifically which programs and people were involved in the new policy, many are offended and confused by 200. Undocumented people will not be denied emergency health care or other emergency services under 200. The new law also does not apply to school-age children in kindergarten through twelfth grade. Nevertheless, confusion and anger abound. Jesus Garcia, an undocumented immigrant from Sonora told the *Arizona Republic* that the proposition already has many immigrants afraid and uncertain. Though he has lived in Arizona for ten years and his three children are American citizens, he says he fears going to a government office. "They don't understand if (undocumented immigrants) receive help, it's not for them, it's for the kids who are U.S. citizens. They're trying to put pressure on immigrants, and it's very dangerous because some won't seek help." Elias Bermudez of the Phoenix's Center of Help, which prepares citizenship documents for immigrants, says they are not clear about which benefits are available and which are not. "The main problem is that immigrants may not want to seek medical care for fear of being deported. It's a slap in the face to the Latino community" (Carroll and Wingett 2004).

POST-200 LITIGATION AND IMPLEMENTATION

Within weeks of its approval, Arizona Attorney General Terry Goddard offered a narrow interpretation of the new law and limited the application of 200 to five welfare programs administered by the state. As of this writing, the FAIR-funded Yes on Prop 200 organization has recently asked the courts to expand the application of 200 to all state benefits. Pullen contends that the spirit of the law was more far-reaching than Goddard allowed. He is advocating that the entire slate of state and local services be denied to unauthorized immigrants, including public schools and library cards. The Mexican American Legal Defense and Education Fund (MALDEF) led the legal charge against 200. MAL-DEF contends that Prop 200 violates federal law because it requires state and local government employees to check the immigration status of anyone seeking public benefits and to turn over the undocumented to immigration authorities. The law also discourages qualified immigrants from seeking public benefits they are entitled to receive under federal law. MALDEF's lawsuit includes several undocumented plaintiffs who say they fear losing benefits for their U.S.-born children if the law becomes effective.

In early January 2005, the Ninth Circuit Court of Appeals denied MALDEF's emergency motion to block the major portions of 200. The sections of 200 that deal with voting are being dealt with separately by the Department of Justice. It remains to be seen whether or not the new voting policies violate federal voting rights law.

While the courts and agencies figure out whether 200 will be expanded or contracted, the state has proceeded to implement at least some aspects of the initiative. Governor Napolitano issued an executive order that directs executive branch agencies affected by Proposition 200 to institute an audit to confirm the application of the new law. According to the governor's website, reports of those audits were due March 30, 2005. The Arizona Department of Economic Security (DES) administers the five programs that are directly affected by 200: General Assistance, Sight Conservation, Neighbors Helping Neighbors, Utility Repair, and Replacement Deposit and Supplemental Payment Program. DES staff members are now required to ask applicants to verify their legal status by providing an approved form of identification including birth certificates, passports, or driver's licenses from states in which legal status has been verified. Undocumented people applying for any of these programs will be reported to the DES Office of Special Investigations. These bureaucrats inform the federal office of Immigration and

Customs Enforcement. According to Governor Napolitano's office, training on the new policies and reporting procedures for more than 2,000 employees was completed on December 17, 2004 (Arizona Governor's Office, 2004).

At the state level, some degree of uniformity should emerge once the court battles are resolved. At the local level, however, governing bodies may choose to give additional validity to 200, therefore creating further tension and legal complication. For example, despite the fact that the Department of Justice had not rendered a decision on the legality of 200's voting regulations as of the time of this writing, the Phoenix City Council and Mayor recently adopted a new code and changed the city charter to require that city voters show identification at the polls (Wingett 2005).

IMMIGRATION REFORM—COMING SOON?

Part of the reason that Arizona voters approved Prop 200 is because the federal government had yet to offer concrete assistance to the state on the matter. President Bush and congressional leaders had promised to take up legislation that would offer relief to border states and move toward a resolution on the complex problem of unauthorized migration to the United States. President Obama offered the same promise, but as of this writing has found Congress as uncooperative on the matter as Bush did during his terms in office. The stage has already been set for a contentious debate on the issue, and various solutions are up for consideration. Some politicians view immigration reform as more Border Patrol crackdowns, like those of the 1990s. Others advocate creating a pathway to citizenship for the tens of millions already residing in the country. It is possible that congressional immigration legislative action will either invalidate or bolster Arizona's host of restrictive immigration policies. It will be interesting to observe how Arizona immigration politics continues to influence federal debate, campaigns, and policy agendas.

While this chapter only considers the Arizona case, it is clear that more and more states are struggling with this issue and will look to

Arizona as a model for policy solutions or political missteps—depending on the given states' point of view. It will be worthwhile to observe the political fallout and long-term policy impacts in the state. The outside interest groups and vocal opponents have created a tense social and political atmosphere. Will voters continue to support this approach to addressing immigration, and if so, for how long? What are the long-term implications for Latinos in the state and what range of choices do they have to respond to these laws, which clearly target them? A more comprehensive understanding of state immigration reform efforts, and Latino-targeted policies for that matter, requires further investigation in a multitude of states. A sophisticated data analysis of public support for these policies over time and across states may offer some power in predicting which contexts are most likely to support or oppose such policies. The unique political and social context found in Arizona paved the way for Proposition 200. New streams of immigrants to the state made many uncomfortable for a number of reasons. The anti-immigrant and anti-terrorist rhetoric fueled anti-Latino policy efforts that were based on those that had been successful in the past. National nativist lobbies provided the organizational and campaign expertise to help make Proposition 200 successful. As the state continues to produce more policy that requires courts to weigh in on their legitimacy, Arizona residents must now contend with the ethnic, social, and political tension their vote choices have created.

APPENDIX

I. Proposition 200 as presented on the 2004 Arizona Ballot[9]

PROPOSED BY INITIATIVE PETITION

OFFICIAL TITLE
AMENDING SECTIONS 16-152, 16-166 AND 16-579, ARIZONA REVISED STATUTES; AMENDING TITLE 46, CHAPTER 1, ARTICLE 3, ARIZONA REVISED STATUTES, BY ADDING SECTION 46-140.01; RELATING TO THE ARIZONA TAXPAYER AND CITIZEN PROTECTION ACT.

DESCRIPTIVE TITLE
REQUIRES: PROOF OF CITIZENSHIP WHEN REGISTERING TO VOTE; REJECTION OF VOTER REGISTRATION NOT AC-COMPANIED BY PROOF OF CITIZENSHIP; SHOWING IDEN-TIFICATION BEFORE RECEIVING A BALLOT; STATE AND LOCAL GOVERNMENTS TO VERIFY IDENTITY OF APPLI-CANTS FOR CERTAIN STATE AND LOCAL PUBLIC BENE-FITS; AND GOVERNMENT EMPLOYEES TO REPORT APPLICANTS WHO VIOLATE IMMIGRATION LAW.

A "yes" vote shall have the effect of [1] requiring a person to submit evidence of United States citizenship when registering to vote, [2] requiring the county recorder to reject any voter registration that is not accompanied by proof of citizenship, [3] requiring voters to present a photo identification with name and address or two other forms of identification with name and address before receiving a ballot at the polling place, [4] requiring state and local governments to verify the identity and eligibility of applicants for state and local public benefits that are not federally mandated, [5] requiring government employees to report violations of United States immigration law by applicants for public benefits, [6] making it a class 2 misdemeanor if a government employee fails to make the required report and [7] permitting private lawsuits by any resident to enforce provisions relating to public benefits.

YES ❏

A "no" vote shall have the effect of retaining the current laws regarding citizenship when registering to vote and not requiring voters to show identification documents at the polls prior to voting, and keeping the current requirements when applying for public benefits.

NO ❏

II. State Legislative Council Description (Official State Interpretation) of Proposition 200 Presented in Official State Voter Guide

Proposition 200 would require that evidence of United States citizenship be presented by every person to register to vote, that proof of identification be presented by every voter at the polling place prior to voting, that state and local governments verify the identity of all applicants for certain public benefits and that government employees report United States immigration law violations by applicants for public benefits.

Proposition 200 provides that for purposes of registering to vote, satisfactory evidence of United States citizenship includes:

- an Arizona driver or nonoperating identification license issued after October 1, 1996.
- a driver or nonoperating identification license issued by another state if the license indicates that the person has provided proof of United States citizenship.
- a copy of the applicant's birth certificate.
- a U.S. passport, or a copy of the pertinent pages of the passport.
- U.S. naturalization documents or a verified certificate of naturalization number.
- a Bureau of Indian Affairs card number, tribal treaty card number or tribal enrollment number.
- other documents or methods of proof that may be established by the federal government for the purpose of verifying employment eligibility.

The county recorder shall indicate this information in the person's permanent voter file for at least two years. A voter registration card from another county or state does not constitute satisfactory evidence of United States citizenship. A person who is registered to vote on the date that Proposition 200 becomes effective is not required to submit evidence of citizenship unless the person moves to a different county. Once a person has submitted sufficient evidence of citizenship, the person is not required to resubmit the evidence when making changes to voter registration information in the county where the evidence has been submitted.

Proposition 200 requires that prior to receiving a ballot at a polling place, a voter must present either one form of identification that contains the name, address and photograph of the person or two different forms of identification that contain the name and address of the person.

Proposition 200 requires that a state or local governmental entity that is responsible for administering "state and local public benefits that are not federally mandated" must:

- verify the identity and eligibility for each applicant for the public benefits.
- provide other state and local government employees with information to verify immigration status of applicants applying for public benefits and must also assist other state and local government employees in obtaining immigration status information from federal immigration authorities.
- refuse to accept any state or local government identification card, including a driver license, to establish identity or eligibility for public benefits unless the governmental entity that issued the card has verified the immigration status of the applicant.
- require all state and local government employees to make a written report to federal immigration authorities upon discovering a violation of federal immigration laws by an applicant for public benefits. An employee or supervisor who fails to make the required report is guilty of a class 2 misdemeanor, potentially punishable by a jail sentence of up to 4 months and a fine of up to $750, plus applicable surcharges.

Any resident of this state would have standing to bring a court action against the state, a local governmental entity or an agent of a state or local governmental entity to remedy a violation of the public benefits verification law including bringing an action to compel a government official to comply with the law. Proposition 200 does not define the term "state and local public benefits that are not federally mandated."

NOTES

1. April 23, 2010, Arizona Governor Jan Brewer signed Senate Bill 1070 into law setting off national controversy. As the *New York Times* notes, the bill's most controversial provision "would make the failure to carry immigration documents a crime and give the police broad power to detain anyone suspected of being in the country illegally" (Archibold 2010).

2. Specific ballot text is provided in chapter appendix.

3. Validating citizenship for voter registration is distinctive from other state and national efforts to require voter identification when actually voting. The Prop 200 provision created a new legal requirement for people to become registered voters altogether.

4. Success here defined only in terms of a legislative victory for bill authors and proponents, not an assessment of implementation or impact on state residents.

5. The National Conference of State Legislatures (NCSL), a non-partisan research center, began tracking and reporting new state immigration legislation beginning in 2005. Their annual reports, available at www.ncsl.org/default .aspx?tabid=19897, verify this point. Vested groups on both sides of the immigration debate provide supporting information indicating Arizona is a high volume immigration regulation state, still NCSL reports remain among the most comprehensive and clearly non-partisan to date.

6. From 1986 to 1992 the state enacted and rescinded a law observing the Martin Luther King Jr. holiday a total of six times via ballot initiative, governor executive orders and bills initiated in the legislature. National attention to the odd statewide controversy over the holiday reached a crescendo when the National Football League withdrew Super Bowl 27 from the state in protest of their failure to recognize MLK Day. The final decision to recognize the holiday occurred via ballot initiative in 1992 (Alozie 1995).

7. Campaign finance details collected at: http://www.followthemoney .org/database/StateGlance/ballot.phtml?m=232.
Contributions over $10,000 on record at the Arizona Secretary of State website: http://www.azsos.gov/election/2004/Info/ballotmeasurenotifications_1.html#.

8. State, county and precinct data on Arizona election outcomes collected from the Arizona Secretary of State, Elections Division website.

9. All 2004 Ballot Information is archived at the State of Arizona Secretary of State website. Documentation quoted here and additional information included in the Voter Guide are located online at: http://www.azsos.gov/election/2004/info/PubPamphlet/english/prop200.htm.

REFERENCES

Alozie, Nicholas. 1995. "Political Tolerance Hypotheses and White Opposition to a Martin Luther King Holiday in Arizona." *Social Science Quarterly* 32 (1): 1–16.

Altheide, David. 2009. *Terror Post 9–11 and the Media*. New York: Lang Publishers.

Andreas, Peter. 2000. *Border Games: Policing the U.S.-Mexico Divide*. Ithaca: Cornell University Press.

Archibold, Randal C. 2010. "Arizona Enacts Stringent Law on Immigration." *New York Times.* April 23, A1.

Arizona Governor's Office. 2004. "Frequently Asked Questions Re: Prop 200." Press Release. December 22. http://www.governor.state.az.us/press/0412/04_12_22a.htm. Last accessed March 12, 2005.

Arizona Secretary of State. 1998. *1988 Ballot Propositions Publicity Pamphlet in English.* http://www.azsos.gov/election/1988/Info/PubPamphlet/PubPam88.pdf.

———. 2000a. *2000 Ballot Propositions Publicity Pamphlet in English.* http://www.azsos.gov/election/2000/Info/pubpamphlet/english/prop203.htm#pgfId-1.

———. 2000b. *2000 Notification of Contribution to Ballot Measure Committees.* http://www.azsos.gov/election/2004/Info/ballotmeasurenotifications_1.html#.

Beck, Roy, and Steven Camarota. 2002. *Elite vs. Public Opinion: An Examination of Divergent Views on Immigration.* Washington, DC: Center for Immigration Studies.

Benson, Matthew, and Robbie Sherwood. 2006. "Lawsuit Questions Illegality of ID Rules for Elections." *Arizona Republic.* May 10. http://www.azcentral.com/arizonarepublic/local/articles/0510voting-lawsuit0510.html.

Bernick, Joe. 2004. "Arizonans Challenge Racist Ballot Measure." *People's Weekly World.* December 4. http://peoplesworld.org/arizonans-challenge-racist-ballot-measure.

Blumenthal, Max. 2004a. "White Noise." *The American Prospect.* August 31. http://prospect.org/article/white-noise.

———. 2004b. "Backlash on the Border." *Salon.com.* October 18. http://www.salon.com/news/feature/2004/10/18/arizona_immigration/.

Brader, Ted, Nicholas Valentino, and Elizabeth Suhay. 2008. "What Triggers Public Opposition to Immigration? Anxiety, Group Cues, and Immigration Threat." *American Journal of Political Science* 52 (4): 959–78.

Bustos, Sergio. 2003. "Bill to Aid Immigrant Jail Costs Falls Short" *Tucson Citizen.* December 9. http://tucsoncitizen.com/morgue2/2003/12/09/164619-bill-to-aid-jail-costs-of-immigrants-falls-short/.

Campo Flores, Arian. 2010. "Will Arizona's Tough Immigration Law Fuel Hispanic Turnout for Democrats?" *Newsweek.* May 20. http://www.thedailybeast.com/newsweek/2010/05/20/will-arizona-s-tough-immigration-law-fuel-hispanic-turnout-for-democrats.html.

Carroll, Susan, and Yvonne Wingett. 2004. "Proposition Is Now Law in Arizona." *Arizona Republic.* December 23.

Chavez, Leo. 2008. *Latino Threat: Constructing Immigrants, Citizens and the Nation.* Palo Alto: Stanford University Press.

Cornelius, Wayne. 2001. "Death at the Border: Efficacy and Unintended Consequences of U.S. Immigration Control Policy." *Population and Development Review* 27 (4): 661–85.

———. 2005. "Controlling 'Unwanted' Immigration: Lessons from the United States, 1993–2004." *Journal of Ethnic and Migration Studies* 31 (4): 775–94.

Cornman, Sheryl. 2004. "Arizona Illegal Immigration Costs Arizona Taxpayers 1.3 Billion per Year." *Tucson Citizen.* June 22.

Diaz, Elvia, and Robbie Sherwood. 2005. "Prop 200's Minimal Effect." *Arizona Republic.* June 5.

Ellis, Richard. 2002. *Democratic Delusions: The Initiative Process in America.* Lawrence: University Press of Kansas.

Espenshade, Thomas J., and Maryanne Belanger. 1998. "Immigration and Public Opinion." In *Crossings: Mexican Immigration in Interdisciplinary Perspectives,* edited by Marcelo M. Suarez-Orozco, 365–403. Cambridge, MA: Harvard University Press.

Gallup Poll. 2004. February 2–12.

Gamble, Barbara S. 1997. "Putting Civil Rights to a Popular Vote." *American Journal of Political Science* 41 (1): 245–69.

Garcia, John A. 2003. *Latino Politics in America: Community, Culture, and Interests.* Lanham: Rowman and Littlefield.

Hanson, Gordon H. 2007. *The Economic Logic of Illegal Immigration.* New York: Council on Foreign Relations.

Hayes, Michael T. 1992. *Incrementalism and Public Policy.* New York: Longman.

Hee Lee, Michelle Yi. 2010. "Appeals Court Strikes Down Voter ID Law." *Arizona Republic.* October 27. http://www.azcentral.com/arizonarepublic/news/articles/2010/10/27/20101027voters1027.html.

Hill, Joshua, Willard Oliver, and Nancy Marion. 2010. "'Shaping History' or 'Riding the Wave'? President Bush's Influence on the Public Opinion of Terrorism, Homeland Security, and Crime." *Journal of Crime and Justice* 38 (5): 896–902.

Judis, John. 2006. "Border War." *New Republic.* January 16. http://www.tnr.com/article/politics/76209/border-war.

Leal, David. 2007. "Latino Public Opinion: Does It Exist?" In *Latino Politics: Identity, Mobilization, and Representation,* edited by Rodolfo Espino, David L. Leal, and Kenneth J. Meier, 27–43. Charlottesville: University of Virginia Press.

Lorey, David E. 1999. *The U.S.-Mexican Border in the Twentieth Century.* Washington, DC: Scholarly Resources.

Malone, Julia. 2004. "Immigration Costs US Men." *Arizona Daily Star.* May 4.

Marrero, Pilar. 2010. "Latinos de Arizona Unidos Contra la Ley." *La Opinión*. May 7. http://www.impre.com/laopinion/noticias/la-california/2010/5/7/ latinos-de-arizona-unidos-cont-187313-1.html.

Martinez, Oscar. 1998. *Border People: Life and Society in the US-Mexico Borderlands*. Tucson: University of Arizona Press.

McCain, John. 2004. "Prop 200 Less Than Worthless to Arizona." *Arizona Republic*. October 24.

Moser, Bob. 2003. "Vigilante Incident List." *Southern Poverty Law Center Intelligence Report*. Spring (109).

Muller, Thomas E. 1994. *Immigrants and the American City*. New York: New York University Press.

Pew Hispanic Center. 2010a. *Statistical Portrait of the Foreign-Born Population in the United States, 2008*. Washington, DC: Pew Hispanic Center.

———. 2010b. "Table 1. Characteristics of the Population in Arizona, by Race, Ethnicity and Nativity: 2008." http://pewhispanic.org/states/pdf/ AZ_08.pdf.

Pierson, Paul. 1993. "When Effect Becomes Cause: Policy Feedback and Political Change." *World Politics* 45 (4): 595–628.

Rau, Alia. 2010a. "Immigration Law Crafted by Rising Star Activist." *Arizona Republic*. May 31. http://www.azcentral.com/12news/news/articles/2010/ 05/31/20100531arizona-immigration-law-kris-kobach.html.

———. 2010b. "Proposals to Deny Citizenship to Illegal Immigrants' Children in the Works, Lawmaker Says." *Arizona Republic*. October 19. http:// www.azcentral.com/news/articles/2010/10/19/20101019deny-us-citizen ship-to-children-of-illegal-immigrants-russell-pearce-national-pl.html.

Seper, Jerry. 2002. "Border Rancher Fights to Stem Flood of Aliens." *Washington Times*. September 25. http://www.washingtontimes.com/news/2002/ sep/25/20020925-090844-9084r/?page=all.

Smith, Daniel A., and Caroline J. Tolbert. 2004. *Educated by Initiative: The Effects of Direct Democracy on Citizens and Political Organizations in the American States*. Ann Arbor: University of Michigan Press.

Southern Poverty Law Center, 2001. "Blood on the Border." *Intelligence Report*. Spring (101).

Strand, Paul. 2005. "Borderline: Teetering Tensions on the Mexico Border." Christian Broadcast Network. January 4.

Wingett, Yvonne. 2004. "Prop 200 Win Inspires Other Groups Across U.S." *Arizona Republic*. November 7.

———. 2005. "Phoenix Council, Mayor Okay on Prop 200." *Arizona Republic*. January 5.

Winograd, Ben. 2004. "Crossing the Border: Again and Again and Again." *Tucson Citizen*. November 5. http://tucsoncitizen.com/morgue2/2004/11/ 05/209307-crossing-the-border-again-and-again-and-again.

Wright, Wayne E. 2005. "The Political Spectacle of Arizona Prop 203." *Education Policy* 19 (5): 662–700.

T H I R T E E N

Proposition 200 in Arizona

Déjà vu All Over Again

MANUEL AVALOS AND LISA MAGAÑA

A decade after the passage of Proposition 187 in California, a move to block undocumented immigrants from receiving public services in Arizona developed as a backdrop to the 2004 election. The heightened sense of concern about undocumented immigration has in part been due to a downturn in the state economy, the increasing influx of immigrants in what is now the busiest undocumented immigration corridor into the U.S., and the incredible growth of the Arizona Latino population (of which close to 40 percent are non-citizens) between 1990 and 2000.[1]

With increasing numbers of Latino immigrants in Arizona, the state has seen mounting frustration with the country's failed immigration enforcement policies in a post–9/11 environment. A citizen group, Protect Arizona Now (PAN), successfully placed a citizen initiative on the ballot for the 2004 general election. This initiative, known as Proposition 200, was titled the "Arizona Taxpayer Citizen Protection Act." If passed, it would require individuals to provide: (1) proof of citizenship

347

when registering to vote;[2] (2) the presentation of identification at polling places; and (3) proof of immigration status when applying for state public welfare benefits. In addition, it would require government workers to alert immigration officials of suspected undocumented immigrants seeking benefits.

Provisions were also implemented to discourage immigrants from voting illegally. PAN asserted that too many illegal immigrants were coming into the United States to commit voter fraud, despite the fact that no cases of immigrant voter fraud were ever found. Arizona became the first state to ask for proof of citizenship when registering to vote, requiring a birth certificate, passport, or tribal identification.

Protect Arizona Now received substantial financial support from three national anti-immigrant groups: the Federation for American Immigration Reform (FAIR), Americans for Better Immigration, and POP.STOP. The goal of this coalition of anti-immigrant groups was to use Arizona's vote to spread their restrictionist agenda: a militarized border, a significant decrease or end to legal immigration, the deportation of undocumented immigrants, and opposition to amnesty or guest worker proposals (Crawford 2004). The nativist sentiment at work at that time in Arizona, expressed as a growing distrust of immigration policy and an increasing desire to tighten laws that keep others out, was a reaction to the large numbers of immigrants already in the country and the feeling of loss of control over the community makeup.

A study conducted by the Southern Poverty Law Center (SPLC) asserts that anti-immigration groups typically coalesce and have open ties to racist organizations. The SPLC maintained that these groups believe that immigrants "are responsible for nearly all the country's ills, from poverty and inner city decay to crime, urban sprawl and environmental degradation." The SPLC also found that some of these anti-immigrant organizations are convinced that there is a secret plot by the Mexican government and Latino Americans to take back the Southwest from the United States (SPLC 2001).

The SPLC further maintained that FAIR, the major financial funder of the pro-Prop 200 campaign, is one of the country's most established anti-immigration groups and has not hidden from an openly racist identity. Dan Stein, for instance, the group's executive director, said that certain immigrant groups are engaged in "competitive breeding" aimed at diminishing white power. Rick Oltman, FAIR's western representative, spoke before and worked with the Council of Conservative Citizens. Garrett Hardin, a FAIR board member, felt that helping "starving Africans is counterproductive and will only encourage population growth." Overall, the SPLC found that FAIR blames immigrants for crime, poverty, disease, urban sprawl, and increasing racial tensions in America (SPLC 2001).

Opposition to Proposition 200 came from a broad-based and bipartisan coalition of political leaders and organizations representing business, labor, health care, the Latino community, and various religious denominations. These included Latino advocacy groups (Alianza Indigenia Sin Fronteras, Arizona Hispanic Community Forum), the Arizona Chamber of Commerce, the ACLU of Arizona, AFL-CIO Arizona, the Arizona Democratic Party, and the Arizona Education Association (Diaz 2004). They formed the No on 200, Arizonans for Real Immigration Reform (ARIR) committee. The committee was chaired by former Arizona Attorney General Grant Woods and included substantial monetary support from the Service Employees International Union (SEIU). Also joining the opposition to Proposition 200 were Democratic Governor Janet Napolitano and Republican U.S. Senator John McCain. The ARIR committee focused their campaign on what they perceived as 'unintended' consequences, specifically the cost to implement the act (Marson 2004).

Despite this widespread bipartisan opposition to Proposition 200, Arizona voters approved the ballot initiative by 56 percent. The popularity of Proposition 200 among voters in Arizona is reminiscent of Proposition 187's popularity among California voters almost a decade ago. Given the well-funded and organized opposition to Proposition 200 from diverse sectors in Arizona political life, three questions arise that this chapter will investigate: (1) what influence did the Latino vote have on Proposition 200, (2) what influence did nativist sentiment have on the outcome of Proposition 200, and (3) why was the bipartisan coalition unable to defeat the proposition?

VOTING FOR PROPOSITIONS

Prior research on the role race plays in policy and citizen initiatives involving racial ethnic groups and immigration have identified two competing theories; social conflict theory and contact theory. Social conflict theory argues that increased interaction between racial/ethnic groups produces friction which breeds ethnic stereotyping and racial antagonism, which results in political conflict (Giles and Hertz 1994; Glaser 1994; Giles and Buckner 1993; Fossett and Kiecolt 1989; Giles and Evans 1985; Key 1949). In contrast, social contact theory argues that intergroup contact reduces intergroup conflict (Kinder and Mendelberg 1995; Sigelman and Welch 1993; Stephan 1985).

Recent research on Proposition 187 allows for a closer examination of the role that race plays in explaining the vote over immigration policy (Valenty and Sylvia 2004; Hood and Morris 2000; Alvarez and Butterfield 2000; Tolbert and Hero 1996). In 1996, Tolbert and Hero analyzed the vote on Proposition 187 within their framework of racial/ethnic diversity theory. The results of their analysis indicated that voting on Proposition 187 was consistent with group conflict theory. Tolbert and Hero found a direct relationship between the size of the Latino population and support for Proposition 187; as the size of the Hispanic population increased, the level of Anglo support for Proposition 187 increased.

A study of the politicization of Proposition 187 by Alvarez and Butterfield (2000) also supported the racial conflict theory and identified the important roles of Governor Pete Wilson and the poor state economy in the 1994 passage of Proposition 187. In a study of Proposition 187 and Proposition 209 (an anti-affirmative action initiative), Valenty and Sylvia (2004) also found that an increased concentration of Hispanics increased the levels of Anglo support for both propositions, further supporting social conflict theory.

In contrast, Hood and Morris (2000) examined the racial/ethnic component of Anglo voting on Proposition 187. They found no evidence of a positive relationship between the size of the Hispanic population and Anglo support for Proposition 187, but they did find a strong relationship between Asian context and Anglo voting, lending support for the social contact hypothesis.

DATA

The unit of analysis for this study is the voting precinct for Maricopa County. Sixty-one percent of the population of Arizona resides in Maricopa County, as does 65 percent of the state's Latino population.

The data used in this study were based on voter registration rolls and the canvass of the vote by precinct for the 2004 general election. Precinct level data include percent turnout, percent vote on Proposition 200, percent vote for Kerry and Bush, percent registered Democrat, and percent registered Republican. Census tract data matched to precincts in Maricopa County include percent voting age of the Hispanic population and percent voting age of the non-Hispanic white population.

ANALYSIS

To examine the effect of the Latino vote on Proposition 200, precincts with 70 percent or more voting age population (VAP) Latinos were selected for analysis. Thirty-six of the 40 precincts with over 70 percent VAP Latinos were located in four legislative districts: 13, 14, 15, and 16. Three of the legislative districts (13, 14, and 16) were majority-minority Hispanic VAP districts (see Table 13.1). In District 15, Latinos were the largest VAP minority group (35 percent).[3]

To test social diversity/conflict theory, all precincts with 70 percent or greater non-Hispanic white VAP population in legislative districts 13–16 (28 precincts in total) were selected as well as homogenous Anglo Legislative District 8 in Scottsdale and Fountain Hills.

Analysis of the precinct data reveals that as the percentage of Anglos in precincts increases, the greater the support for Proposition 200. This is true whether one examines the vote in heavily populated Anglo precincts in Phoenix legislative districts 13–16 or when one examines the 97 percent Anglo precincts in legislative district 8.

Table 13.1. Demographic Characteristics of Select Legislative Districts in Maricopa County, 2000

District	13	13%	14	14%	15	15%	16	16%	8	8%
Total Pop	168,187		171,137		170,479		168,938		170,656	
Latino	101,517	60.4	109,457	63.9	70, 122	41.1	109,245	64.7	7,785	4.6
NH White	48,833	29.0	43,410	25.6	78,613	46.1	30,970	18.3	155,132	90.9
NH Black	11,165	6.6	8,456	4.9	9,122	5.4	22,420	13.3	941	1.1
VAP	108,826		112,351		125,205		111,696		137,953	
Latino 18+	58,832	55.1	65,290	58.1	43,573	34.8	66,628	59.7	5,301	3.8
NH White 18+	37,188	34.8	35,289	31.4	66,687	53.3	25,623	22.9	127,012	92.1
NH Black 18+	6,362	5.9	5,196	4.6	6,072	4.9	15,134	13.6	1,425	1.4
Total Minority	119,354	70.9	127,727	74.6	91,866	53.9	137,968	81.7	15,444	9.1
Total Minority 18+	69,638	65.2	77,062	68.6	58,518	46.7	86,073	77.1	10,941	7.9
Democratic Registration	22,286	52.9	18,971	52.7	23,326	44.4	29,722	65.4	22,927	24.1
Republican Registration	11,810	28.0	10,085	28.1	23,326	44.9	7,653	16.8	54,194	57.0

Source: Data from Arizona Independent Redistricting Commission, www.azredistricting.org.

Fifty-three percent of voters in the heavily Anglo-populated precincts in legislative districts 13–16 and 57 percent of voters in Scottsdale/Fountain Hills voted in favor of Proposition 200. Race rather than party registration seems to be driving the vote for Proposition 200. While prior research analyzing voter choice on Proposition 187 suggests that partisanship was a strong determinant of voter choice, this does not appear to be the case in voter choice for Proposition 200 (Cain and MacDonald 1996; Hood and Morris 2000; Valenty and Silva 2004).

Registered Democrats and Republicans in all heavily populated majority Anglo precincts voted similarly for Proposition 200 whether they lived in Phoenix, Scottsdale, or Fountain Hills. The presidential vote also does not appear to drive levels of support for Proposition 200, although the vote for President Bush in district 8 is more closely aligned with the vote for Proposition 200 than it is in the heavily Anglo populated districts 13–16 (see Table 13.2).

Despite the bipartisan support against Proposition 200 from popular and well-known Democrats and Republicans, the ARIR coalition was unable to influence the majority of Anglo Republican and Democratic voters to defeat this proposition.

We know from previous research that when racial categories become intertwined with political initiatives (for example, affirmative action, immigration, etc.), voting for the proposition can become an opportunity to discriminate against particular populations without being socially reprimanded or accused of bigotry (cf. Dovidio and Gaertner 2000; Sears 1988). One can hide one's true attitudes about racial groups by championing political initiatives that appeal to universal abstract principles such as justice, egalitarianism, fairness, and equity.

Protect Arizona Now utilized the issue of equity, fairness, and voter fraud as a strategy to gain support from Arizona voters for Proposition 200. Throughout the early fall of 2004, the supporters of Proposition 200 maintained that the initiative was not about targeting ethnic groups, racism, or discrimination (Diaz 2004). Instead, they argued that Proposition 200 was about issues involving fairness: allowing illegal immigrants (lawbreakers) to undercut the wages of U.S. citizens; trimming taxpayer costs to illegal immigrants utilizing social services;

Table 13.2. Canvas of the 2004 Vote for Selected Precincts and Demographic Groups

Precincts	Percent Latino VAP	Percent Registered Demo	Percent Registered Republican	Percent Voter Turnout	Percent Vote Kerry	Percent Vote Bush	Percent Yes Vote Prop 200
Heavily Populated Latino Precincts in Districts 13–16	74.4	58.3	14.9	50.7	67.9	30.8	44.3
Heavily Populated Anglo Precincts in Districts 13–16	18.2	42.1	32.4	73.5	73.5	43.3	53.4
District 8	2.3	24.9	51.5	87.7	41.8	58.9	57.2
Maricopa County	24.8	31.2	43.5	78.2	41.7	56.0	57.5

Source: Arizona Secretary of State, www.azsos.gov//election/2004/Info/ElectionInformation.

and protecting the integrity of the election system by preventing illegal immigrants from committing voter fraud. However, a PAN television ad containing images of border jumpers and crime scenes that ended with "Arizona is sick and tired of illegal immigration" was very reminiscent in spirit to the Proposition 187 racialized anti-immigrant advertisement ten years ago in California that declared "they keep coming."

Contemporary theories of psychological racism (cf. Dovidio and Gaertner 2000; McConahay 1986; Sears 1988) would support the notion that when a racial/ethnic group is constructed negatively, say, as those who break the law, it is easier to rally against them and avoid being labeled a racist. For example, if a Mexican immigrant has come to this country illegally, by definition, that person is a criminal. Such a label psychologically makes it easier to vote for a proposition like 200. While it ostensibly discriminates against Latinos (legal or undocumented), it becomes possible for Anglo voters to vote for the initiative under the guiding principle of being against voter fraud, as opposed to being anti-Mexican or anti-Latino.

The research on modern racism "under the guise of fairness and equity" has produced some interesting findings in the area of public policy attitudes, particularly immigration. Some scholars maintain that genuine opposition to public policies may not be motivated simply by racism or bigotry, rather protesting some of these policies may be motivated by the "impression" that these initiatives are unfairly appealing to principles of justice, egalitarianism, and equity, to name but a few. This notion of fairness and equity applies "seamlessly" to immigration policies and may explain why some Latinos support what is, in fact, anti-Latino legislation. For example, if an immigrant has entered the United States illegally, by definition, that person has been engaged in criminal behavior. Researchers maintain that these labels make it psychologically easier to discriminate against members of their own ethnic group. "I don't dislike Latino immigrants, I just don't think it is fair to break the law (Short 2004)." For Latinos, this creates an interesting dilemma; sharing a phenotype (Latino) with a stigmatized other ("illegal" Mexican immigrants) renders one susceptible to prejudice and discrimination. Consider the following story published in the *Arizona Republic* (Amparano 1999):

Joshua Ramirez. . . . [is] a fourth-generation American of Mexican descent. His family didn't immigrate, illegally or otherwise. Yet people assume that's how he got here. "I get the wetback comments. . . . I'm asked to produce proof of citizenship when I apply for a job—and I don't even speak Spanish." . . . Ramirez remembers the night he was kicked and punched by a gang of boys who swore at him and told him they don't like "illegal aliens. . . . I was leaving a restaurant. . . . It was closing time and I was walking to my car at the far end of the parking lot. They jumped me. I never called police. I just thought it would be too much of a hassle."

Recognizing the potential threat of discrimination and increased racism if Proposition 200 were approved, many Latino leaders and community organizations entered the political fray over Proposition 200. Fearing, however, the kind of backlash that some believe propelled Proposition 187 to victory a decade earlier, Latinos were very careful not to label Proposition 200's supporters as racists. They also avoided displays of Mexican nationalism, such as those that occurred during the demonstrations and the march from East Los Angeles to downtown Los Angeles in the fall of 1994, where Latino protesters waved Mexican flags, sparking complaints that the protests were un-American.

Instead, the Latino community joined forces with mainstream politicians and bipartisan supporters who framed opposition to Proposition 200 in terms of its unintended consequences. Former Attorney General Grant Woods, chairman of the coalition of ARIR, repeatedly argued that Proposition 200 "will have a whole series of unintended consequences and it won't prevent one illegal alien from coming across the border. It does nothing for real immigration reform" (Marson 2004). He further argued that "What it does do is drive up the cost of government in this state and it will have the consequences of having government intrude in the lives of average, everyday Arizonans on a daily basis" (Marson 2004).

An analysis of voter turnout and vote on Proposition 200 in heavily Latino populated precincts in metropolitan Phoenix reveals that while the majority of Latinos (55.7 percent) voted "no," to defeat Proposition

200, 44.3 percent of Latino voters voted in favor of the proposition. It is also apparent that Proposition 200 did not mobilize large numbers of the Latino electorate to the polls on election day. Turnout in the Latino precincts in Phoenix (50.7 percent) was markedly lower than both the heavily populated Anglo precincts (73.5 percent) in the same legislative districts and turnout was over 37 percent lower than the affluent homogenous Anglo precincts (87.7 percent) in Scottsdale and Fountain Hills. How might we explain this lack of overwhelming support for the defeat of Proposition 200 by the Latino electorate?

One argument is that economic self-interest explains why many Latinos voted for Proposition 200. We know from previous studies over the last forty years that there have always been divergent opinions in the Latino community over support for more restrictive immigration policy (de la Garza et al. 1992; Gutiérrez 1995; Rodriquez and Nunez 1986). A study by Gutiérrez (1995) traced the debate between Mexican American and immigrant labor though the 1970s and documented how Latino political organizations in the Southwest fought immigration in order to preserve wage levels and jobs. A study using 1980s survey data from the Latino National Political Survey revealed that 75 percent of Mexican Americans agreed that there were "too many immigrants" in the United States, suggesting support among the Mexican American population for more restrictive immigration policies (de la Garza et al. 1992). Finally a study in south Texas by Rodriquez and Nunez (1986) found evidence to support how social class and economic standing explained support for anti-immigration legislation among Mexican Americans. These researchers found that Latinos who voiced support for stronger controls on immigration and limiting access to public services for undocumented immigrants were from lower socioeconomic status (SES) backgrounds (Rodriquez and Nunez 1986).

Since the vast majority of Latinos who live in legislative districts 13–16 are working-class and low-SES residents, one could argue that Latinos were as inclined as any voters to protect their economic livelihoods. Even though the proposition focused on government services for undocumented immigrants, the proposal offered blue-collar, working-class voters the chance to express their frustration over competing with undocumented workers willing to accept lower pay.

Exit poll results of 1,881 voters conducted for the Associated Press by Edison Media Research and Mitofsky International (2004) lends some support for the economic self-interest argument. Exit poll results revealed that support for Proposition 200 was highest among the lowest wage earners (72 percent)—those making less than $15,000 in 2003. Almost two-thirds (60 percent) of respondents earning $50,000 or less also supported Proposition 200. In contrast, voters earning between $100,000 and $200,000 (55 percent) were the only demographic group to vote no on Proposition 200 (Associated Press 2004).

An alternative explanation for why 44 percent of Latinos may have voted for Proposition 200 may be gleaned from a study of the Latino vote in the similar anti-immigrant initiative, Proposition 187 in California almost a decade earlier in 1984 (Newton 1998). In this study Newton found support for a discriminatory self-interest argument as to why Latinos opposed proposition 187. Newton argued that Latinos who were of lower SES backgrounds were most likely to face discrimination based on Proposition 187 in California, as would have been the case in Arizona with Proposition 200.

In an analysis of Latino respondents in a California Field Institute poll in 1994, the author found a significant political cleavage within the Latino community on the dimension of ethnic identity measured by language usage and citizenship. Newton found that Latinos who were recent immigrants, Spanish speakers, and disproportionately poor opposed Proposition 187 because they were the most likely to face discrimination with the passage of the measure. Latinos who were U.S. born and spoke English perceived no threat from Proposition 187 and were more likely to support its passage (Newton 1998).

The Latino legislative districts in our analysis certainly lend some support for these similar findings in the analysis of Proposition 187. Legislative districts 13, 14, and 16 represent some of the oldest historical Latino neighborhoods in Phoenix, as well as neighborhoods with large populations of immigrant residents. Latino low-income and predominately Spanish speaking enclaves exist along with more bilingual and predominately English-speaking middle-class Latinos in densely populated neighborhoods in these legislative districts. Those Latinos who are poor, working class, and predominately Spanish speakers certainly were more likely to face discrimination with the passage of Proposition 200 than more English-speaking middle-class Latinos. In the final analysis it is most likely that a combination of both the economic self-interest argument as well as the discriminatory self-interest argument explain why 44 percent of Latinos supported Proposition 200.

■ ■ ■

What is clear from the analysis of the Latino vote on Proposition 200 is that the Latino community was divided. Contrary to many expectations, a substantial minority of Latino voters (44 percent) supported the proposition. This can be explained by a combination of economic self-interest and discriminatory self-interest arguments. Furthermore, this vote outcome was not likely due to a turnout effect. Greater voter mobilization of the Latino electorate would not have changed the overall outcome of the vote.

Nevertheless, exit poll results by Edison Media Research and Mitofsky International (2004) reveal that the overwhelming support for Proposition 200 came from white males (60 percent), Republicans (70 percent), the ideologically conservative (70 percent), voters who made their decision to vote more than a month prior to the day of the election (64 percent), and respondents who identified terrorism and moral values as the most important issues in the election (64 percent). As in California a decade ago, it was déjà vu in Arizona with Proposition 200.

NOTES

1. The 2000 Census count revealed that the Arizona population grew more than three times as fast as the rest of the nation. During the 1990s, Arizona increased its total population by 1.5 million while the Latino population increased by an amazing 88 percent (from 688,000 in 1990 to over 1.2 million in 2000). During the decade, the Latino population increased its proportion of the statewide population from 18.7 percent in 1990 to over 25 percent in 2000 (U.S. Census 2000).

2. On October 27, 2010, the U.S. Ninth Circuit Court of Appeals invalidated the proof of citizenship requirement in a 2–1 decision. The three-judge panel declared that the proof of citizenship requirement conflicted with the intent of the Help American Vote Act (HAVA), which aimed to increase voter

registration by streamlining the process with a single form and removing state-imposed obstacles to registration.

3. Of the 16 Latino members of the state legislature, seven are in districts 13–16: Senator Richard Miranda (D), Representatives Steve Gallardo (D) and Martha Garcia (D) in District 13; Representative Robert Meza (D) in District 14; Representative David Lujan (D) in District 15; Senator Linda Aguirre (D), and Representative Ben Miranda (D) in District 16.

REFERENCES

Alvarez, R. Michael, and Tara L. Butterfield. 2000. "The Resurgence of Nativism in California: The Case of Proposition 187 and Illegal Immigration." *Social Science Quarterly* 81 (1): 167–80.

Amparano, Julie. 1999. "The Taunts, and the Stings, Never Go Away." *Arizona Republic.* July 26, D1.

Associated Press. 2004. "Prop. 200 Won Support from Blue-Collar Workers." *Arizona Republic.* November 3.

Brischetto, Robert R., and Rodolfo O. de la Garza. 1983. *The Mexican American Electorate: Political Participation and Ideology.* Austin: University of Texas Press.

Cain, Bruce E., and D. Roderick Kiewiet. 1984. "Ethnicity and Electoral Choice: Mexican American Voting Behavior in the California 30th Congressional District." *Social Science Quarterly* 65 (1): 15–27.

Cain, Bruce E., D. Roderick Kiewiet, and Carole J. Uhlaner. 1991. "The Acquisition of Partisanship by Latinos and Asian Americans." *American Journal of Political Science* 35 (2): 390–422.

Cain, Bruce E., and Karin MacDonald. 1996. "Nativism, Partisanship, and Immigration: An Analysis of Prop 187." Presented at the Annual Meeting of the American Political Science Association, San Francisco.

Crawford, Amanda. 2004. "Prop. 200 Gains Fans, Foes Nationwide." *Arizona Republic.* October 22, B1.

de la Garza, Rodolfo O., Louis DeSipio, F. Chris Garcia, John Garcia, and Angelo Falcon. 1992. *Latino Voices: Mexican, Puerto Rican, and Cuban Perspectives on American Politics.* Boulder: Westview Press.

Diaz, Elvia. 2004. "66% in state favor anti-immigrant issue." *Arizona Republic.* September 10, B1.

Dovidio, John F., and Samuel L. Gaertner. 2000. "Aversive Racism and Selection Decisions: 1989 and 1999." *Psychological Science* 11 (4): 315–19.

Edison Media Research and Mitofsky International. 2004. Election 2004 Exit Poll Results. www.edisonresearch.com/home/archives/2004/11/view _election_2.php

Fossett, Mark A., and K. Jill Kiecolt. 1989. "The Relative Size of Minority Populations and White Racial Attitudes." *Social Science Quarterly* 70 (3): 820–35.

Giles, Micheal W., and Melanie Buckner. 1993. "David Duke and Black Threat: An Old Hypothesis Revisited." *Journal of Politics* 55 (3): 702–13.

Giles, Micheal W., and Arthur S. Evans. 1985. "External Threat, Perceived Threat, and Group Identity." *Social Science Quarterly* 66 (1): 50–66.

Giles, Micheal W., and Kaenan Hertz. 1994. "Racial Threat and Partisan Identification." *American Political Science Review* 88 (2): 317–26.

Glaser, James M. 1994. "Back to the Black Belt: Racial Environment and White Racial Attitudes in the South." *Journal of Politics* 56 (1): 21–41.

Gutiérrez, David G. 1995. *Walls and Mirrors: Mexican Americans, Mexican Immigrants, and the Politics of Ethnicity.* Berkeley: University of California Press.

Hood, M. V., and Irwin L. Morris. 2000. "Brother, Can You Spare a Dime? Racial/Ethnic Context and the Anglo Vote on Proposition 187." *Social Science Quarterly* 81 (1): 194–207.

Key, V. O. 1949. *Southern Politics in State and Nation.* New York: Knopf.

Kinder, Donald, and Tali Mendelberg. 1995. "Cracks in American Apartheid: The Political Impact of Prejudice among Desegregated Whites." *Journal of Politics* 57 (2): 402–24.

Marson, B. 2004. "No on 200 Group Targets 'Unintended' Outcomes." *Arizona Daily Star.* September 10.

McConahay, J. B. 1986. "Modern Racism, Ambivalence, and the Modern Racism Scale." In *Prejudice, Discrimination, and Racism,* edited by J. F. Dovidio and S. L. Gaertner, 49–59. San Diego: Academic.

Newton, Lina. 1998. "Why Latinos Supported Proposition 187: Testing the Threat and Cultural Identity Hypotheses." Irvine: University of California Irvine.

Rodriquez, Nestor, and Rogelio T. Nunez. 1986. "An Exploration of Factors That Contribute to Differentiation Between Chicanos and Indocumentados." In *Mexican Immigrants and Mexican Americans: An Evolving Relation,* edited by Harley L. Browning and Rodolfo O. de la Garza, 138–56. Austin: University of Texas Press.

Sears, David O. 1988. "Symbolic Racism." In *Elimination Racism: Profiles in Controversy,* edited by Phyllis A. Katz and Dalmas A. Taylor, 53–84. New York: Plenum.

Short, Robert. 2004. "Justice, Politics, and Prejudice Regarding Immigration Attitudes." *Current Research in Social Psychology* 9 (14): 193–209.

Sigelman, Lee, and Susan Welch. 1993. "The Contact Hypothesis Revisited: Black-White Social Interaction in an Urban Setting." *Social Forces* 71 (3): 791–95.

Southern Poverty Law Center (SPLC). 2001. "Anti-Immigration Groups." *Intelligence Report* (101, Spring).

Stephan, Walter. 1985. "Intergroup Relations." In *Handbook of Social Psychology*, edited by Gardner Lindzey and Elliot Aronson, 599–658. Reading: Addison-Wesley.

Tolbert, C. J., and R. F. Hero. 1996. "Race/Ethnicity and Direct Democracy: An Analysis of California's Illegal Immigration Initiative." *Journal of Politics* 58 (3): 806–18.

Valenty, Linda O., and Ronald Sylvia. 2004. "Thresholds for Tolerance: The Impact of Racist and Ethnic Population Composition on the Vote for California Propositions 187 and 209." *Social Science Journal* 41 (2): 433–46.

Welch, Susan, and Lee Sigelman. 1993. "The Politics of Hispanic Americans: Insights from National Surveys." *Social Science Quarterly* 74 (1): 76–94.

FOURTEEN

Are Anti-Immigrant Statements Racist or Nativist?

What Difference Does It Make?

RENÉ GALINDO AND JAMI VIGIL

The topic of immigration continues to receive considerable attention as the press media reports on demographic shifts, proposed immigration laws and policies, and accounts of popular reaction to immigrants including reports of anti-immigrant statements. A key question in the press media reports of anti-immigrant statements has been whether or not the statements were racist. However, these press media accounts have generally side-stepped the question of whether or not the statements were nativist. Given that immigrants are the targets of anti-immigrant statements, failure to mention nativism by the press media is notable. The focus on racism and the absence of nativism in press media accounts is telling and reflects a historical amnesia of the recurring patterns of nativism across previous eras of anti-immigrant sentiment in the history of the United States (Perea 1997). Behdad (2002, 117) noted this historical amnesia in the following two questions: What is it about nativism and xenophobia that liberal America wants to forget?

And what role does the forgetting of nativism play in the construction of national consciousness in the United States? An additional question raised in this study of press media accounts of anti-immigrant statements is whether the term "racism" has come to replace the term "nativism" in the post–civil rights era. The answers to these three questions hold important consequences since interpreting anti-immigrant incidents as either racist or nativist leads to very different policy and social justice outcomes (Sanchez 1997).

These two concepts, racism and nativism, although always a part of the American social and political landscape, were each especially prevalent in the public discourse during two distinct and separate historical periods. Racism in the current era was made a pressing issue in racial/ethnic societal relations by the civil rights movement of the 1960s. Nativism, like racism, also has a very long-standing history in America, being the prominent societal response to mass immigration during different periods of immigration such as the Americanization period of the first two decades of the twentieth century (Higham 1955). The dramatic immigration growth of the last two decades of the twentieth century and accompanying anti-immigrant sentiment have provided an occasion for the reemergence of nativism as a major force in America, and it is increasingly appearing as anti-immigrant animus and restrictionist policies (Perea 1997).

Cases of anti-immigrant statements during a period of renewed nativism provide an opportunity to examine the dynamics of the nativism that is directed against Latinos. Unlike the European immigrants who were the targets of nativism at the turn of the twentieth century, the nativism of the current era is directed against a group of immigrants who are predominantly people of color from Latin America and other non-European countries. The ethnic/racial backgrounds of these immigrants, which differ from the European immigrants, highlight the complexity of the nativism directed against them, which involves an intersection of both racism and defensive nationalism. In spite of the different histories of Latino immigrants and African Americans, anti-immigrant statements and other forms of nativism directed at Latinos are understood by the press media through the black and white dichotomy developed from the African American historical experience

(Sanchez 1997). This tendency to view discrimination in terms of Blacks and Whites to the exclusion of Browns and other people of color is termed "racial dualism" (Cameron 1997). Such a view ignores the racist policies and the history of discrimination that is unique to Latinos. For example, Mexican-origin Latinos in the Southwest offer a unique history of the intersection of racism and nativism due to both their historic presence in the United States and their recent immigration. As long-term residents, they have faced discriminatory policies such as segregation, and as recent immigrants they have been targeted by restrictionistic policies such as Arizona's Proposition 200. This distinct history of Latino discrimination and racialization calls for a different lens than the one offered by the black and white dichotomy (Sanchez 1997). To develop such a lens, the differences and interactions between nativism and racism in anti-immigrant incidents need to be analyzed.

At a minimum, there are three important reasons for drawing distinctions between racism and nativism. First, discrimination that is based on nativism is often not recognized as discrimination when only viewed through the lens of black and white racism. The non-recognition of discrimination based on nativism obscures current and historical patterns of discrimination directed against Latinos. Secondly, discriminatory practices, such as restrictionist policies, will continue as long as the defensive nationalism that drives nativism remains unexamined. Finally, the exclusionary definition of national identity defended by nativism will continue to define cultural and linguistic diversity as alien to the nation. Drawing attention to nativism as a term, ideology, and political practice will make visible previous and current patterns of prejudice and discrimination directed against immigrants that was undertaken under the cover of defensive nationalism.

Racism and nativism overlap and interact in complex ways, which can be understood only by analyzing specific cases. The interaction between nativism and racism will be examined here in the context of press media coverage of two incidents involving anti-immigrant statements, with a special focus on editorials—the unsigned opinion pieces that represent the newspaper's official position. Editorials are unique and particularly telling in that they express the analysis, interpretations, opinions, and recommendations of the newspaper's editorial board (Vermeer 2002). Editorial recommendations are influential because they are directed at both the political elite as well as the general public (van Dijk 1991). As such, editorials are considered authoritative expressions of how given events should be understood and reacted to, as well as the important policy implications arising from the particular situation. Newspapers and news magazines have been productive sites for the analysis of immigrant issues as illustrated by several studies.

In an analysis of abstracts of newspaper articles from the *New York Times* and the *Los Angeles Times,* Keogan (2002) examined how undocumented immigration was portrayed in those two contrasting settings. He found divergent cultural orientations toward immigrants, with the *Los Angeles Times* viewing undocumented immigrants as a "threat" and assigning them a negative social status. In contrast, the *New York Times* presented undocumented immigrants more positively by linking contemporary immigrants to immigrants from the mythic past. In another study, Coutin and Chock (1996) analyzed newspaper articles to identify how immigrant identities were constructed. They described their findings with the phrase "legalization narratives" that described the shift in immigrant identities from threats to immigrants on the path toward citizenship. In another study of newspaper representations of immigrants, Santa Ana, Morán, and Sánchez (1998) examined the metaphor representation of the discourse of immigration used by the *Los Angeles Times* in their articles and editorials. They found that although the *Los Angeles Times* editorials were anti–Proposition 187, they were not pro-immigrant, and both the editorials and articles shared a view of dehumanized immigration. In a study of news magazine cover illustrations of immigration, Chavez (2001) found that immigration was cast primarily as a national crisis, and alarmist images of immigration grew in frequency and became the dominant cover illustrations during the 1980s and 1990s.

An examination of nativism and its relationship to racism, nationalism, and nation-building is presented before the analysis of the press media coverage of the two cases of anti-immigrant statements is discussed.

NATIVISM

Nativism is generally defined as the favoring of native-born citizens over immigrants (Higham 1955). It is an "intense opposition to an internal minority on the grounds of its foreign connections," with modern nationalism serving as the energizing force of the intense opposition (Higham 1955, 4). Nationalism, expressed in the continual process of nation-building, which marks distinctions between those who are inside from those who are outside of the nation, is the driving force behind nativism (Higham 1955). However, nationalism does not simply cause nativism. Rather, nationalism by definition includes a nativist or anti-foreigner component that creates an imagined sense of a national community based on distinctions between insiders and outsiders (Behdad 2002).

Nativism consists of more than personal grudges or individual anxieties. It is a body of interconnected ideas about American government and society, about the past and future of the United States, and about who counts as an American (Knobel 1996). More than just xenophobic attitudes of a few isolated individuals, nativism has been one of the most sustained social movements in the United States, spanning over 150 years (Knobel 1996). Opposing allegedly excessive "foreign" influences in American life, probably the most memorable slogan to come out of this movement has been "America for Americans" (Knobel 1996). Through nativism and nativistic organizations, prejudice is disguised as patriotism and individual indignation and anxiety and fear of others has been converted into coordinated action (Knobel 1996). Nativist movements sought, and continue to seek, to reinforce their narrow view of a national culture and purport to protect national unity or security against perceived threats from immigrants. Different cultural traits or activities of immigrants are considered "foreign," or "un-American," and a threat to the nation (Higham 1955). A perceived failure to assimilate, such as continuing to speak a non-English language, is considered un-American and as evidence of disloyalty to the nation.

Throughout U.S. history, three types of nativism, based on readily identifiable traits can be seen: (1) political nativism, under which political activity or views were thought to be a threat to the nation, such as in the case of refugee radicals during the "Red Scare" thought to be promoting class-warfare; (2) religious nativism, directed against members of a particular religious denomination, specifically Catholics; and (3) racial nativism, where members of a particular ethnic group were targeted based on physical features or cultural traits, including language (Higham 1999). Of these three types, racial nativism has been the most prominent and long-lived, and has given rise to fraternal organizations and political parties that seek to ensure a certain ethnic make-up of the country (Knobel 1996, xviii). These organizations try to control the ethnic composition of the nation not only because foreigners are perceived as different but also possibly because they are reminders of struggles for equity in the past as well as foreshadowing a future in which cultural and linguistic diversity will be among its defining features (Fox 2002). Nativism becomes especially rampant during times of national stress and fear, as in times of war, economic recession, or demographic shifts stemming from unwanted immigration. Nativistic attitudes respond to stress and fear by triggering "restrictive laws aimed at persons whose ethnicity differs from that of the core culture" (Perea 1995).

The term "nativism" is often associated with the anti-immigrant sentiment that occurred at the turn of the nineteenth century, during a time of mass immigration from Europe. However, over the past few years, anti-immigrant sentiment focusing on ethnicity and language has again become a regular feature of American discourse as illustrated recently by the anti-immigrant Proposition 200 in Arizona that was passed in 2004. In another recent example, Harvard professor Samuel Huntington (2004) charged that Mexican immigrants were the greatest threat to American national identity and that they have the potential to divide the nation into two peoples, Anglo versus Hispanic, with two cultures and two languages, English and Spanish.

The current racialized nativism directed against immigrants is driven by three fears (Sanchez 1997). Current manifestations of racial nativism are marked by antipathy toward non-English languages driven by a fear that linguistic diversity will undermine national unity (Galindo and Vigil 2004). This fear has resulted in restrictionistic policies such as the English-only and anti-bilingual education initiatives. A second fear is that multicultural policies, such as affirmative action, favor communities of color and are considered "un-American" because they run counter to the ideology of meritocracy. A fear also exists that these policies encourage the maintenance of distinct racial and ethnic identities. A third fear embodied in California's Proposition 187 and Arizona's 200 is that immigrants are a drain on public resources such as education and health care. Across these three fears, immigrants are construed to be threats to the nation.

Increased nativism was particularly evident following the national tragedy of September 11, 2001. Among the numerous consequences of September 11, and the following "war on terror," was the view of immigrants as threats to national security. Several national structural and policy changes occurred post–September 11 based on this new view of immigrants and immigration matters. One particular structural change was the elimination of the Immigration and Naturalization Service and the transfer of immigration functions from the Department of Justice to the newly created Department of Homeland Security. The decision to grant authority to the Department of Homeland Security over immigration underscored the message that all immigrants will first be considered possible threats to national security and, only secondly, as newcomers (Tumlin 2004). This current linkage between terrorism, national security, and immigration is a contemporary manifestation of the political variety of nativism identified by Higham (1999) and is similar to other instances of political nativisms such as the demands in 1880 by labor movements to exclude "revolutionary foreigners" and the Red Scare of 1919–1920 (Behdad 2002).

Immigration policy is viewed primarily as a means for fighting terrorism since September 11, and immigration policy has lost its own independent policy agenda apart from anti-terrorist measures (Tumlin 2004). No new immigration policies have been created independently from terrorism policies since September 11 (Tumlin 2004). The national view of immigrants as threats to national security, and the accompanying policy shift from immigration to terrorism, has strengthened the stance of anti-immigrant border vigilantes who can now mask their nativism with patriotism by claiming the more acceptable concern over national security and border enforcement (Bauman 2002; Shore 1997).

The effect has been to reinforce and legitimize prejudices and stereo-types by labeling Latinos and others attempting to cross the border as security threats to the nation.

NATIVISM VERSUS RACISM

Inadequate attention has been paid to the distinctions between racism and nativism. As a result, nativism and discrimination against immigrants is seldom differentiated from racial discrimination against non-immigrants. While nativist discourse is linked with racist discourse, important differences exist that lead to different consequences. As Sanchez (1997, 1013) states, "while nativistic discourse is often decidedly linked to racial discourse, they are not one and the same and they often lead in different directions." First, nativism and racism differ in their definitions and goals. Although both nativism and racism are based on fear, nativism demands assimilation through the elimination of undesirable cultural, linguistic, religious, or political traits. In contrast to the concept of racism, nativism "divides insiders, who belong to the nation, from outsiders, who are in it but not of it" (Higham 1999, 384). Racism, on the other hand, is more concerned with distinctions between the "civilized and barbarian than with boundaries between nation-states," and with maintaining a lower societal status for those groups considered to be inferior (Higham 1999, 384).

Although nativism is often racialized, and is thus racist, in its essence nativism espouses assimilation into the dominant culture through elimination of "foreign" traits—such as languages other than English, whereas racism entails exclusion from the dominant culture as illustrated by the Jim Crow laws. Nativism operates as a result of revisions of national history that ignores the historic presence of cultural and linguistic diversity such as the presence of Spanish and indigenous languages in parts of what are now the Unites States that predate the arrival of the English language. The Spanish language is now considered "foreign" in states where the names of cities and geographic locations indicate otherwise.

Increasingly, immigrants today are from Latin America, Asia, and Africa. These immigrants more often than not possess physical, cultural, and linguistic differences distinct from the dominant American society, and it is this combination of differences that makes the nativism faced by today's immigrants unique. Anglo society views Latinos, with their Spanish language and surnames, their non-Anglo culture, and their different physical appearance, as foreign and different (Perea 1995). These differences prevent full acceptance by the dominant society, regardless of how long these immigrants have been in the United States. As Perea (1995, 977) notes, "[A]n important part of the public image of the Latino is the Latino as alien: an immigrant, a recent arrival, a foreigner not really belonging to, or in, America." Although at times considered members of different racial groups, European immigrants did not face the same barriers of entry into American society because they were white. Ultimately, the European immigrant could assimilate.

At the international level, "xenophobia" is the general term used for anti- immigrant sentiment, and definitional distinctions have also been made between anti-immigrant sentiment and racism. At an international conference sponsored in part by the United Nations, racism was defined as an ideological construct that assigned a given race a position of power over others on the basis of physical characteristics or cultural attributes, where the "'superior' race exercises domination and control over others" (International Labour Office 2001, 2). In contrast, xenophobia described attitudes, prejudices, and behaviors that reject, exclude, or vilify persons based on the perception that they are outsiders or foreigners to the society or national identity. According to Hobsbawm (1992), the dramatic societal changes introduced by globalization, transnationalism, and immigration have positioned xenophobia to become the mass ideology of the current era. As a consequence, the national community will continue to be defined on the basis of exclusion, labeling those who do not belong or should not belong to the nation.

A second key distinction between racism and nativism is that nativism is fuelled by nationalism. Unfavorable reactions to personal or cultural traits are not necessarily nativist but may still be racist. It is only when combined with hostile, defensive, and fearful nationalism that they become nativist (Higham 1955). Nationalism is the driving force behind nativism, peaking during times of nation-building efforts. Within this context, when nation-building efforts appear to falter, such as during times of increased immigration, nativism appears as expressions of tension directed against immigrants (Higham 1999). The identification of internal threats to the nation is both a characteristic of nativism and an integral to nation-building in which national unity is achieved at the expense of excluded internal racial, religious, or ethnic groups (Marx 1998, 275). National allegiances create a common prejudice against internal minority groups and cast them as "foreigners." Such allegiances reinforce national unity at the cost of reproducing inequality and continued conflict—an expense that continues to be deemed worth the cost, as illustrated by the popular support for anti-immigrant state ballot initiatives. Anthony Marx (1998, 275) states, "Countering prejudice to build a truly inclusive or civic nation was more difficult. When internal conflict emerged or reemerged, the crutch of exclusion was too handy to ignore." Although distinct in their basic definition, racism and nativism intertwine during processes of nation-building when immigrants happen to also be people of color.

NATIVISM AND LATINOS

Nativism directed against Latinos continues to reproduce their social positions as "foreigners" who do not belong to the nation. Even politically elite Latinos, such as Congressman Luis Gutierrez, are not immune from the nativist refrain "go back where you came from" (Roman 1998). In addition to expressions of individual nativist sentiment, federal policy resulted from nativist attitudes during the repatriations of the Great Depression and during "Operation Wetback" of the 1950s when thousands of Mexicans, including some who were citizens, were sent back to Mexico (Hoffman 1974; Garcia 1980). In addition to anti-immigrant initiatives, a primary expression of nativism directed against Latinos is language discrimination. Examples of language discrimination include work-place restrictions against the use of other languages; anti-bilingual education initiatives passed in California, Arizona, and Massachusetts; and Official English initiatives, such that government agencies cannot provide language assistance to non-English speakers, for instance during driver's license examinations (Moran 1997; Chen 1999).

Language discrimination can serve as an acceptable method of discriminating against a certain group without explicitly resorting to race (Chen 1999). Not always as blatant as in the past, discrimination against Latinos is often now directed by proxy in targeting the Spanish language (Johnson and Martinez 2000). As an example, Johnson and Martinez (2000) point to voters who supported the anti-bilingual Proposition 227 in California as discriminating against Mexicans by proxy since the largest bilingual education programs were for Spanish speakers. Juan Perea (1992) drew similar conclusions noting that strong popular support for language restrictionism, such as Proposition 227, not only indicated an affirmation of English as a symbol of national identity, but also a devaluing of Latino culture and of the Spanish language. Such devaluing of the Spanish language, an important and highly visible symbol in its own right, reproduced the nativism and negative mode of incorporation that the Mexican-origin community had experienced for over a century (Perea 1992).

The characterization of languages-other-than-English as "un-American" is central to anti-bilingual education and English-only policies and to the two anti-immigrant cases analyzed here. This dimension of nativism is also illustrated by legal precedent and court rulings, which prohibit the exclusion of possible jurors on the basis of race, but not on the basis of language. In the United States, while it is no longer acceptable to discriminate against persons on the basis of race, it is still acceptable to discriminate against persons solely on the basis of their membership in a linguistic minority. In *Hernandez v. New York,* 500 US, 352 (1991), the U.S. Supreme Court held that a prosecutor's use of peremptory challenges during jury selection to exclude all bilingual, English and Spanish-speaking, Latino jurors was constitutional—even if the exclusions resulted in all potential Latino jurors being excluded. In this case, all of the excluded jurors also spoke English; they were fully bilingual. The prosecution argued that because one of the witnesses would be testifying in Spanish, they believed that the bilingual, Latino jurors would not adhere to the office English translation of the witness's testimony. In essence, it was assumed that the Latino jurors would not be able to comply with the court's order to follow the English version of the witness testimony should they believe that the English version differed from what they understood the Latino witness to say. All jurors were asked if they would abide by the English version, and all said that they would. Language discrimination cases are not always covered by legal protections against discrimination such as Title VII of the Civil Rights Act or the Equal Protection Clause of the Fourteenth Amendment. This lack of coverage is illustrated by contradictory court rulings, which differ on whether language discrimination is a form of national origin discrimination (Locke 1996). The result is that Latinos may be discriminated against resulting in the arbitrarily denial of state privileges on the basis of language.

THE TWO CASES

The interplay between nativism and racism will be examined through press accounts and editorials of two cases of anti-immigrant statements. The first statement was made in 2002 by country-western musician Chad Brock. The second account was made in 2004 and included statements by the Maryland comptroller and governor. These two cases are well suited for analysis because both news articles and editorials were written in several newspapers in response to each incident. In combination, the articles and editorials provided background information, analysis, and recommendations. The background to the cases developed from the news articles will be presented in the following sequence: (a) the incident, (b) call for an apology, (c) the clarification, and (d) support for the statement. The analysis of the editorials follows the background sequence for each case.

Case Number 1—The Brock Incident

Chad Brock, a country-western singer and former professional wrestler, drew media attention and the ire of the Latino community as a result of comments he made during his concert at the Colorado Independence Stampede in Greeley, Colorado (about sixty miles north of Denver with 77,000 residents), on July 4, 2002. Brock complained to the crowd of about seven thousand during a break between songs, "Why should we adapt? You are coming over to our country. We don't speak Russian. We don't speak Spanish. We speak English here." The *Greeley Tribune* additionally noted that Brock said, "get the hell out" ("Singer's Words Reveal Discord," July 10, 2002). Many Latinos walked out of the concert while other members of the audience cheered Brock's comments. For Latinos in Greeley, his statement reopened old wounds of Mexican segregation and Ku Klux Klan activity in Greeley (Riley, 2002a, July 14).

The Call for an Apology. Latino activists denounced Brock's comments and were upset that Greeley officials had not condemned his statements. The Independence Stampede rodeo had already gained ill will with the Latino community due to its decision of a few years to cancel "Fiesta Latina," a portion of the rodeo dedicated to Mexican music and performances. Latino activists met with representatives from Greeley's Human Relations Commission to air their complaints against Brock. They also held a news conference where Latino leaders demanded an apology from city officials, the event sponsors, and the Stampede organizers. Jorge Amaya, director of the Northern Colorado Latino Chamber of Commerce, stated, "For some reason the Stampede seems to bring out the worst in the community. It seems like this is the time of year when the closet racists come out" ("Singer's Comments Draw Fire from Latino Activists," 2002, July 9). He also said that the real problem was a lack of willingness on the part of community leaders to condemn Brock's statement. Another Latino, Roberto Cordova, a local college professor, said that Brock's comments were "bigoted, inflammatory, and hateful" (Riley 2002b, July 9). The mayor of Greeley, Jerry Wones, was not inclined to condemn Brock's comments, stating that although they were ill-advised, Brock had the right to make them. A spokesperson for the rodeo told the press that they were not pleased that the incident had happened and the marketing director, Kyle Holman, said Brock had the right of free speech but that his opinions were not necessarily those of the Greeley Independence Stampede (Riley 2002b, July 9).

The Clarification. Shortly after the incident, Brock stated that his comments were meant to express his pride in being American and were spurred by a recent court decision regarding the phrase "under God" found in the Pledge of Allegiance. Brock directly addressed the charge of racism, stating, "I am not a racist. I wasn't directing the comments toward any particular group. I was speaking my mind as an American during the 4th of July holiday. But I had no idea that there were so many Hispanics in Greeley. I didn't mean to offend anybody" (Riley 2002b, July 9). While he was sorry that his comments were offensive to some, he would not apologize. He also added, "I had the guts to speak out, but I think a lot of people feel the same way" (Riley 2002b, July 9). Brock elaborated that his comments were general in nature and not directed at any one community, "I'm sorry I touched a nerve. I'm not pointing to the Mexican community, I'm not racist. I'm just an American speaking out. If my comments stirred that much, something needs to be addressed in that community" (*Greeley Tribune* 2004, July 9). Claiming that his comments were covered by the principle of free speech, Brock stated, "that's the beauty about this country. We can say what we feel" (*Greeley Tribune* 2004, July 9).

Support for the Statement. Support for Brock's comments was documented on the *Greeley Tribune* website, which received more than 1,622 replies in response to the question, "Do you think that Chad Brock's comments about immigrants were appropriate during Friday night's concert at the Greeley Independence Stampede?" Approximately 75 percent of the votes supported his comments. Critiques of Brock's comments by members of the Latino community were documented at public meetings and in press interviews. One example comes from a Latino veteran who challenged Brock's assertion that he was speaking as a patriot, "It bothers me when people use patriotism to mask their racism" (Garner 2002, July 10). The editorials written in response to Brock's statements will next be examined preceded by a brief explanation of their analysis.

Analysis of Editorials. Editorials typically address policy-relevant issues and make policy recommendations based on their analysis. On occasion they comment on specific incidents as in the cases of the Brock and Ehrlich statements. In cases like these two, the object of analysis is not an issue, but controversial statements and their policy implications. The editorials presented their interpretation of the controversial statements, including whether they consider the statements to be racist, and made recommendations on how to respond to such statements. Editorials that respond to controversial statements use reported speech, meaning direct or indirect quotations, to develop their argument. Reported speech is typically understood as direct or indirect quotation but it may be more broadly considered as "speech within speech and message within message and at the same time it is speech about speech and message about message" (Voloshinov 1971, 149).

In the analysis of the editorials presented here, identifying the functions of reported speech was the principal focus given the status of the editorials as the newspapers' official message about the message contained in the anti-immigrant statements. Reported speech is understood here in its more general meaning to encompass the editorials' interpretations of what the words meant, the editorials' positive or negative evaluations of the messages, and the editorial characterizations that described the controversial statements as in the *Greeley Tribune's* characterization of Brock's statement as a "tirade" or the *Rocky Mountains News'* characterization of "patriotic homily." These characterizations are both interpretations and evaluations of the controversial statements that reflect the editorial's point-of-view. They are the building blocks of the editorials' message about the controversial message. The functions of reported speech in the editorials were analyzed to identify how they were used to: provide background on the incident, explain and evaluate the statements, dismiss the message, or persuade the readers to the editorial's point-of-view. The analysis also utilized van Dijk's (1991) three-part functional categories to identify the editorials' interpretations and conclusions regarding the statements. The functional categories divide editorials into the following sections: Definition of the Situation, (what happened); Explanation and Evaluation (why did it happen); and Conclusion/Moral (what should be done).

Brock Editorials. The *Greeley Tribune's* (GT) editorial, "Singer's Words Reveal Discord" (2002, July 10), defined the situation as a controversy that resulted from immigrant-bashing. The *Denver Post's* (DP) editorial, "Y'all Don't Come Back" (2002, July 10), defined the situation as one in which an offense had been committed and to which Latino activists requested an apology, and *The Rocky Mountain News* (RMN) editorial (2002, July 16), "Is Speaking English a Sign of Patriotism," called it a case of a confused connection between speaking the English language and patriotism.

The GT editorial in its opening paragraph wrote that there must be a good country-western song amid the controversy—called "brouhaha" by the GT—that was sparked by "Brock's tirade." The GT editorial lamented that a song would be the only good thing so far to come out of the controversy. In calling the discussion a "brouhaha," the GT editorial foreshadowed its final recommendation: the need for reasoned discussion on the topic of immigration with more listening and less name calling. The DP interpretation was that Brock had given a "boorish performance" that offended Latinos as well as the editorial board. For its part, the RMN editorial's interpretation was that Brock delivered a "patriotic homily."

In the "Defining the Situation" section, the GT labeled Brock's statements "immigrant bashing," which drew responses from extremists from both sides of the political spectrum. According to the RMN, Brock's comments were based on an "irrational connection" between speaking English and defending national symbols (the Pledge of Allegiance). Brock told those who did not like his views, to "get the hell out." Brock's statements were further characterized by the GT as "drivel" that displayed his ignorance. While acknowledging Brock's free speech, the GT called on community leaders to state that "hate-filled speech" was not welcomed in Greeley. In contrast to the GP, neither the DP nor the RMN called for public condemnation of Brock's comments. The GT editorial backed its call for a public condemnation of Brock's statement by negatively evaluating his speech as a tirade, immigrant bashing, and drivel. The editorials' message about Brock's message was that it was ultimately hate-filled speech. The DP took a different position from the GT categorizing Brock's statements as "political speech." Although it considered Brock's comments "misguided" as political speech, the DP thought that it should not be condemned.

In spite of calls from the Latino community for an apology, the RMN and DP wrote that they never thought that Brock was a racist. The DP quoted directly from Brock's letter to the editor, "I'm not a racist. I was not directing the comments toward any particular group. I was speaking my mind as an American." Brock claimed his American identity in defense of his comments, as if those offended by his comments were not also Americans and part of the nation. Brock's quote in the DP editorial was preceded and followed by reference to the Latinos who were offended and to their growth in Greeley where the Latino population doubled during the 1990s, clearly indicating that they were the affected community.

After defining the situation in evaluative terms, the GT editorial presented its recommendation that the best response to ignorance was reason. It called on Hispanic activists to help sort out the mess left behind by Brock. However, the GT wrote that Latinos' calls for the Stampede organizers to apologize were misguided. The GT next offered an explanation for Brock's speech. The editorial noted that entertainers were often outrageous and the GT recalled Brock's former occupation as a wrester. It explained that "bluster" was common in that profession and that other musical entertainers were also outrageous. The DP also turned to Brock's wrestling past to explain his lack of manners and sensitivity but also stated that it took "umbrage at his loutish misuse of an entertainment venue to insult immigrant communities on the nation's birthday." The GT editorial softened its characterizations of Brock's speech in the paragraphs where it explained the Brock incident. Instead of its previous characterization as immigrant bashing and as a tirade in the "Defining the Situation" section, in the "explanation" section of the GT editorial, Brock's speech now became merely "bluster" that was common in professional wrestling. The shift in tone did not appear in the DP and RMN editorials, instead the DP discussed the topics of political speech and the RMN discussed tensions over immigration policy.

The GT further developed its explanation by shifting from the topic of entertainment to free speech. It stated that the First Amendment covered the words that people did not want to hear. The editorial returned to its theme of reasoned discussion and wrote that immigration policy was a complex problem that demanded discussion and not finger pointing. In another characterization of Brock's speech, the GT wrote that by "blurting out his frustrations," Brock tapped into the concerns and questions of many Americans regarding the recent large wave of immigration, the unclear border policy, and the cost-benefits of immigration. The GT wrote that understanding complex immigration issues was not advanced by jingoistic slogans such as "America: Love it or Leave it." Explaining the larger message of the Brock incident, the editorial wrote that the country's strength lies in dissent without fear of jail (for those who make statements) or pressure to leave (for those who disagree with statements).

The GT defended its editorial analysis of Brock's "off-the cuff political position" that could be easily dismissed as inconsequential by noting that intense community reaction warranted the attention. However, not much attention was given in the editorials to the reaction of Latinos. The GT editorial next shifted from explaining Brock's speech to challenging his logic by critiquing the fundamental flaw behind Brock's statement. The GT wrote that Brock assumed that immigrants did not want to learn English. The editorial replied that they do, but that it took time. While English will always be the language of the country, the GT recommended that bilingualism should be encouraged for all. The RMN also commented on this topic noting that Brock had implied that immigrants were cultural separatists when in fact they were "following the trail blazed long ago by millions of previous immigrants." The RMN also noted that the complete acquisition of English by immigrants takes more than one generation. The RMN further explained that the presence of non-English languages in the United States was at one of its highest levels.

In contrast to the other two editorials, the RMN alone challenged Brock's logic in linking the speaking of English to patriotism. Quoting from Brock's letter, "if Americans and immigrants to this great nation were to embrace being American (in all its aspects) as we did after the September 11 tragedy, the solidarity might better protect us all from the evil deeds of outsiders. What better way to embrace being American than to speak the language of its government, people and mainstream populace?" The retort from the RMN was that it could think of better ways, including having people embrace and understand its representative government. The RMN message about Brock's message was that it was a false equation between speaking English and American patriotism.

The RMN criticized not only Brock's logic but also the indirectness of his message. If Brock thought that the numbers of immigrants threaten national unity, the RMN wrote that he should say so instead of insulting members of his audience. Also, if Brock's point was that a common language fosters social cohesion, the RMN agreed and the RMN thought that the vast majority of immigrants would also agree. The RMN concluded that these false assumptions were the reason some Hispanics took offense at Brock's statements.

In its conclusion, the GT editorial assumed the voice of the majority and advocated the middle road, which was shared by "most Americans," in spite of the "shouting from those on the fringes of the political spectrum." In this middle of the road position, Anglos could question immigration policy without being called racists and Hispanics could speak out against injustice without being told to leave. In response to the "brouhaha" that followed the Brock incident, the GT and the RMN recommended, "a lot less name-calling and a lot more listening." The DP recommended that the Stampede "never book him, or the horse he rode in on again," but the DP did not identify the horse as racism and/or nativism.

Case Number 2—The Ehrlich Incident

On May 5, 2004, the governor of Maryland, Robert Ehrlich, was quoted as saying on a radio talk show that multiculturalism was "crap" and "bunk" and that he rejected the idea of multiculturalism. He further stated that young immigrants should learn English and assimilate into American culture. The governor stated, "Once you get into this multicultural crap, this bunk, you run into a problem. With respect to this culture, English is the language. Should we encourage young folks here to be assimilated, to learn the culture and values? Of course" (Mosk 2004, May 8). Ehrlich had been asked to react to comments made one day earlier by State Comptroller William Schaefer, who had complained about the trouble he had communicating with a Spanish-speaking McDonalds employee. Schaefer stated, "Then I got a bag, and instead of having English on it, it had Spanish and German and every other language. I don't want to adjust to another language. This is the United States. I think they ought to adjust to us" (Nitkin 2004a, May 9).

Call for an Apology. Community groups, Montgomery County Council members, and state lawmakers held a news conference on May 11 and demanded in English, Korean, and Spanish an apology. Hispanic leaders called Ehrlich's comments divisive, destructive, and shocking. One leader, state delegate Ana Sol Gutierrez (D-Montgomery), a first-generation immigrant from El Salvador, stated, "I think what the governor said absolutely is offensive. It's also a dangerous comment. What I am sensing is that these kinds of comments from leadership, from people who are in high-level positions, are really fuelling an environment that is very dangerous and negative. It says it is okay to consider people who are different as something less" (Mosk 2004, May 8). A group of Hispanic, Native American, and African American civil rights activists in Baltimore also demanded apologies from Ehrlich and Schaefer (Nitkin and Pelton 2004 May 14).

The Montgomery County Council adopted a resolution on May 11, 2002, that was also critical of Ehrlich's comments (Montgomery County Council 2002). The resolution acknowledged that Montgomery County was the home to nearly half of all foreign-born residents of Maryland and had the state's most diverse population. Additionally, it acknowledged that the United States was a diverse country. The county council defined multiculturalism as the appreciation and celebration of multiple cultures rather than a single culture. Multiculturalism also meant tolerance for languages other than English and other religions, races, and national origins. The action section of the resolution expressed deep concern over the Governor's "ill-chosen remarks" because they could contribute to a climate of intolerance toward limited English speakers, those that speak with accents, minority groups, and those who practice minority religions. The council reaffirmed pride for its open door to diverse communities and for the American and Maryland values of tolerance, acceptance, and multiculturalism. The resolution suggested to the governor that the phrase, "I'm sorry" was appropriate to the occasion.

Baltimore Mayor Martin O'Malley delivered a rebuttal in Spanish (a language he had not studied since high school according to Nitkin 2004b, May 13) to the governor's comments on his weekly radio show. The mayor gave recognition to the immigrant ancestors of most Americans who struggled for decades to learn English and suggested that people should remember this during encounters with immigrants who are learning English (Barker and Pelton 2004, May 12).

The Clarification. The governor's press secretary clarified his comments stating that Ehrlich believed that ethnic groups were important to the fabric of life in Maryland but that ethnic groups "needed to develop a singular culture as Americans and speak English" (Mosk, 2004, May 8). The governor himself later clarified his position and said that ethnicities were valued but that Americans shared a singular culture. He further stated that people should not separate themselves into different cultures and that this country was a melting pot. Immigrant advocates challenged the governor to back up his comments by funding adult English as a second language classes for immigrants at a greater rate. In another attempt to clarify his comments, the governor stated, "With regard to this culture, English is the language. Can [immigrants] obviously honor their ethnic traditions and languages at home and other places? Of course. They are not mutually exclusive. The point here is there is a major distinction between ethnic pride, which is appropriate, and multiculturalism, which is damaging to the society in my view" (Nitkin 2004a, May 9). He also said the goal should be a common culture with a common language and not ethnic separation, which was "utter common sense" (Johnson and Mosk 2004, May 12).

For his part, Schaefer let his spokesperson clarify his comments by stating that the criticism directed at the governor's and his comments missed the point that people serving customers should be able to speak English. While the comptroller was sympathetic toward immigrants, he did not think that it was fair to customers nor the employee not to be able to transact business because of a language barrier (Barker and Pelton 2004, May 12). At one of his meetings, Schaefer passed out bumper stickers that said, "Schaefer, He Says What You Think." Neither Ehrlich nor Schaefer offered an apology in response to the demands of community members and elected officials. Ehrlich would not apologize for the words or tone of his remarks but reaffirmed the importance of ethnic groups to Maryland and the United States (Carson 2004, May 11).

Support for the Statement. The Ehrlich-Schaefer incident received widespread press media attention with 68 articles written within two weeks of the statements (Siedt, 2004). This broad coverage gave the incident considerable attention. Support for Schaefer's comments came in the form of public comments. Schaefer's office received 220 phone calls and emails with only 10 being critical of his statement (Mosk 2004, May 8).

Analysis of Editorials. Three editorials on the Ehrlich incident were located. The *Washington Post* (WP) editorial, "Un Big Mac Por Favor" (2004, May 13), defined the situation as a misunderstanding of definitions in which the multiple meanings of the term "multiculturalisms" were mixed-up by Ehrlich. The *Maryland Gazette* (MG) editorial "Venting by Ehrlich, Schaefer not best use of English" (2004, May 15), defined the situation as another of Schaefer's outbursts and tirades that was "amplified" by Ehrlich's statements. "No Bunk" (2004, May 13) by the *Baltimore Sun* (BS), defined the situation as one in which inappropriate comments were made by the governor.

Of the three editorials, The *Baltimore Sun*'s "No Bunk" was the most unique and consequently will be analyzed separately. The editorial consisted of only a short statement: "Maryland is a society of many cultures. The comments by Governor Robert L. Ehrlich Jr. and Comptroller William Donald Schaefer were highly inappropriate. Maryland needs more people of all talents, no matter their country of origin. And that's no bunk." This one statement was reproduced in the editorial six times, each time in a different language starting with German, the language of Ehrlich's ancestors, followed by Spanish, French, Russian, Korean, and finally English. These six languages represented the predominant ethic groups in Maryland. The different languages and scripts visually communicated the message regarding diversity that the editorial expressed. The editorial interpreted Ehrlich's comments as inappropriate and appropriated Ehrlich's term "bunk" in support of cultural and linguistic diversity in its final sentence. It used Ehrlich's own words to reject his message.

In its opening paragraph, the WP editorial critiqued Ehrlich in a general recommendation that serious politicians stay away from the terms "crap" and "bunk." It then specifically recommended that Governor Ehrlich consider staying away from the term "multiculturalism" which the WP recalled had been characterized by Ehrlich as "crap" and "bunk." In contrast, the MG's opening paragraph focused on Schaefer and his "outburst" at his weekly meetings where "Mount Schaefer" erupted on a regular basis, drawing attention to his words rather than his work. Schaefer's immigrant comments had already drawn media attention when the Governor decided to "pitch in" with the "rumblings" still being felt at the time of the MG editorial. The MG's characterizations of Schaefer commented critically on his patterns of prior verbal behavior.

The MG provided the requisite background regarding Schaefer's "complaint" in its definition of the situation. It quoted his words, "the person who was waiting on me didn't speak English. I had to go through a long process of trying to order something . . . I don't want to adjust to another language. . . . This is the United States. I think that they should adjust to us . . . the schools should say, 'English first, then Spanish,' or whatever language they are." Presenting its interpretation of the meaning of Schaefer's message, the MG wrote that if he meant that immigrants had to learn English to succeed, then the MG agreed. However, the MG noted that it was not one of Schaefer's better "tirades" and that he should look for better targets than low-wage workers in grueling jobs. According to the MG, "many of us" trace our history back to hard working immigrants who originally spoke languages other than English. Although the MG agreed with the content of Schaefer's message, it evaluated the form of the message as a "tirade."

In the Explanation and Evaluation sections, the editorials provided an examination of how Ehrlich used the term "multiculturalism." According to the MG, Ehrlich "amplified" Schaefer's words when the governor stated, "I reject multiculturalism." Both the MG and the WP noted that Ehrlich's message was not clear because Ehrlich did not provide a definition of multiculturalism, leaving both editorials to provide one. Both editorials understood the multiculturalism that Ehrlich critiqued as the notion that immigrants do not have to "learn our language and adjust to our values, and that government will force society to adjust to them" (MG). The MG negatively dismissed such a definition as "folly." The WP wrote that another distinct definition of multiculturalism from cultural separatism was tolerance, and that Ehrlich's comments appeared to critique the tolerance definition when he meant to critique the cultural separatism definition. The WP presented its view that it did not think Ehrlich had meant "anything quite so bigoted and offensive," countering one possible interpretation of his message.

Like the GT in the Brock case, the MG bemoaned the lack of a constructive approach to a pressing issue facing society that was illustrated by both Schaefer and Ehrlich statements. The MG's message on the larger context of the incident was in the form of a question, "Where do we draw the line between respect for cultures and language immigrants bring with them, and insistence that they learn English and assimilate enough of our customs and values to carry their own weight here?" Both the MG and the WP recommended, as a constructive approach, that English language classes be provided to immigrants. The WP cited the under-funding of this area in the Erhlich administration with a waiting list of approximately 2,000 in Montgomery County alone. In their negative evaluation of both Ehrlich and Schaefer, the MG wrote that the problem will not be solved by "venting at multiculturalism and fast-food servers" or throwing "crude insults" at cashiers (WP). Both the WP and MG were critical of Ehrlich and Schaefer's comments, but unlike the Brock incident, the calls for apology were not mentioned in either editorial.

In their analysis of the Brock and Ehrlich cases, the editorials engaged in a work of interpretation, attempting to decipher the message of their statements. Across both cases, the editorials' negative evaluations of the anti-immigrant statements were expressed through the terms tirade, venting, boorish performance, insult, immigrant bashing, and drivel. In spite of these negative evaluations, none of the editorials supported the community calls for an apology. They also either made excuses for the comments, as in the Brock case, or gave the benefit of the doubt, as in the Ehrlich case, that the statements were not meant to be bigoted. Common also across both incidents, the editorials in their final recommendations concluded that the statements were not a constructive contribution to the national questions raised by immigration.

The issues of free speech in the Brock case and multiculturalism in the Ehrlich case were central in the editorials' interpretations of the statements. These issues along with the consequences in both cases of calling anti-immigrant statements either nativist or racist will be discussed in order to further examine the editorials' interpretations.

FREE SPEECH

Although several of the editorials found the comments made by Brock, Ehrlich, or Schaefer either offensive, insulting, or bigoted, they did not call the comments racist or nativist. In the Brock case, only one of the three editorials called for community leaders to publicly state that "hate-filled speech" was not welcomed in Greeley. Two editorials considered his comments as political speech or individual expression and thereby protected by the First Amendment. Only one of the five editorials came even close to calling the comments either racist, nativist, or both. The *Greeley Tribune* used a term similar to nativism by likening Brock's comments to jingoistic, or anti-immigrant, slogans. By not using the term "nativist," the *Greeley Tribune* however failed to connect Brock's comments with those recurring eras of anti-immigrant legislation and sentiments found across the history of the United States.

The editorials failed to identify the comments as racist or nativist because they considered them to be speech protected by the First Amendment. Brock himself also invoked the First Amendment in a letter to the editor where he stated, "We as Americans have the right and the freedom to speak" (Brock 2002, July 12). The *Greeley Tribune* presented its understanding of the First Amendment by stating that it was meant to protect not only speech that is agreed to by the majority, but rather that its strength was in protecting words that people do not want to hear. However, that interpretation did not keep the *Greeley Tribune* from being the only newspaper to call for the content of Brock's comments to be publicly condemned due to their harmful public effect. Congress itself has on one occasion condemned hate speech. In spite of concerns on the part of some members of Congress that the Constitution was being hurt, House passed, by a vote of 361–34, a resolution condemning racist, anti-Catholic, and anti-Semitic comments made by a member of the Nation of Islam as racist speech (Hook 1994, February 26). A closer look at the issue of free speech is needed in order to understand the editorial's interpretations of the Brock incident.

Traditionally acts such as assault and battery have been punishable by law but words have been considered acts of individual expression. A current debate exists among legal scholars concerning whether racist hate speech should be included as one of the limits of the First Amendment. Understanding what constitutes racist hate speech can help develop criteria from which to judge Brock's comments. Racist hate speech is "[s]peech or conduct aimed at a group of historically disenfranchised; speech that reviles, ridicules, or puts in intensely negative light a person or group on account of who they are" (Leder and Delgado 1995, 5). Linda Greene (1995) defined it as the use of epithets and similar words with which the speaker intends to cause emotional harm and grievous insult. The purpose of racist hate speech is the subordination of one people by another (Leder and Delgado 1995).

Many legal scholars have called for a re-examination of the traditional understandings of the First Amendment in light of racist hate speech, noting that free speech is already curtailed by competing state interests such as in the case of libel or plagiarism, or by other rights, such as equal protection (Leder and Delgado 1995). These scholars support the regulation of racist hate speech because it "demoralizes and silences its victims while denying them credibility in the eyes of the public at large" (Leder and Delgado 1995, 6). Instead, they propose that racist hate speech should be viewed as a form of discrimination. Greene (1995) also questioned whether hate speech should be considered free speech. She recalled the connection between hate and violence with racial epithets that were visible in film footage of demonstrations during the civil rights era. Such film footage had a strong impact on its viewers and made it clear that hate speech was harmful and that it was the audible reminder of the ideology of racial supremacy, enforced inferiority, and the rejection of equality. For Greene (1995), protecting racist hate speech through the First Amendment devalues and weakens equality for historically excluded groups while granting privilege for historically dominant groups. The free speech argument provides a lofty rationale for behavior that is difficult to defend. The result is that racial harassment becomes protected through privilege and subordination is maintained through harassment and intimidation (Greene 1995).

The definition of racist hate speech presented by Leder and Delgado (1995) includes directing comments toward a historically disenfranchised individual or a group. Brock addressed this issue when he defended his comments by saying that he did not single out any one group. He stated, "If I had said, 'All Mexicans get out. We don't want you here,' then I would have said the wrong thing, and I would apologize. But I didn't address any specific race and I won't apologize" (Garner 2002, July 15). In contrast to Brock's interpretation that he didn't single out a group, Latinos in attendance at his concert felt singled-out enough to get up and walk out. While not labeling it racist or hate speech, the *Denver Post* did identify Brock's comments as offensive to Latinos and to the editorial board and insulting to immigrant communities in general. However, the *Denver Post* did not clarify on what grounds the comments were offensive.

In the Brock case, the *Denver Post* and the *Greeley Tribune* explained his comments by referring to his previous career as a professional wrestler. The *Rocky Mountain News* did not consider Brock a racist, merely confused over the nature of patriotism and all the foreign languages that he had been hearing. These excuses, which may have been made to justify or legitimize Brock's comments, are exactly the type of rationales described by Greene (1995) that protect the privilege of members from dominant groups to continue racial-ethnic harassment.

MULTICULTURALISM

Ehrlich's comments linked the topic of immigration, which has characterized this country's development across its history, with the notion of multiculturalism, which in the current era became prominent in the public discourse as a result of the 1960s civil rights movement. The connections between immigration and multiculturalism may not be readily apparent, given the historical differences. However, Geyer

(2003), a newspaper columnist, also made this connection by calling multiculturalism a set of suppositions underlying an advocacy approach to legal and illegal immigration. Others have linked multiculturalism to nationalism by writing that multiculturalism is an "anti-western" ideology that undermines national unity (Starr 2004), is anti-nationalistic, and repudiates the idea of a national identity (Rorty 1994). In comments such as these, multiculturalism and diversity are seen to undermine national unity. This view of multiculturalism can be understood by the contrasting definitions of nationalism presented through the terms "ethnic" and "civic nationalism."

The nationalistic critique of multiculturalism by Ehrlich and others illustrates the distinctions between civic and ethnic nationalism. In this critique, the affirmation of diversity through the notion of multiculturalism is taken to be anti-nationalistic and anti-patriotic. Ethnic nationalism presumes that national unity requires cultural-linguistic uniformity. In contrast, civic nationalism views common political principles as the basis for national unity rather than cultural-linguistic homogeneity (Benhabib 2004). Equality under civic nationalism is not based on sameness, but on respect for difference (Benhabib 2004). Civic and ethnic nationalism represent poles on a continuum that can be illustrated by ethnic cleansing at one end and official multicultural policies and access to citizenship for immigrants on the other. The English language in the United States operates as the symbol of the common ethnic identity presumed under ethnic nationalism and English-only and anti-bilingual education efforts can be understood as attempts to enforce through the power of law the cultural-linguistic homogeneity demanded by ethnic nationalism. The *Rocky Mountain News* editorial challenged Brock's ethnic nationalism that presumed an English language–based patriotism and countered with its own civic nationalistic view of patriotism that called for an understanding of and participation in the country's representative government.

Governor Ehrlich's critique of multiculturalism was grounded in the popular image of the melting pot, which symbolizes national unity through cultural-linguistic uniformity. The melting pot image was first used in the early decades of the twentieth century when strong anti-immigrant sentiment emerged during the social movement known as

Americanization that spawned assimilationism and restrictionist policies that limited the participation of immigrants in certain sectors of society such as teaching (Ross 1995). Politicians use rhetoric such as the melting pot image to gain support from the strong emotional resonance of that image. But listeners who respond strongly to the image may not be aware of the historical legacies, such as restrictionism, that are resurrected through such discourses and the potential harm that they can create. Enough memories of the civil rights fight against racism remain in people's consciousness that attacks against the larger goal of societal equity for minority groups would be challenged. However, that does not prevent politicians from using images like the melting pot to challenge pro-diversity views such as multiculturalism. Like the 1960s, the early decades of the twentieth century witnessed social turmoil regarding national identity stemming from mass European immigration. However, across time that turmoil and the Americanization movement became historically distant.

Nativism has become a forgotten prejudice as a result of historical amnesia of the Americanization era. Attitudes developed during the Americanization era toward national identity that can be described as ethnic nationalism continue to feed today's anti-immigrant political and popular rhetoric. Another result of historical amnesia of the Americanization period is that multiculturalism is viewed as a product of liberal 1960s policies. Like nativism, "multiculturalism" also has a long history and was termed "cultural pluralism" during the Americanization period. Opponents of nativism during that time period who were educators developed the area known as intercultural education. In a similar fashion to current day multicultural educators, the interculturalists believed that diversity enriched society (Banks 2005). The lack of a critical examination in the press media of nativism and of the mixing of immigration and multicultural discourses helps produce a post–civil rights era in which: (a) multiculturalism may be considered a recent liberal anti-nationalistic invention by some, (b) multiculturalism is publicly attacked as an outdated notion in spite of its long history and the societal goal of equity, and (c) the historic legacy and recurring patterns of anti-immigrant sentiment in the history of the United States remain invisible.

NATIVISM OR RACISM—DOES IT MAKE A DIFFERENCE?

The discourse concerning anti-immigrant statements in the press media is filtered through the lens of raced-based prejudice, but these statements are actually concerned with nativism and nationalism and may be considered acts of banal nationalism (Billig 1995). Charges of racism draw attention to acts of discrimination but not to the process of nation-building, which involves forging national unity at the expense of an internal minority. Evidence of this process of forging allegiances for national unity in the Brock case was the 75 percent approval rating that Brock received on the *Greeley Tribune* website and Schaefer's bumper sticker, "Schaefer say what you think." Another aspect of nation-building is the manipulation of symbols to reproduce a narrow definition of national identity. The primary symbol of national identity referred to in both the Brock and Schaefer cases is the English language. In the Brock case, nation-building was also flagged by the 4th of July celebration during which his comments were made. Brock defended speaking English while supporting another national symbol, the Pledge of Allegiance. The *Rocky Mountain News* did not accept Brock's argument of patriotism and challenged his nationalist connection between patriotism and speaking English. In nation-building discourse, patriotism is often a cover for nativism and its use stirs up turmoil as illustrated by the reactions to the statements (Billig 1995). As the Chicano veteran stated in the Brock case, "It bothers me when people use patriotism to mask their racism" (Garner 2002, July 10). Prejudice or bigotry, the term used in the editorials, is camouflaged by nativism through its defense of national symbols such as the English language (Shorris 2004).

While society frowns on discrimination based on race, discrimination based on nationalism and fuelled by nativism is not always recognized as discrimination. The symbolic-indexical function of a language to represent a national or ethnic group is not always recognized, and that makes discrimination on linguistic grounds publicly acceptable whereas discrimination on ethnic or racial grounds would not be (Woolard 1998). Attitudes toward immigrants and linkages that were established during the Americanization period, such as the English language as the key symbol of national identity, appear today as having always existed and as self-evident and not as historically based social constructions. The result is that defense of the English language as a national symbol reaffirms definitions of national identity on ethnic rather than civic terms. An important consequence of not understanding nativism is that anti-immigrant statements are not considered to be discriminatory. In both cases analyzed here, the calls for apologies by community members went unheeded and the editorial boards saw no need for an apology. Not recognizing prejudice based on nativism makes it difficult to challenge the view that immigrants are an internal threat to the nation and these attitudes in turn contribute to restrictionistic policies directed against immigrants who are blamed for societal ills (Massey 2004).

■ ■ ■

Like the Americanization period, the current immigration era has raised questions about national identity resulting from demographic shifts. Immigration from Latin America, Africa, and Asia has changed the face of the nation, with Latinos becoming the nation's largest minority group. As this demographic shift is made, it is not yet clear whether popular understandings of national identity will ever expand to embrace the cultural and linguistic diversity represented by the new immigrants or whether those traits will continue to be considered foreign to the nation. Will conceptions of national identity and unity continue to be understood as requiring the cultural and linguistic uniformity demanded by ethnic nationalism? Or, will civic nationalism be recognized as the needed foundation for national unity in an increasingly diverse society? Answers will begin to emerge as the public, the media, and politicians are able to understand and respond to the legacy of nativism as they understand the legacy of racism.

The civil rights era taught the nation that public discussion must continue to identify and understand forms of racism as they emerge in practice and policy. However, the immigration era that followed has not benefited as much as might be expected from this legacy. The lack of benefit may be due to the difference between eliminating societal barriers stressed under the civil rights model and expanding definitions of national membership called for in anti-nativistic efforts. From a legal and policy perspective, the civil rights model sought to eliminate barriers to access by addressing the effects of past discrimination through policies such as affirmative action (Moran 1997). However, respect for and the positive view of the cultural and linguistic contributions of minority groups to society may not have received adequate attention. A pluralistic model is needed in addition to the civil rights model to achieve the goal of a discrimination-free society that values cultural-linguistic diversity (Moran 1997). Under a pluralistic model, the right of Latinos to speak Spanish would be respected, even if they also speak English. In addition, the cultural and linguistic markers of Latino identity would not have to be eliminated—as demanded by nativism—for Latinos to be considered part of the nation and be able to insist on equal treatment in schools and in the workplace.

Another reason that the recent period of immigration has not benefited more from the gains of the civil rights era is the lack of understanding of nativism's role in producing anti-immigrant policies and practices. Campaigns to raise awareness of nativism, such as the South Africa national "Roll Back Xenophobia" campaign are needed. This campaign involved activities on the part of governmental, religious, civic, and media organizations along with training for police and union officers (International Labour Office 2001). While the melting pot image is a well-known and commonly used phrase, its links to the strong anti-immigrant actions of the Americanization period remain unknown to the majority of the public. The historical recovery needed for a new understanding of nativism will be a challenge, especially since nations are selective of their history as is indicated by the old saying, "getting one's own history wrong is part of being a nation" (Renan 1990).

NOTE

Originally published in *Latino Studies* 4 (2006): 419–47. Only minor formatting, spelling, grammatical, and similar copyediting changes have been made. The research reported here was supported in part by the Spencer Foundation and is gratefully acknowledged. The views expressed herein are solely those of the authors. The feedback provided by Elizabeth Kozleski on an earlier version of this chapter is also gratefully acknowledged.

REFERENCES

Banks, Cherry. 2005. *Improving Multicultural Education: Lessons from the Intergroup Education Movement.* New York: Teachers College Press.

Barker, Jeff, and Tom Pelton. 2004. "O'Malley Rebuts 'English' Remarks; As Mayor Criticizes Ehrlich, Immigrants Rally for Apology from Governor." *Baltimore Sun.* May 12, B1.

Bauman, Zygmunt. 2002. "The Crises of the Human Waste Disposal Industry." *Tikkun* 17 (5): 41–44.

Behdad, Ali. 2002. "National Identity and Immigration." In *Beyond Dichotomies: Histories, Identities, Cultures, and the Challenges of Globalization,* edited by Elisabeth Mudimbe-Boyi, 201–29. Albany: State University of New York Press.

Benhabib, Seyla. 2004. *The Rights of Others: Aliens, Residents, and Citizens.* New York: Cambridge University Press.

Billig, Michael. 1995. *Banal Nationalism.* London: Sage Publications.

Brock, Chad. 2002. "One Singer's Opinion (letter to editor)." *Denver Post,* July 12. www.denverpost.com. Last accessed July 19, 2002.

Cameron, Christopher. 1997. "How the Garcia Cousins Lost Their Accents: Understanding the Language Of Title VII Decisions Approving English-Only Rules as the Product of Facial Dualism, Latino Invisibility, and Legal Indeterminacy." *California Law Review* 85 (5): 1347–93.

Carson, Larry. 2004. "Politicians Show Support for Multiculturalism; Schaefer, Ehrlich Remarks Draw Strong Reaction at a Council Meeting; Howard County." *Baltimore Sun.* May 11, B1.

Chavez, Leo. 2001. *Covering Immigration: Popular Images and the Politics of the Nation.* Berkeley: University of California Press.

Chen, Edward. 1999. "Labor, Law, and Language Discrimination." *Asian Law Journal* 6: 223–29.

Coutin, Susan, and Phyllis Chock. 1996. "Your Friend, the Illegal: Definition and Paradox in Newspaper Accounts of U.S. Immigration Reform." *Identities* 2 (1–2): 123–49.

Fox, Richard. 1992. "Comment: Twice-Told Tales from India." *Anthropology Today* 8 (1): 11–13.

Galindo, Rene, and Jami Vigil. 2004. "Language Restrictionism Revisited: The Case against Colorado's 2000 Anti-Bilingual Education Initiative." *Harvard Latino Law Review* 7: 27–61.

Garcia, Jorge. 1980. *Operation Wetback: The Mass Deportation of Mexican Undocumented Workers in 1954*. Westport: Greenwood Press.

Garner, Joe. 2002. "Discord in Greeley: Singer's Remarks Ignite Race Debate at City Forum." *Rocky Mountain News,* July 10. www.insidenver.com. Last accessed October 7, 2002.

Geyer, Georgia Anne. 2003. "Taking a Realistic Look at Immigration." *San Diego Union-Tribune*. August 15, B8.

Greene, Linda. 1995. "Racial Discourse, Hate Speech, and Political Correctness." *National Forum* 75 (2): 32–35.

Higham, John. 1955. *Strangers in the Land*. New Brunswick: Rutgers University Press.

———. 1999. "Instead of a Sequel, or How I Lost My Subject." In *The Handbook of International Migration: The American Experience,* edited by Charles Hirschman, Philip Kasinitz, and Josh DeWind, 383–89. New York: Russell Sage Foundation.

Hobsbawm, Eric. 1992. "Ethnicity and Nationalism in Europe Today." *Anthropology Today* 8 (1): 3–5.

Hoffman, Abraham. 1974. *Unwanted Mexican Americans in the Great Depression: Repatriation Pressures, 1929–1939*. Tucson: University of Arizona Press.

Hook, Janet. 1994. "House Denounces Remarks as Racist Speech." *Congressional Quarterly Weekly Report* 52 (8): 458.

Huntington, Samuel. 2004. "The Hispanic Challenge." *Foreign Policy* (141): 30–45.

"'I'm not a Racist' Country Singer Says." 2002. *Greeley Tribune,* July 9. www.greeleytrib.com. Last accessed October 7, 2002.

International Labour Office. 2001. *International Migration, Racism, Discrimination, and Xenophobia*. New York: International Labor Office, International Organization for Migration, Office of the United Nations High Commissioner for Human Rights.

"Is Speaking English a Sign of Patriotism?" 2002. *Rocky Mountain News,* July 16. www.insidedenver.com. Last accessed July 16, 2002.

Johnson, Darragh, and Matthew Mosk. 2004. "Immigrant Remarks by Ehrlich Still Burn; Local Leaders Want an Apology." *Washington Post*. May 12, B01.

Johnson, Kevin, and George Martinez. 2000. "Forging Our Identity, Transformative Resistance in the Areas of Work, Class, and the Law: Discrimination by Proxy, the Case of Proposition 227 and the Ban on Bilingual Education." *University of California-Davis Law Review* 33 (4): 1227–1300.

Keogan, Kevin. 2002. "A Sense of Place: The Politics of Immigration and Symbolic Construction of Identity in Southern California and the New York Metropolitan Area." *Sociological Forum* 17: 223–53.

Knobel, Dale. 1996. *America for the Americans: The Nativist Movement in the United States*. New York: Twayne Publishers.

Leder, Laura, and Richard Delgado. 1995. *The Price We Pay*. New York: Hill and Wang.

Locke, Steven. 1996. "Language Discrimination and English Only Rules in the Workplace: The Case for Legislative Amendment of Title VII." *Texas Tech Law Review* 27: 34–101.

Marx, Anthony. 1998. *Making Race and Nation*. New York: Cambridge University Press.

Massey, Douglas. 2004. "Review: Samuel P. Huntington: Who Are We? The Challenges to America's National Identity." *Population and Development Review* 30 (3): 543–48.

Montgomery County Council. 2002. "Comments by the Governor of Maryland Regarding Multiculturalism, May 5. Resolution No. 15–606." www .montgomerycountymd.gov/council.

Moran, Rachel. 1997. "What If Latinos Really Mattered in the Public Policy Debate?" *California Law Review* 85 (5): 1315–45.

Mosk, Matthew. 2004. "Calls Multiculture Idea 'Bunk'; Radio Show Remarks Offend Latino Leaders." *Washington Post*. May 8, B1.

Nitkin, David. 2004a. "Ehrlich Calls Multiculturalism 'bunk,' Damaging to Society." *Baltimore Sun*. May 9. www.baltimoresun.com. Last accessed December 21, 2004.

———. 2004b. "Ehrlich Has No Apology as Immigrants Protest; 'Multiculturalism is Bunk' Not View for Governor." *Baltimore Sun*. May 13, A1.

Nitkin, David, and Tom Pelton. 2004. "Ehrlich Says He Didn't Mean to Offend; But Governor Reiterates Multiculturalism Position." *Baltimore Sun*. May 14, B4.

"No Bunk." 2004. *Baltimore Sun*. May 13, A20.

Perea, Juan. 1992. "Demography and Distrust: An Essay on American Languages, Cultural Pluralism, and Official English." *Minnesota Law Review* 77: 269–373.

———. 1995. "Los Olvidados: On the Making of Invisible People." *New York University Law Review* 70 (4): 965–77.

———. 1997. *Immigrants Out! The New Nativism and the Anti-Immigrant Impulse in the United States*. New York: New York University Press.

Renan, Ernest. 1990. "What is a Nation." In *Nation and Narration,* edited by Homi Bhabha, 8–22. New York: Routledge.

Riley, Michael. 2002a. "Greeley Ethnic Divide Resurfaces: Singer's Remark Reopens Wounds, Local Reactions Revive Debate." *Denver Post*. July 14, B1.

———. 2002b. "Singer's Remark Riles Hispanics Greeley Debates 'English' Comment." *Denver Post*. July 9, B1.

Roman, Ediberto. 1998. "The Alien-Citizen Paradox and Other Consequences of U.S. Colonialism." *Florida State University Law Review* 26 (1).

Rorty, Richard. 1994. "The Unpatriotic Academy." *New York Times*. February 13, D14.

Ross, William. 1995. *Forging New Freedoms: Nativism, Education, and the Constitution, 1917–1927*. Lincoln: University of Nebraska Press.

Sanchez, George. 1997. "Face the Nation: Race, Immigration, and the Rise of Nativism in Late Twentieth Century America." *International Migration Review* 31 (4): 1009–30.

Santa Ana, Otto, Juan Morán, and Cynthia Sánchez. 1998. "Awash under a Brown Tide: Immigration Metaphors in California Public and Print Media Discourse." *Aztlan* 23 (2): 137–76.

Shore, Chris. 1997. "Ethnicity, Xenophobia, and the Boundaries of Europe." *International Journal on Minority and Group Rights* 4: 247–52.

Shorris, Earl. 2004. "A Nation of WASPS." *The Nation* 278 (May 31): 21–22.

Siedt, Debra. 2004. "MD Comptroller Berates Journalists for Coverage." *Daily Record,* May 20. www.lexis-nexis.com. Last accessed December 12, 2004.

"Singer's Comments Draw Fire from Latino Activists." 2002. *Rocky Mountain News*. July 9, 7A.

"Singer's Words Reveal Discord: Community Leaders Need to Change Tune, Lead Talks in Healthier Direction." 2002. *Greeley Tribune,* July 10. www.greeeleytrib.com. Last accessed October 7, 2002.

Starr, Paul. 2004. "The Return of the Nativist." *New Republic* 230 (June 21): 23, 25–29.

Torres, Maria De Los Angeles. 1998. "Transnational Political and Cultural Identities: Crossing Theoretic Borders." In *Borderless Borders: U.S. Latinos, Latin Americans, and the Paradox of Interdependence,* edited by Frank Bonilla, Edwin Melendez, Rebecca Morales, and Maria de los Angeles Torres, 169–82. Philadelphia: Temple University Press.

Tumlin, Karen. 2004. "Suspect First: How Terrorism Policy Is Reshaping Immigration Policy." *California Law Review* 92 (4): 1175–1240.

"Un Big Mac Por Favor." 2004. *Washington Post*. May 13, A28.

van Dijk, Teun. 1991. *Racism and the Press*. New York: Routledge.

"Venting by Ehrlich Not Best Use of English." 2004. *The Maryland Gazette*. May 15, A8.

Vermeer, Jan. 2002. *The View From the States: National Politics in Local Newspaper Editorials*. New York: Rowman and Littlefield.

Voloshinov, V. N. 1971. "Reported Speech." In *Readings in Russian Poetics,* edited by Ladislav Matejejka and Krystyna Pomorska, 149–75. Ann Arbor: Michigan Slavic Publications.

Woolard, K. 1998. "Introduction—Language Ideology as a Field of Inquiry." In *Language Ideologies: Practice and Theory,* edited by Bambi B. Schieffelin, Kathryn A. Woolard, and Paul V. Kroskrity, 1–15. New York: Oxford University Press.

"Y'all Don't Come Back." 2002. *Denver Post.* July 10, B6.

Immigrants and Leadership

FIFTEEN

Latino Youth Activists in the Age of Globalization

MARIA DE LOS ANGELES TORRES

The relationship between youth and nation building has long been a concern of political philosophers. In *The Republic,* Plato wrote about the social impact of children's education, particularly on those who would grow up to be future rulers, so as to ensure the creation of a just society (Plato 1941). During the next centuries philosophers would debate the nature of childhood and how to best educate children (Gay 1964; Rousseau 1956; Kant 1960). Eventually, childhood would emerge as a social category (Aries 1962; Stone 1977).

Modern nation-states tied their political processes to the actions of citizens and therefore became preoccupied with developing the "good citizen." Children were the key to this social experiment. Children's education came to occupy center stage in the early 1900s as social theorists advocated the idea that without good citizens, democracy could not be constructed (Mann 1965; Dewey 1916). Modernism placed children at the center of political debates because they were viewed as the future of society. Not surprisingly therefore, society's protection of children increased. In spite of their protected status, however, children per se were not given political voices. As much concern as there has been about the role of children and their education in nation-building projects, democratic theory does not contemplate a role for children in the public arena (Kulynych 2001). Indeed, some have vehemently opposed a public role for children, claiming that the privacy of their world should be protected (Elshtain 1995).

It was not until the 1960s that social scientists began asking how children viewed politics. They found that children do have a political life that, in part, begins with a sense of place, usually the nation, and includes feelings about authority figures and knowledge about political processes and issues (see Greenstein 1965; Hess and Torney 1968; Easton and Dennis 1970; Sigel 1969).

Children's political development is closely tied to their overall development (Piaget 1932). There seem to be certain stages of development in political attitudes, although these vary for youth of different backgrounds and nationalities (Jahoda 1963). In addition, a variety of socializing agents from parents, to teachers and peers, influence their political behavior (Jennings and Niemi 1974). Class differences can change the ways in which political socialization unfolds (Hirsch 1971), and some traditions matter (Connell 1971; Jennings and Niemi 1981).

The seminal studies of children's political lives were conducted at a time when the modernist paradigm influenced the definition and the operation of both politics and childhood. The practice of politics was organized primarily within the borders of nation-states, and it had meaning in many people's lives, including children's. In his study *The Political Life of Children,* Robert Coles (1986) relates how a few dozen children from seven different countries construct their political world. He found that the children constructed political worlds that were different from country to country and suggested that a child's political life was influenced by national political cultures. In addition, children are assumed to be innocent, living in a world that is still somewhat demarcated by limited access to information. In his view, adolescence is a transition period to adulthood that society must carefully monitor.

Since then, important economic and cultural changes in the world have affected the structure of politics and identity and consequently our notions of childhood (see Cannella and Kincheloe 2002; Kaufman and

Rizzini 2002). This new age of postmodernity is characterized by the declining ability of nation-states to bind our economies, cultures, and, to a certain degree, our politics. Economies, cultures, and people cross borders. In the Western Hemispheres the most important movement of people is from Mexico to the United States. In addition, innovations in transportation have made it easier to travel from one part of the world to another increasing contact among people of different backgrounds. Changes in technology have radically changed the ways that information is presented and distributed, as such changing the boundaries that contained childhood (Postman 1994).

Our notions of racial and ethnic identities—so integral to the political process itself—are also in flux. More youths, for example, now embrace multiple identities. The place of youth and our concerns about them have also undergone drastic changes (Grossberg 2001). In many countries, for example, public education is no longer considered central to the future of the nation.

In addition, the organization and meaning of politics are changing. The nation-state is not the exclusive organizer of our economies, politics, or selves, especially for immigrant children. Some argue that cities are the critical links in a new global economy and consequently the space for meaningful politics may have shifted away from national politics to city and local politics (Sassen 1991). The meaning and the promise of political participation has also undergone a drastic decline. For instance, the United States has the lowest voter registration and turnout rate of all the affluent countries in the world.

In the United States, concern about faltering civic participation has led some to predict the end of democracy, a system of government that requires active and informed engagement by its members (Putnam 2001). These concerns have given rise to a preoccupation around civic engagement and particular youth (Flanagan and Sherod 1998; Buckingham 1999). Although youth are often considered uncaring, uninvolved, and cynical in their political attitudes, a great many care deeply about their communities and have increased their levels of activism over the last several years. In addition, many community groups have organized to support youth activism; in Chicago, for instance, numerous organizations have geared projects toward youths that encourage them to participate in their communities.

THE PROJECT

In 2004 I began to interview youths in the Chicago area who were actively involved with their communities. I began this research for several reasons. First, we know more about disaffected youths than about those who are engaged. The aim of the project was to listen and record these young people's stories of how and why they got involved, as well as who supported and worked with them. I also wanted to understand how they defined politics, who they thought had legitimate authority over their lives, what issues they felt were important to young people, and how they viewed their world and their place in it. This study is a way to understand civically engaged youths in the context of a global postmodern world.

There were several key events marking the time period preceding the study and during the time the interviews were conducted, which may have certainly influenced their interest in politics (Gimpel et al. 2003). One was the contentious 2000 U.S. presidential election whereby the outcome was determined by a very narrow margin and the Electoral College winner actually received fewer popular votes than the loser—only the fourth time this has occurred in American history—and despite widespread concerns of voter disenfranchisement in minority communities. This rare political event had a profound impact on many young people. Immediately afterward, the September 11 terrorist attacks and invasion of Afghanistan and Iraq in the aftermath shook the nation. The highly charged 2004 presidential election again piqued political interest across the United States and brought to light the deep political and ideological divide in the American electorate. In addition, the election of an African American to the U.S. Senate (only the fifth in U.S. history) from Illinois provided a unique moment for the state.

METHODOLOGY AND DATA

The project began with a series of meetings with directors and organizers of community organizations that work with youths. Located throughout the city, these organizations serve a range of racial and ethnic communities and engage youth in a variety of ways. The organizers, often young adults themselves, were asked to help identify youths who were active and interested in participating in this project. I attended a series of initial meetings with youth organizers and with the interested youths as well as organized events including film screenings, poetry slams, political discussions, meetings, and retreats.

Forty youths were interviewed; nineteen identified themselves as Latinos (this paper will focus on the Latino students). Specific themes were used to guide the interviews including basic personal background questions, a series of questions about their political histories, what issues were important to them, their ideas about authority, rights and responsibilities, their political beliefs, and their place in the world. While most of them wanted to have their names used, some chose not to do so.

The interviews were transcribed and given back to the youths who were asked to elaborate on their interviews in an essay, which would provide an opportunity for them to develop their narratives and share them with other youth activists throughout the city. We invited everyone to write an essay based on their interview, and ten did so. We met individually with the students on two occasions and talked about what each one thought was important to share with others and how they could best write about their experiences. Their essays were published and a publication conference held to which community organizers, teachers, and parents and relatives were invited to attend.

Latino Youths: A Profile

On average, the Latino community is one of the youngest in the United States; the median age of the Latino population is 29.5 years compared to the overall U.S. population of 35.3.[1] The individual ethnic groups show that Cubans are outliers among several very young populations: the median age for Mexican immigrants is 24.2 years; for Puerto Ricans, 27.3 years; for Central Americans, 29.2 years; and for Cubans, 40.7 years.[2]

In 1990, Latino youths were the largest sector of non-white youths.[3] Latino teenagers have been the fastest growing sector of all youths since 1999. By 2001, 18 percent of all babies born in the United States were Latino. In the next 17 years, nearly half the growth among Latinos will result from second-generation births. By 2020, immigrants' children will outnumber them 21.7 million to 20.6 million, and nearly 18 million will be third generation according to the Pew Center Study. Currently, 39.1 percent of the U.S. Latino population is foreign-born, 32.4 percent is of native parentage, and 28.5 percent is of foreign or mixed parentage.[4] The numbers are significant in various ways. For the first time in three decades, children of immigrants are the largest percentage of the Latino population. This group represents a potentially impressive influx of Latinos into the political system as well as on the future makeup of the Latino community itself.

Despite the political promise in this population growth, several concerns arise that may compromise their numerical strength. Poverty, education, language, and legal status are among the most important factors that determine their ability and/or their proclivity to vote.

Latino children are more often poverty stricken than other groups of youths. Latino children comprise 18 percent of the total children in the United States, but 30 percent of all children under the poverty rate are Latino. While many parents work, they are concentrated in low paying service jobs and must pay to sustain larger families than the U.S. average. In addition, these families often lack adequate housing and health care and live in violent neighborhoods where gang-related activity is high.

Education is one of the most important issues facing Latino youth today and into the future; the number of school-aged Latino children will more than double between the years 2000 and 2010. Although public officials and academic researchers focus their attention on the high drop-out rate among Latino students, the second generation's educational attainment is higher on average than the first generation, indicating that the demands for higher education will increase.

Learning a second language is challenging for immigrant youths and for those whose parents have immigrated, particularly in a country where retaining one's native tongue is not valued. Most of the bilingual programs throughout the United States are aimed at getting children to forget their native tongues and teaching them a new one in the process; many of the children never fully acquire either.

Although the fastest growing segment of the Latino population is born in the United States, the many immigrants, both legal and undocumented, contribute to the precarious nature of who they are in U.S. society. While technically undocumented children are not deported, they can be held indefinitely in INS-financed institutions. In practicality, undocumented youth cannot apply for financial aid and therefore have a hard time going to college; for this reason, state legislators in many states have begun to address the question of financial aid for undocumented students.

While special issues particularly affect Latino youths, they are also uniquely situated. They understand different languages and cultural as well as the conceptual underpinning of these phenomena due to their need to negotiate in a Latino home environment and an English-speaking external environment, giving them a unique advantage in a multicultural world. In addition, the majority of them will be eligible to vote once they turn eighteen.

The ability of a community to leverage public and private resources to meet their needs depends in part on their political effectiveness. Their sheer numbers indicate that Latinos potentially hold the key to electing presidents and state officials. While this potential is not yet realized, the fact that U.S.-born youths are the fastest growing sector of the Latino community makes it important to understand their politics.

For Latinos in general, engaging in the electoral arena is influenced by education; higher educational attainment indicates greater involvement in the electoral process as well as other civic activities. The majority of Latinos are registered Democrats, although national differences exist; for example, slightly more Puerto Ricans are Democrats and markedly more Cubans are Republicans. Younger Latino voters (defined as eighteen- to thirty-year-olds), like adults, are more likely to identify themselves as Democrats (Center for Information and Research on Civic Learning and Engagement). Latino youth turnout is generally lower than other groups of youths; like them, turnout has declined in the last few years. In addition, although there are national differences among the voters (for example, Cuban American youths turn out at a higher percentage than others), youth turnout is still significantly below the older voters in their communities. About half of Latinos fifteen to twenty-five think that voting is not an important activity and that they are not taken into account during elections. As a group, they trust government less. The 2008 presidential election and the war in Iraq, however, have piqued the political interests of all youths, including Latinos (Vanishing Voter Project, Harvard University).

The Politically Engaged Youth

The youths interviewed in this study come from the city of Chicago. They are all involved in organizations that are either youth-focused or youth-run. All of the organizations have youth organizers whose goal it is to increase young people's political and community engagement. Chicago has a long tradition of community organizing and including youths as part of the community. Although the project did not draw a statistical sample, I was interested in ensuring class, racial, ethnic, and gender diversity in the group, in addition to immigrant status.[5]

At the time of the interviews, the youth ranged in age from 11 to 19. They shared some common personal characteristics; all had a special awareness of their status as youth and the special qualities they bring to the political process because of their age. They feel they have power when they are working with youth organizations and that they can make a difference when they act together in one voice. They are highly motivated and committed to learning both in and out of school. They watch the news, read newspapers, and oftentimes discuss politics with friends and family. Said one youth, "My main goal in politics is to be objective . . . to learn the facts and present them to others."

They are high achievers, many reporting high grades in school, or at least in classes they really liked. All of them said they had plans to go to college. This strong sense of self also influenced their activism. While they believe in or are part of a group process, most feel that an individual can make a difference and they have a strong sense that by engaging, they themselves can make a difference in the world. Some said that, alone they could only be heard, but if they had a powerful group behind them, they could actually accomplish something

Learning and internalizing racial and ethnic identity is part of the process of becoming self-aware; this awareness was marked in Latino youths we interviewed. As Maceo from Video Machete described it,

"When I was younger, race was not relevant. I did not know what color I was. I knew we ate different foods at home, that you rolled the r's in our last name. Until I started hearing words, racial slurs, and started to understand what they were, why some people go to do something and others not. And why some people in class got yelled at more than others." Multiracial kids find that they are constantly battling racism from multiple communities and unable to find a voice that allows their complexities to emerge. Maceo, whose father is African American and mother is Cuban, says that kids at his school insisted he did not look Latino.

Latino youths usually define themselves first by their national origin and secondly as Latinos. Jessica from Mikva Challenge defined herself as "Mexican even though I was born in the United States. It is a way of carrying on my parents and grandparents' heritage. I want to keep it going." Jennifer from the Southwest Youth Collaborative said, "I am Puerto Rican, I don't deny it, but I don't rub it in people's face. We are all humans, and we all have needs." For Luis, also from the Southwest Youth Collaborative, Mexican did not sound right. "I grew up over there, and I am totally different then they are. I would call myself Latino." For others, Latino is used strategically as a way of uniting various individuals without offending certain members of the group. For example, Gisela from the Interfaith Leadership Project in Cicero made a conscious choice not to leave anyone out: "What unites us is our native language, Spanish."

For some immigrants, identifying themselves as "American" is problematic. Mayra from Tepochcallli in Little Village said, "I came to the United States at three, I don't want to be American, because when I think of an American I think of the American dream, and this is unattainable . . . it's just a dream. America has failed minorities."

These youths have global points of reference. They are aware of the plight of youths in other countries; those who have had the opportunity to travel abroad shared experiences that confirmed that they were different then most youths. They are aware that they live in the most powerful country in the world, and they have a sense of responsibility to make sure that it does not abuse its power or ruin the environment. Luis from Southwest Youth Collaborative says, "I think we don't understand poverty as it is experienced in other parts of the world, like in Mexico, but I am like them in that we are all Mexicans. And I know what it is like to move from place to place." Jo from Southwest Youth Collaborative compared U.S. youths and those in other countries: "Youth from all around the world have one commonality: wanting to love and be loved. And that while there were similarities amongst all youth in the world . . . there were marked differences in a variety of areas from the speed in which kids are forced to grow up to educational and political opportunities." One main difference these youths mentioned between the U.S. political culture and that of many other countries was that this society permits dissent, even if it is often muted.

GETTING INVOLVED

Early Influences

All these youths were involved politically in some activity, and each had stories to tell about political influences in their lives. They were asked about early political influences, how they got involved, and what motivated them to stay engaged. Of the forty youths interviewed, only two had parents who were actively involved in political activities.

In most families, politics was a common topic of conversation even if parents themselves were not activists. Maceo recalled that, "We talked politics at dinner all the time. My parents would give me a book to read and we would discuss it and then they would give me another one."

While activist parents are the exception, the one experience the youth seem to share is that they had a parent at home who respected them and their ideas, listened to them, let them speak up at home, and let them express their points of view. It was not so much that politics and political activism was encouraged, but rather that they were respected as individuals. Jessica from the Mikva project expressed it like this: "I was the first kid, and grandkid in my family, and because of that I was never treated like a kid . . . I was never told 'don't do that,' rather 'go ahead, do it.'" Another youth recalled, "My parents have strong political opinions, but I always felt that even if we disagreed, they still took my opinions into consideration. I was allowed to express mine."

It is not that all parents wanted their children involved in politics; indeed in some cases parents counseled against it for a variety of reasons, including the feeling that political activities would take them away from their studies. Immigrant parents worried that their children's political activism would draw the attention of the government to the members of their family who were undocumented. But even in these situations, youth reported that they felt respected by their families. The fact that they speak English and have more knowledge of U.S. society makes them brokers between their private familial context and the public sphere. In effect, this gives them a special status within the family; as such, these youths felt respected by their family members, if not supported in their activism.

Other youths attributed familial values and traits that led them to activism. One young woman said that her parents gave her a strong will. When she was little, Griselda, a member of the Interfaith Leadership Project in Cicero, remembers that her grandfather taught her the importance of giving back to people by reading her stories of good Samaritans. "I always saw myself giving something back to humanity."

How Youths Get Involved

Schools influence political development in a variety of ways. Several of the youths we interviewed mentioned specific teachers who introduced them to civics lessons. For instance, Henry and Omar from Tepochcalli talked about one teacher at Farragut High School in Chicago's Little Village who taught a special class on law and politics and spent a lot of time with students after school. "He taught us about laws, and what our rights are." Civics teachers throughout some Chicago public schools worked closely with the Mikva Challenge organization to get students to identify the issues they face and set up a specific program to address them. In several cases, a teacher introduced the student to the political organization they ultimately joined.

Some youths mentioned books they read in school that influenced their political development. Jennifer from Southwest Youth Collaborative remembers reading Howard Zinn's *A People's History of the United States* and thinking, "we need to get involved and know more about our history." Another read a book on Hiroshima: "That got me more into politics. And then when Bush won even though Gore got more votes, I started to look around at my surroundings so I could do something to try to change things that I did not agree with."

One school in particular actively creates an environment that is inclusive of students and their families and encourages responsible social action. InterAmerican, a premier dual language school for Kindergarten–eighth grade on Chicago's north side, helps families get involved and supports kids and teachers. Lilian of Video Machete and a student there described it as follows, "Most of the students are Latino and it helped them form an identity. The teachers also help get kids thinking about issues, researching them, understanding them."

Students find other paths for political involvement as well. For example, Jennifer went to a cultural event with a friend and became interested in the notion of a youth organization that tries to make changes. For others, like Daisy and Jesse from Brighton Park, a community organizer knocked on their door and invited them to a meeting.

Community organizations provide a place for youths to develop skills while they begin to become politically active. Through their respective projects, these youths found enthusiastic and supportive community organizers who taught them important political skills including surveying, lobbying, and writing press releases. Most importantly for many of the youths, the organizations introduced them to other young people from across the city.

Why Youths Become Involved

The youths we interviewed mentioned personal motives for their involvement in political action including a sense of responsibility for their families and communities, a desire to change unfair situations, and the feeling that they can effect social change. Henry from Little Village said, "What really motivates me to get involved is my family, the problems that my family have deep down inside the family, the financial problems, other things, I don't want them to continue facing hardships, and it makes me want to help and change the things that affect them, and not just for my family, but other families in the communities as well who have similar problems."

The need to be involved was also awakened by youth finding themselves in situations they felt were inherently unfair. Dante, a sixth grader at InterAmerican and a member of the Video Machete collective said, "My mom is in a wheelchair, and they towed our car and when we called a taxi no one wanted to pick us up because she had a wheelchair. This was so unfair. I wanted to change things." Jennifer said, "I guess I feel that I need to change things. The last election sparked me to know more, and why I was angry, I felt cheated in some way, but I did not understand what had happened between Bush senior and Saddam Hussein, so I realized that I needed to know more."

Some youths felt that the broader community did not recognize their personal significance, which led them to activism. Cristina, of Young Chicago Authors, stated the following, "I know that there are things that need fixing, where you don't feel represented, particularly as young persons, and I want to fight to fix things, even if I do not know as much as I will when I am older and have more experience." Maceo is motivated in part by the possibility of getting people to think differently. "I am involved in making videos because I might change people's point of view, change their opinions, and the way they look at things."

For some, activism is seen as a way to obtain very practical outcomes. Daisy from Brighton Park said, "I got involved in the Youth Council of Brighton Park, and I also worked local elections because we wanted an alderman who would help us get a youth center." Another youth felt strongly that if she was going to complain, she needed to get involved.

Positive experiences from being involved encourage them to continue their activism. Cristina from Chicago Young Authors, expressed the following, "I got invited to go to a protest during the trade talks. There was an amazing surge of energy. I realized that this was about the world."

Early political victories also encouraged optimism about social activism. After a group of three youths from Cicero's Interfaith Leadership Project convinced a local businessman to donate a building to their organization, they were excited about all the programming they were going to be able to provide other youths. Those involved in the Barack Obama campaign for Senate were ecstatic about his victory. "This showed me that someday I can be a Senator too," said one volunteer. Early setbacks also seemed to increase their determination. The group from Brighton Park wanted to work harder after they were involved in a local campaign that resulted in the election of an alderman who was not responsive to their needs. "We helped get him elected and he turned his back on us. Now we have to find a better person."

References to altruistic motivations were scarce, although one student said, "I got involved because I like helping people." Religion, although identified by most as a family practice, does not seem to play a significant role for the youths interviewed. Cristina, who had gone through the initiation rites of Santeria, was an exception. For her, religion was a centering experience that allowed her to reach out to others.

ISSUES AND POLITICAL ACTIVITIES

While a range of concerns was important to these youths, the interviews revealed several prominent issues. While some were closely linked to the goals of the organizations, we went beyond their particular organizational activities in the interviews to try to understand which issues greatly affected them and which issues they felt affected youths in general. These youths were careful not to generalize; many cautioned that these were their personal opinions and did not necessarily reflect what other youths may identify as key issues in their lives.

Education

Not surprisingly, education was the foremost concern. Specific issues included the lack of resources, the inadequate curriculum, and the inability to provide input regarding school affairs. The most critical problems affecting some of the youths were educational services and resources. One student expressed his disappointment in then Illinois Governor Blagojevich who ran on a platform promising more funding for public education and then did not deliver on his promise. Another mentioned the problems her teachers faced as they attempted to teach in an overcrowded school. One blamed overcrowding on school closings due to the No Child Left Behind Act. Others said that they and other students were limited in their collegial aspirations because the lack of college counselors meant less information and support during the increasingly complicated college application process. The youth working with Southwest Youth Collaborative had spent the summer surveying fellow students and trying to prioritize these issues. The next step was to organize more students to go see the principal and, if necessary, the board to ask for more funding for their schools. Dante said he felt sorry for his teacher who used her own salary to buy school supplies for her students. He felt that she should get a higher salary. Other youths pointed to inequitable distribution as the culprit for unequal education. Students did not mention curriculum in general, except to state that oftentimes it did not include the histories of particular communities.

For many of the students, not having a voice in the decisions that affect them was the most serious problem in education. Jennifer put it this way: "Everyone talks about educational changes, but they are adults, we are the ones who are in school, and we are the ones affected by decisions, so they should count on us . . . it would make us more responsible for what is going on in our schools."

Students at Morton East High School in Cicero advocated changes in the function of their student council—they wanted the council to be more than an event planner. Students from Farragut High School in Little Village had been involved in a walk-out protesting school conditions. Mayra felt that she lost her rights once she set foot in her school: "You know we have rights outside of school because we are citizens, but once we get inside the school, they take half of our rights away. Our privacy is gone and so is our right to protest."

Immigration

The Latinos interviewed were directly affected by immigration policies since they were either immigrants themselves or children of immigrants. These youths mentioned the Dream Act in particular, which has been introduced at the federal and state levels. In the last couple of years, many immigrant rights organizations have advocated for the passage of the Dream Act, which seeks to guarantee higher education to any student who graduates from a U.S. high school regardless of their immigration status. Mikva Challenge students studied and debated the legislation. Although a law that would encourage illegality troubled one youth, all the others who mentioned immigration issues felt that youths should not be denied education because of their legal status. Another said, "The Dream Act after all is a way to make sure that undocumented students receive a chance to be educated. Don't we want everyone to stay in school?" The group from Mikva Challenge went on to organize a rally in support of the Dream Act, inviting U.S. Senator Dick Durbin who pledged his support at the rally.

Immigration policy concerns extended beyond their impact on these specific youths, particularly after September 11. Many youths felt that INS officials unfairly targeted Muslim Americans, and others felt that their communities experienced a spillover effect—September 11 became the federal government's excuse for targeting all immigrant communities. It also fostered existing racism against immigrant communities. Luis from Southwest Youth Collaborative said, "It is racism to deny someone a job because he is Mexican and has no papers. But this has been happening more and more." The group working with Video Machete spent the summer of 2003 looking at the impact of the Patriot Act on their communities. They were keenly aware of the connections between foreign policy and local issues.

War

The invasion of Afghanistan and the Iraq war played prominent domestic roles during the time we conducted the interviews. None of the youths interviewed had made anti-war efforts their primary engagement, yet many were critical of the war and questioned its logic, some were concerned about its impact on youths, and some felt that the United States was imposing its will on others.

Dante, who had helped organize a protest against the war at his school, thought the war was inherently illogical: "He sent out tanks that used up a lot of oil for gasoline, just to get more. This wastes a lot. I don't think it is right to sacrifice a lot of lives just to get a substance to save the country. You know we could get solar-powered cars." Lilian from Video Machete helped organize a walkout in her school; she said, "You know this whole war is a grudge. Instead of killing people Bush should have sat down with Hussein and worked things out. He needs to listen to the UN that said not to go to war. Now there is a war, death, and the economy is falling."

Students questioned why the United States would spend money on a war when there were so many poor in the United States. They felt that we should help others, not kill them. "How can the United State defeat violence with violence?" asked Jennifer from the Southwest Youth Collaborative.

The war's immediate impact on youth was clear; because military recruitment is down, the Defense Department is pressuring recruiters who go out into poor communities with promises of education and training. In one school, Jennifer said, "Counselors were telling kids who are not doing well that they should sign up for the military . . . instead of helping them get into a university they are telling them to go to the military." Luis felt ambivalent about the war, but felt that the troops needed to be supported—his two closest friends were in Iraq.

Empowerment and Rights for Their Communities

While many of these youths see themselves as members of a youth community, their geographic communities are important centers for their politics as well as their identities. Communities in Chicago are closely defined by the ethnic and racial composition of their residents. When youth speak of their communities, they are referring to their ethnic group as well.

While many of these youths expressed their dismay regarding equal opportunities and rights for all neglected communities, be they African American or gay and lesbian, they are keenly aware that their communities are not treated fairly. One of the students from the Southwest Youth Collaborative said, "I hate to go back to the Latino thing. But it exists. There are a lot of people who have more power than Latinos, and they ignore them. They don't know we exist historically or otherwise. This leads to the abandonment of the community and its needs and as such becomes a rallying point." Mayra, from Little Village, summed up her feelings, "I don't think we really have democracy. We don't get equal rights. Our public schools are not funded as well as suburban schools, we are not seen as equals."

Racial profiling and targeted repression by the police tends to affect youths disproportionately, especially in immigrant and African American communities. Some of the youths we interviewed have had personal experience with it, including Omar, who related the following incident: "One day we were crossing the street and there were these gangbangers, and the cops stopped us, and one smacked me around, broke my pen on my back and got ink all over my jacket. You know even if we have rights, if cops want to stop you because of how you look, they do." Cicero in particular has ordinances that prohibit more than three youths from gathering in public spaces. Over 90 percent of youths in Cicero are Latino. A young Latina from the Interfaith Leadership Project puts it plainly, "it is a law that targets us."

Several of the youths were aware that, while they may be specific targets because of their age and background, their entire community is oppressed. Henry from Little Village, says, "The cops in my community have power over certain people because they are not citizens and many do not know their rights."

The Marginalization of Youths

In part due to their political nature, most of the youths we interviewed do not see themselves reflected in popular culture's portrayals of youth and are committed one way or another to help change negative images; their public image is very important to them. Cultural representation is integral to their politics, particularly when it intersects with racial and ethnic categories that either negatively portray them or narrow the multiplicity of their backgrounds. They see a connection between how they are portrayed and their lack of voice, sensing that these images affect how adults speak to them and report about them, reinforcing a vicious circle.

A more complex form of stereotyping occurs for youth of color, because both their age and their background are compounded. Youth of color are "portrayed as gang bangers . . . stereotypes [that] make it very hard to work yourself up the ladder." Mayra from Little Village says it is all youth in her community who are stereotyped because they are

Mexican: "They think we cannot have a good community because all Mexican youths are violent."

Young women face special stereotypes. For some of the young women, gender inequities within their religion and culture are barriers to becoming full members of society.

Almost all the youths were committed to combat these images. Some choose to do so by reaching out to adults in their communities. For example, Henry said, "One particularly rewarding experience was bringing together the parents of the youth in our organization and having them involved, and at the same time having them recognize the importance of the work their children were doing."

The youths in Video Machete were being trained in filmmaking. "Video Machete is my way to say exactly what I want to say. . . . It is not so much persuasion, but the chance to have our voice heard." Youth in Little Village went straight to the point and started an organization called *Stop Ignoring Youth.*

THEIR POLITICAL IDEAS

The interviews included questions about political beliefs, definitions of politics, views of authority, rights and responsibilities, and their notions of citizenship, concluding with questions about good government and hopes for a future political situation. Several issues became apparent, including their concepts of how politics should be practiced and how to define good government, as well as their perspective on community and authority. These issues are discussed in greater detail below.

The Idea and Practice of Politics

Generally, politics is viewed as much more than simply participating in elections. For some it was a "feeling," a sense of commitment that harkened back to the sixties, but that also had a programmatic element to it as Jessica from Mikva Challenge described: "politics is a mission statement about things you want to achieve for yourself and your community." A few characterized politics as an altruistic endeavor. Politics "should be making life better for people." "Politics is making decisions which benefit mankind and society. Politics is a process of trying to make things better." "Politics is relating to the world and people."

Most of the youths saw politics as a process: "A way of analyzing and deconstructing the world around us and being conscious of what is around us." A way to "make sure that you are heard and that other people's feelings and ideas are heard." "The way a community works." "Politics is the most efficient way to make the world work." "Politics is a process, people are competing with each other over ideals and values, on who is a citizen and how they should live and how they can succeed. It's a lot of important people coming together trying to solve problems and often causing more." A few saw politics as something outside their reach—a government and politicians that have power to control and affect their lives. "Government mostly represents people who are doing well in society, they do not represent people who are suffering and dying to get better." "Politics is people deciding what is right for others, we are supposed to be democratic, but we are not included."

While some of the youths do not see themselves as part of government, they would like to think they could influence governmental decisions. In discussing formal politics, Dante, the youngest person interviewed, believed that elections could hold politicians accountable. Few of the youths were enthusiastic about conventional politics in general, however. Jessica, from Mikva Challenge described this perspective: "I never saw politics as bad. My family voted. And there were good guys and not so good guys."

Many see government as embedded in the rule of law and, as such, is something that is continually changing and needs to take social changes into account. Still, they say this should include a democratic process that brings people together to discuss and debate issues since all individuals have opinions that count. These Latinos thought that the vote was something everyone should have regardless of legal status.

Defining Political Community

These students define political community to include multiple sites. They see themselves as members of a physical neighborhood community, as community members of their youth organization, and as members of their school communities, although how affectionate they are toward the schools seems to depend on how inclusive it is of their voices.

Conceptually, many feel that the broader political community should be more inclusive of everyone, especially immigrants who are left out of the political process. Those from immigrant communities felt strongly that everyone who contributes to society should be allowed to vote regardless of their legal status. Mayra from Little Village said, "They are working for the country and usually the ones who work hardest and for less pay, therefore they should at least be allowed to have a voice in politics." This is closely tied to the idea that everyone is a human being and should be treated as such. Omar added, "The worth of human beings should not be measured by how they look, but rather who they are."

As far as the inclusion of youths in formal political communities, the youths were divided. Those who viewed their fellow classmates as uninformed and uncaring thought that those who are not informed should not be allowed to participate, as being informed was an important aspect of their political beliefs. Some, however, felt that by sixteen, most youths can make informed decisions. If you are able to drive, why not vote? For Jessica, the issue was straightforward: "Since governmental decisions affect everyone, then everyone should be involved somehow, including children."

Authority

Politics cannot be fully understood without introducing the notion of authority. Therefore, these youths were asked who the authority figures were in their lives and how their authority was granted. They understand the difference between private authority ("My parents have authority") and public authority. While their right to challenge authority could be limited in their private worlds, they felt they had the right to challenge public authority figures

As far as public authorities, one youth commented: "The president of the United States has authority because of his title, but he has not done anything in my mind really to gain much respect from him. So I would counter his authority on purpose to show him he does not have any." "Teachers have day-to-day influence on young people. But still if a teacher makes a decision I don't agree with, I will set up a meeting and talk about why I disagree. We try to work it out."

Despite recognizing limits on their ability to act, many of the youths had a strong sense of self. They admitted for instance that teachers had the authority to choose the books they read in class, but they were the ones who chose what they read otherwise. "There are rules, but I decide what to do." And there was a strong sense that no one had authority over one's individual choices. "I feel that my personal convictions about religion, politics, music, learning, belong to me and no one has authority over them." In addition, they indicated that the people granted authority to their leaders: "Authority is not something you are naturally born with. It is something you have to acquire through the respect of other people, through actions and not just words."

Rights and Responsibilities

Political entitlement generates rights and responsibilities. Youths were asked what rights they felt they had. Overwhelmingly, they answered through notions of rights embedded in law. Across the board, all youths felt strongly that they had the right to express themselves. "I have the right to be heard and respected," Cristina says, "And I can protest, I can ask questions, challenge authority—that does not mean beating up on people, but I can always have a dissenting opinion that is mine and I can always assert myself." Citing the U.S. Constitution, many added that they had all the rights given to all Americans. The youths also felt that they had the right to participate in governmental decisions. They had the right to contest and protest in order to hold politicians accountable. Some also felt strongly that they had a right to defend themselves against false accusations, and that they had the right to the truth as to what goes on in government. Other forms of rights not embedded in U.S. law were discussed, but it is interesting to note that the only social right mentioned by some of the youths was the right to what one called "a fine education."

Many of the students felt the limits of their rights. "You have the right to say whatever as long as it does not physically hurt someone, even if it hurts emotionally." For instance, while they had the right to protest, they needed to be respectful. Dante related a story of a school walkout he had helped organize. He was critical of one "kid who went crazy and kicked a reporter. That was stupid." Dante felt that he did not have the right to say bad words in anger.

Many also felt that their rights were unfairly limited: "The Patriot Act has certainly limited many of my rights." "Rights are abstract. When it comes to organizing in schools for instance, I can't do that without risk of getting kicked out." They thought that many of their rights were limited because of their age, especially in regard to their right to vote. Some felt very strongly that the voting age should be lowered to allow youth to have a voice in electoral politics.

Some felt that, while they may have rights in the public sphere, as long as they were living at home, their parents conditioned their rights. One youth who helped organize a school walkout was warned by his mother not to walk out himself because it was disrespectful to the teachers. "I have the right to organize a protest, but then I have to listen to my mother." They understood certain limitations on their rights, but clearly felt that there were a series of personal rights they were entitled to, including their ability to choose their dress, their manner of speaking, their ability to introduce themselves to others without masking who they are, and to choose their friends.

These activist youth have a keen sense of political, social, and personal responsibilities attached to their notion of rights. For these students, political responsibilities include being informed about the world so that they can better act on their beliefs, and specified that they got into political work because they were motivated to make change in the world. Several mentioned formal participation; for example, Daisy felt that it was her responsibility to vote. Another youth saw that it was his to keep elected officials accountable, "especially if we helped elect them." Cristina felt she had the "responsibility to share my ideas with others, and to promote arts in different places so that others could have the same opportunities they have had in cultural programs to learn how to express themselves."

Some felt responsible for the youth community: "I think I have responsibility to show people that young people are more than just the kind that slack off and we do take things seriously and we do understand that there are things in the world besides social circles." "I'm responsible for myself, but I have to definitely take into account my actions and how they will be perceived by others because it will affect how all youth are perceived." "I feel strongly that my responsibility is to change the image that others have of young people." Some based their responsibility on their gender and racial/ethnic background. Lilian said, "I don't want to be pitied as a little Mexican girl, I want to show them I can be just as smart."

In addition to feeling responsible for representing their gender, ethnicity, race, and culture in the broader society, these students felt they needed to conscientiously represent a constituency. Cristina felt she had ". . . responsibility to the people I represent, other young people and Latinos, to other women, and people who practice my religion, other writers. In other words," she added, "I need to be a role model."

Many youths felt their responsibilities also included personal commitments like obeying their parents, helping out in the house, performing well in school, and keeping safe. Cristina added, "and if I am reckless, not involve others in my recklessness." Henry felt extremely responsible to his family. "My family has gone through some very difficult stages, and it's my responsibility to be there to support them." Jennifer summoned it up, saying, "I have the responsibility to respect myself and others."

Future Visions

The sum of these youths' political views can be discerned from their hopes for the future and their visions of what a good government could be. Although each student had very specific perspectives, their responses can be summed up in terms of their definitions of a good government: inclusive, helpful, responsive, honest, and locally and globally responsible, providing services to those that needed them. Lastly, these youths desired a government that took them into account. Some examples of these sentiments include the following:

- Generally good governments were described as responsive and honest. "A good government is one that communicates with people and does not hide what they are doing."
- "Just government would be one in which politicians are held accountable to their voters, not the president. And a higher level of consciousness and morality would help."
- Latino youth in particular thought a good government would be more inclusive of immigrants. Mayra expressed the following: "You know the United States has forgotten that it was immigrants and slaves that built its greatness. Immigrants need to be included, after all they are the ones who work the hardest."
- Omar thought that, "Ideally we would put a lot more faith in working-class people, not just rich ones, it should be about people. Therefore it should be more diverse. In sum, a democratic government would include everyone."

These youth activists believed that government had a role to play in providing services, particularly to needy communities. Government should look after people who need to be looked after.

- Maceo expressed the following: "I would like to see health care for everybody and a good education. In my ideal world, I would like a society built on principles in which people had the ability to live with dignity, to have certain control over their lives, not to be powerless, where there was a better distribution of wealth and government was there to make sure that some people are not falling under, like medical insurance of some kind."
- There is also a sense that a powerful country has responsibilities to weaker ones. For instance, Omar from Little Village said, "I would like to see the United States help other countries, not go to war with them. To help them build up their economies. So they would not be poor." Jennifer said, "I would try to get all these different types of people to come together and realize that we are the same, we are linked in this world."
- They also want a world in which they are taken into account. Jessica expressed the following: "I want a world in which people had

faith in students because we are the ones getting education." Cristina, the young poet, said, "In my ideal world, my stories would affect people, because people will listen more to people who look like me. In an ideal society I would be heard."

▪ ▪ ▪

This project documents the trajectory of civically engaged youths, giving them an opportunity to talk about their political activism and beliefs. By listening to them, we hoped to learn how to encourage civic engagement, especially among young people. Engagement after all is a necessary activity for the health of democracies and for youths themselves (Levine 2007). Although the youths interviewed came from different organizations and communities, their strong sense of personal efficacy supports their activism and they all have plans to eventually go on to college.

Their introduction to political activism has many sources. Although most were from working-class families that were not involved in politics, all shared a parent whom they felt listened to them, gave them permission to think independently, and made them feel valued. Their parents did not necessarily support their activism—indeed, first-generation immigrant parents were concerned that their children's activism would draw unwanted attention to their families—rather, they gave their children permission to speak up and develop their own opinions. Children of immigrants had a special role as the bridge between their families and U.S. society, which conferred on them a degree of authority about U.S. society that was valued and respected. Being valued at home contributes to creating a strong sense of self and, perhaps most importantly in relation to activism, that their ideas have merit.

As other scholars have noted (see, for example, Andolina et al. 2003), schools and community organizations play similar roles. Youths learn about compelling subjects and acquire skills that help prepare them to be leaders and introduce them to issues that may become their particular passions. Activist youth meet other committed youths and learn political skills in various community organizations, including school organizations. Through community-based activities, they begin to feel empowered as youths and as informed citizens. They meet youths from other communities, which encourages them to be more open and forthcoming in accepting the differences in others: "I feel that I have learned to appreciate and listen to different views." Of particular importance to many of the youths we interviewed, their encounters with public officials allowed them to present their cases and argue for changes in particular policies. These encounters left a lasting impression that, through hard work and informed politics, they could make changes in the political system or, at least, they could stand up and be heard. Community organizations provide stimulating political environments in which budding activism can develop and find a more collective expression.

Overwhelmingly, these youths view the law as the means to protect their rights, particularly through freedom of speech and expression. While a few mentioned collective rights (such as education and health care), the right to protest and act politically was on the top of their list, as long as protestors are thoughtful and respectful of other political points of view; tolerance of others' beliefs was extremely important to nearly all of the youths interviewed. They discuss rights and their political styles in the deeply embedded democratic tradition of debate and dissent. In addition, they felt that it was their responsibility to become well informed through valid research in order to present their cases clearly and convincingly to others.

In addition to the keen sense of responsibility to their families and their studies all these youths felt, they were very concerned about their responsibility for representing their communities, which is closely tied to their perception that popular images of youth in general, Latino youths in particular, portray them as uncaring and apolitical at best and violent at worst. As scholars have noted these stereotypes keep Latino youth marginalized (Montero-Siebuth and Villaruel 2000). They were motivated to become active in order to challenge these perceptions through their personal example. For these youth, "identity politics" based on ethnicity or race is coupled with age awareness, which helped them to create a multi-ethnic youth community; most felt that their need to represent racial and ethnic communities reflects the legacy of a political society that has defined inclusion and exclusion on the basis of these cultural divides. Personally, some of the young women also felt that they have to fight gender-biased stereotypes in order to be heard, even if they do not have to represent all young women. These students have also embraced politics that transcend national borders, as they have become informed about global issues. In particular, they are aware that the world's perception of the United States is changing, and they feel a need to respond on a global level. The majority of these youths, however, tend to engage in politics that unfold in very local settings—schools and neighborhoods—even when they are more global in nature. *The* community becomes an important arena for their politics (Noguera et al. 2006).

With a few exceptions the young people interviewed for this study have opted not to engage in conventional politics. In this way their political behavior is not much different than the community in general (Garcia Bedolla 2005). However, they do engage in many other ways. From making films, to participating in meaningful philanthropy, to organizing educational advocacy groups, their activism is the type of political activity that creates engaged citizens and can help us understand how to bring children and young people into the political process (Bennett 2003; Rutherford 1998). In addition, this activism is the training grounds for learning practical and analytical skills that, in the future, may be used in more conventional forms of politics.

These youth activists are not pursuing the types of utopian projects that characterized the New Left of the 1960s (Keniston 1968). The politically active youths who are either children of immigrants or immigrants themselves are focused on local issues, yet are aware of their global implications; they seek a responsive government that will listen to them in a more ideal democracy. Perhaps their working-class families ground them in reality-based politics in comparison to the New Left, or maybe they have more realistic expectations from the political process itself, but the youth activists of the twenty-first century seem more sobered than their counterparts two generations ago.

In conclusion, these interviews illustrate that the home environment is the most important predictor of how active they will become in the public arena. While efforts to increase political participation in Latino communities usually concentrate on adult participation and aim at registering the unregistered and naturalizing the resident, in order to encourage deeper community involvement in politics, educational campaigns aimed at helping parents encourage their children to have a public voice may be the most effective strategy for increasing public participation in Latino communities.

NOTES

1. http://www.ahaa.org/Mediaroom/finalfacts0303.htm.

2. http://www.census.gov/prod/2001pubs/c2kbr01-3.pdf.

3. http://www.census.gov/population/socdemo/hispanic/ppl-165/tab01-1.txt.

4. http://www.census.gov/prod/2002pubs/p23-206.pdf.

5. In total forty youths were interviewed for this project. The original group consisted of twenty youths identified by organizers from the following organizations: Southwest Youth Collaborative, Video Machete, Chicago Young Authors, Interfaith Leader Project, Tepochcalli, Multicultural Youth Project, Girls Best Friend Foundation, Sisters Empowering Sisters, Brighton Park Neighborhood Council, and Chicagoans Against War. Another fifteen youths were interviewed; these were identified through Mikva Challenge and their Social Justice Project.

REFERENCES

Andolina, Molly, Krista Jenkins, Cliff Zukin, and Scott Keeter. 2003. "Habits from Home, Lessons from School: Influences on Youth Civic Engagement." *PS: Political Science and Politics* 36 (2): 275–88.

Aries, Philip. 1962. *Centuries of Childhood: A Social History of Family Life.* Translated by Robert Baldick. New York: Vintage Books.

Bennett, Robert. 2003. *Talking It Through: Puzzles of American Democracy.* Ithaca: Cornell University Press.

Buckingham, David. 1999. "Young People, Politics, and News Media: Beyond Political Socialization." *Oxford Review of Education* 25 (1 and 2): 171–84.

Cannella, Gaile S., and Joe L. Kincheloe, eds. 2002. *Kidworld: Childhood Studies, Global Perspectives, and Education.* New York: Peter Lang.

Center for Information and Research on Civic Learning and Engagement. 2006. "The 2006 Civic and Political Health of the Nation: A Detailed Look at How Youth Participate in Politics and Communities." http://www.civicyouth.org/PopUps/2006_CPHS_Report_update.pdf.

Coles, Robert. 1986. *The Political Life of Children*. Boston: Atlantic Monthly Press.

Connell, R. W. 1971. *The Child's Construction of Politics*. Melbourne: Melbourne University Press.

Dewey, John. 1916. *Democracy and Education: An Introduction to the Philosophy of Education*. New York: Macmillan.

Easton, David, and Jack Dennis. 1970. *Children in the Political System*. New York: McGraw-Hill.

Elshtain, Jean Bethke. 1995. "Political Children." In *Feminist Interpretations of Hannah Arendt,* edited by Bonnie Honig. University Park: Penn State University Press.

Flanagan, Constance, and Lonnie Sherod. 1998. "Youth Political Development: An Introduction." *Journal of Social Issues* 54 (3): 447–56.

Garcia Bedolla, Lisa. 2005. *Fluid Borders: Latino Power, Identity, and Politics in Los Angeles.* Los Angeles: University of California Press.

Gay, Peter, ed. 1964. *John Locke on Education*. New York: Columbia University Press.

Gimpel, James, J. Celeste Lay, and Jason Schuknecht. 2003. *Cultivating Democracy: Civic Environments and Political Socialization in America*. Washington, DC: Brookings Institution Press.

Greenstein, Fred. 1965. *Children and Politics*. New Haven: Yale University Press.

Grossberg, Lawrence. 2001. "Why Does Neo-Liberalism Hate Kids? The War on Youth and the Culture of Politics." *Review of Education/ Pedagogy/Cultural Studies* 23 (2): 111–36.

Hess, Robert, and Judith Torney. 1968. *The Development of Political Attitudes in Children*. New York: Doubleday Anchor Books.

Hirsch, Herbert. 1971. *Poverty and Politicization: Political Socialization in an American Sub-Culture*. New York: Free Press.

Honig, Bonnie, ed. 1995. *Feminist Interpretations of Hannah Arendt*. University Park: Penn State University Press.

Jahoda, Gustave. 1963. "The Development of Children's Ideas about Country and Nationality. Part II: National Symbols and Themes." *British Journal of Educational Psychology* 33: 143–53.

Jennings, Kent, and Richard Niemi. 1974. *The Political Character of Adolescents*. Princeton: Princeton University Press.

———. 1981. *Generations and Politics: A Panel Study of Young Adults and Their Parents*. Princeton: Princeton University Press.

Kant, Immanuel. 1960. *Education*. Ann Arbor: University of Michigan Press.

Kaufman, Natalie Hevener, and Irene Rizzini, eds. 2002. *Globalization and Children: Exploring Potentials for Enhancing Opportunities in the Lives of Children and Youth*. New York: Kluwer Academic.

Keniston, Kenneth. 1968. *The Young Radicals: Notes on Committed Youths.* New York: Harcourt, Brace and World.

Kulynych, Jessica. 2001. "No Playing in the Public Sphere: Democratic Theory and the Exclusion of Children." *Social Theory and Practice* 27 (2): 231.

Levine, Peter. 2007. *The Future of Democracy: Developing the Next Generation of American Citizens.* Civil Society: Historical and Contemporary Perspectives. Boston: Tufts University Press.

Mann, Horace. 1965. *On the Crisis in Education.* Edited by Louis Filler. Yellow Springs: Antioch Press.

Montero-Siebuth, Martha, and Francisco Villaruel, eds. *Making Invisible Latino Adolescents Visible: A Critical Approach to Latino Diversity.* New York: Routledge.

Noguera, Pedro, Julio Cammarota, and Shawn Ginwright, eds. 2006. *Beyond Resistance! Youth Activism and Community Change: New Democratic Possibilities for Practice and Policy for America's Youth.* Critical Youth Studies. New York: Routledge.

Passel, Jeffrey, and D'Vera Cohn. 2008. "U.S. Population Projections: 2005–2050." Washington, DC: Pew Hispanic Center. http://www.pewhispanic.org/2008/02/11/ii-population-projections/.

Patterson, Thomas E. 2002. *The Vanishing Voter: Public Involvement in an Age of Uncertainty.* New York: Knopf.

Piaget, Jean. 1932. *The Moral Judgement of the Child.* London: Routledge.

Plato. 1941. *The Republic of Plato.* Translated by Francis MacDonald Cornford. London: Oxford University Press.

Postman, Neil. 1994. *The Disappearance of Childhood.* New York: Vintage Books.

Putnam, Robert. 2001. *Bowling Alone: The Collapse and Revival of American Community.* New York: Simon and Schuster.

Rousseau, Jean-Jacques. 1956. *Emile.* Selections translated and edited by William Boyd. New York: Columbia University Press.

Rutherford, Jane. 1998. "One Child, One Vote: Proxies for Parents." *Minnesota Law Review* 82 (6): 1464–1525.

Sassen, Saskia. 1991. *The Global City.* New York: Columbia University Press.

Sigel, Roberta. 1969. *Learning about Politics: A Reader in Political Socialization.* New York: Random House.

Stone, Lawrence. 1977. *The Family, Sex, and Marriage in England, 1500–1800.* New York: Harper and Row.

Strama, Mark. 1998. "Overcoming Cynicism: Youth Participation and Electoral Politics." *National Civic Review* 87 (1): 71–77.

SIXTEEN

The Emerging Community Leadership and Transnational Politics of Mexican National Immigrants in New England

MARTHA MONTERO-SIEBURTH

The presence of Mexican nationals[1] in the United States has been historically, socially, and politically well documented and researched during the past one hundred years (Suro 2005; C. Suarez-Orozco and M. Suarez-Orozco 2001).[2] Waters and Jimenez (2005, 119) argue that "Mexicans are the only immigrant group to span the Great European Migration, the post 1965 era of immigration, and the period in between," covering close to one hundred years.

Yet the dimensions of their impact in terms of their growing numbers in the United States, identities, settlement patterns, social and cultural modalities, as well as their integration into U.S. society have become more recently debated from U.S. and Mexican perspectives, as immigration issues intensify and the passage of Arizona's Law SB 1070 granting the state and local police power to enforce immigration calls into question the role of the federal government (Archibold 2010; Corchado and Solis 1999; Custerd 2003; Edwards 2003).

434

Mexicans have been one of the largest and most continuous Latin American immigrant populations to the United States and are the largest single source of new arrivals (Suro 2005; Camarota 2004). Despite their long-term presence, the surge in large-scale migration of Mexicans is a recent phenomenon, increasing the U.S. population seventeen-fold since the 1970s. The Mexican immigrant population in the U.S. was then less than 800,000 but by 2008 had risen to 12.7 million (Camarota 2001; Guzmán 2000 U.S. Census 2000 Brief; Passel and Cohn 2009a). While Mexican immigrants have declined since the mid-decade,[3] due to the impact of the recession and many returning to Mexico, they still account for 32 percent of all immigrants living in the United States (Passel and Cohn 2009b). Mexicans make up close to 59 percent of the share of unauthorized immigrants, a situation that has persisted over the past three decades, and 74 percent of their children are born in the U.S. and are U.S. citizens according to Passel and Cohn (2009a).

This increase in numbers of undocumented immigrants as well as evident anti-immigrant sentiment has placed immigration reform at the center of heated political debates. Measures ranging from stronger legal enforcement of immigration policies such as those of Arizona and other states, to building a reinforced wall along the entire U.S.-Mexican border, to increasing INS raids are all responses advanced to stop what is being referred to as an "invasion" of the United States (see Montero-Sieburth and Meléndez 2007).

The supply and demand for workers has engendered much of the massive exodus of Mexicans each year. But family reunification has also added to an increase in their numbers. In recent years, the wars between the drug cartels and the high criminality experienced throughout Mexico have caused a social diaspora of many seeking secure lives in the United States.

Since the 1960s after the Bracero program ended, Mexicans continued to leave Mexico. In the 1980s, 200,000 immigrants per year left for the United States, growing to 300,000 per year in the 1990s and from 2006 to 2008, such numbers rose to about 400,000 a year (Leite, Angoa, and Rodriguez 2009; Alba 2002; Instituto Nacional de Estadística, Geografía e Informática; INEGI 2003).

Mexico's overall population has been highly affected by such emigration: 2.1 to 1.5 million citizens emigrated to the U.S. from Mexico between 1980 and 1990 and 3.3 million citizens left Mexico between 1990 to 2000, and close to 1.6 million citizens moved to the U.S. during 2004–2006 (López Vega 2003). The settlement patterns have also dramatically changed during the past twenty years. Research by the National Council of Population in Mexico (CONAPO) and the Pew Hispanic Center reflect these new trends: (1) a reduction in the circular migration leading to greater permanency of Mexicans in the United States, Mexicans are staying in their newfound areas;[4] (2) an increase in the flow and stock of documented and undocumented Mexicans, with many having entered legally but overstaying and others simply entering irregularly; (3) a greater heterogeneity in the makeup of the immigrant profile—a higher percentage from urban centers, with greater numbers of females and higher educational levels; (4) greater occupational and sector work diversification with shifts from agricultural to construction and service-oriented work; and (5) growth in the number of Mexican-sending regions and receiving states in the United States, with Mexicans from non-traditional states such as Chiapas, Puebla, and Oaxaca joining the northward trek to the United States; and settling in states beyond the Sunbelt, to include Alabama, Mississippi, South Carolina, Wyoming, Oregon, Washington, Iowa, and Michigan. This has lead some social scientists in Mexico and the United States to comment on the "reconquista" (reconquest) of California and other states (M. Suarez-Orozco 2001; Hondagneu-Sotelo 2003).

The New England area[5] has also been affected by such trends. Over the past thirty years, a combination of factors has brought tremendous demographic changes (Marcelli 2001) which have been identified by Miren Uriarte and Charles Jones (2002): (1) "white flight" and out-of-state migration, as many European whites leave the area to move to nearby states such as New Hampshire and Vermont, or farther away to the South and West; and (2) greater diversification of incoming groups. The flow of immigrants to New England has offset the economic losses that some states, including Massachusetts, have experienced.

During 1990 to 2000, the demographic profile surveyed by the Federal Reserve Bank of Boston indicated that New Englanders represented a smaller share of the total U.S. population, dropping from 7.3 in 1990 to 5 percent. However, New England represented a larger fraction of baby boomers, between the ages of 45 to 54 years, than the rest of the United States.

While five of the six New England states have lagged relative to U.S. population growth, Connecticut and New Hampshire[6] have seen the greatest gains in population head counts. New Hampshire's population has tripled since 1900, doubling from 1960 to 2000 (FRBB) and it has grown at a rapid pace since the 1960s, whereas Connecticut's growth in population was rapid in the 1940s, 1950s, and 1960s, and tapered off in recent decades. Southern New England, including Massachusetts, Connecticut, and Rhode Island, are particularly more racially diverse than northern states, where all but 3 percent of their total populations are white (Demographic Profile of the Federal Reserve Bank of Boston 2005).

The arrival of Mexican immigrants,[7] while relatively new in New England, has been documented through newspaper and anecdotal data: in Rhode Island since the 1920s,[8] Maine since the late 1980s,[9] Connecticut since the 1950s,[10] New Hampshire and Vermont since the 1990s,[11] and Massachusetts since the 1960s (Fieldnotes 2004–2005). However, recent documentation of the Mexican population of New England parallels the greatest surge of Mexicans in this area since the 1990s (Marcelli 2001). Current communication about Mexicans is disseminated by Julio César Aragón, a former assessor of the political bureau of the Institute of Mexicans Abroad and a community member highly invested in Mexican and U.S. politics.

Mexicans settled in New England sporadically in towns such as Framingham or East Boston, Massachusetts, or by transplanting entire towns from Mexico to New England. Families from Sombrerete, Zacatecas, clustered around the Nashua-Manchester, New Hampshire area. Residents from El Refugio, Jalisco, now into their second and third generation, settled in East Boston, Massachusetts. Residents from Alfayayucan, Hidalgo, made Central Falls and Pawtucket, Rhode Island, their home (Rico 2001). Poblanos from the state of Puebla continue to thrive in Lynn and Waltham, Massachusetts (Fieldwork data March 2004; Creuheras 2001; Smith 2006).

Although visible throughout New England, Mexicans accounted for 2 percent or 26,000 of the 1,376,317 total foreign-born immigration populations in New England (Marcuss and Borgos 2004). Yet these numbers do not represent actual numbers of documented and undocumented Mexicans based on observations conducted in Mexican communities and the statements made by leaders interviewed in this study. True figures are more likely double these numbers (Fieldwork notes May 2005). The sheer numbers of Mexican restaurants,[12] *panaderias* (bakeries), mariachi bands, and *tiendas de abarrotes* (grocery shops) that have sprung up throughout New England to keep up with the growing demands for Mexican products and services attest to such growth.

Based on the 2000 U.S. Census, Mexicans account for 5.2 percent, or 60,173 of the total 875,225 Latino population in the New England area made up of 9.6 percent Puerto Ricans, 3.5 percent Cubans, 2.2 percent Dominicans, 4.8 percent Central Americans, 8 percent South Americans, 17.3 percent other Latinos, and 0.3 percent Spaniards. Based on the 2008 U.S. Census Bureau's American Community Survey (ACS), Mexicans made up less than 5 percent in several states: Massachusetts (1.4 percent), Rhode Island (3.1 percent), Vermont (2.6 percent), New Hampshire (2.6 percent), Maine (0.5 percent), and Connecticut (3.0 percent) (Terrazas, 2010).

While their numbers are small, they are nevertheless growing at a fast rate as the statistics of several cities in New England, which have doubled or tripled their numbers between 1990 and 2000, illustrate. Mexicans in Boston grew from 2,640 to 4,126 (56.3 percent); Mexicans in Chelsea grew from 120 to 660 (450 percent); Lynn's Mexicans grew from 167 to 853 (410 percent). Mexicans grew in Central Falls from 91 to 677 (644 percent); in Pawtucket from 254 to 581 (128 percent); and in Providence from 738 to 2,237 (203 percent). Nashua's Mexicans grew from 554 to 1,306 (135 percent), and in Manchester from 391 to 1220 (212 percent). Mexicans in Bridgeport grew from 402 to 2,687 (568 percent), in New Haven from 781 to 3,483 (345 percent), in Norwalk from 182 to 1,897 (942 percent), and in West Haven from 76 to 451 (493 percent) (U.S. 2000 Census).

Given this growth, an examination of how Mexicans settling in New England have been organizing over the past twenty years, how the directors and presidents of Mexican community-based organizations (CBOs) report the development of leadership infrastructures, and how they simultaneously maintain political transnational ties to Mexico, is eminent in undertaking this study.

PURPOSE

Because gaining entry as an outsider to Mexican communities is made difficult by identifying who is a Mexican, and is further complicated by the sensitivity surrounding their legal status, this study attempts to provide a first cut description and approximation of leadership perspectives from directors and presidents of Mexican organizations and potential political actors within the New England area.

The intent is not to present a representative sample of the Mexican community since this would require a longitudinal and concentrated study of Mexicans in each of the New England states, but rather, identify such "leaders," as proxies to these communities who can report on the salient issues affecting Mexicans, identify the leadership strategies they are using in managing Mexican organizations, and describe the political strategies they employ drawn from their migration and transnational experiences as Mexicans residing in New England. To that end, this study concretely focuses on: (1) the conceptualization of leadership shared by these leaders, (2) the leadership styles that these nascent and seasoned leaders rely on, (3) the types of relationships and support these leaders need from the Mexican Consulate, the Mexican government, and the U.S. government, (4) the social and political networks that these leaders are developing, their roles within that context, and the implications for the future of Mexican immigrants in New England. Among the basic questions this study explores are:

1. What type of leadership is emerging from the work of directors and presidents of Mexican community organizations and how can it be characterized?

2. What kinds of leadership styles are evident and how are these described by such leaders?
3. What kinds of relationships do these Mexican immigrant nationals have with the Mexican Consulates in the New England area?
4. What expectations do these Mexican leaders hold for the Mexican Consulates, the Mexican government, and the U.S. government?
5. What does the research of these nascent and seasoned Mexican leaders indicate about the local and transnational political leadership for future Mexicans in New England?

The survey and in-depth interviews highlight the demands Mexicans are facing at the local grassroots level (particularly in Boston, Massachusetts, Providence, Rhode Island, and Nashua, New Hampshire), the development of leadership through their organizations, the attainment of the right to vote for the president of Mexico in the United States, and the political and democratic transnational bridges being created.

RESEARCH METHODS AND THEORETICAL LENS

A combined qualitative and quantitative approach was used to gather data on identified Mexican leaders within the New England communities.[13] This consisted of a three-hour in-depth interview undertaken with twelve male and female Mexican leaders of community-based organizations during 2004–2005. As directors or presidents of Mexican organizations, they acted as proxies in identifying the needs of the Mexican communities, and the types of leadership and organizations being developed.

The interview questions addressed the background of the identified leaders including their education and work experiences, as well as information regarding their organizations including membership characteristics, members' education and standard of living, leadership aspects including the role of women in such organizations, decision-making, leadership styles, conceptualization of leadership, the role of the organizations with the Mexican communities, their relationship with the

Mexican Consulate and their expectations of the Mexican Consulate, the government of Mexico, and the United States.

An additional survey, in which half of these identified leaders participated, was administered to Mexicans who attended a seminar from the Institute of Mexicans Abroad on the programs and actions being implemented. Sponsored by the General Consulate of Mexico in Boston in collaboration with the Gaston Institute for Latino Community Development and Public Policy, on December 11, 2004, the seminar focused on educational, cultural, and community program information. Of the sixty participants who attended the seminar, twenty-one (twelve males and nine females) responded to the survey, with six participating in the in-depth interviews which were analyzed by Bertha Lucia Fries, a master's degree graduate in the Program for Creative and Critical Thinking of the Graduate College of Education of the University of Massachusetts–Boston, and this author.

The survey served as a backdrop of the general perspective of the status of Mexicans in New England at that time. Data of the more recent changes in the Mexican community have been gathered through Internet information shared by Julio Cesar Aragon, Lazos, a Mexican government sponsored website, and frequent visits to the Boston area. Drawing on the data provided by the General Consulates of Boston and New York of a list of identified "leaders" and using a snowball sample, a total of twelve male and female leaders out of twenty-five were selected. Leaders within the states of Vermont and Connecticut were not identified given the fact that the only viable Mexican organization in Vermont became inactive after 2001, and the three organizations headed by Mexicans in Connecticut were also not viable since one was a sports organization, the other existed only for a short period, and a new organization was in the process of becoming established at the time this research took place. Reported herein is the information on the Mexican national immigrant leaders of the social, civic, and legal organizations that were viable in Rhode Island, New Hampshire, Massachusetts, and Maine.

Once interviews were transcribed, mapping using matrix analysis was conducted to identify any of the emergent themes. These were tied to the extant literature for political incorporation and transnationalism of immigrants found in the research of Guarnizo, Haller, and Portes (2003), Jones-Correa (1998, 2004), Barreto and Muñoz (2003), Cano (2004), Cano and Délano, 2007, and Cano and Délano (2004). A more in-depth explanation of the settlement patterns of Mexicans in New England and the relationship of CBOs to leadership development is found in another publication (Montero-Sieburth 2007a).

While the sample populations of Mexicans in both the survey (N=27) with twenty-one seminar participants and six leaders and interviews (N=18 with twelve leaders and six seminar participants) were quite small, an overview of the Mexican community was able to be captured.

FINDINGS

Overview of Survey Findings

The administered survey[14] to Mexican participants, who had been invited from the rosters of registered Mexicans at the General Consulate of Mexico in Boston, was intended to gather data on the demographics, economic issues, educational levels, and leadership concerns of the Mexicans in New England participating in the seminar. This was a first cut analysis of the issues that affected a broader population. Those answering the survey were Mexicans from New Hampshire, Vermont, Rhode Island, Maine, and Massachusetts since these were under the jurisdiction of the General Mexican Consulate of Mexico in Boston. No participants from the state of Connecticut were included, since they are under the jurisdiction of the General Mexican Consulate of Mexico in New York.

The general demographics of the survey indicated that even though attending participants represented the Eastern, Central, and Western states of Mexico, 70 percent came from the federal district of Mexico, with the majority being "Chilangos," or Mexico City dwellers. Half of the participants reported they were married while the rest were single, divorced, or separated. A large majority were between 18–19 and 30–40 years of age with only four between 45–64 years of age. Seventeen percent reported they had no children, 17 percent had children ages one to five, 33 percent had two children, 25 percent had three, and 8 percent had five children. Close to 78 percent of the children were born in Mexico and 22 percent in the United States. These respondents represented the states of Massachusetts, Rhode Island, and New Hampshire[15] where most Mexicans tend to be concentrated in New England. Forty-seven percent came from cities with over 500,000 inhabitants, whereas 26 percent lived in medium size cities of 100,000, 11 percent lived in rural areas, and the remainder were equally distributed across small towns and suburban areas.

In terms of their length of stay in the United States, few had been in the U.S. less than one year, and greater numbers had been in the U.S. between one to five years. Close to 14 percent reported they were in the United States more than five years, 20 percent more than ten years, and 20 percent close to twenty years. Those who had been in the United States over ten years appeared to be more likely to stay.

Educationally, fifteen of the twenty-one had studied at a university: four had master's degrees, one had a doctorate, two had completed technical studies, one had completed preparatory school, two completed secondary school, and one completed primary school. This was noteworthy since in 2000, more New Englanders attained higher educational status than other residents in the United States—21 percent of the region's population earned a college degree and 11 percent earned advanced degrees (Demographic Profile of the Federal Reserve Bank of Boston 2005).

The majority reported they spoke Spanish, yet 77 percent reported they were not yet bilingual while 23 percent identified as being fully bilingual. Spanish was preponderantly used at home with children speaking more Spanish than English, and only 18 percent equally speaking Spanish and English.

None of the respondents were unemployed, 75 percent worked full time, 5 percent part time, and 20 percent were not in the labor force and were not seeking employment. Of those not in the labor force, 38 percent were housewives, 50 percent were students, and 13 percent were volunteers. Occupationally, 11 percent were administrators, 11 percent were consultants, 11 percent were laborers, 6 percent were child-care providers/elder-care providers, and the rest were project coordinators, entrepreneurs, jewelry workers, special education teachers, and salespersons. Their personal net incomes were reported to cover the following ranges: 24 percent earned less than $20,000 a year, 47 percent earned between $20,000 and $49,000, 18 percent earned between $50,000 and $74,000, and 12 percent earned above $74,000 a year. Their family net incomes were reported in the following ranges: 53 percent earned between $20,000 and $49,000 per year, 27 percent between $50,000 and $74,000 per year, and 7 percent above $74,000 per year. Eighty-one percent rented apartments or houses while 10 percent owned homes. All sent monthly remittances of less than $100 to over $300 to Mexico.

Of the twenty-one respondents, 29 percent reported they were U.S. citizens, 6 percent were currently soliciting U.S. citizenship, 12 percent were soliciting permanent residency, 24 percent were planning to become U.S. citizens, and 29 percent did not plan to become citizens. Only 22 percent voted in the last national U.S. election, and 78 percent did not vote, signaling that even those who are U.S. citizens do not always vote. Eighty-three percent of the respondents voted in the previous Mexican election prior to the absentee vote granted to Mexicans, while 17 percent did not.

Seventy-five percent identified Mexico as the country that best represents them and 25 percent responded that the U.S. and Mexico equally represented them, but none identified being solely represented by the United States, indicating the preservation of a strong national Mexican identity.

About half felt that the media negatively represented Mexicans. Only 3 percent thought Mexicans were positively represented and the rest were neutral. Yet close to 90 percent felt they could influence such images, while 10 percent felt they could not. Despite the negative media portrayals of Mexicans, most felt they could positively influence the media, indicating the need for further exploration of this issue.

When asked about discrimination, 95 percent stated they felt it was frequent against Mexicans, and only 5 percent stated there was none. Yet in relation to discrimination practices among Mexicans, 55 percent stated they were frequent or continuous, whereas 45 percent stated they were occasional.

To summarize, Mexicans surveyed had a wide range of back-grounds, occupations, and incomes, but by and large they tended to be educated, were in the labor workforce, sent remittances to Mexico, and settled permanently in New England after their initial ten years. They considered themselves bilingual, but frequently used Spanish at home and with their children. They identified preferentially as Mexicans, not as North Americans, and considered discrimination evident toward Mexicans, but also significant among Mexicans. Many were dual citizens, but voted more often in Mexico than the U.S. They considered the media images of Mexicans as negative, yet felt they could overturn and change this negative imagery into positive. Leadership responses were combined with in-depth interviews of the Mexican leaders of organizations and are represented in the following sections.

The In-Depth Interviews

A total of twelve (six male and six female) participants were identified as leaders from six organizations for the in-depth interviews because they have either been directors or presidents of Mexican organizations or had been identified by the General Consulates of Mexico in Boston and in New York as leaders. The leaders who represented viable Mexican organizations were primarily from Maine, New Hampshire, Massachusetts, and Rhode Island, but not Connecticut or Vermont. The demographic, linguistic, social, and economic composition of these leaders consisted of the following:

- All were first-generation Mexicans in the United States, except one born in the United States, who returned to Mexico, and was brought back to the U.S. as a child. When an adult, that leader reclaimed his Mexican citizenship. All these leaders were in the United States from seven to twenty-four years, having arrived between the ages of eleven and forty-seven years. More than half lived elsewhere in the United States before New England, and seven of the twelve were U.S. citizens.
- Like other Mexicans, they were from northern, southern, central, eastern, and western Mexico, but five were from Mexico City and

all but one volunteered in one of the six organizations throughout New England. The non-volunteer worked through his own business directly with the Mexican community on issues of social and legal needs.

- These leaders varied widely in their educational backgrounds: one completed primary school, four completed secondary or preparatory school, two had bachelors' degrees, four had master's degrees, and one a medical degree. Of the twelve, four continued to study and one was completing a doctorate.

- Eight of these leaders classified themselves as middle class, two as working class, and two as upper class. They were dentists, business administrators, urban planners, child-care providers, car salesmen, jewelry cleaners, language teachers, special education teachers, agricultural workers, lawyers, and legal rights advocates. Their incomes ranged from baseline existence above the U.S. poverty level to being comfortable and affluent; five rented and seven owned homes—and of these, two owned more than one house.

- Seven reported being fully bilingual in Spanish and English; two were additionally fluent in French and other languages. Four were fluent in English and one was not fluent in English. All were Spanish speakers able to read and write in Spanish, but a few had difficulties with Spanish orthography. Language skills appeared to be influenced by the number of years they had been in the United States.

- Ten of the twelve used computers on a weekly basis; four used the computer extensively in advanced programming (for example, creating posters and graphics, using urban planning programs and producing legal programs), six used the computer for daily communication and two did not use computers. One leader spent six hours daily communicating missives and Mexican concerns to a wide network of Mexicans and non-Mexicans.

The demographic profile of these leaders showed that while they represent a wide range of backgrounds and interests, language skills and professions, they were by and large educated, were computer literate, had full-time employment, were financially stable with some being even affluent, and others having a limited but acceptable standard of living. All spoke Spanish, considered themselves to be bilingual and were somewhat proficient in English. More were homeowners than renters. All were involved in Mexican community social, civic, and cultural activities.

Conceptualization and Types of Leadership

Different interpretations are attributed to the interpretation of "who" is a leader within the Mexican communities of New England. The General Consulates of Mexico in Boston and New York provided lists of leaders that not only identified the presidents of Mexican organizations, but also included entrepreneurs, religious leaders, and non-Mexicans highly committed to Mexican concerns. The community affairs coordinators from the Institute for Mexicans Abroad (IME) in each of the Consular offices identified as "leaders" of the Mexican communities focal people as point persons or persons who had the power to "convoke" or congregate people and who were shop owners, restaurant owners, religious leaders, and information point persons. The Consular officers talked about Mexican "leaders" in a symbolic manner, anointing those capable of living up to such a role, on the basis that they could provide a social and communal space for people to gather and congregate, this included directors of dance groups and even mariachi bands.

Whether such individuals saw themselves as leaders or not, was not the issue. Rather, they were entitled to the role given through the perception that was shared by others. Such perceptions of "leaders," were confirmed by the survey results. When asked how they defined leadership in their community, 3 percent associated this with a restaurant owner who they felt was able to gather people together, 15 percent referred to educators as leaders, 18 percent used such a word to describe information bearers within the community, 24 percent used the term for those persons who were recognized by the community, and 41 percent used it for those who advocated for the needs of people and helped with their problems.

Moreover, when asked if there were leaders within the Mexican community, 55 percent responded in the affirmative and 45 percent in the negative. When asked if they were leaders within their community, 45 percent said yes, and 55 percent said no. Yet when asked whether Mexicans were represented in the leadership throughout New England, 25 percent said yes and 75 percent said no, implying that many felt that while there were leaders in New England, Mexicans were not represented. In fact, 48 percent considered Mexican leaders to be marginalized in New England while 52 percent did not think this was the case. As to the organization of Mexican leaders in New England, 80 percent said no and 20 percent said yes, projecting a lack of unity among Mexicans. Fifteen percent stated that Mexicans frequently shared projects between themselves and other Latinos, 65 percent responded "only on occasion," and 20 percent said never, showing the lack of interaction between Mexicans and other Latinos in project sharing. In terms of discrimination, close to 55 percent of the Mexicans reported frequent and continuous discrimination against Mexicans, while 45 percent reported occasional discrimination. When asked the same question about discrimination amongst Mexicans, close to 95 percent reported frequent and occasional statements of discrimination toward Mexicans, and only 5 percent stated never. In responding to the question on how the media represents Mexicans, 45 percent regarded the image as negative, 41 percent thought it was neutral, and only 14 percent found the images positive, yet 90 percent felt they could influence such image making compared to 10 percent who felt they could not.

These leaders' responses to the in-depth interview questions revealed that the majority of these Mexican leaders characterized their leadership as a vocation which they were born to fulfill, acquired on the basis of their experiences or crafted from the commitments made to Mexicans. Male leaders distinguished female leadership styles from their own styles and described the leadership of Mexican women as "decisive, continuous, feminine, and visionary" and stated these were attributes they did not have. Instead, they identified male leadership with the attributes represented by such leaders as César Chávez or Benito Juárez and were humbled when they were called "leaders." They stated that what was important "was not how they viewed or defined themselves, but how others saw and judged them." Mexican women leaders were more outspoken and one spoke of leadership in the following way: "I do not define myself as a leader, but as a person who likes to problem-solve issues and who likes challenges and takes them on to see them come to fruition. So for me a leader has to have satisfaction and pleasure in being one." Another characterized the leadership of women as "the motor of the Mexican community's consciousness." Thus the leadership for this cohort is not only differentiated by ascribed or inherent attributes but also by gender.

These findings indicate that the leadership of Mexican organizations is driven by: (1) *symbolically imbued leaders,* those who are attributed the role simply because they symbolize participation within the Mexican communities; (2) *self-appointed leaders,* those who claim their leadership based on the power of information they hold, knowing their constituents, and being capable of resolving problems; and (3) *leaders by default,* those who assume such a role because no one else steps in to make decisions and carry out actions.

Differences in leadership styles are apparent between the nascent and more seasoned and established leaders. The nascent leaders appear to have gained much of their leadership ideas and strategies as university student organizers when they were in Mexico, from their current job situation where leadership skills and training are part of their work, or from their affiliations with other organizations including board membership.

For some, the leadership they experienced in Mexico became reproduced in their new communities; in other cases, they tried out new modalities through the functions and activities of their organizations or boards, or learned leadership skills on the job. The more established leaders leaned toward patterns of *compadrazgo* (god parenting) and *cacicazgo* (patron or chief of group) brought from Mexico; the less seasoned leaders tended to use newly appropriated strategies from boards, imitating some of the Anglo processes. The more progressive leaders seemed to incorporate what might be identified as bicultural strategies that secure the support of their constituents in the Mexican communities and members from the Consulate of Mexico and at the same time, procure the interests of local people and politicians in the communities where they live. Such dexterity allows them to be local as well as transnational, catapulting their interests beyond New England.

The Relationship of Organizations to Leadership Development

Without doubt, Mexican leadership in New England has grown in spurts and over time encouraged by the interest of Mexican community members, professionals, students, and the growing support from the General Consulate of Mexico in Boston including the initiatives of the Institute of Mexicans Abroad (see Montero-Sieburth 2007a). Students within private and public universities and music schools throughout New England have formed groups and organizations that represent Mexican interests. Mexican communities have developed organizations linked to the celebration of religious festivities. The General Consulate of Mexico in Boston has also galvanized Mexicans through specific initiatives, activities, and delivery of seminars. Because the role of student groups, Mexican organizations linked to religious groups, and the General Consulate of Mexico is discussed in depth elsewhere (see Montero-Sieburth 2007a), this chapter discusses how Mexican nationals are emerging as leaders and their roles in transnational politics.

From 1980 to the present, various community groups and individuals have developed six Mexican organizations. These organizations are of four types: (1) organizations that serve immigrants at the grass-roots levels on specific personal issues such as labor force access, housing, and so on; (2) organizations that help migrant workers who need legal or social support; (3) organizations that provide social and cultural regeneration of cultural activities and civic functions; and (4) organizations that act as springboards for leadership development.[16] Each organization had its own vested groups, small in numbers, but able to organize events and functions that drew large numbers of Mexicans and Latinos. The organizations served as a template for these leaders to either test out their newfound skills or to hone in on their developed leadership based on earlier experiences and practices in Mexico. Many of these leaders had not had the opportunity to acquire the knowledge and skills they needed to successfully implement a vision, such as growing an organization, learn how to use parliamentary procedures, identify board members, develop the organization's mission and vision, create yearly plans, and hold monthly meetings. In other cases, the village democratic models used in Mexico were replicated in New England. But such a model was often patriarchal and created many challenges for the leadership of women, giving rise to the belief that Mexicans still needed to develop a culture of civic empowerment (Hondagneu-Sotelo 2003).

While these organizations experienced similar ebb and flow patterns like many other U.S. community organizations in their boards and membership, some developed strong infrastructures and others quasi or no infrastructures.[17] They were identified as symbolically significant for the activities that Mexican nationals celebrated. Within such organizations, the attributes that characterize leaders included the ability to mobilize members, to act in response to crises, and to convoke Mexicans around cultural and civic celebrations.

In 2001 the Federation of Organizations of Mexicans in New England was founded as an umbrella non-profit organization to conduct greater outreach to other emerging Mexican organizations in New England, model leadership, identify critical issues, and train potential leaders. Over the years, the Federation focused on the *matricula* or identity card, remittances, the absentee vote in Mexico, and educational scholarships for Mexican youth (O'Neil 2003).

The General Consulate of Mexico in Boston played a role in supporting the growth of these organizations since the 1990s by shifting from an official, authoritative stance to a more communal, invitational stance, allowing Mexicans to seek the Consular officers for needs that went beyond their visas and passports. The Consulate responded by issuing the *matricula,* or identification card. One of the most debated issues in the United States, the Mexican government supported its nationals through the Consulate and the card was used to obtain automobile licenses or open bank accounts.[18] Through the use of mobile consulates, the General Consulate of Mexico in Boston conducted greater outreach, offered direct services to the Mexican communities, supported civic celebrations, and presented collaborative fora and seminars to update Mexicans on the types of social, economic, and cultural programs in finances, education, and community growth that the Institute of Mexicans Abroad (IME) made available.

The IME's representative within the Consulate served as a liaison to the Mexican students, organizations, and communities, and communicated via internet information about events, special seminars, and activities for all registered Mexicans. This feature made the presence of Mexico and the Mexican government evident and influential in New England. Thus the combined efforts of student groups and leaders, the Mexican organizations linked to religious and civic celebrations, the Consular office, and the Institute of Mexicans Abroad did much to link professionals and working class Mexicans with organizations having something to offer.

Each of the leaders contacted for this study was at a different stage of development. Their organizations provided a wide variety of services: two were at the grassroots level attempting to meet individual and community needs, one used social or cultural events as a catalytic and centering experience, another focused on the development of students' professional careers and brought speakers to their universities, one provided legal support for migrant workers, and one worked at a sophisticated political level with strategies and networks that included other Latinos and non-Latino groups. Still needed was the type of leadership training and development of a core of Mexican collective rather than individual leaders, who would train their followers in a multiplier effect, and develop coalitions with Puerto Ricans, Dominicans, Colombians, and non-Latinos.

Relationships and Support from the Mexican Consulate, the Mexican Government, and the U.S. Government

The survey and the in-depth interviews clearly showed that these leaders depended on the support from the Mexican Consulate. While the Consulate provides for the mobile consulates that meet identified needs, some have more mobile consulates than others depending on the lobbying done by the presidents and directors of these organizations. Hence, a database that captures a more accurate count of the growth of Mexicans in urban and rural communities would match resources to needs and favor those most in need. Many of the leaders demanded that their role as clients of the consulate be acknowledged and legitimized. They felt that while the General Consulate of Mexico in Boston had made an outreach effort, much more needed to be done. As one of the directors expressed, "they don't understand that we are growing by the minute and that we need to be heard now, not tomorrow."

These leaders wanted support from the Mexican government in being recognized as a potentially significant group, especially since the absentee vote in Mexico was spearheaded through the initiatives of one of the leaders of these organizations. This same leader wrote a missive during the election period for the president of Mexico where he decried the Mexican government's lack of listening to "the forgotten ones" in New England. He was also able to request that the Mexican government recall one of the General Consuls assigned to Boston who was not paying attention to Mexican compatriots by writing a scathing letter to the secretariat of the government and raising sufficient signatures for the Consul's removal.

These leaders sought a relationship with the U.S. government of greater respect and appreciation for the role that Mexicans played in U.S. communities and in the economy. As a group, these leaders endorsed the idea of providing amnesty, the worker's program, and a stronger bilateral relationship that benefits Mexicans and Americans and directly addresses immigration and the consideration of amnesty for undocumented Mexicans. While the idea of constructing a wall on the border between Mexico and the United States was considered a direct affront to Mexicans throughout the United States, one of the leaders in New England stated, "The wall will not keep Mexicans out, it will simply make them more ingenious" (personal communication, December 10, 2005).

Leaders' Roles and Their Social and Political Networks

In their role as leaders, these Mexicans have fostered social and political networks using the following strategies: (1) *grassroots politics,* in which they work directly with individuals and groups within the Mexican communities to meet an immediate crisis or other compelling problems; (2) *cultural and social networking,* in which they develop, expand, and nurture the activities and functions groups play in promoting Mexican social, cultural, and educational events; and (3) *strategic politics* in which they use local, national, and international influences to bear upon issues of greater transnational meaning, such as the presidential election in Mexico, remittances, immigration, and educational scholarships, and so on. Strategic politics is limited to leaders who have identified how the local politics of the towns and cities they live in operate and can negotiate their entry into internationally influential spheres. They find ways to meet the needs of the Mexican community by lobbying for scholarships or funds, procuring funding for local amenities such as the creation of the César Chávez statue and park, or by meeting with local police and U.S. immigration officers to reduce raids on undocumented workers. At the same time, these leaders use their understanding of such social and cultural capital to also make demands of the Mexican government via their representative roles as counselors and community advocates supported by IME and by aligning themselves with other Mexican groups around voting initiatives, the use of the absentee vote, and presidential elections.

At the grassroots level, several of these leaders expressed being overwhelmed and burnt out from trying to meet all of the growing demands of their constituents. Delegating responsibilities was not a tactic often used, since these leaders did most of the required tasks. This led to frequent turnover in the directorships of these organizations and to limited influence beyond the local community. To date, only three or four of the original twelve leaders are active, with the rest having given up on struggling with keeping their organizations abreast.

Establishing cultural, social, and educational activities, exchanging information, and building the Mexican community's foundation was extremely important, but required skills and efforts related to galvanizing community members through non-political processes and not necessarily developing political leadership skills.

Only a few of the leaders interviewed were able to develop both their immediate, own personal causes and local networks and national or international platforms that influence public policy—skills needed in strategic politics. Those few who were politically knowledgeable made inroads with local, state politicians and key stakeholders. In this regard, the Consul General of Mexico in Boston played an important role as he/she sought counsel and support from these leaders, but also advanced their issues and helped catapult them into representative roles. The founding of the Federation of Mexican Organizations in

New England was in great part due to the initiatives of former Consul General Hector Vasconcelos, the late Carlos Rico, consul general who crystalized it, and Elizabeth Canali, its first president with notable organizational board and directorship knowledge. In addition, the seminars and meetings called forth by the Institute of Mexicans Abroad served to inform and update the Mexican community on changes taking place in Mexico, and to foster a degree of unity and response to their local communities. As one consular officer remarked, "Reaching Mexicans is no small feat. We are so different and have such diverse agendas that to get people to the table takes enormous energy and commitment" (personal communication from field interview, March 2005).

Needed strategies in developing Mexican nascent leadership in New England for the future need to: (1) reach out to the recent arrivals, (2) understand the other Latinos and seasoned Mexican leaders who have galvanized their communities, and (3) develop mentoring programs and leadership training through a cohesive platform that empowers Mexicans. Community-based organizations can play a role in creating spaces where leadership emerges and evolves to become a political community platform for action is highly significant.[19]

IMPLICATIONS OF TRANSNATIONAL POLITICS OF MEXICANS

The arrival of Mexicans in New England has changed from transitory to permanent. As Mexicans have made New England their home, their identity as a group has become consolidated through the development of organizations, the continuous celebration of religious, civic, social, and cultural events, and their growing political involvement (DeSipio et al. 2003). As Jones-Correa (1998, 132) has remarked about Latin American organizations oriented to the home country, "the autonomous space they create here lends itself (perhaps unintentionally) to the expression of multiple identities that allow them to avoid the closure demanded by formal politics."

Among the transnational implications that can be drawn are the way that (a) the organizations foster experimentation for political development and (b) how the leaders within these communities extend their understanding of their power through dual frames, for their local communities and in Mexico. Heeding the needs of their Mexican constituents, (c) these Mexican leaders galvanize their members around critical situations, while simultaneously maintaining connections to Mexican politics. They recognize (d) the power of remittances and the ways it affects their communities here and there. They make use of (e) transportation and (f) telecommunication to live dual existences.

Mexican leaders in New England continue to be affiliated to parties in Mexico. Some still hold the Institutional Revolutionary Party (PRI) in high regard, despite its loss to the National Action Party (PAN) in 2000 and 2006. Others recognize the PAN for generating needed change and vision, and a small non-vocal group advocates for the Party of the Democratic Revolution (PRD), initiated by Cuauhtémoc Cardenas, while others are still concerned with the underdogs. These leaders keep the political party affiliations they knew in Mexico, but once naturalized, make choices at the local and national levels that will directly bear on their life in the United States. Few interviewees, if any, wanted to discuss their Mexican party affiliations, but were less reticent in identifying themselves as Republicans or Democrats. These findings, as well as the survey results regarding voting, fit Nancy Foner's (2001) notion of dual engagement in politics,[20] which does not make their engagement in Mexico or the U.S. exclusive. In addition, these findings support the Guarnizo, Portes, and Haller (2003) study of Colombians, Salvadorans, and Dominicans, which found that Latinos do not necessarily shed their loyalties or identities after they emigrate and continue to be politically active in the host country if they were already active in their home country.

With regard to gender roles, this study demonstrates that the three women leaders are more politically active than the three male leaders within their communities, and have attained important positions that afford them prominence. Support for the development of their leadership in strategic politics is necessary and inroads by Oiste, one of the political development groups in New England, through leadership workshops is a first step.

For many, English fluency becomes a vehicle for political participation as they parlay their knowledge of Mexico to local politicians, while also demanding recognition from Mexican officials in the United

States and politicians in Mexico. Even in cases where leaders lack English fluency, by meeting the sheriff or counselor of the city and by knowing and working with key people, they participate at the local level. The glue that holds the Mexicans in New England together is the characterization of culture and social, values, manifested through celebrations of national festivities, social, and civic events—the commemoration of César Chávez, or September 15, for example. At a deeper level, local situations, such as setting up a local soccer football junior team, the crisis created by the earthquakes in Mexico, the death of a *paisano* (countryman) who needs burial in Mexico, or the deaths of so many through the drug wars, or the needs of an indigent family or of a sick child needing medical assistance, draw families, merchants, and the community together to pool their resources and offer support. Multiple examples were cited by our interviewees of local restaurant owners providing soccer or marathon shirts with their logo, mothers raffling tickets or selling Mexican food at a *kermes,* (fundraising fair), local tortilla factories paying for Mexican dancers' dresses, the local artists donating television time to keep Mexicans informed, or the folkloric ballet performing dances for a worthy cause. Family members, arriving from Mexico also contribute to this sense of culture maintenance by bringing back suitcases full of inexpensive soccer outfits, the *canastitas* (little baskets) and *golosinas* (sweets) for the *Posadas,* or the *mole* and other food dishes (Fieldnotes March 2005).

Like other Mexicans elsewhere, the Mexicans in New England exhibit the traits that Manuel Orozco (2003) argues affect the global economy, that is, the five T's: transfers of remittances and grants, transportation, tourism, telecommunication, and nostalgic trade. I would argue that remittances, transportation, and telecommunication are central in allowing these Mexicans, as diverse and dispersed as they are, to maintain a strong sense of culture and national identity tied to Mexico and its political scenarios on the one hand, and to develop the grounding and political knowledge that helps them integrate politically into the New England landscape on the other.

Although remittances have diminished greatly during the current economic recession, in 2005 the total amount of Mexican remittances in the United States was $18 billion (Suro 2005), and in 2003 the total remittances sent by foreigners living in New England was close to $775 million, which is 3 percent of the total volume of U.S. remittances (Marcuss 2005). The remittances of Mexicans in New England are small in comparison but nevertheless significant in the linkages they create.

Remittances alone play a significant role particularly in rural Mexican economies and in developing needed hometown infrastructure and opportunities (de la Garza, Orozco, and Baraona 1997; DeSipio et al. 2003).[21] This study identified that the members' remittances in at least in two of the six New England organizations led to decisions that affected the rebuilding of schools and the expansion of water sources in two of the former hometowns and villages. Such initiatives seem to have a circular democratizing effect: local officials write emails, internet and letters that identify specific needs of their hometowns in Mexico; the directors of these Mexican organizations in New England make decisions and take actions to help. As a response, fund-raising activities are put into action to accumulate monies within the Mexican communities, which are sent to their respective towns and cities, thereby setting up the infrastructure that builds schools, etc.

Notwithstanding, the Institute for Mexicans Abroad (IME) provides financial and educational programs and establishes *plazas communitarias* ("community schools") in New England to serve Mexican nationals, which also stimulates linkages as Mexicans realize they can create many of these infrastructures in their own local contexts to aid those communities. Such relationships help to foster the transnational processes that Cano (2004, 5) alleges to exist at "the federal government level, local and state level and . . . exerts influences on the immigrant community of the sending state and on the government structure of the receiving state, within a context of urban politics." At the same time, through its Advisory Counsel (Consejo Consultivo del IME), the IME fosters personal networks among Mexican government officials and local U.S. politicians, as well as church and community leaders (Cano and Delano 2004; Cano and Delano 2007).

Remittances also appear to have a role in influencing the local political participation that Barreto and Muñoz (2003, 444) have identified appears to take place for non-citizens. They state: "an immigrant who has come to the United States for more opportunities, but continues to stay in close contact with his host country by sending money home, is someone who is more likely to get involved in politics in America."

Several of the Mexican leaders were aware that politicians and policymakers in Mexico hold remittances in high regard. These leaders felt they had a say in what happens in Mexico since they were "footing the bill" in keeping Mexico economically and socially stable. One leader remarked: "Mexico's government should recognize that part of Mexico's economy is based on the money that families send home, and that is what keeps Mexico above water" (personal communication, February 2005). At the same time, these leaders also recognize the economic power that Latinos have in the United States and the interest that financial and lending companies, such as Wells Fargo, have in courting them. The Mexicans in New England who saw investment practices and commodities made easily in the United States and abroad shared these same visions (Crowley 2001) and also suffered the consequences of these during the current economic crisis.

The flow of remittances indirectly influences Mexico's non-restriction of immigrants to the United States insofar as the remittances are viewed as safeguards for continued Mexican economic development and stability on the one hand, and contribute to poverty reduction on the other, a feat that then President Fox credited to his administration.[22]

Greater access and availability of air travel, direct routes to Mexico, and reduced costs have also contributed to the transnationalism of Mexicans in New England. Establishment of direct routes between Boston and Mexico by Aero Mexico and other airlines has made it possible for Mexicans to come and go easily. Airline travel, once a commodity of the elite and wealthy, has become accessible for many through cost reductions. Travel to Mexico is not only affordable and easily obtained through Internet and travel agency purchases, but is promoted via television and radio. The availability of favorite novelas (Spanish-language novels) as well as the Latino television networks (such as Univision) helps to foster this sense of a "borderless" Mexico. The celebration of the Virgin of Guadalupe on December 12 can be viewed from Mexico as it is taking place in New England via multiple channels. Advertisements that link Mexicans to family and culture in Mexico are extensive.

Aware of this market, the telephone companies have made it possible for telecommunications to thrive. Mexicans residing in Mexico who receive transnational remittances tend to have about three times the number of telephone conversations with relatives abroad during the week than those not receiving money (Suro 2003). For many Mexicans in New England, family in Mexico becomes both an extraneous motivation in their individual work and social and cultural practices, but also an internal encouragement for advancement, demonstrated by residual gains for the family and communities in Mexico.

■ ■ ■

Although this study was exploratory in presenting a general overview of the Mexicans in New England, it is significant in highlighting how Mexican nationals are beginning to shape their emergent leadership along local and national linkages to Mexico. Through the leadership of their organizations, student groups, and support from the General Consulate of Mexico, as well as through counselors sponsored by the Institute of Mexicans Abroad (IME), these Mexicans are acquiring the types of knowledge and skills to lobby, negotiate, and arbitrate for changes in their own New England backyards. Mexican organizations provide a platform for leadership development and the extension of democratic processes; the next step needs to examine how such initiatives are consolidated and refined to develop political incorporation and accountability theories. Several of the seasoned Mexican leaders acknowledged the need for legal status, education, and leadership training as vehicles for harnessing the political power of their local communities as well as the need to build coalitions with Puerto Ricans, Dominicans, and Colombians. Nascent Mexican leaders need to be mentored and supported at the local level through the Mexican organizations, socially and culturally grounded through the support of Mexican student groups as collaborators and pipelines to education, and by the Mexican Consulate in Boston and the IME through their information sharing, program development, and leadership training to help link Mexicans in New England to Mexico.

NOTES

The research in this study was funded by the Gaston Institute of the University of Massachusetts–Boston under the directorship of Andres Torres. This research has contributed to the development of several publications identifying the presence of Mexicans in New England.

1. Mexicans in New England and in this study are defined as follows: (1) *Mexican nationals* refers to those who are in the United States of Mexican nationality with U.S. visas. These include students at diverse universities, many of whom have scholarships from the Mexican government, and are transient in nature; visitors and tourists who are in the United States for limited periods who often visit their families, and general visa holders. Once they graduate, some of the students obtain work permits as professionals in the public and private sector, receive H–1B visa program authorizations, or solicit their alien registration card once they have completed the required five year stay. (2) *Mexican nationals with U.S. permanent residence* have lived in the U.S. for more than the five year limit to obtain U.S. citizenship and have rights to study, work, but not vote. (3) *Mexican dual nationals,* many of whom became American citizens after being in the States, but because of the change in law in Mexico in 1993, have opted to regain their Mexican nationality, which has been sustained since 1996 without time limits. For these dual nationals, travel with a U.S. and or Mexican passport provides them with greater flexibility, yet for some U.S. politicians this practice is unfavorable. (4) *Undocumented Mexicans* are unauthorized to work in the United States, but have access to a social security card, are in the labor force, pay taxes, and make up much of the informal infrastructure in child care, elder care, house and office cleaning services, restaurants, and residential care facilities where their legal status is not questioned. (5) *Migratory Mexicans* are brought to work in the food industries managed by diverse employees, or are seasonal cranberry, potato, broccoli, onion, or other produce workers who return to the southern United States or Mexico based on bilateral agreements between the United States and Mexico and who use H2-B visas.

2. See the growing literature on first- and second-generation immigrants, for example: Suárez-Orozco and Suárez-Orozco (1995); Suárez-Orozco and Paéz (2002); and Suárez-Orozco and Suarez-Orozco (2001).

3. Aaron Terrazas notes that there has been a substantial decline between 2008–2010 of the Mexican population entering the United States. Close to 142,000 Mexicans departed for abroad according to Mexico's National Survey of Occupations and Employment (ENOE).

4. The circular migration, once most commonly undertaken by single males who came to the United States to earn dollars and returned to their

towns or villages in Mexico, has changed due to several factors: (1) immigration law changes, (2) family reunification, and (3) the creation of community bases in the United States. The present circular migration embodies families and includes females and children who accompany husbands and single females. Provided they can legally return, have the money to do so, are able to take the whole family and can do so within the parameters of their work, Mexicans tend to return to Mexico annually or biannually. If they can't travel, they save until the *día de santo* (saints day), or the birthday of a beloved family member. This pattern was also observed for many Mexicans in New England, particularly around Christmas and Easter.

5. According to Federal Reserve Bank of Boston, New England's Demographic Profile for 2000 was less racially diverse than the rest of the United States: 87 percent of its population is considered white compared to 75 percent nationally.

6. See Camayd-Freixas, Karuch, and Letjer (2006).

7. The Mexicans who live in New England range from privileged students at academic institutions to professionals, entrepreneurs, businessmen, contractors, house cleaners, day laborers, and even prisoners according to former Consul General Carlos Rico (2001). Included among these are a Nobel Prize winner, several prosperous restaurant owners, a number of established professionals, many students, service oriented workers including housecleaners and elder care helpers, a myriad of musicians and artists, and numerous potato and cranberry pickers.

8. See the report by Miren Uriarte and Charles Jones (2002), "Growth of Latino Population," in *Rhode Island Latinos: A Scan of Issues Affecting the Latino Population of Rhode Island.* eds. Miren Uriarte, Maria Estela Carrion, Charles Jones, Natalie Carithers, Juan Carlos Gorlier, and Juan Francisco Garcia (Boston: Mauricio Gaston Institute for Latino Community Development and Public Policy), 23–26. See also Martha Martinez (2002).

9. As reported by Benjamin Guiliani, President of the Maine Migrant Workers' Advocacy Group in Portland, Maine.

10. Personal records of Martha Montero-Sieburth who lived in Norwich, Connecticut, during the 1950s–1960s and recalls Mexican gatherings of professional and working class people in homes and during Latin American celebrations.

11. As reported by Margarita Fernandez-Letowski, president of the Mexican Association of New Hampshire, and her board members (Field notes 2005).

12. In 2006 well over eighty Mexican restaurants were listed in the Boston greater metropolitan area yellow telephone directory with smaller taquerias (taco bars) set up throughout towns and cities. Note that not all are owned by Mexican nationals, but many Central Americans and North American entrepreneurs own these eateries.

13. Additional sources included: (1) Census data for Massachusetts, New Hampshire, Vermont, Maine, Rhode Island, and Connecticut; (2) web searches of documents from the Mexican government and from published reports and research studies; (3) anecdotal accounts from Mexican community members, newspaper articles; and (4) data provided by the General Consulate of Mexico in Boston with jurisdiction over New Hampshire, Maine, Vermont, Rhode Island, and Massachusetts and the General Consulate of New York with jurisdiction over Connecticut.

14. An earlier questionnaire was developed by Latino Leadership Opportunity Program students of the Gaston Institute under the guidance of Professor Jorge Capetillo, faculty in the Sociology Department and researcher in the Gaston Institute. It was disseminated at a September 2004 Latino Public Policy Conference. That survey was reviewed by Professors Capetillo and Montero-Sieburth, and was updated and translated from English to Spanish by Montero-Sieburth for use at the December 11, 2005, seminar. The survey, entitled: "Intake Questionnaire for Participants in the Seminar for the Exchange of Information and Opinions on the Mexican Community in New England," was administered and the data was analyzed by Martha Montero-Sieburth and Bertha Lucia Fries, a master's candidate in the Critical and Creative Thinking Program of the University of Massachusetts–Boston during spring 2005.

15. The single representative from the state of Maine, a director of his own organization, was not able to attend, hence his perspective as a leader was not included in the survey, but was later captured in the in-depth interviews.

16. The Maine Migrant Workers' Advocacy Group, Inc., an organization serving migrant workers in Maine founded during the early 1980s, is the oldest and most targeted to meeting legal and social needs of migrant Mexican workers. The rest of the Mexican organizations are more directed towards meeting the social, cultural, civic, and educational needs of Mexicans in New England. The Mexican Organization of New England (OMNI) was the first of such organizations, founded in 1992 in Boston, Massachusetts, to promote Mexican cultural and social events of a civic and social nature. The Social, Cultural, and Mexican Sports Organization of Rhode Island, originally founded in 1995 as a sports organization working within church to plan related social and cultural activities, has taken on a more political agenda because its only president in power since its founding has connections with the local politicians in Rhode Island and the Mexican government through the Institute of Mexicans Abroad. The Mexican Free Association of Rhode Island is an offshoot of the previous organization, created by a team of directors in 2001 and officially founded in 2003 to attend to more concrete community needs which include providing aid to families, paying for medical needs, sending remittances to rebuild schools, and funding of social and civic activities. The Mexican New Hampshire

Granite State Organization was founded in 1999 to help Mexicans in the Nashua-Manchester area with information, the mobile consulates, access to obtaining their driver's licenses, and other community needs, and Fronteras Unidas was founded in 2003 to help Mexicans and other Latinos access needed information, social services, and training in obtaining loans and their drivers' license.

17. Some of the apparent infrastructural issues are how Mexicans decide to create their boards, follow Roberts Rules of Order, develop their board and committee membership and member functions, and conduct their business meetings. In some cases, this is new knowledge learned on the job and from workplace experiences where the responsibilities demand organization. In other cases, they learn from joining other organizations and becoming board members. Seasoned organizers tend to expand on the democratic principles they brought from Mexican experiences as students or organizers or adapt into their leadership style as they develop the organization.

18. The identification card has been in use since 1871, yet in recent years it has become the focus of much heated debate at local and national levels (Donohue 2003).

19. Mexicans are politically split; while they tend to maintain strong ties to Mexican party affiliations, once they are able to vote in the United States, they generally support the Democratic Party. Within New England, however, Republicans have a strong Mexican following and several of the directors of the organizations identified as Republicans.

20. See also Foner, Rumbaut, and Gold (2000).

21. In 2003 President Vicente Fox remarked that remittances were Mexico's "biggest source of foreign income, bigger than oil, tourism or foreign investment." http://www.signonsandiego.com/news/mexico/20030924-2051-us-mexico.html.

22. According to the World Bank's June 2004 Report No. 28612-ME, "Mexico, Poverty in Mexico: An Assessment of Conditions, Trends and Government Strategy," extreme poverty in Mexico in the 2000–2004 period was reduced to 17.6 percent in 2004, yet much of this reduction took place in rural communities, whose rate of poverty declined from 42 percent to 27.9 percent although urban poverty stagnated at 11 percent.

REFERENCES

Alba, Francisco. 2002. "Mexico: A Crucial Crossroads." *Migration Information Source.* Updated March 2004. http://www.migration.org/Profiles/display.cfm?id=211. Last accessed February 15, 2006.

Archibold, Randal C. "Arizona Enacts Stringent Law on Immigration." *New York Times,* April 23, 2010.

Barreto, Matt A., and Jose A. Muñoz. 2003. "Reexamining the 'Politics of In-Between': Political Participation among Mexican Immigrants in the United States." *Hispanic Journal of Behavioral Sciences* 25 (4): 427–47.

Camarota, Stephen. 2001. "Immigration from Mexico: Assessing the Impact on the United States." Washington, DC: Center for Immigration Studies.

———. 2004. "Economy Slowed, but Immigration Didn't: The Foreign-Born Population, 2000–2004." Washington, DC: Center for Immigration Studies.

Camayd-Freixas, Yoel, Gerald Karuch, and Nelly Letjer. 2006. "Latinos in New Hampshire: Enclaves, Diasporas, and an Emerging Middle Class." In *Latinos in New England,* edited by Andres Torres, 1–17. Philadelphia: Temple University Press.

Cano, Gustavo. 2004. "Urban and Transnational Politics in America: Novus Ordo Seclorum?" Paper prepared for delivery at the Annual Meeting of the American Political Science Association, Chicago, September 2–5.

Cano, Gustavo, and Alexandra Délano. 2004. "The Institute of Mexicans Abroad: The Day After . . . After 156 Years." Paper prepared for delivery at the 2004 Annual Meeting of the American Political Science Association, September 2–5.

———. 2007. "The Mexican Government and Organized Mexican Immigrants in the United States: A Historical Analysis of Political Transnationalism (1845–2005)." *Journal of Ethnic and Migration Studies* 33, no. 5 (July): 695–725.

Consejo Nacional de Población (CONAPO). n.d. "Migración mexicana hacia Estados Unidos." http://www.conapo.gob.mx/mig_int/03.htm.

Corchado, Alfredo, and Dianne Solis. 1999. "Mexicans Reshaping America." *Dallas Morning News,* September 19.

Creuheras, Santiago. 2001. "The Poblano Diaspora: The View from New York." *ReVista* (Fall): 42–43.

Crowley, Cathleen F. 2001. "As Latino Population Surges, So Does Its Power, Influence." *Eagle Tribune.* July 1.

Custerd, Glynn. 2003. "North American Borders: Why They Matter." Washington, DC: Center for Immigration Studies.

de la Garza, Rodolfo, Manuel Orozco, and Miguel Baraona. March 1997. "Binational Impact of Latino Remittances." Claremont: Tomás Rivera Policy Institute.

Demographic Profile of the Federal Reserve Bank of Boston 2005.

DeSipio, Louis, Harry Pachon, Rodolfo O. de la Garza, and Jongho Lee. 2003. "Immigrants at Home and Abroad: How Latino Immigrants Engage the

Politics of their Home Communities and the United Status." Vol. 55. Claremont: Tomás Rivera Policy Institute.

Donohue, Brian. 2003. "Mexico's ID Cards Ignite a Controversy." *Star-Ledger*. May 15.

Edwards, Will. 2003. "The Case for Immigration." *International Herald Tribune*. February 2.

Foner, Nancy. 2001. "Immigrant Commitment to America, Then and Now: Myths and Realities." *Citizenship Studies* 5 (1): 27–40.

Foner, Nancy, Rubén G. Rumbaut, and Steven J. Gold, eds. 2000. *Immigration Research for a New Century*. New York: Russell Sage Foundation.

Guarnizo, Luis Eduardo, William Haller, and Alejandro Portes. 2003. "Assimilation and Transnationalism: Determinants of Transnational Political Action among Contemporary Migrants." *American Journal of Sociology* 108 (6): 1211–48.

Guzmán, Betsy. The Hispanic Population 2000. Census 2000 Brief, U.S. Washington, DC: U.S. Department of Government and Statistics.

Hondagneu-Sotelo, Pierrette, ed. 2003. *Gender and U.S. Immigration: Contemporary Trends*. Berkeley: University of California Press.

Instituto Nacional de Estadística, Geografía e Informática (INEGI). 2003. Anuario Estadístico de los Estados Unidos Mexicanos.

Jones-Correa, Michael A. 1998. *Between Two Nations: The Political Predicament of Latinos in New York City*. Ithaca: Cornell University Press.

———. 2004. "Understanding Immigrant Politics: Lessons from the U.S." *Migration Information Source,* 1–4. http://www.migrationinformation.org.

Leite, Paula, María Adela Angoa, and Mauricio Rodríguez. 2009. "Emigración Mexicana a Estados Unidos: Balance de los Últimas Décadas." http://paisano.gob.mx/pdfs/articulo_1.pdf. Last accessed January 2011.

López Vega, Rafael. 2003. "La Población Mexicana en los Estados Unidos." México: Consejo Nacional de Población.

Lowell, Lindsay, and Roberto Suro. 2002. "How Many Undocumented? The Numbers behind the U.S. Migration Talks." Washington, DC: Pew Hispanic Center.

Marcelli, Enrico. 2001. "Legal Immigration to New England during the 1900s. Latinos in Massachusetts: Immigration." Boston: Mauricio Gaston Institute, University of Massachusetts-Boston.

Marcuss, Mamie. 2005. "International Remittances: Information for New England Financial Institutions." Boston: Federal Reserve Bank of Boston, 1–19.

Marcuss, Mamie, and Ricardo Borgos. 2004. "Who Are New England's Immigrants?" Boston: Federal Reserve Bank of Boston. http://www.bos.frb.org/commdev/c&b/2004/fall/Immigrants.pdf. Last accessed May 2005.

Martinez, Martha. 2002. "The Latinos of Rhode Island." In *Rhode Island Latinos: A Scan of Issues Affecting the Latino Population of Rhode Island,* edited by Miren Uriarte, Maria Estela Carrion, Charles Jones, Natalie Carithers, Juan Carlos Gorlier, and Juan Francisco Garcia, 35–50. Boston: Mauricio Gaston Institute for Latino Community Development and Public Policy.

Montero-Sieburth, Martha. 2007a. "The Roles of Leaders, Community and Religious Organizations, Consular Relationships, and Student Groups in the Emerging Leadership of Mexican Immigrants in New England." *Journal of Latinos and Education* 6 (1): 5–33.

Montero-Sieburth, Martha. 2007b. "'Si Se Puede' Newcomers: Mexicans in New England." In *Latinos in a Changing Society,* edited by Martha Montero-Sieburth and Edwin Melendez, 58–92. Westport: Greenwood Publishing.

Montero-Sieburth, Martha, and Edwin Meléndez, eds. 2007. *Latinos in a Changing Society.* Westport: Greenwood Publishing.

O'Neil, Kevin. 2003. "Consular ID Cards: Mexico and Beyond." Migration Information Source, April 1.

Orozco, Manuel. 2003. "Hometown Associations and Their Present and Future Partnerships: New Development Opportunities?" Report commissioned by the U.S. Agency for International Development, Washington, DC. September.

Passel, Jeffrey S., and Cohn, D'Vera. 2009a. "A Portrait of Unauthorized Immigrants in the United States." Washington, DC: Pew Hispanic Center.

———. 2009b. "Mexican Immigrants: How Many Come? How Many Leave?" Washington, DC: Pew Hispanic Center.

Rico, Carlos F. 2001. "The View from New England: A Preliminary Portrait." *ReVista* (Fall): 42–43.

Smith, Robert Courtney. 2006. *Mexican New York: Transnational Lives of New Immigrants.* Los Angeles: University of California Press.

Suárez-Orozco, Carola, and Marcelo Suárez-Orozco. 1995. *Transformations: Migration, Family Life, and Achievement Motivation among Latino Adolescents.* Palo Alto: Stanford University Press.

Suárez-Orozco, Carola, and Marcelo M. Suarez-Orozco. 2001. *Children of Immigration.* Cambridge, MA: Harvard University Press.

Suárez-Orozco, Marcelo M. 2001. "Mexican Immigration," *ReVista* (Fall): 40–41.

Suárez-Orozco, Marcelo M., and Mariela M. Paéz. 2002. *Latinos: Remaking America.* Los Angeles: University of California Press.

Sum, Andre M., Johan Uvin, Ishwar Khatiwanda, Dana Ansel, Paulo Tobar, Frimpomaa Ampaw, Shelia Palma, and Greg Leiserson. 2005. *The Changing Face of Massachusetts.* Boston: Massachusetts Institute for a New Commonwealth.

Suro, Roberto. 2003. "Remittance Senders and Receivers: Tracking the Transnational Channels." Washington, DC: Pew Hispanic Center.

———. 2005. "Attitudes toward Immigrants and Immigration Policy: Surveys among Latinos in the U.S. and in Mexico." Washington, DC: Pew Hispanic Center.

Terrazas, Aaron. 2010. "Mexican Immigration in the United States. Migration Information Source. http://www.migrationinformation.org/USFocus/print.cfm?ID=767.

United States 2000 Census.

Uriarte, Miren, and Charles Jones. 2002. "Growth of Latino Population." In *Rhode Island Latinos: A Scan of Issues Affecting the Latino Population of Rhode Island,* edited by Miren Uriarte, Maria Estela Carrion, Charles Jones, Natalie Carithers, Juan Carlos Gorlier, and Juan Francisco Garcia, 23–46. Boston: Mauricio Gaston Institute for Latino Community Development and Public Policy.

Waters, Mary C., and Jimenez, Tomas R. 2005. "Assessing Immigrant Assimilation: New Empirical and Theoretical Challenges." *Annual Review of Sociology* 31:105–25.

CONTRIBUTORS

RICARDO AINSLIE is a native of Mexico City, Mexico. He earned his bachelor's degree at the University of California at Berkeley and his Ph.D. in Clinical Psychology at the University of Michigan. He is currently a Professor in the Department of Educational Psychology at the University of Texas at Austin where he is a Fellow in the Charles H. Spence Centennial Professorship in Education. He is also an Affiliate Faculty of the Center for Mexican American Studies and the American Studies Program at the University of Texas. Drawing from psychoanalysis as well as books, articles, and film, his work explores the intersection of individual psychology, social processes, and culture. He has published articles and books on the psychodynamics of culture, the psychology of the immigrant experience, and "cultural mourning." His documentary films include *Looking North: Mexican Images of Immigration* (2006) and *Ya Basta* (a 2007 film about crime in Mexico in the wake of the country's transition to democracy). His most recent book is *The Fight to Save Juárez: Life in the Heart of Mexico's Drug War*.

MARÍA DE LOS ANGELES TORRES is director and professor of Latin American and Latino Studies at the University of Illinois in Chicago. She received her Ph.D. from the University of Michigan, Ann Arbor. She taught political science at DePaul University in Chicago from 1987 to 2005. She was a faculty associate at Notre Dame's Institute for Latino Studies, 2000–2001 and was a research fellow at Chapin Hall University of Chicago 2002. She is the author of two books, *The Lost Apple: Operation Pedro Pan, Cuban Children in the US and the Promise of a Better Future* (Boston: Beacon Press, 2004) and *In the Land of Mirrors:*

The Politics of Cuban Exiles in the United States (Ann Arbor: University of Michigan Press, 1999). She also edited *By Heart/De Memoria: Cuban Women's Journeys in and Out of Exile* (Philadelphia: Temple University Press, 2002) and co-edited *Borderless Borders: U.S. Latinos, Latin Americans, and the Paradox of Interdependence* (Philadelphia: Temple University Press, 1998). A co-authored book, *Citizens in the Present: Civically Engaged Youth in Three American Cities: Chicago, Rio and Mexico City*, is forthcoming from the University of Illinois Press.

MANUEL AVALOS is Director of Research Partnerships and Innovation at the University of North Carolina at Wilmington (UNCW). He is also a Professor in the Department of Public and International Affairs at UNCW. His academic research focuses on questions of racial inequality in the Americas and the political representation and incorporation of the Latino electorate at the state, local, and national levels. His publications include articles in *Sociological Perspectives, Harvard Journal of Hispanic Policy*, and *Policy Studies Journal* as well as chapters in Roberto de Anda, ed., *Chicanas and Chicanos in Contemporary Society*, and Rodolfo de la Garza and Louis DeSipio, eds., *Ethnic Ironies: Latino Politics in the 1992 Elections, Awash in the Mainstream: Latino Politics in the 1996 Elections*, and *Muted Voices: Latino Politics in the 2000 Elections*.

GILBERTO CÁRDENAS, the Executive Director of the IUPLR, is also Director of the Institute for Latino Studies (ILS) and Assistant Provost at the University of Notre Dame. He is Professor of Sociology at the University of Notre Dame and holds the Julian Samora Chair in Latino Studies. Author of *Los Mojados: The Wetback Story* (University of Notre Dame Press), he is also the editor or coeditor of three other books, including *Health and Social Services among International Labor Migrants* (CMAS/University of Texas Press) and *La Causa: Civil Rights and the Quest for Equality in the Midwest* (Arte Público/University of Houston Press). Dr. Cárdenas is the author of several dozen articles and book chapters and twenty reports. He is currrently the editor of the Latino Perspectives series of the University of Notre Dame Press, and he has served on the editorial boards of many journals. He has received grants from the Joyce Foundation, the Pew Charitable Trust, the U.S. Department of Health and Human Services, the Annie E. Casey Foundation, the Kellogg Foundation, the Smithsonian Institution, the Ford Foundation, and the U.S. Department of Education. He received his Ph.D. in Sociology from the University of Notre Dame.

MARISOL CORTEZ is a community scholar located in San Antonio, Texas. She holds a Ph.D. in Cultural Studies from the University of California, Davis, which she applies in her work as an organizer with the Esperanza Peace and Justice Center and as an instructor in the Sociology Department at Texas A&M–San Antonio. In this way she aims to ground her research and teaching within community struggles for social and environmental justice, with much of her writing focused on the cultural and ideological dimensions of environmental crisis. In previous publications, she has examined the environmental politics of embodiment, cultures of waste disposal, and movements for environmental justice in California and Texas; current projects explore the environmental history of San Antonio within a framework of Chicana/o bioregionalism.

LOUIS DESIPIO is an Associate Professor in the Departments of Political Science and Chicano/Latino Studies at the University of California, Irvine (UCI). He is the author of *Counting on the Latino Vote: Latinos as a New Electorate* (Charlottesville: University Press of Virginia, 1996) and coauthor, with Rodolfo O. de la Garza, of *Making Americans/Remaking America: Immigration and Immigrant Policy* (Boulder: Westview Press, 1998). He is also the author and editor of an eight-volume series on Latino political values, attitudes, and behaviors. The most recent volume in this series, *Beyond the Barrio: Latinos in the 2004 Elections,* was published in 2010 (University of Notre Dame Press). DeSipio's research focuses on Latino politics, the process of political incorporation of new and formerly excluded populations into U.S. politics, and public policies such as immigration, immigrant settlement, naturalization, and voting rights.

DAPHNY DOMINGUEZ AINSLIE of Rockport, Texas, earned her bachelor of arts degree and her Master of Education in Counseling at the University of Texas at Austin. She earned her Doctorate in Psychology from Our Lady of the Lake University in San Antonio, Texas.

She completed her training at the Central Texas Veterans Health Care System of the Department of Veterans Affairs, where her clinical and research interests center around post-traumatic stress disorder, trauma, and substance use. She is currently in private practice in Austin, Texas.

RODOLFO ESPINO is an Associate Professor at Arizona State University. He received his bachelor of arts from Luther College and his master of arts and Ph.D. from the University of Wisconsin–Madison. His primary research and teaching interests are in the fields of minority politics, political behavior, and political methodology. His dissertation focused on the Congressional Hispanic Caucus and Latino representation in Congress, specifically focusing on how institutional and electoral forces both hinder and facilitate the representation of Latinos. This work received the American Political Science Association's Award for the best dissertation on race and politics. He is presently engaged in a number of research projects, some of which include an examination of Latino political empowerment, the campaign rhetoric of Latino candidates and Spanish political campaign ads, and the political behavior of whites in response to Latinos. He is also the coeditor of *Latino Politics: Identity, Mobilization, and Representation* (University of Virginia Press, 2007). Aside from research on Latino politics, he conducts work that examines bias in survey-item response, the effect of civic education on political participation, and the political participation of language-minority Americans.

RENÉ GALINDO is an Associate Professor in the School of Education and Human Development at the University of Colorado at Denver. He earned a Ph.D. from Ohio State University in 1990. His recent publications have appeared in the *Harvard Latino Law Review, The Journal of Latinos and Education,* and the *Texas Hispanic Journal of Law and Policy.*

JOHN A. GARCIA accepted a position in 2010 as Research Professor at the Institute for Social Research, University of Michigan. His appointments are with the Inter-University Consortium for Political and Social Research (ICPSR) and the Center for Political Studies (CPS). He was previously Professor of Political Science at the University of Arizona (since 1972). His primary areas of research have been in the area of American politics, concentrating specifically on minority group politics (especially Latinos), political mobilization and participation, urban governments, survey research, and policy implementation and formation. He has published articles and book chapters in these fields for the past forty years. He was coauthor of *Latino Lives in America: Making It Home* (Temple University Press, 2009), and his textbook, *Latino Politics: Community Formation and Political Empowerment* (Rowman and Littlefield, 2003), is undergoing revisions for the second edition (expected 2011). Professor Garcia was one of the principal investigators of the original 1979 National Chicano Survey, one of the four principal investigators on the 1989–1990 Latino National Political Survey, and one of the six coprincipal investigators of the recently completed Latino National Survey, which was the largest political survey of Latinos in the U.S. He has extensive expertise on Latino demographic change and its political effects and the methodological issues of both sample-design and census-taking among Latinos. His works bridge basic and applied research, as evidenced by his participation on the decennial Census advisory committee and Inter-University Consortium for Political and Social Research (ICPSR).

RAFAEL A. JIMENO is the Diane D. Blair Professor of Latino Studies and Assistant Professor of Political Science at the University of Arkansas, Fayetteville. His research and teaching interests include research methods, political behavior, party identification and ideology, racial and ethnic politics, and Latino and immigration politics. His most recent work includes research into the dynamics of Latino linked fate, as well as research into the preimmigration preferences of Latino immigrants and how those impact their preferences in the United States. He received his Ph.D. in 2010 from Arizona State University, Tempe.

DAVID L. LEAL is an Associate Professor of Government, Faculty Associate of the Center for Mexican-American Studies, and Director of the Irma Rangel Public Policy Institute at the University of Texas at Austin. His primary academic interest is Latino politics, and his work explores a variety of questions involving public opinion, political behavior, and public policy. His publications include over fifty journal articles and book chapters on these and other topics. He is also the co-editor of *Latinos and the Economy, Beyond the Barrio: Latinos and the 2004 Elections, Immigration Policy and Security,* and *Latino Politics: Identity, Mobilization, and Representation.* He was a Spencer/National Academy of Education Post-Doctoral Fellow and an American Political Science Association Congressional Fellow. He is a member of the editorial boards of *Social Science Quarterly, American Politics Research,* and *State Politics and Policy Quarterly* and a former cochair of the American Political Science Association's Committee on the Status of Latinos y Latinas in the Profession. He received his Ph.D. in Political Science from Harvard University in 1998.

JOSÉ E. LIMÓN is the Notre Dame Professor of American Literature at the University of Notre Dame and the former Mody C. Boatright Regents Professor in American and English Literature and Director of the Center for Mexican-American Studies at the University of Texas at Austin. His academic interests are varied and include cultural studies, Chicano literature, anthropology and literature, Mexicans in the United States, U.S.-Mexico cultural relations, critical theory, and folklore and popular culture. He has published articles in a wide range of scholarly journals and is the author of several books. *Mexican Ballads and Chicano Poems: History and Influence in Mexican-American Social Poetry* (University of California Press, 1992) received an Honorable Mention award from the University of Chicago Folklore Prize for "distinguished contribution to folklore scholarship." *Dancing with the Devil: Society and Cultural Poetics in Mexican-American South Texas* (University of Wisconsin Press, 1994) won the 1996 American Ethnological Society Senior Scholar Prize. He is also the author of *American Encounters: Greater Mexico, the United States, and the Erotics of Culture* (Beacon Press, 1998). He has received fellowships from the National Endowment for the Humanities, the Stanford Humanities Research Center, and the American Council of Learned Societies. He received his Ph.D. from the University of Texas at Austin.

LISA MAGAÑA is an Associate Professor in the School of Transborder Studies at Arizona State University. She has published in the area of immigration and Latino public policy issues. Author of *Straddling the Border* (University of Texas Press) and *The Politics of Diversity* (University of Arizona Press), she has been a Research Associate at the Tomás Rivera Policy Institute and a visiting Lecturer and Assistant Professor at Pitzer College, UCLA, and Williams College. She received her doctorate from the Center for Politics and Economics at Claremont Graduate University.

SYLVIA MANZANO is Senior Project Manager for Latino Decisions, a Latino public opinion research firm. She taught at St. Mary's University in San Antonio, Texas, and Texas A&M University and holds a PhD in political science from the University of Arizona. Her academic research on Latino and state politics issues have appeared in many academic outlets, including *Political Research Quarterly, State Politics and Policy Quarterly, Politics and Gender,* and *Urban Affairs Review*.

MARTHA MONTERO-SIEBURTH is currently a Research Fellow at the Institute for Migration and Ethnic Studies in the Department of Sociology and Anthropology at the Faculty of Social and Behavioural Sciences and a lecturer at the Graduate School of Social Sciences of the University of Amsterdam and at Amsterdam University College. She is Professor Emerita of the Department of Leadership in Education at the Graduate College of Education at the University of Massachusetts–Boston, where she taught in the Leadership in Urban Schools Doctoral Program and the Educational Administration Master's Program until August 2007. Montero-Sieburth has conducted extensive research on Latinos and their communities in the United States, especially Mexicans in New England. She has studied Latin Americans in Spain, second-generation Dutch Turkish students in the Netherlands, and most recently is completing a study of Mexicans in the Netherlands. She was a Fulbright Senior Scholar at the University of La Laguna, Canary Islands, in 2006–2007, and received the 2005 Hispanic Research SIG Elementary, Secondary, or Postsecondary Education Award of the American Educational Research Association, where she recently completed serving on the International Relations Committee. Her edited volumes include *Latinos in a Changing Society* (with Edwin Melendez, Greenwood Publishers, 2007), *Making Invisible Latino Adolescents Visible: A Critical*

Approach to Latino Diversity (with Francisco Villarruel, Routledge, 1999), and *The Struggle of a New Paradigm: Qualitative Research in Latin America* (with Gary L. Anderson, Garland Press, 1998). She has over two hundred articles dealing with Latinos, Latin Americans, policies and practices in schools, intercultural and multicultural education, the educational similarities and differences of U.S. Latinos, and second-generation Dutch of Turkish and Moroccan backgrounds. Forthcoming is "Education of Immigrant Youth—A Twenty-First Century Challenge" (in Jan Rath and Marco Martiniello, *An Introduction to Immigrant Incorporation Studies,* IMISCOE, University of Amsterdam).

JESSICA NÚÑEZ DE YBARRA currently serves as a Public Health Medical Officer III at the State of California Department of Public Health (CDPH) in the Division of Communicable Disease Control in the Office of Workforce Development. Her primary role is to provide technical support for division-level preparedness, communication, and training efforts—including providing oversight for the CDPH Public Health Laboratory Director Training Program (LabAspire). She also assists in the development and formulation of policy recommendations in areas such as health care reform implementation and public health emergency response. She previously served as a Deputy Public Health Officer in the Kern County Department of Public Health and as Director of its Office of Public Health Preparedness. She is presently a volunteer Assistant Clinical Professor at the University of California, Davis (UCD) School of Medicine's Department of Public Health Sciences. She has served as a lecturer in the UCD Chicano/a Studies Program. She received her Medical Doctorate from UCD and her degree of Master in Public Health from the University of California, Los Angeles. She is Board Certified in Public Health and General Preventive Medicine.

RAYMOND V. PADILLA holds an undergraduate degree from the University of Michigan and a master of arts and Ph.D. from the University of California, Berkeley. He is Professor Emeritus in the Department of Educational Leadership and Policy Studies at the University of Texas at San Antonio and cofounder and former director of the Hispanic Research Center at Arizona State University. Through his research and teaching, he has contributed to the fields of bilingual education, Chicana/o Studies, higher education, and qualitative research methods. Professor Padilla is the developer of the Expertise Model of Student Success (EMSS), which uses qualitative research methods to construct empirical models of student success. He is also the developer of HyperQual, SuperHyperQual, and HyperQual Lite software for the management and analysis of qualitative data. The results of his research have been presented at major national and international conferences and applied at various colleges and universities. His publications have appeared in numerous books, journals, and electronic media. His most recent book is *Student Success Modeling: Elementary School to College* (Sterling: Stylus Publishing, 2009).

ADRIAN D. PANTOJA is Professor of Political Studies and Chicano Studies at Pitzer College, a member of the Claremont Colleges. His research interests are in immigration studies and Latino politics. His numerous articles have appeared in journals including *Political Research Quarterly, Political Behavior, International Migration,* and *Social Science Quarterly,* as well as in edited volumes. His current research looks at the intersection between religious identities/beliefs and Latino political behaviors and attitudes.

EMILY PRIETO is the Director of the Latino Resource Center at Northern Illinois University. She received her Ph.D. from the School of Education at the University of California, Davis, in 2007. Her major field of study is language, literacy, and culture. As Director, she works with Latino youth on campus and in the surrounding area to support recruitment and retention of Latino students, especially in areas where they are underrepresented. Additionally, her current research interest focuses on the behavioral and psychological factors influencing risk factors associated with HIV transmission and drug use among female sex workers in Tijuana, Mexico. She also studies pedagogies used in community-based education of vulnerable populations. She serves as an Adjunct Professor teaching courses on topics such as U.S.-Mexico border relations and multicultural education. She recently was awarded a Fulbright Fellowship to teach and conduct research at the University of Ibadan in Nigeria.

JAVIER M. RODRIGUEZ is a Ph.D. candidate in Political Science at the University of California, Los Angeles. His research is focused on the study of human adaptability, both in immigrant and African American communities in the United States. He asks how adaptability impacts a community's chance to improve its sociopolitical standing. Two lines of research derive from this question: how pre-immigration factors influence the political socialization paths of immigrants in the United States; and how mortality gaps and health inequalities between African Americans and whites affect their voter turnout disparities.

HARRIETT D. ROMO is a professor in the Sociology Department at the University of Texas at San Antonio (UTSA). She is the Director of the UTSA Mexico Center and the Child and Adolescent Policy Research Institute at UTSA. She received her Ph.D. at the University of California, San Diego. Her research focuses on Latino families and children. She has published work on undocumented Mexican immigrant children, Latino high school graduation, early childhood literacy, border families, and racial and ethnic relations. She coordinated the first IUPLR research grant program on Latino Public Policy Research at the University of Texas at Austin. She teaches courses on the sociology of education, racial and ethnic relations, immigration and borders, and qualitative research methods. Her chapter is based on research funded by the Rockefeller Foundation to study the transnational community in San Antonio, Texas.

JILL STRUBE received her Ph.D. in Public Administration from Florida International University (FIU). From 2006–2010, she was the Program Coordinator for the Irma Rangel Public Policy Institute at the University of Texas at Austin. Previously, she was the Associate Director in charge of transportation-related public policy projects at the Metropolitan Center at FIU. She has also done extensive work on the issues of homelessness, affordable and public housing, useful practices in service provision, and community indicators. She has published several articles and reports on these topics. Her dissertation, "Fiscal and Organizational Determinants of Transportation Outcomes: A Quantitative and Qualitative Analysis of Sustainability Factors," was funded through a Housing and Urban Development grant. She currently works as the

Grants Administrator for the City of Smithville, Texas, and is applying her research to the practical efforts of planning and building capacity for sustainability in a small community.

ADELA DE LA TORRE is Professor of Chicana/o Studies and Director of the Center for Transnational Health at the University of California, Davis. From 1996–2002, she was the Director of the Mexican American Studies and Research Center at the University of Arizona. Prior to her Arizona appointment, she was Professor of Health Care Administration and Chair of Chicano and Latino Studies at California State University, Long Beach, and an Executive Fellow in the Office of the Chancellor of the California State University system. She also served as a syndicated columnist for the *Los Angeles Times*. Her commentaries addressing economic, political, educational, health care, and immigration issues have grounded her empirical work in developing practical public policy applications on matters affecting the Latino community. Her publications and research focus on community-based health disparities that impact the Latino community as well as national, binational, and transnational policies that fuel these growing disparities. She has completed studies on the impact of education on the occupational location of Hispanics. She is the author of two books published by the University of Arizona Press: *Sana, Sana: Mexican Americans and Health,* and *Moving from the Margins: A Chicana's View of Public Policy.* She is the editor of the University of Arizona Press series on Mexican-American Studies and the coeditor of two books: *Speaking from the Body: Latinas on Health and Culture* (University of Arizona Press, 2008) and *Building with Our Hands: New Directions in Chicana Scholarship* (University of California Press, 1993). She received her Ph.D. in Agricultural and Resource Economics in 1982 from the University of California, Berkeley.

JAMI VIGIL received a J.D. from the University of Colorado Law School in 2002. She is the Executive Director and Managing Attorney for Socorro: Legal Services for Immigrant Women and Children, a nonprofit that provides free legal and educational services. She clerked for the Honorable Justice Alex Martinez on the Colorado Supreme Court and is a practicing attorney in the area of immigration law.